Global London on screen

Manchester University Press

Global London on screen

Visitors, cosmopolitans and migratory cinematic visions of a superdiverse city

Edited by

Keith B. Wagner and Roland-François Lack

MANCHESTER UNIVERSITY PRESS

Copyright © Manchester University Press 2023

While copyright in the volume as a whole is vested in Manchester University Press, copyright in individual chapters belongs to their respective authors, and no chapter may be reproduced wholly or in part without the express permission in writing of both author and publisher.

Published by Manchester University Press
Oxford Road, Manchester M13 9PL

www.manchesteruniversitypress.co.uk

British Library Cataloguing-in-Publication Data
A catalogue record for this book is available from the British Library

ISBN 978 1 5261 5756 0 hardback
ISBN 978 1 5261 9119 9 paperback

First published 2023
Paperback published 2025

The publisher has no responsibility for the persistence or accuracy of URLs for any external or third-party internet websites referred to in this book, and does not guarantee that any content on such websites is, or will remain, accurate or appropriate.

EU authorised representative for GPSR:
Easy Access System Europe – Mustamäe tee 50,
10621 Tallinn, Estonia
gpsr.requests@easproject.com

Typeset
by Cheshire Typesetting Ltd, Cuddington, Cheshire

To Jiyung Jung: let our London adventures live on forever in memory.
With indefatigable love,
Keith

This book is also dedicated to Roland-François Lack: a pioneer in cinema and the city studies, a dear friend to many and a wonderful and witty human being. You are very missed.

Contents

List of figures	*page* ix
List of contributors	x
Acknowledgements	xv
In memoriam: Roland-François Lack	xvi

Introduction: Global London on screen: visitors, cosmopolitans and migratory cinematic visions of a superdiverse city 1
Keith B. Wagner

1 'God is everywhere!': engineering the immigrant landscape of Emeric Pressburger's *Miracle in Soho* 25
  Jingan MacPherson Young

2 Dropping out: interiority, claustrophobia and decadence in cosmopolitan London cinema of the 1960s and 1970s 44
  Kevin M. Flanagan

3 On location in 1970s London: an interview with Gavrik Losey 61
  Paul Newland

4 Outside in: *Twilight City* and the birth of global London 72
  Malini Guha

5 'Where I come from, we eat places like this for breakfast': Aki Kaurismäki's *I Hired a Contract Killer* as transnational representation of local London 93
  Claire Monk

6 Bollywood's London: the moral-political undertow of London's Hindi cinema presence 107
  Shakuntala Banaji and Rahoul Masrani

7 Brazucas on screen: the Brazilian diaspora in London as depicted in Henrique Goldman's *Jean Charles* 124
   Stephanie Dennison

8 A critical analysis of the Nollywood film *Osuofia in London* 140
   Uchenna Onuzulike

9 Poetics of double erasure: British East/South-East Asian cinema and *Lilting* 158
   Victor Fan

10 Global Hollywood and the London set piece 174
   Lawrence Webb

11 Performative liveness in *Lost in London*: cinematic streaming and the digital happening in globalising London 192
   Michael A. Unger and Keith B. Wagner

12 Borders and cosmopolitanism in the global city: *London River* 210
   Ana Virginia López Fuentes

13 Utopia as a cosmopolitan method in Alfonso Cuarón's *Children of Men* 228
   Mónica Martín

Epilogue: The rise of sourdough bread: *The Street*, gentrification and Brexit 243
Charlotte Brunsdon

Index 260

Figures

9.1 Henri Bergson's first schema of time, from Henri Bergson, *Matière et mémoire: Essai sur la relation du corps à l'esprit* (1939; repr., Paris: Presses Universitaires de France, 2019), p. 115. *page* 166
12.1 Finsbury Park and the cosmopolitan canopy, *London River* (dir. Rachid Bouchareb, 2009). 217
12.2 Ousmane crossing the bridge to live with Elisabeth in Jane's flat, *London River* (dir. Rachid Bouchareb, 2009). 220
12.3 The flat as a 'borderscape' when the police arrive to take DNA samples, *London River* (dir. Rachid Bouchareb, 2009). 222
14.1 The poster for the film showing a repeated shot of Hoxton Street looking south towards the City of London, *The Street* (dir. Zed Nelson, 2019). 244
14.2 Cakes and cake prices in Anderson's the Bakers, *The Street* (dir. Zed Nelson, 2019). 247
14.3 Errol and his garage: last man standing, *The Street* (dir. Zed Nelson, 2019). 250

Contributors

Shakuntala Banaji is Professor and Director of Graduate Studies in the Department of Media and Communications, London School of Economics and Political Science. She has published widely on youth, audiences, Bollywood and internet civic participation. Her books include *Reading Bollywood: The Young Audience and Hindi Film* (Palgrave, 2006) and *Children and Media in India: Narratives of Class, Agency and Social Change* (Routledge, 2017).

Charlotte Brunsdon is Professor of Film & Television Studies at the University of Warwick. While at Warwick, Professor Brunsdon has taught visiting semesters in the USA at Duke University and the University of Wisconsin–Madison, and been visiting scholar at other universities including Stockholm, Queensland, Southern California, New York, Northwestern and Murcia, lecturing and presenting research at many other universities. She has been Principal Investigator on the AHRC-funded 'Projection Project' (2014–18), was a founder member of the Midlands Television Research Group and co-edited the book series Oxford Television Studies, also serving on the editorial boards of *Visual Culture in Britain*, *Film Quarterly*, *Screen* and *Feminist Media Studies*. She is the author or co-editor of more than eight books, including *Television Cities: Paris, London, Baltimore* (Duke University Press, 2018), *Law and Order BFI Television Classic* (Palgrave Macmillan, 2010), *London in Cinema: The Cinematic City since 1945* (BFI, 2007), *The Feminist, the Housewife and the Soap Opera* (Clarendon Press, 2000), *Screen Tastes: Soap Opera to Satellite Dishes* (Routledge, 1997), *Feminist Television Criticism* (Open University Press, 1997) and *Everyday Television: Nationwide* (with David Morley; BFI, 1978).

Stephanie Dennison is Professor of Brazilian Studies at the University of Leeds. A founding member of the Centre for World Cinemas and Digital Cultures, she has published on World Cinema (e.g. *Remapping World Cinema*, Wallflower, 2006 and *The Routledge Companion to World*

Cinema, Routledge, 2017), transnational cinema (e.g. *Contemporary Hispanic Cinema*, Tamesis, 2013) and Brazilian cinema (e.g. *Remapping Brazilian Film Culture*, Routledge, 2020). She is President of ABIL (the Association of British and Irish Lusitanists) and a founding member of REBRAC (European Network of Researchers in Brazilian Cultural Studies).

Victor Fan is Senior Lecturer at the Department of Film Studies, King's College London and Film Consultant of the Chinese Visual Festival. He is the author of *Cinema Approaching Reality: Locating Chinese Film Theory* (University of Minnesota Press, 2015) and *Extraterritoriality: Politics and Hong Kong Cinema, Television, and Video Art, 1967–Present* (Edinburgh University Press, 2019). His articles have been published in peer-reviewed journals and anthologies including *World Picture Journal*, *Camera Obscura*, *Journal of Chinese Cinemas*, *Screen*, *Film History* and *Comparative Literature and Culture*. Besides being an academic scholar, Fan is also a composer and film director. His film *The Well* was an official selection of the São Paolo International Film Festival; it was also screened at the Anthology Film Archives, the Japan Society and the George Eastman House.

Kevin M. Flanagan teaches in the English department at George Mason University. He is editor of *Ken Russell: Re-viewing England's Last Mannerist* (2009) and has published essays in the *Journal of British Cinema and Television*, *Framework*, *Critical Quarterly* and *Adaptation*. He recently co-edited a dossier in *Screen* on architectural documentaries on British television.

Malini Guha is Associate Professor of Film Studies at Carleton University. Her research and teaching are broadly concerned with spatiality and the cinema, with an emphasis on postcolonial and post-imperial modes of mobility, migration, displacement and settlement. Recent publications include a chapter on the narratives of return in the films of Ousmane Sembene and Djibril Diop Mambety in *Cinematic Homecomings: Exile and Return in Transnational Cinema* as well as her monograph *From Empire to the World: Migrant London and Paris in Cinema*, published by Edinburgh University Press in 2015. Her current research project addresses the history of location shooting in the city of Kolkata.

Roland-François Lack was Senior Lecturer in French Culture and Film. His research interests included cinema and place; French and Swiss film; nineteenth-century poetry and poetics; and Francophone literature.

Dr Lack's monograph, *Poetics of the Pretext: Reading Lautréamont*, was published by Exeter University Press in 1998. His work also appeared in *Film History: An International Journal*, *Studies in French Cinema*, *Romanic Review*, *French Forum*, *Journal of European Studies* and *Literature Film Quarterly* and in the anthologies *Moving Pictures/Stopping Places: Hotels and Motels on Film*, *Le Paradis français d'Eric Rohmer* and *Cinematic Urban Geographies*.

Ana Virginia López Fuentes works as a lecturer at the Department of Education Sciences, University of Zaragoza, Spain. She holds BA degrees in Infant Education and Primary Education, with a bilingual English–Spanish specialism. Since 2016, after completing an MA in Cinema and Literature in English, she has been working in film studies. In May 2021 she obtained a PhD in English Studies from the University of Zaragoza with a dissertation on the potential of cosmopolitanism in twenty-first-century Disney animation films to promote inclusive education. Her latest publications include 'Analysing the Potential of Disney-Pixar Films for Educating Young Children in Inclusive Values' (*International Journal of Inclusive Education*, 2021) and 'Transcending the Border: The Encounter with the Other in *Tinker Bell and the Secret of the Wings*' (*Atlantis*, 2021). Her main research interests include inclusive education, film studies, cultural studies and the use of digital media to promote inclusion in the classroom.

Mónica Martín is a lecturer in the Department of English Studies at the University of Zaragoza. Her research interests include utopia and dystopia in cinema, cosmopolitan hopes in twenty-first-century films, social movements, feminism, ecocriticism and the sociology of globalisation. Her PhD thesis (2020) analyses cosmopolitan aspirations in contemporary movies, exploring how films of globalisation illustrate the rebirth of utopia, conceived as an open method grounded in egalitarian and ecological principles. She is a member of the research project 'From Utopia to Armageddon: The Spaces of the Cosmopolitan in Contemporary Cinema'.

Rahoul Masrani is visiting fellow and guest teacher in LSE's Department of Media and Communications. His doctoral research is an in-depth study of global cities and the interconnecting discourses of romance, multiculturalism and neoliberalism in London on screen. He is turning this research into a monograph, *The 'Reel' London: Symbolic Power and Cinema*.

Claire Monk is Professor of Film and Film Culture at De Montfort University. She has published widely on the heritage film, post-1970 British cinema and the cultural politics of both, and is co-editor of *British*

Historical Cinema (Routledge, 2002). More recently, she has contributed a chapter to the edited collection *Upstairs and Downstairs: British Costume Drama Television from The Forsyte Saga to Downton Abbey* (Rowman & Littlefield, 2014) and an article to *Shakespeare Bulletin: The Journal of Early Modern Drama in Performance* (2014).

Paul Newland is Senior Lecturer at the University of Worcester and Director of Research and Knowledge Exchange for the College of Arts, Humanities and Education. He previously worked at Bath Spa University and Aberystwyth University. His research specialisms span English literature and film studies. He has published extensively on British cinema and cinema and the city; these works include *British Art Cinema* (with Brian Hoyle) (Manchester University Press, 2019), *British Rural Landscapes on Film* (Manchester University Press, 2016), *British Films of the 1970s* (Manchester University Press, 2013), *The Cultural Construction of London's East End: Urban Iconography, Modernity, and the Spatialisation of Englishness* (Rodopi, 2008).

Uchenna Onuzulike is an assistant professor in the Department of Communications at Bowie State University. His research foci lie in (critical) intercultural communication, media literacy, ethnic and diasporic identities, communication theories, organisational communication, transnational media and globalisation; interrelationships of religion, culture, folk belief and language; and Nollywood/film analysis and criticism.

Michael A. Unger is Associate Professor of Film Practice at Sogang University in Seoul, South Korea. He is a writer, director and editor of documentaries, shorts, music videos and experimental work screened and broadcast in the United States and Asia. His latest documentary, *Far from Forgotten*, is part of the permanent collection at the National Museum of Korean Contemporary History in Seoul, Korea. He has published work on documentaries, film directors and Korean popular culture in academic journals such as *Journal of Popular Music Studies, Asian Cinema, Journal of Film and Video, Studies in Documentary Film* and other periodicals in the United States, the United Kingdom and Korea.

Keith B. Wagner is a visiting professor at Sungshin Women's University in Seoul, South Korea. He was formerly Assistant Professor of Film and Media Studies at University College London and held a visiting professorship in the College of Liberal Studies at Seoul National University. He is the co-editor of *Neoliberalism and Global Cinema: Capital, Culture and Marxist Critique* (Routledge, 2011), *China's iGeneration: Cinema and*

Moving Image Culture for the Twenty First Century (Bloomsbury, 2014), *Korean Art from 1953: Collision, Innovation, and Interaction* (Phaidon, 2020) and *Fredric Jameson and Film Theory: Marxism, Allegory and Geopolitics in World Cinema* (Rutgers University Press, 2022). His monographic study entitled *Cinema of Labor Insecurity: Precarity on Screen in the Global North and South* will be published in 2023. His work has also appeared in *Media, Culture & Society*, *Radical History Review*, *Visual Communication*, *Quarterly Review of Film and Video*, *Globalizations*, *Race and Class*, *Journal of Film and Video*, *Animation: An Interdisciplinary Journal*, *Critical Arts*, *Labor History*, *Inter-Asia Cultural Studies* and *Third Text* and in the anthologies *Screening China's Soft Power*, *Japanese Animation: Transnational Industry and Culture in Asia* and *Rediscovering Korean Cinema*.

Lawrence Webb is Lecturer in Film Studies at the University of Sussex. He is author of *The Cinema of Urban Crisis: Seventies Film and the Reinvention of the City* (Amsterdam University Press, 2014), co-editor of *Global Cinematic Cities: New Landscapes of Film and Media* (Wallflower Press, 2016) and co-editor of *Hollywood on Location: An Industry History* (Rutgers University Press, 2019). His work has also appeared in *Cinema Journal*, *Post-45* and *Oxford Bibliographies in Cinema and Media Studies*. He is an editorial board member of *Mediapolis: A Journal of Cities and Culture*.

Jingan MacPherson Young was awarded her PhD in Film Studies from King's College London in 2020. She also holds a Master of Studies in Creative Writing from Oxford University and a BA in English with Film Studies from King's College London. Her first monograph, *Soho on Screen*, was published by Berghahn Books in 2022. She is currently a lecturer in Digital Entrepreneurship at King's College London.

Acknowledgements

The following works are reprinted in this collection with permission from the author and publisher:

López Fuentes, Ana Virginia. 'Borders and Cosmopolitanism in the Global City: London River', *Journal of English Studies*, 16 (2018), pp. 165–83.

Martín, Mónica. 'Utopia as a Cosmopolitan Method in Alfonso Cuarón's *Children of Men*' *Utopian Studies*, 32.1 (2021): pp. 56–72.

Monk, Claire. 'Where I Come From, We Eat Places Like This for Breakfast': Aki Kaurismäki's *I Hired a Contract Killer* as Transnational Representation of Local London', *Journal of British Cinema and Television*, 6.2 (August 2009), pp. 267–81.

Newland, Paul. 'On Location in 1970s London: Gavrik Losey', *Journal of British Cinema and Television*, 6.2 (August 2009), pp. 302–12.

Onuzulike, Uchenna. 'A Critical Analysis of the Nollywood Film *Osuofia in London*', *Journal of International and Intercultural Communication*, 11.1 (2018), pp. 81–95.

I would like to express my gratitude to my excellent and erudite research assistants in Seoul: Jinha Choi and Handeul Kim. Matthew Frost, David Appleyard and Paul Clarke at Manchester University Press have been immensely supportive, attentive at every stage and wonderfully considerate as the book moved through different stages of production. A wonderful experience throughout! I also owe a debt of gratitude to all the contributors for their compelling and erudite chapter contributions: thank you for bringing new dimensions to the study of cinema and the city particularly, and to global studies more generally.

In memoriam: Roland-François Lack (1960–2021)

London was, undoubtedly, Roland's cultural oyster. He seemed most animated when discussions turned to the city's vast, dense topography, particularly when those spaces converged with film, especially 1960s art cinema shot all around the capital. This was one of his main areas of academic expertise. Michelangelo Antonioni's film *Blow-Up* was a film he could pick apart by geolocation, giving precise postcodes and naming (now razed) architecture as Thomas (David Hemmings), the film's protagonist, traversed the city on foot and by car. This left his students in awe and gave them an exciting new way to analyse film. Newer, more global films such as Rachid Bouchareb's *London River* saw Roland recite shops that had closed after the film completed in Finsbury Park or, if a flat had been newly painted, he was all too giddy to mention this aesthetic difference. Sadly, such engrossing film commentary was cut short as Roland passed away on 19 February 2021.

Roland spent most of his life in the leafy enclaves north of the River Thames – with brief spells in Oxford and Sussex – with his topophilia extending passionately, but not more intimately, to Paris and its suburbs. Much of his life's work sought to map and analyse these two great cities and the many films attached to each milieu. Many scholars have labelled Roland a 'literal topologist' because of the A–Z Atlas of London he carried in his head – he could conjure details of the most obscure streets and zones in London with precision, like a walking GPS, chirping out a compressed cultural history of that exact spot and an anecdote from his past that often placed him in the very location under discussion. His creation of Cine-Tourist, a website that linked maps and film in an intriguing way, had much buzz about it on its launch, matching his contemporary flaneurist tendencies with the Easter egg hunt for a precise film's location that he so loved to discover and then digitally archive. His pastime often consisted of city walks or taking the Tube or bus to the various film locations scattered throughout London's boroughs, giving new meaning to filmed urban appreciation. He gave back to the London community too by giving accessible public talks to seniors and cinephiles at cultural centres and the Highgate Society. But he was much more than a scholar putting real/digital pins into locations on a map/screen: Roland would bore down into films, re-screen and exhaustively read about many locations and places in London, providing a sharp geocultural, social and aesthetic appraisal of those filmic locations, thinking that is indebted as much to Henri Lefebvre as it is to newer cinematic geographers such as Mark Shiel and John David Rhodes.

Like he was to so many others, Roland was an inspiring mentor to me, a once-in-a-lifetime colleague and dear friend. Our friendship began after my hire at University College London in 2016. Over the years, I had the great privilege to co-convene a module that would fortify some of the very conceptual parameters of this book. At UCL, Roland and I taught a very popular undergraduate module titled 'Of, On, In London: Stage and Screen', and again, his formidable knowledge of location, architectural history, cultural contexts and aesthetic sensibility was on full, formidable display. But his ability to be self-deprecating, to make a silly joke at his own expense or to lament his absentmindedness complemented his intellectual sharpness. But sometimes he was just entertaining, like fumbling a film title – delivering a lecture in my presence on the Finnish noir shot in London, *I Hired a Contract Killer*, calling it instead *I Hired an Axe Murderer* (confusing it with the Mike Myers comedy *So I Married an Axe Murderer*); this brought laughter during this lecture before he seriously returned to the task at hand – dissecting cinematic urban space. Other times, Roland's sudden glee in recollecting a personal experience at a given London location lent a personal history layered over his cultural history, making listening to him highly enjoyable; sometimes his playfulness would surface as he would recall a racy-looking Giallo movie poster or an actor's name that triggered a memory of his at the iconic Muswell Hill movie theatre. Muswell Hill was also Roland's home for nearly his entire life.

One of my greatest memories of Roland was his ability to be both provincial in his views about London, making him the perfect co-editor to get me out of my obsession with London's inter/multiculturalism and global processes and conditions (he dubbed me affectionately 'global Keith'), and his highly sympathetic view toward London's globalising demography, iconicity and place as megacity, that it is a broker to innumerable cultural exchanges and frictions. One personal story about Roland as this book got off the ground five years ago is worth recounting. Roland was a keen jazz enthusiast. One Sunday in 2018 he invited me to a jam session at a home in Archway in North London. To my great surprise, the crowd that gathered at the Archway home was diverse in age, ethnicity and even personal style, with the musicians themselves supported by our at-the-door donations. I later learned this home, with its built-in music studio, was a favourite haunt for up-and-coming jazz musicians. As we sat enjoying the smooth and spontaneous jazz flow, I looked around the room and felt great comfort in London's feeling of globalness and the music as glocal practice. Roland, whether he would agree with me or not, was a kind of ambassador to London: a scholar, a lifelong resident and someone who took time to enjoy all locations on the map that he could, often getting lost and then joking about it, connecting that tale with how he found another street in another London-shot film.

Keith (Seoul, 2022)

Introduction:
Global London on screen: visitors, cosmopolitans and migratory cinematic visions of a superdiverse city

Keith B. Wagner

Global London on screen offers exciting inscriptions about life in a global city through the medium of cinema. It pivots on the relocalisation and delocalisation of iconic, familiar and less seen spaces in London – where neighbourhoods and cultures captured by filmmakers from around the globe are seen afresh. This prompts a kind of bemused reflection and awe due to the city's multisited cinematic experiences. Analysing both London's cinematic high periods of cosmopolitan and multicultural worldliness on film and some of its less laudable migratory histories, exclusionist enclaves and brushes with crime and terrorism, this book explores numerous archetypal, but also less seen zones that span the post-war period to the late 2010s. Told through different urban imaginaries by visitor filmmakers from Algeria, France, Sweden, Italy, Poland, Finland, Nigeria, Mexico, Brazil, Hungry, South Korea, Cambodia, China, India, Canada and the United States, these films continue to destabilise and confront conceptions of English or British non-global London. Seldom has an eclectic group of London films been conceptualised to challenge the universalist preconceptions about London's hegemonic cultural status to outsiders, while also being wary of a kind of British ascendant localism engendered in the complexities of this nation's most famous city. It is here that London's globality through film shows 'neither absolute nor impervious agents, communities or locales', as Bhaskar Sarkar explains about the term global itself.[1] I borrow Sarkar's notion of 'the global' to prescribe a sense of place and multiple points of origin where London's ability to foster a 'range of outcomes – collaboration, competition, neutral indifference' – is contingent on those very ambivalences.[2] It is a city that does not value one thing over another; it is a place that allows cultures to flourish, collide and occasionally find contestation. While other cities around the world claim some type of national order above all else, London uncharacteristically does not.

Like most cities – large and small – London thrives on its constant state of transmogrification. It is through unexpected, unquantifiable and sometimes unwanted processes and conditions transmitted by globalisation that this city changes daily. Thus, the effects of globalisation on cities like London have triggered profound changes to its social fabric, demography and topography. But these elements happen at different scales, and the global scale of London, to borrow from Saskia Sassen, is one of the densest in the world: it is a global city, a city state, a European city (pre-Brexit), the capital of England and power centre of the United Kingdom and the Commonwealth, a set of thirty-two boroughs, near endless quaint streets and bustling thoroughfares, and home to more than eight million people. Many city films inhabited by visitors to London – from the Global South and North – thus convey, sometimes implicitly or in other cases defiantly, the need to jettison the simple binary between local and global, to instead see London through scale and density of expression and experience. To see it as a multifaceted meeting ground unlike any other metropole on earth – this is one reason why so many people subscribe to London's unmatched globalism.

A trinity of outcomes takes shape on screen in the London films covered in this book: (i) a hybrid view of London where visitor filmmakers delocalise certain elements and environs of the city with local help, whether through co-productions with the British film industry, EU or overseas investment or through specific location shooting by a non-British filmmaker, all with an intention to distribute these films internationally as part of a foreign film industry's genre of city films set abroad; (ii) the multisited view of London's superdiverse demography and milieus, its cosmopolitan communities or a larger event or condition that necessitates a global understanding of a film's supranational ambitions – these films usually sit outside of conventional national cinema taxonomies and are sometimes referred to as 'global art cinema'[3] or 'global cinema';[4] and finally, (iii) the least represented but important preservationist view of London: the city shown from a hyper-local perspective that points to London's diversity as well as its tight-knit ethnic communities, sometimes conscious to their segregation and cultural essentialism as enclave. Approaching this topology holistically, these three types of film present a polyvalent view of London's different urban imaginaries and continue to confront, creolise and coexist alongside conceptions of English or British non-global London made by indigenous filmmakers for decades.

London as 'illimitable' cultural and filmic space

Like earlier perspectives on cinematic London, this book equally values 'what the city signifies, the stories that recur as London stories'.[5] Yet what makes the cinematic moments here different is that, while continuing to see London as a lasting beacon and site whose highly photogenic qualities on screen have mystified, perplexed and challenged audiences for more than a century, *Global London on screen* simultaneously presents a mélange of films by foreign directors that portray everyday life; from the fantastical, odious or extraordinary circumstances that are captured culturally and lend substance to claims of the city's superdiversity. While social relations continue to disembed themselves even in the shadow of deglobalisation and particularly Brexit's ravaging of London's connection to Europe since 2016, the films examined in this collection show the 'pulsations of intersocietal interaction networks' that have been occurring in London long before those two shocks disrupted the city's globality.[6] As one of the greatest urban outposts for global worldliness, our view of London in this collection is determined to interlard this city with globalisation, rejecting claims that the latter is a homogenising force on culture and urban life.

Films shot in London belong to this city's photogenic supremacy, a legacy that is forged largely through media; it is a city that has been viewed billions of times. Today people encounter global London not only through cinematic and televisual renditions over the decades but also, more recently, through the action of clicking and scrolling, often aimlessly and repetitiously, through social media focused on the capital. Instagram and TikTok are abuzz with the London-look: tourist traps like the London Eye snapped and uploaded, posh restaurants in Knightsbridge, people hanging about in Piccadilly Circus or shopping on Oxford Street, influencers strutting around Selfridges while livestreaming themselves with luxury goods, capturing these interior spaces in London that are similarly well known; all these visual snippets present a global recycling of this city's vast spaces. Yet unremarkable London sees users post in the humblest of places: the millions of bedrooms scattered throughout the city that serve as confessional spaces, creative workshops or intimate interludes to voyeurism. Banality is part of London's imagery and reimagined cityscape too.

As people are continuously drawn to London's topography from abroad, this book looks at the integral role that cinema has continued to play even as social media becomes more dominant and COVID-19 eviscerated tourism for a two-year period from 2020 to roughly early 2022. Before this pathogenic virus spread, we must recall, the capital claimed the highest number of sojourns for decades. Time will tell if London keeps this title, but it appears unrivalled as the world opens back up. For now, at least looking back to pre-2020, London-inspired imagery holds to what psychogeographer Peter Ackroyd calls its 'illimitable' production and what I see as the increasing global circulation of those very images.[7] Yet this idea that images of London can never render this UK city as all-knowable is true. What we provide here is a slice of that extraordinary iconography and images that show multi-origin people in what Steve Vertovec has called the 'diversification of diversity'.[8] In all this mixing, we also refrain from the temptation to push London's globalism to mere abstraction or to envision it through a crude tiering or boosterism. We emphasise that the exponential growth in the use of London as location by filmmakers in Western and non-Western contexts is rarely discussed in these sorts of terms and is worth paying critical attention to, especially as the global turn evaporates across many disciplines.

Part of London's appeal is no doubt down to its being a space to globetrot and where many globetrotters call home. These citizens of the world actively seek out interracial and multilingual people and those customs present themselves in this global city – making it so quintessentially intercultural – thus corresponding to it being a microcosm of a highly mobile, changing world. London's aura of indispensability to the world lies in how it is captured by many not born there nor well-versed in its cultural history but who nonetheless reinscribe it, remake it, and reimagine it to their unique purposes, making it a metropole of great envy. As a virtual and real place where power and technology, spatial change, tradition and diversity collide, you can find just about 'anything ethnic and cultural in this multilingual capital'.[9]

Talking about diversity in terms of community interactions, culture shocks and acculturation, or about London being a peripatetic hub for cosmopolitan elites, we must also acknowledge its dubious elements as a global city and sketch its dark side, beyond it being enjoyed as a place of tourism and patronage. Such positive views of this city often obfuscate those on wayward journeys in the capital, suffering from xenophobia or physical and psychological abuse by those with more power. Many films show a new geography of dislocation and exclusion through narratives that purposefully disorientate, exemplifying those who are forced illegally to migrate into the capital and find themselves in all sorts of demeaning work, often invisible to most of us. As a result, a set of horizontal zones, made by cross-cultural, hybrid urban imaginaries, have come into view and structure discussions in this collection. *This* London is best thought of in terms of aesthetics, activities, ideologies and subjectivities, either by characters or inferred by directors, that help build new meaning through the following genres which are built into the city film: noir films by émigré directors sifting through Soho's nightlife; art cinema's American and European auteurs documenting the Swinging London of the 1960s and the claustrophobia and decadence of London in the 1970s; multicultural London told by radical Black British filmmakers in the 1980s; nondescript, grungy London seen through the eyes of a Scandinavian director in the 1990s; and a new cross-cultural, multiethnic group of films from East and South Asia, Africa and Latin America, alongside Hollywood blockbusters set in this megacity. Each of these tropes and motifs – taken together – mediate for audiences what Andreas Huyssen argues are 'sites of inspiring traditions and continuities, as well as the scene of histories of destruction, crime, and conflicts of all kinds'.[10] That filmed urban spaces, particularly those collected here, can amplify or contest different forms of global integration – often messy and erratic – shows that they also speak to London's unparalleled culture of tolerance. When viewed from such a supranational register, a uniquely cross-cultural group of films is detectable and exemplified by filmmakers who have come to London to produce representations of this city. Thus, we carry on a theoretical tradition in which urban space interrogated through cinema postulates the effects of globalisation on the processes of urbanisation.[11]

Unrivalled placeness: London's global media activities and infrastructure

In addition to its prestige as a place, London outpaces most other urban milieus because it is shaped by capital. It was rapid urban redevelopment in the Docklands under Margaret Thatcher's neoliberal revolution in the 1980s that created a second financial centre for the capital. British neoliberalism wasn't sustainable without globalisation's diffusion of culture into this very specific East End locale. For example, *The Long Good Friday* (1980) provided a prophetic vision of the Docklands with Bob Hoskins' and Helen Mirren's gangster characters wishing, unsuccessfully, to turn this riverfront area into a London Las Vegas; to make the city global before anyone thought of it in these terms. It wasn't long before financial professionals quickly pounced on London's centrifugal position in global capitalism. This rise as a financial hub brought about London's thorny relationship with the art world, facilitating, to a degree, the rise of global art stars who studied and lived in the capital. The young British artists (YBAs) brought this tripartite fusion of city, finance and art into full view: their trendsetting move to repurpose a warehouse in the Docklands for their *Freeze* exhibition in 1988 catapulted London to the centre of the art world, knocking New York down to second place. By the 1990s, gentrification became a key battleground in this part of London which was often explored as backcloth theme in art cinema: *I Hired a Contract Killer*, shot around the area of the Docklands now known as Canary Wharf, is imbued with the spirit of 'social conflict over the urban regeneration of the warehouses, wharves and docks'.[12] By the 2000s, the skyscrapers in Canary Wharf themselves became a character and phallic projection in the raunchy opening scene to *Basic Instinct 2*, a German, Spanish, British and American co-production, utilising the space for psychosexual and psychogeographic reasons: 30 St Mary Axe or 'the Gherkin' becomes an obvious phallic set piece, one that darts up into the London skyline in perverse defiance. Much the same, Ben Wheatley's 'terror towers' of Brutalist design in the 1970s-set skyscraper film *High-Rise*, located fictively on the River Thames, use London-inspired architecture – Ernö Goldfinger's 31-storey Trellick Tower – as allegory of egalitarian built-space gone tragically awry.

Cultural content like film and art can be perceived as part of this city's value and brand in an increasingly global marketplace, forces not exclusive to London's intangible cultural contributions. This is how urban milieus build their own cultural capital through the proliferation of screen media in collusion with or supported by the flow of capital. Urban realms may also be construed as *globalising* because they are not only alpha integrative points for global culture but also locations for intense media production that reinforce a sense of technological englobement – a sense that we are all interconnected. Media historians have chronicled this development: from telegraph cables in the nineteenth century to television's satellite transmissions in the 1960s and 5G infrastructure bouncing information in milliseconds from one end of the planet to the other in the twenty-first century. London was central to this englobing of information and thus boasts an international prominence through its formidable broadcasting achievements over the last two centuries like no other city on earth. Making sense of this information and thus shaping it are London's creative industries – institutions that nurture homegrown and global talent, attracting many film and television stars, and leading to this media capital's prominence as a highly desirable location. As a place, destination and cluster of creative industries, not unlike Global Hollywood and its conglomerate restructuring, Global London also becomes a premier place for location shooting precisely because it is a vital node in our transnational mediascape, coupled with the unparalleled tax incentives to lure productions to this city.[13] We must remember that Los Angeles is not just a tourist destination due to its media infrastructure – film studios like Columbia Pictures and Universal Pictures, music label giants like Interscope Records and the Walt Disney Company's original Burbank studio, which all attract throngs of fans; these studios and company headquarters are also places that you can inhabit and see as part of the city's urban fabric. A taxi driver might shout out an important piece of history linked to architecture or green space – from Waterloo Bridge to Regent's Park. But in younger cities like Los Angeles, people pay entry into studio lots in Burbank to walk history and find a relation between behind-the-scenes production in the hanger-like lots and enclosed studios. Learning from another media capital like Los Angeles, commodifying the production of space and part of the larger transmedia immersion related to screen media, London has caught on with its Harry Potter World UK theme park and has opened its own infrastructure to consumers beyond our direct focus on filmmakers using London's geography. Its concentration of media activities and infrastructure via Pinewood Studios, Shepperton Studios and Longcross Studios on the edges of the city's zonal limits show the world just how involved the British film industry is with Hollywood productions, past and present, and its own blockbuster industry.[14]

Media conglomerates and new networks also make London a global beacon for broadcasting: ITV, Sky, Channel 4, CNN International and Bloomberg are all headquartered here; and social media and internet giants Facebook and Google have moved into King's Cross, with the Chinese-owned TikTok opening offices in the capital as well. In political-economic terms for global film production, London remains the single most popular destination for overseas filmmaking over the last twenty years, which accounts for a large portion of these industries' production shoots in the British capital. When the focus is narrowed to top-grossing films, particularly the genre of action blockbusters, espionage, travelogue and romantic comedy (rom-com) films, along with art cinema and independent films, London holds impressive numbers, far above any other city worldwide: London outperformed Los Angeles as well as New York, Paris and Tokyo as the production location for box office hits.

It is this distinction between real place and cinematic place in film studies,[15] where London leaks out its *globally felt* and *active* internationalisation,[16] that one sees the capital's magnetism attracting attention to its mystique and recognisability, to its public and private institutions, creating feelings of wanting to know and experience what London can offer. London thus summons talent away from other cities, in what Hall and Hubbard argue is a feature of an 'entrepreneurial city';[17] its brand and base of international headquarters remain unmatched and suit Rem Koolhaus's notion of a generic city; its vast demographic scale and constantly changing social groups overshadow Europe, Asia and Africa, with the Latin American city of Rio de Janeiro the only place coming to rival, slightly, London's interculturalism.

Elsewhere, London's power relations between world cities – shown with the London Mayor's office describing London as the city that other cities look up to – aligns with *The Economist* naming London 'Europe's only properly global city' in 2012.[18] The British capital is also the hub of the gold standard in journalism and music history worldwide, from the broadcast news colossus the BBC to the Royal Albert Hall as venerated concert venue. Enshrining all this culture, one must not forget London's architectural benchmarks, from the medieval cathedrals to the Victorian and Edwardian Gothic Revival, from the city's Brutalist phase of concrete structures in the post-war period to its millennial neo-futurist-styled superstructures that remain, if viewed collectively, unmatched globally. Even London's real estate valuation, bloated and linked to speculation across all seven continents, exceeds any other city in our world system due to its perceived unbeatable investment potential. But this has also led to a housing crisis, with London leading the world in the number of empty flats not being used to house needy citizens, which leads to how economic variables must also be discussed alongside cultural ones. This is especially true when thinking about London's enduring, influential visions registered by filmmakers that are heightened by the city's 'globally-oriented producer service firms' and the creative industries that make such claims more resolute.[19]

The global city paradigm à la London

Not all cities stand to benefit equally in economic terms. Some fare better than others financially. Analysis of financial variables comes to structure Saskia Sassen's pathbreaking book *The Global City: New York, London, Tokyo*. In it, Sassen argues that the 'global city' paradigm is a leading conceptual marker by highlighting these cities' specialised services and the financial goods they produce. She argues that the global city can be characterised as a social and urban entity that exudes several vital characteristics and functions, casting New York, London and Tokyo's supremacy over other megacities. Five tenets order her logic: 'as a center of global flows; performs multiple and significant *world city functions*; detains *central command roles* within such functions; maintains an *urban order* that balances local and global; projects such order towards the global through *entrepreneurial activities*'.[20] Thus, New York, London and Tokyo are unmatched in terms of their global accumulation, an accurate claim by Sassen, with their financial districts known as citadels to capital. As such, zones of these cities are known to outperform other financial exchanges across the globe and serve as centres through which flow workers, information, commodities, cultural prestige and other non-economically relevant variables. Left out of Sassen's critical focus, however, are the non-economic goods propelled by globalisation, goods which also demarcate increases in cultural value.

Providing examples outside of the scope of this book which fit into this global city paradigm and are useful to keep with the city film moniker, the anthology film *Tokyo!* (2008) exudes a certain globality of intention. When auteurs Bong Joon-ho from Korea and Michel Gondry and Leos Carax from France directed three vignettes about Tokyo, their short films challenged the orderly and harmonious stereotypes of Japan's largest city. The omnibus film provided a strange, delirious and violent atmosphere that spoke to larger issues of domestic terrorism (Aum Shinrikyo's sarin gas attack), precarity (underemployment since the 1990s recession) and exclusion (*hikikomori*) known acutely to locals in Tokyo. In New York, the sinister final shot of Manhattan's skyline in *The American Friend* (1977) by German filmmaker Wim Wenders presents one of the most unforgettable set pieces in cinema history: New York never loomed so ominously in the backdrop of any Hollywood film. This final scene of estrangement from another world-famous skyline is gathered from the hulking, then newly built World Trade Center towers, suggestive of what Merrill Scheiler calls 'a spatial ideology, in the form of grand skyscrapers that are but a veneer to oppressive ideologies'.[21] We must remember that New York City's hard edge and negative reputation were actively being rejuvenated by a powerful elite and a new mayor determined to scrub away crime but also the lower classes from this borough. Like these intriguing cinematic New Yorks and Tokyos, India has long appropriated and seen London as a second home and place of unmatched opportunity – and sometimes oppression. *Dil Diyan Gallan* (2019) takes London as a romantic interlude, conjuring its social media appeal alongside the hi-def images of London's mostly posh cityscape. As a global melodrama – transnational in scope – its Indianness reclaims previous West End and central London spaces and architecture as its own: a Bollywood travelogue film, with splashes of earlier British rom-coms. Like *Tokyo!*, depictions of a global city do not have to be flattering nor do they have to integrate their characters into the multicultural fabric – outsiders exist too, in their own enclosed social spaces, 'promoting a sense of distinctiveness'.[22] The two central protagonists in this Punjabi love story, Natasha and Laddi, float through exquisite spaces in the most pristine areas of London's on-screen visuality: Marylebone, Mayfair and the Southbank; another way that the cityscape is used to show characters and people inhabiting a polyethnic playground.

London's 'locational non-substitutability' for film studies

Historically, London's many cityscapes on film have since the post-war period commanded an air of cosmopolitan worldliness. Its semi-preserved cartographic placeness – of which New York and Tokyo seem less able to boast due to architectonic losses associated with gentrification or war – set this city apart. But London has felt urban renewal and conflict as well, with large and small fissures to its urban fabric coming to reconfigure or raze (sometimes through terrorism) certain sections of this city. Still, obsessive preservation of the built environment put London on a higher order. Here the ringfencing, quite literally, of listed buildings in London has become a staple in the British heritage mandate and identifiable treasures, adorned with blue plaques that give an enduring global presence to these landmarks. These round sapphire gems that are hidden among ordinary buildings provide historical recognition that outnumbers the recognisability of other buildings, elsewhere in other cities. Without question London is place-dependent, establishing its uniqueness through a kind of 'locational non-substitutability'.[23] London in its filmic form promotes the urban environment and its uniqueness, while also stressing comparison to other cities and their iconic cityscapes. For example, New York's Chrysler Building and Empire State Building and Tokyo's Imperial Palace and Docomo Towers are landmarks that pale in comparison to the instantly recognisable Gothic Houses of Parliament or the neoclassical assuredness of Buckingham Palace; even The Shard, a new addition to the skyline, has equally mesmerised those who visit it or view it virtually. Locational non-substitutability comes into sharp relief again when compared to New York, as Vancouver in Canada offers producers in Hollywood a substitute for the Big Apple. London, on the other hand, counts its urban agglomeration as nearly impossible to simulate. More contemporary urban views of London remain etched into our collective memories: the postmodern corporate structures such as the commercial skyscraper on 20 Fenchurch Street (aka 'the Walkie Talkie') and the Leadenhall Building (aka 'the Cheesegrater'). In many ways, London has changed but paradoxically stayed very much the same. These skyscrapers and regal-looking buildings suit London-based blockbusters' use of the city. Elsewhere, visual knowledge of London extends to more mundane, clichéd iconography such as the city's archetypal red buses and phone boxes which populate many foreign and domestic filmmakers' *mise-en-scène*.

In film studies, London has been a subject and character of limited interest, occasionally given over to intense discussions about its geographical and cartographical character. Charlotte Brunsdon's *London in Cinema* is one of the only books to carefully articulate London's many national cinematic faces – from *Passport to Pimlico* (1949) and *The Long Good Friday* (1979) to *My Beautiful Laundrette* (1985), *Naked* (1993) and *28 Days Later* (2002), among many other London-based films that are culturally deconstructed. Her dual notion of 'fresh views of familiar landmarks or attempts to eschew them altogether in favour of accent and character as ways of establishing setting' resonates in this collection in a variety of ways.[24] Many of the visitor films shot in globalising London reconfigure the 'hardware of familiar places', providing not overheard accents in front of or inside historic buildings, but subtitles and the appropriation for nationalistic purposes of those very landmarks. The London 2012 Olympics exemplify a perfect symmetry between sport, finance and tourism that enabled the capital to further brand itself. But film as much as television played a role in this, widening the appeal of London to a number of fans of the games. The widest possible ambit for Olympics-themed films were commissioned in a series of short films: 'These featured dysfunctional but compassionate families (Leigh's *A Running Jump*), freerunners and BMX-ers (Max & Dania's *What If*), and aerial shots of the city interspersed with news footage of the 7/7 bombings and the 2010 riots (Kapadia's *The Odyssey*).'[25] These slice-of-life films return the viewer to the centrality of London: it is a place of family ties, athletic competition and terror-induced tragedy, known to most cities at some point in time, but in London such phenomena just seem more mundane, iconic or macabre when on screen.

For more global resonances of Olympic London, take Korean filmmaker Kim Dal-Joong's *Pacemaker* (2012), the first and only South Korean film to feature London in its glorious, touristic and landmark stateliness. But the film also becomes part of a Korean cinematic event culture as it imagines success going into the 2012 Olympics held in the British capital. Its cinematographic elements capture the regal scenery of Westminster's lordly architecture, the Strand roadway with its iconic Savoy Hotel and the City of London's handsome churches, many designed by Christopher Wren. All this cartographic sumptuousness made in central London is captured via a mounted camera on a truck that simulates the marathon route: it bestows much social capital and ornamental prestige on London but also grants a Koreanised London through its *Chariots of Fire* sport-like pageantry.

Complementing Brunsdon's pathbreaking original monograph on cinematic London is the rich contextual studies of different films *in* London found in Pam Hirsch and Chris O'Rourke's *London on Film*. Their collection focuses on a set of homegrown cinematic Londons, understanding this city as 'variously glamourous and grimy, cosmopolitan and parochial, ultramodern and rooted in the inclusive and the deeply divided'.[26] Thoroughly ordered, the films covered in this book thus align with British filmmakers or émigré visionaries who worked or are working currently within this very system, calling the United Kingdom or even London their permanent home. Although discussions of various London diasporas and ethnic communities are absent in Hirsch and O'Rourke's edited collection, immigrant communities are called attention to, with a particular focus on their new lives in London. Outside of their book and our coverage, yet another useful example of visitor filmmaking in London is Po-Chih Leong's *Ping Pong* (1986). In this Sinophone British film, we are given a deceitful, money-obsessed DINK (double income, no kids) couple living in the newly crowned financial epicentre of the world – London. More specifically, a view towards where those money-managers reside, in Mayfair, with minority communities clawing their way in, makes this a fascinating picture of British-style neoliberalism. These anglicised Hong Kongers embody a new conflation in the Thatcher era; intriguingly, these East Asian entrepreneurs, not unlike Stephen Frears's Pakistani British small business–owners in *My Beautiful Laundrette* (1985), make the preconceived, xenophobic notion that ethnic minorities cannot be Thatcherites ring hollow. We know they can. Asian cinema in London – specifically Indian and Chinese Cambodian films shot in the capital – finds a unique diasporic coverage and place in this book.

London films, according to Ian Christie, also take viewers vicariously through the city's shifting cultural geography.[27] Many vicarious views of London are tied intimately to place-based location: postcodes on an A–Z London map detailed by Roland-François Lack and his topographic survey of Michelangelo Antonioni's film *Blow-Up*, or Google Earth coordinates on mobile phone apps. The films analysed in this book show a penchant for reinventing and displaying locales that are ready for imminent destruction, urban redevelopment or ongoing gentrification, or studio sets made up of interiors of flats or nightclubs that were scrapped decades ago. Borough-based London is often given to a grungy decay, with signs of physical damage and blight functioning as visual motif, one that finds its way into some of the films discussed, making the city 'appear strange',[28] ruinous, an 'off-centre location'[29] or unidentifiable.

Multicultural and superdiverse London: opportunity and disadvantage

A great deal of the films about London in this edited collection seem more tactical in how they intuit the potential of London to offer multi-ethnic experiences as well as the positive and negative outcomes of global processes as they manifest themselves in individual filmic worlds. These very experiences and processes are often articulated beyond mere 'film location' or the fetishisation of an auteur and 'their ambivalent relationship to location'.[30] Moreover, this is a collection that tries to pinpoint the possibilities – and pitfalls – of London's worldmaking on screen. With such worldmaking one must adhere to various forms of cosmopolitanism – an outlook, a convivial way to interpret a kind of closeness to the edge. The term 'global village' could be used to describe London throughout the twentieth and twenty-first centuries because it evokes this spirit of world citizenship or what Kant called enlightened humanism, something that is fragile and morphs into an ethical position, yet is continually upheld in this megacity.

Furthering questions of London's extraterritoriality, I positively appropriate Emily Apter's notion of oneworldedness for some of the films in this collection. Not to imply American-produced globalisation/ McDonaldisation of global processes, rather I transfer this to apply to the visualities of global London films: London is a microcosm of the world and compositely refracts many communities and diasporas, groups that make the capital their home. Apter refers to oneworldedness as requiring 'the match between cognition and globalism that is held in place by the paranoid premise that "everything is connected"'.[31] London as epicentre for cultural outwardness seems to annotate Apter's notion: we find that the city's importation of other cultural identities and activities also happens to make it global. From the London Korean Film Festival held across the city in various screening spaces since 2012 to Brazil Day held annually in Trafalgar Square, the Chinese Lunar New Year celebration and avid American-football fans cramming into Wembley Stadium to watch an imported sport – these, among countless other multicultural events, showcase London as an emporium of *imported* choice. But provincial London, comprised of many small ethnic villages and their strident appeal for difference, finds room for discussion here too. Some filmmakers play with cognition and globalism, of the world out there lost in a vast hinterland; others resist the creolisation of their culture in this megacity; others still develop London's interconnectedness through narrative, industrial, linguistic and social integration of some kind. Because these filmmakers come from the Global North and South, men and women who stand outside of the British film industry, rather than exude a homogeneity of culture they instead actively engage with a global consciousness of where they are in the world and where their projected worlds often intersect with real London. In other words, London-based filmmaking often 'resists the ideas of globalization as complexity and engages in an exploration of the intimate relationship between location and globality as it plays out within the confines of the cinematic image'.[32]

One can understand the scale of London's enormous diversity through the policies and discourses of multiculturalism. For decades, multiculturalism as written into policy in the UK was about the accommodation between majority and minority communities: to frame rights, equal treatment and non-discrimination as key conceptions of coexistence. As a theory, multiculturalism was born out of burgeoning ideas about identity politics, postcoloniality and race as intrinsically linked to the wider UK and in particular London. In their landmark study *Unthinking Eurocentrism: Multiculturalism and the Media*, Ella Shohat and Robert Stam confirm that artistic, cultural and political alternatives through a wide range of non-Eurocentric media including Third World films, rap videos and indigenous media, overlooked in popular culture and in academia before the 1990s, need to be accessed and given proper attention. Their mediation on multiculturalism is best understood as the self-representation of difference in media, indebted to Stuart Hall's writing from a decade earlier related to the marginalisation of Black British talent on and off screen. To promote polycentrism over ethnocentrism via a showcase of marginal groups – sometimes via their commodification, disaffiliation or cosmeticisation by a dominant national culture, even the filmmakers themselves – is to find different ethnic groups enframed as simply foreign or spatially and institutionally materialised. Such an unequal playing field is implied in the cross-cultural possibilities embedded in many films in Europe, the United States and more recently in Asia. These ethnic groups don't often retain control of the film worlds we see them in nor does their adopted homeland make it easy on them. This, however, is where our book departs from what may be an Anglocentric view of filmmaking in Britain and London, as an Angloscape of white British ancestry is rethought and intersects with multicultural London. If we look back at history, this book also *unthinks* Anglocentric media produced in London.

Similarly, the city has housed an influx of non-indigenous people – its demographic multitude – which pushed at the edges of what is perceived as its Anglo-Saxon identity for centuries. As Steven Vertovec explains, this is what truly shaped London's multicultural identity.

> Nineteenth-century poets like Wordsworth described London's heterogeneity of peoples, while in an 1880 book *The Huguenots*, Samuel Smiles called London 'one of the most composite populations to be found in the world' (Holmes 1997: 10). Irish in the nineteenth and twentieth centuries and Jews from throughout eastern Europe in the late nineteenth and early twentieth centuries comprised significant immigrant influxes. Yet it was the post-war large-scale immigration of African-Caribbean and South Asian peoples which particularly prompted the recognition of difference throughout public policy. British policy-makers responded with various strategies for a kind of diversity management strategy that came to be called multiculturalism.[33]

In contemporary London, the city itself becomes a gathering point for hundreds of diasporas, something contemplated through attempts to 'organize diversity'.[34] Here, filmic representations of such polyvalent identities (from queer to differently abled to heteronormative) and ethnic groups (from Hasidic Jews to Japanese British, among hundreds of other communities) are schema that come to dismiss the promotion of urban monoculturalism. The dichotomy of not getting 'locked in' to notions of single ethnicity and accommodations between majority and minorities in London, in Chek

Wai Lau's words, is just one route to plurality in the wider UK and in this megacity.[35] But a commitment to a stronger sense of a whole community, in terms of 'societal cohesion and national citizenship', is also actively being shaped, pursued and idealised ideologically and filmically *in* London.[36] This occurs through a form of superdiversity, understood not only through demographic expansion but also by way of sociocultural exchanges. London's established multicultural characteristics encode it as a superdiverse urban metropole. But the population's heterogeneity has historical precedence.

To help make this multicultural superdiversity implicit or explicit, groups of non-resident overseas filmmakers show a preference for mobility over indigeneity; but some of these filmmakers also exude a propensity towards multilingualism, anti-discrimination and coexistence in the places they film in London. Other filmmakers that resist assimilation are defiant and champion insular ethnic communities within the wider patchwork of London's superdiverse demography. Yet nearly all of these filmmakers work in one space and culturally inhabit another, wary of flaunting their foreignness; nor do we accentuate it for them. In other ways, some visitor filmmakers operate like migrants new to London, emphasising through their various films that 'in contemporary globalization the differences between localities have lessened and the variety within localities has increased'.[37] London becomes a 'global broker' of sorts, allowing these polychromatic experiences, conditions and attitudes to accumulate as an outcome of globalisation's effects on urban life in this megacity and present themselves on screen.[38]

Moving beyond what may be perceived as mere platitudes to London's polycultural exchanges, some factual aspects of this city's globality need to be stated. Let us begin with the crude metric of tourism. In 2013, 33 million people visited London, while 'international visitors also spent over £3.37 billion on shopping, hotels, restaurants and visiting attractions during the summer, up five per cent compared to the same time last year'.[39] Its uncontested touristic appeal (pre-COVID-19) makes London, in the words of Andrew Church and Martin Frost, a powerhouse of leisure in England, and they argue that: 'Tourism in London plays a complex economic and social role that appears simultaneously both to enhance and to challenge the global city role and competitiveness.'[40] Films based during the New Labour period tended to predominantly sketch London as a touristic wonderland – *Sliding Doors* (1998), *Martha, Meet Frank, Daniel and Laurence* (1998), *Tube Tales* (1999), *Notting Hill* (1999) – or render the city a slick, gangland topography as associated with *Lock, Stock and Two Smoking Barrels* (1998), *Face* (1999) and *Sexy Beast* (2000), shot in East and West End London. In an essay entitled 'Citylife: Urban Fairy-tales in Late 90s British

Cinema', Robert Murphy sets out to examine some of the broader narrative antecedents of such films as *Four Weddings and a Funeral*, *Sliding Doors* and *Notting Hill*, as well as considering their underlying political significance within British culture. Murphy suggests that an

> examination of the narrative patterns of several 1990s British romantic comedies testifies to the influence of fairy tales and folk tales on the distinguishing features of the scenarios, particularly in their emphasis on the setting of a 'magical quest' to be participated in by modern-day kinds of princesses and princes, alongside their constructing of alternative, attractive surroundings in which true lovers can discover each other (often depicting London, unexpectedly, as an 'enchanted village' in the process).[41]

But other films have tried to see it from the foreigner's gaze, unafraid to move beyond mawkish love stories or lad-focused gangland tales.

Social class diversity, especially in London, is massively affected by neoliberal globalisation: London as wonderland hides it and the gangland movies exploit it for profit. Yet, London is a place disproportionately favouring the more well-heeled: 'From a city dominated by a large working class in the early post-war decades, the decline of manufacturing and port-related industries from the 1960s onwards has been accompanied by an equally marked increase in both the size and in the proportion of its white-collar middle class, the great majority of whom work in the service sector' from the 1990s onwards.[42] But in terms of diversity, globalisation's effects in London are extreme and largely unmatched comparatively, though still contradictory, as gaps between the BAME (Black, Asian and Minority Ethnic) and other white precariats keep widening as well. As with any city, at any juncture in history, the world pours into London through diplomatic channels; it is mobile and agile to accommodate those uprooted for work or family, is mercantilist and, more dubiously, becomes a bulwark for the slave trade, illegal migration and deportation. It also has sectors suffering from underemployment, toiling away in precarious jobs or experiencing the anxieties of stagnating incomes.

We would be remiss not to acknowledge that London's globality came at a price and has a cruel anomic past. The Windrush generation and many who were refused permanent residency status in recent years exemplify the troubling persistence of institutional racism found in the UK, and its effects on London throughout history. London is linked to England's blood-soaked imperium. Many of the Windrush generation who came to London after arriving in Birmingham in the 1960s made the capital their home. After residing for nearly sixty years, some had their residency revoked and were made to uproot from London and other cities and leave for Commonwealth nations, places that many knew little of or had never set foot in before. London's ongoing decolonisation has shed light on its strategic place in the British Empire, where measures of atonement for those crimes against its colonial subjects are gaining credibility.[43] Not enough has been done and clearly the reparations awarded to some of the Windrush generation are paltry in comparison to their suffering. These recent and important decisions have remunerated the victims, of course, but these payoffs, to put it bluntly, are insignificant to this ethnic community and others who have experienced institutional racism over the decades. Yet London's accountability for its past injustices is better than most cities worldwide because tolerance and empathy is often born out of those dark moments for this city and this nation. This growing awareness of past injustices makes London a place of continued tolerance; even its past, bleaker version that saw heinous exclusion, Booth-like living standards and exclusionary policy must be considered in the assimilation of a global consciousness of cultures beyond one's own, learned from those rotten lessons in history anchored in London.

Newer films shot in London, though brutal in their capture of the poorer strata of life in the capital and far away from Mayfair, need brief explication. One excellent example is *She, a Chinese* (Xiaolu Guo, 2012). The female protagonist, Li Mei, goes through a painful and at times impetuous self-discovery, captured via this wayward Chinese immigrant drifting through life and English and European lovers in millennial London. Guo's film echoes *Dirty Pretty Things* (2002), directed by Stephen Frears, which concentrates on two 'illegals' – a Turkish woman and a Nigerian doctor-turned-precariat – employed under the table in a shabby three-star London hotel. Their marked exploitation in the labour market is underpinned by a criminal network that preys on asylum seekers and migrants desperate for a European Union passport. These places on film also speak to what Nikos Papastergiadis refers to as a city with an accelerating 'turbulence of migration';[44] here, movement is disruptive, stressful and often leads to feelings of displacement and alienation. Indeed, London can be a lonely place for the newly arrived and many of the films analysed in this collection emphasise this feeling of homesickness and exploitation. Guo's *She, a Chinese* and Frears's *Dirty Pretty Things* both fight against a *mobile gaze* or *destination-scape* of London's boroughs and cityscape, and are imbued, instead, with seedy and lesser seen spaces: tiny and scruffy studio and shared flats, cluttered gardens and nondescript maintenance rooms, dimly lit car parks, taxi stands and bathrooms in hostels and rundown hotels. Such severe exclusion in London's unfair housing system also finds room for discussion in this collection.

Chapter summary

Invariably, London's place-based film shooting has mandated that cultural globalisation's coordinates are unimpeded. The majority of films covered in this book benefitted from London's once continuous process of globalism. Times are different now as London was off-limits for many in the years 2020 and 2021 because of the COVID-19 pandemic, thus preventing new cinematic imagery from circulating unceasingly. Coming to grips with nearly two years of devastation, coupled with the disconnectedness brought on by COVID-19 as a biosocial inhibitor to cultural openness and the resulting deceleration of cultural globalisation, also caused by deglobalisation[45] – and in particular location shooting – became the main catalyst for wishing to publish this book. Thus, the closure of the number one travel destination in the world – when the city was in lockdown – meant that earlier visual manifestations of London became more symbolically coveted, with people gazing longingly at London on screen for two-plus years. Simulacra of London were in, while sojourns during that disconnected period were largely out. In such grim times, it is microscopic points of view about places in London's past explored by filmmakers that make the city a place of global opportunity and openness.

Despite London being given the dual accolade of leading tourist destination and instantaneous and unmistakable mediatic global city, Heathrow Airport would sit dormant, like most international airports. It remained largely passenger-less throughout 2020. Only in the spring of 2022 did this transportation hub on the outskirts of Zone 6 and fourteen miles west of central London come slowly back to life; only a trickle of motion compared to the tens of thousands of passengers that shuttled through its gates each day in pre-pandemic times. Lost, temporarily, was the euphoria of seeing loved ones and friends passing through the Heathrow arrival gates. *Love, Actually* (2003), by Richard Curtis, captured this precise sentiment in its mawkish epilogue: the Christmas-themed romantic comedy shows its fictive characters gleefully greeting one another in the world's most recognisable airport. Such glittery glamour or even the economy-class of travel and reunions with loved ones seemed very far away from reality. Still, we must remember that London has survived plagues and invading armies, aerial bombardments and terror attacks, even cultural catastrophes like Brexit. To mourn a city's subtle cultural demise via the pandemic or through an ill-timed political ideology requires us to recognise its high period in terms of its measurable global cultural contribution.

We draw upon the term art cinema as the key mode of filmmaking that is analysed in this book. Rather than cinema telegraphing a city's domestic and dominant character, its larger-than-life-presence and stereotypical imagery, a pre-eminence that usually favours one ethnic majority and national imagined community over others, many of the films analysed in this collection counter this notion. Thus, visitor filmmakers tend to make art cinema films, recognised by their international aesthetic that provides a renewed sense of this global city. These cityscapes honed by filmmakers challenge precise geographical, ethnic and historio-cultural contexts. In Chapter 1 Jingan MacPherson Young historicises the émigré labourers working in London's Soho district and one Hungarian producer angling to bring lesser-told stories to screen. Following in Chapter 2 Kevin M. Flanagan looks at the crumminess of London interiors in the hangover from the Swinging London period and what John Hill calls British cinema's drabbest period – the 1970s. He analyses filmmakers from the United States and Poland who use London interiority as a means of intensifying any number of psychosocial issues, ranging from PTSD in *Repulsion* (1965) to voyeurism *Wonderwall* (1968) to exploitative labour in *Death Line* (1972). Paul Newland provides a sturdy introduction to Gavrik Losey's use of London geography in Chapter 3.

The rise of what Stuart Hall would say is a 'complex structure of relations' is embodied in the Black Audio Film Collective's corpus of experimental film. In Chapter 4 Malini Guha provides a detailed analysis of *Twilight City* (1989) by the BAFC and how this focus on Black British culture shows a multiculturalising London – what she sees as the birth of global London.

Hipsters, gangsters and 1950s retro make an appearance in Aki Kaurismäki's *I Hired a Contract Killer*. In Chapter 5 Claire Monk provides an exhaustive and erudite treatment of the Finnish-directed London noir in all its exquisite parts. Through a deep analysis of *I Hired a Contract Killer*'s mapping of the 'off-centre location' of East London we can understand the slow gentrification of these unidentifiable locales that registers as a double articulation for the nihilism of the film: a pastiche of coolly ambivalent characters and banal urban space.

Londoners living in less accommodating communities, those from different diasporas that are important to the globalness of the capital, often come to counter city policy makers, millionaires and billionaires, think tank wonks, wandering celebrities and embassy attachés and academics whose elevated entitlement puts them above the fray. Those unconcerned with greater lived social realities beyond their boroughs or neighbourhoods want to keep striated difference in place; their communities remain undisturbed as frenetic new groups and individuals culturally recalibrate and creatively disinherit their local histories and traditions, actively renewing and remaking them in the process. Victor Fan in Chapter 9 looks to diasporas from East and South-East Asia that do just that: reclaim urban enclaves for themselves.

In Charlotte Brunsdon's Epilogue, she reverses the trend of looking at transnational or global elements and forces active in London to see *The Street* as a film that articulates gentrification and Brexit, in a community of ethnically diverse Londoners who also wish to relocalise their patch in the capital. The tragedy of the Grenfell Tower fire becomes an internal reference point in *The Street*. This is an important marker because it illustrates how the multicultural precariat class is still suffering due to underfunding on council estates which are hidden in plain sight in posh enclaves in London. These communities are subsumed in the global logic of megacity discourses, which don't account for marginalisation through improper housing maintenance or dislocation by new residents, two inimical problems for London that are highlighted, rigorously, in this chapter.

India and Brazil, part of the BRIC country grouping, together with Nigeria are three countries with their own storied film industries and megacities that are engaged in cross-cultural production, and have each staged films in London. In Chapter 6 Shakuntala Banaji and Rahoul Masrani provide another layer to Bollywood's global proximity to London, showing London's Hindi cinema presence in the capital and using the problems of inter/multiculturalism to show the nationalistic prowess of Hindi culture in the world. For Latin America, Stephanie Dennison's Chapter 7 provides a thorough unpicking of Henrique Goldman's *Jean Charles* (2009), a dramatisation about mistaken identity and splintering multiculturalism after the London bombings in 2005. Uchenna Onuzulike's Chapter 8 brings the film *Osuofia in London* – a Nollywood *Crocodile Dundee* (Faiman, 1986) – to bear on several fascinating trichotomies through the collision of two cultures and their compressed cross-cultural fusion: (i) African/Nigerian/Igbo; (ii) Western/British/Global London. This comedy of errors, full of cultural shocks, is a smart intervention.

Global Hollywood is said to use London as its backyard. Two chapters capture different scales and modes of intention in their narratives to expand the transatlantic cultural relationship between audiences and industries. London is transformed into an action film set piece in Lawrence Webb's Chapter 10, with particular focus on *Mission: Impossible – Fallout*. Liveness is the central premise of the streamed film *Lost in London* (2017) directed by Hollywood A-lister Woody Harrelson. Michael A. Unger and Keith B. Wagner in Chapter 11 see this both as a digital happening, a type of beamed trickery for its livestreamed plot, and as multicultural in its selection of cast and the purposeful cosmopolitan ethos attached to this ambitious film.

Finishing out the collection, in Chapter 12 Ana Virginia López Fuentes theorises the aftermath of the London 7/7 terror attacks in Rachid Bouchareb's *London River* (2009). The film dramatises the difficult task of cultural reconciliation after the heinous London bombings on 7 July 2005, setting the film in Finsbury Park. The French Algerian filmmaker re-visions the city as a persistent intercultural place, explored through two bereaved parents who look for their missing children. These visitors to London – an African French Muslim and a British expat – eventually go into mourning after learning that their twenty-something son and daughter died in the attack; but they take some solace in discovering their children's loving interracial relationship.

Science fiction is discussed in Chapter 13 by Mónica Martín. Her analysis of *Children of Men* turns a cosmopolitan lens on the Mexican-directed but London-shot dystopian thriller about a near future and the threat of global infertility. This global film is also prescient in commenting on the rise of alt-right regimes and their demonisation of immigrant communities that London equally faces through policies introduced by both Labour and Tory parties. In an age of Brexit and anti-immigration across Europe, Martín's decolonial reading of *Children of Men* also prompts readers to overcome whitened and patriarchal forms of cosmopolitanism.

Where all these chapters speak to one another thematically is in their subtle (or ambitious) pursuit of what London means as a superdiverse space and place for filmmaking, persisting beyond British national culture's cinematic imprint. Media of all forms can promote an accumulatory penchant for superdiversity and difference and London speaks to these sociocultural and ethnic principles better than most cities elsewhere in the world. From the late 1990s to the late 2010s, global London on screen became an unrivalled place in the cinematic world system of cities for its versatility and multivalent fulcrum of symbolic exchanges, resistances and assimilation by people and creative types coming to this megacity from all across the globe. A new facet in British cinema history's subnational production, London as site and city film becomes a transnational by-product and a sub-strand of world cinema studies as well.

Notes

1 Bhaskar Sarkar, 'Plasticity and the Global', *Framework: The Journal of Cinema and Media*, 56.2 (Fall 2015), p. 452.
2 Ibid., p. 452.
3 Rosalind Galt and Karl Schoonover, eds, *Global Art Cinema* (Oxford: Oxford University Press, 2010).
4 Keith B. Wagner, 'Globalizing Discourses: Literature and Film in the Age of Google', *Globalizations*, 12.2 (April 2015), pp. 229–43. Keith B. Wagner,

'Global Cinema in the Age of Deglobalization: Trans-territorial Compulsions and the Plenipotentiary Potential of Human Activities in *Cloud Atlas* and *Okja*', *Globalizations* (2023), DOI: 10.1080/14747731.2023.2171624.
5 Charlotte Brunsdon, *London in Cinema: The Cinematic City since 1945* (London: BFI Publishing, 2007), p. 14.
6 Christopher Chase-Dunn and Barry Gills, 'Waves of Globalization and Resistance in the Capitalist World-System: Social Movements and Critical Global Studies', in *Critical Globalization Studies*, ed. Richard P. Appelbaum and William I. Robinson (London: Routledge, 2005), pp. 45–54.
7 Peter Ackroyd, 'London Luminaries and Cockney Visionaries', in *The Collection* (London: Vintage, 2002).
8 Steve Vertovec, 'Super-diversity and Its Implications', *Ethnic and Racial Studies*, 30.6 (2007), pp. 1024–54.
9 Writing a guide to navigate London as a global emporium of choice, I borrow Philip Baker and Jeehoon Kim's subtitle to their book, *Global London: Where to Find Almost Everything Ethnic and Cultural in the Multilingual Capital* (Dublin: Battlebridge Publishers, 2003). For more academic discussions of globalising London, see Tanya Agathocleous, *Urban Realism and the Cosmopolitan Imagination in the Nineteenth Century: Visible City, Invisible World* (Cambridge: Cambridge University Press, 2011); Malini Guha, *From Empire to World: Migrant London and Paris in Cinema* (Edinburgh: Edinburgh University Press, 2015); Maurizio Cinquegrani, *Of Empire and the City: Remapping Early British Cinema* (Oxford: Lang, 2014).
10 Andreas Huyssen, 'Introduction', in *Other Cities, Other Worlds: Urban Imaginaries in a Global Age* (Durham, NC: Duke University Press, 2007).
11 Linda Krause and Patrice Petro, eds, *Global Cities: Cinema, Architecture, and Urbanism in a Digital Age* (New Brunswick, NJ: Rutgers University Press, 2003); Johan Andersson and Lawrence Webb, eds, *Global Cinematic Cities: New Landscapes of Film and Media* (New York: Columbia University Press, 2016).
12 Chris Hamnett, *Unequal City: London in the Global Arena* (London: Routledge, 2003).
13 For the concept of Global Hollywood, see Toby Miller, Nitin Govil, John McMurria and Richard Maxwell, *Global Hollywood* (London: BFI Publishing, 2001).
14 See Andy Pratt, *Clustering the Media Industries in London* (2010). For a wider global purview, see Dwayne Winseck and Jin Dal Yong, eds, *The Political Economies of Media: The Transformation of the Global Media Industries* (London: Bloomsbury Academic, 2011).
15 Mark Shiel, 'Cinema and the City in History and Theory', in Mark Shiel and Tony Fitzmaurice, eds, *Cinema and the City: Film and Urban Societies in a Global Context* (Oxford: Blackwell Publishers, 2001), pp. 8–9. Also see François Penz and Richard Koeck, eds, *Cinematic Urban Geographies* (New York: Palgrave Macmillan, 2017).
16 See the Globalization and World Cities Research Network (GaWC), a think-tank that studies the relationship between world cities in the context of globalisation.

17 Tim Hall and Phil Hubbard, *The Entrepreneurial City: Geographies of Politics, Regime and Representation* (Chichester: Wiley, 1998).
18 Emma Duncan, 'On a High', *The Economist* (12 June 2012), www.economist.com/special-report/2012/06/28/on-a-high (accessed 1 June 2020).
19 Saskia Sassen, *The Global City: New York, London, Tokyo* (Princeton, NJ: Princeton University Press, 1991), p. 4.
20 Ibid., p. 31.
21 Merrill Scheiler, *Skyscraper Cinema: Architecture and Gender in American Film* (Minneapolis, MN: University of Minnesota Press, 2009), p. 60.
22 Peter Kivisto, *Multiculturalism in a Global Society* (Oxford: Blackwell Publishing, 2002), p. 15.
23 Nick Redfern, 'Defining British Cinema: Transnational and Territorial Film Policy in the United Kingdom', *Journal of British Film and Television*, 4.1 (2007), p. 155. The term was first introduced by Kevin R. Cox, 'Introduction: Globalization and Its Politics in Question' in *Spaces of Globalization: Reasserting the Power of the Local*, ed. Kevin R. Cox (New York: Guilford Press, 1997).
24 Brunsdon, *London in Cinema*, p. 21.
25 Pam Hirsch and Chris O'Rourke, 'Introduction: Film London', in *London on Film*, ed. Hirsch and O'Rourke (London: Palgrave Macmillan, 2017), p. 1.
26 Ibid., p. 2.
27 Ian Christie, 'East-West: Reflections on the Changing Cinematic Topography of London', in *London on Film*, ed. Pam Hirsch and Chris O'Rourke (London: Palgrave Macmillan, 2017), pp. 239–40.
28 Hirsch and O'Rourke, 'Introduction', p. 10.
29 Claire Monk, "Where I Come From, We Eat Places Like This for Breakfast': Aki Kaurismäki's *I Hired a Contract Killer* as Transnational Representation of Local London', *Journal of British Cinema and Television*, 6.2 (August 2009), p. 269.
30 Galt and Schoonover, *Global Art Cinema*, p. 7. For notions of location shooting in London, see Neil Mitchell, 'London: City of the Imagination', in *World Film Locations: London*, ed. Neil Mitchell (Bristol: Intellect, 2011), pp. 6–7. For textual foci on London, see Gail Cunningham and Stephen Barber, eds, *London Eyes: Reflections in Text and Image* (New York: Berghahn Books, 2007).
31 Emily Apter, 'Oneworldedness: Or Paranoia as a World System', *American Literary History*, 18.2 (Summer 2006), p. 364.
32 Mads Anders Baggesgaard, 'Picturing the World Cinematic Globalization in the Deserts of Babel', *Journal of Aesthetics & Culture*, 5.1 (2013), p. 2.
33 Steven Vertovec, 'The Emergence of Super-diversity in Britain', Working Paper No. 25, University of Oxford, 2006, www.compas.ox.ac.uk/wp-content/uploads/WP-2006-025-Vertovec_Super-Diversity_Britain.pdf (accessed 10 June 2022).
34 Ulf Hannerz, *Cultural Complexity: Studies in the Social Organization of Meaning* (New York: Columbia University Press, 1992).
35 Chek Wai Lau, 'The Ownership of Cultural Hybrids', in *Interculturalism: Exploring Critical Issues*, ed. Diane Powell and Fiona Sze (Oxford: Interdisciplinary Press, 2004), pp. 121–5.

36 Nasar Meer and Tariq Modood, 'How Does Interculturalism Contrast with Multiculturalism', *Journal of Aesthetics and Culture*, 5.1 (2011), p. 2.
37 Jan Nederveen Pieterse quoting Michael Storper in *Global Multiculture, Flexible Acculturation* (London: Routledge, 2007), p. 68.
38 Recently Patrick Wintour has argued that the United Kingdom can be a 'global broker, not a great power', borrowing from the published white paper by the Chatham House think-tank based in London. Despite the imperialist echoes here, how might films about London be seen as cultural brokers to this city before the political reality of Brexit materialised into law and reality, and COVID-19 kept people marooned and largely immobilised due to fear about the pandemic's spread? The films gathered here when viewed collectively offer London's globality as intercessor to the city's dense and enigmatic richness, something not universally accepted or acknowledged, but instead something that is brokered through these very films.
39 'Famous Londoners Tell VisitLondon.com What Makes the City So Great As London Breaks a Record for Tourists Visiting the City', *Cision PR Newswire* (16 January 2014), http://bit.ly/3nqyujJ (accessed 10 June 2022).
40 Andrew Church and Martin Frost, 'The Employment Focus of Canary Wharf and the Isle of Dogs: A Labour Market Perspective', *The London Journal*, 17.2 (1992), p. 137.
41 Robert Murphy, 'Citylife: Urban Fairy-tales in Late 90s British Cinema', in *The British Cinema Book*, ed. R. Murphy, 3rd ed. (London: British Film Institute, 2009), pp. 357–65; Nigel Mather, *Tears of Laughter: Comedy-Drama in 1990s British Cinema* (Manchester: Manchester University Press, 2006), p. 120.
42 Hamnett, *Unequal City*, p. 8.
43 See John Eade, *Placing London: From Imperial Capital to Global City* (New York; Oxford: Berghahn Books, 2000), p. 2. Also see Cinquegrani, *Of Empire and the City*.
44 See Nikos Papastergiadis, *The Turbulence of Migration: Globalization, Deterritorialization and Hybridity* (Cambridge: Polity Press, 2000).
45 Wagner, 'Global Cinema in an Era of Deglobalization'.

1

'God is everywhere!': engineering the immigrant landscape of Emeric Pressburger's *Miracle in Soho*

Jingan MacPherson Young

Anglo-Italian Julia Gozzi (Belinda Lee) is kneeling at the altar of Saint Anthony of Padua, the patron saint of lost things.[1] She is praying for a miracle. We move to a close-up of her determined face, brilliantly lit by a golden candelabra as she urgently pleads for the return of Michael Morgan (John Gregson), an Irish road labourer and incorrigible breaker of hearts, including her own. Shortly thereafter, her prayers are answered. Outside St Anthony's Church, the water mains beneath asphalt that has been newly laid by Morgan and his road gang burst open, flooding the lane. 'Yes, yes, God *is* everywhere!' proclaims Salvationist postman Sam Bishop (Cyril Cusack) as the locals lament the unforeseen damage to their beloved street. The following morning, Michael returns with the road gang to repair the street and the lovers are reconciled.[2]

This sequence marks the conclusion to *Miracle in Soho*, which was directed by Julian Amyes and released in the summer of 1957. The film was executive produced by Earl St John for the J. Arthur Rank Organisation and co-produced and written by Emeric Pressburger whose original version of the script was written in 1934 under the title *The Miracle in St Anthony's Lane*.

Upon its release, the film was a failure critically and at the box office. Commentators seemed unanimous in their disappointment with the cinematically engineered Soho set designed by Carmen Dillon, who had won an Academy Award for her work on *Hamlet* (Laurence Olivier, 1948). The self-contained, artificially constructed spaces of St Anthony's Lane, where commercial spaces of the pub, restaurant and church are erected side-by-side, add a bygone theatricality to the film. Soho is cinematically mapped as a cosmopolitan quarter, where the area's commercial and moral spaces are two conflicting and artificially constructed mechanisms.

Despite its negative reception, this forgotten film is a rare, big-budget treatment of London's Soho and a significant example of the British film industry's attempt to combat the British public's increased consumption of commercial television through the implementation of cross-marketing and other strategies aimed at appealing to the global marketplace. It also was a film which deliberately linked itself to Soho. The studio behind the film, the Rank Organisation, released the film during the week-long Soho Fair of 1957, going so far as to stage promotional one-offs, such as frivolous competitions where members of the principal cast such as Belinda Lee attended as guests. We can expect Pressburger regularly visited Soho, the physical locus of the British film industry headquarters from the 1930s until the end of the century, and felt inclined to capture the area's cultural diversity on film.[3] How did Pressburger's identity as an émigré filmmaker inform the film's reconstruction of the area? By this period, the Hungarian Jewish filmmaker had been living in Britain for over two decades, having emigrated as a refugee in 1935 before gaining full British citizenship in 1946. The topographical specificity found within Pressburger's final screenplay does suggest a fundamental and instinctive understanding of the urban arrangement of Soho's commercial economies. As a space of 'cultural difference [along with] extremely localised public spaces, complex history, unique customs and characters', Soho makes the ideal transitional site for exploring the immigrant and native interaction on screen.[4] However, the film's chief love story between the hedonist native Michael and the moral immigrant Julia conflicts with the film's underlying critique of urban life and the historical significance of Soho's entrepreneurs, largely immigrants, who provided the 'commercial blueprint for the area's renewal'.[5]

This chapter will discuss the film's reconstruction of Soho's immigrant landscape in the context of post-war commercial development and British cinema's treatment of cosmopolitanism. I argue this is a unique and important film, as a contribution to migrant portraits on screen but also as an attempt to depict Soho's diversity during an intense, transitory period. It is also worthy of reconsideration as a British film which holds an intrinsic relationship to Soho's renewal as a cosmopolitan-bohemian centre on the national and world stage.

Soho cosmopolitanism and British cinema

Soho's reputation for cosmopolitanism was produced by waves of immigration and by foreign entrepreneurs who were chief directors of the development of its commercial geography and cultural diversity. John Eade, who has detailed the area's transformation further in his book *Placing London* (2000), argues that 'In the context of the West End and London … Soho serves to sustain an ethnic boundary between insiders (the English/British majority) and outsiders (a varied minority of foreign, predominantly Continental, exotics.'⁶ The production of Soho's bohemia relied upon the consumption of the area's cosmopolitan atmosphere and blossoming forms of sexual commerce by a group consisting of writers, artists and musicians, who, in turn, constructed and cemented a particular (and subjective) Soho identity in the public sphere.

Although the promotion of 'otherness' in the public imagination helped to establish Soho as a distinctly cosmopolitan quarter and its bohemian tourists promoted its commercial businesses, it largely failed to attract mainstream British and international filmmakers to use Soho as a title setting for their films. As Eade has shown, 'During the twentieth century the link between London and the nation was crucially altered by the collapse of the world's most extensive empire. London's prestige as the epicentre of empire and nation was diminished between the 1950s and 1970s.'⁷ The wave of immigrants after the Second World War marked this transition with 'racialised boundaries between insiders and outsiders'.⁸ Similar transformations played out in Soho, a space which flourished as a result of its historical function as an immigrant locus. However, its role in the promotion of a 'Global Britain' in the immediate post-war period directly contradicted its reputation as a seedy underbelly, which was cemented by popular modes of literature during the 1920s.

From the 1930s onwards, British films did attempt to explore these 'transformations' within the context of national versus global Britain. However, as Ann Ogidi states, Black actors in British films of this period were often depicted as 'token representation(s) of black communities in England'.⁹ British cinema of the 1960s began to open up to the possibilities of more complex stories with films like *Sapphire* (1959) and *Flame in the Streets* (1961). According to Ogidi, 'This was also the decade when Black film pioneers Lionel Ngakane (*Jemima + Johnny*, 1966), Lloyd Reckord (*Ten Bob in Winter*, 1963) and Frankie Dymon (*Death May Be Your Santa Claus*, 1969) were making their first films about the experiences of Black people in the UK.'¹⁰ Similarly, there are only a handful of films depicting the lives of Soho's cosmopolitan, largely European, community. The musical film *Greek Street* (Sinclair Hill, 1930), retitled *Latin Love* for US release, follows a traditional love story between an Italian émigré, Rikki (William Freshman), a café owner who falls in love (perhaps to the point of obsession) with an aspiring English singer, Anna (Sari Maritza).¹¹ Val Guest's satirical comedy *Give Us the Moon* (1944) starred Margaret Lockwood as the leader of a Soho members-only club. Later, *Soho Conspiracy* (Cecil H. Williamson, 1950), which drew inspiration and incorporated footage from Mario Costa's musical film *Mad about Opera* (1948), follows the daughter of an Italian restaurant owner and her fiancé as they attempt to organise a concert to restore a Soho church damaged by the Blitz. Regarding the depiction of non-white European immigrants, *Piccadilly* (E. A. Dupont, 1929) remains the most widely recognised silent British film which featured Chinese characters and is noteworthy for its positioning in London's West End. To date, Soho's Chinatown and its British Chinese community appear only in two films, both released in the 1980s: *Ping Pong* (Po-Chih Leong, 1986) and *Soursweet* (Mike Newell, 1988).

Historically, Soho's bifurcated character rarely joined together to produce a hybrid, cosmopolitan-bohemian artefact. Inspired by local entrepreneurs, council members and London's city planners, the inaugural Soho Fair of 1955 ambitiously plotted to celebrate and exploit Soho's identities to promote itself on the post-war, global stage. From its successful debut, the fair became an annual, televised event organised by Soho's local entrepreneurs. The fair was devised as an attempt to rebrand the area nationally after the sensationalised reports made by the popular press alleging the increase in prostitution and crime in the West End and Soho had fostered a 'climate of disgust over the state of the metropolis'.[12] This occurred during the run-up to the Festival of Britain in 1951 and the coronation of Queen Elizabeth II which took place in 1953, the first televised coronation in history. It involved 'Lavishly illustrated press supplements ... together with the Pathé newsreel footage [that] depicted London as a site of glamorous international and imperial spectacle'.[13] Such 'imperial spectacle' filtered into the distinctly continental forms of entertainment offered by the festival, which included dance, an expansive offering of food from around the world, a float parade and a waiters' race. In many ways, *Miracle in Soho*'s ambitions to produce an authentic rendering of the Soho locality with cinematic spectacle were akin to the Soho Fair's overarching aim of commercial reinvention. This was directly aligned with post-war reconstruction for the metropolis and 'schemes for the beautification of the central area' in the 'interests of national and imperial renewal'.[14]

The Soho Fair does not explicitly feature in *Miracle in Soho*. However, the film has an intrinsic and reciprocal relationship to it. The film was released during the week of the 3rd Soho Fair in July 1957. Events scheduled during the Soho Fair to complement the film's release listed within the weekly London magazine *What's On in London* include the '*Miracle in Soho* Window Dressing Competition' and the 'Belinda Lee Challenge Cup' which took place at Lysbeth Hall in Soho Square.[15] The story is shaped in this image of Soho as a diverse, though traditionally conservative community. This is most evident in the opening sequence of *Miracle in Soho*, where the camera sweeps across grey and brown weather-beaten rooftops with the addition of a voice-over from an unseen (uncredited) male narrator who declares:

> There is an island in the great city of London, a little foreign island called Soho ... Italians live there and Greeks, French, Spaniards and Germans, Czechs and Hungarians, Maltese, Cypriots, Hindus and Muhammads. There's probably an Eskimo or two, certainly a few Scotsmen.[16]

The camera then sweeps across Soho's skyline, before zooming in on the fictional St Anthony's Lane storefronts and apartment windows. These belong to, according to Pressburger's script, 'Negros, Chinese, Spanish Woman, Mrs Mop, Swoboda, Mrs Belucci, Buddy Brown'.[17] This personalised engagement of visible geographical and cultural difference suggests a commodification of the experience of the modern world. The film views Soho as a continental gateway and major thoroughfare to the tourist city (London), serving as an intercultural or contact zone between national and global identities. The use of voice-over and tracking shots, a device used in documentary filmmaking and a technique adopted by many post-war Soho films, mimics the transcultural text of the guidebook and acts as a mediation between cultural differences. Although the film makes an admirable attempt to 'gaze' briefly at the lives of the Soho minority, it functions on a superficial level to add a dash of exoticism without any more overtly complex or meaningful ambitions.

The Making of an Englishman, immigration and exile

In the biography of Pressburger written by his grandson, the acclaimed Scottish director Kevin Macdonald, we learn of the 'peculiar twists of fate' which prevented the original *Miracle in Soho* script, first written in 1934, from going into full production: 'There did indeed seem to be a touch of divine intervention in the fortunes of *The Miracle in St Anthony's Lane* ... It was forever being bought or optioned.'[18] Macdonald also directed and produced a television documentary on his grandfather's life called *The Making of an Englishman*, which first aired on UK's Channel 4 in 1995. The film documents Pressburger's journey to England and further underscores the importance of his identity as an exile-filmmaker in England. Both of Macdonald's biographies of Pressburger further contribute to our understanding of his grandfather's films, for 'like so many other European refugees from Hitler' he became 'more Anglophile than the English'.[19]

By the mid-1950s, the Hungarian Jewish Pressburger had been residing in Great Britain for nearly two decades. The chief protagonists of *Miracle in Soho* emulate and assimilate to Englishness, echoing Pressburger's own story of exile. Born in Hungary as Imre József Pressburger in 1902, his migrant childhood led him to living in Prague, Stuttgart and Budapest following the outbreak of World War I. After arriving in Berlin in the 1920s, he found employment with the German UFA studios and worked on scripts in their dramaturgy department before leaving for France (Paris) in 1933 when working conditions for Jews became more difficult. He arrived in London two years later, becoming a protégé of fellow exile, the producer Alexander Korda of London Films who would later introduce him to the director Michael Powell.

Pressburger's successful working partnership with Powell had come to an end the year before the release of *Miracle in Soho*. Together, the pair produced thirteen films between 1943 and 1955 under the alias of The Archers, the majority of which 'expressed a deep fascination with and affection for Britishness'.[20] Following their separation, Powell's second project was the psychological crime thriller *Peeping Tom* (1960) which utilised Newman Passage in London's Fitzrovia (or north Soho) for its opening sequence in which a young filmmaker Mark Lewis (Carl Boehm) brutally murders a prostitute whilst simultaneously recording the violent act on his camera. Pressburger's second project, following a lost film entitled *Men Against Britannia* (Marcel Hellman, 1957), was *Miracle in Soho*, which he also co-produced.

Kevin Gough-Yates proclaims Pressburger 'one of only two exile scriptwriters who shaped significant careers in Britain', who is 'unique in that the sense of emptiness and dejection that he experienced as an exile'.[21] Interestingly, Pressburger's original script for the film told the story of German exiles in Paris and sought to explore the notion of the miracle as not so much a physical act as one of imagination:

> A few years earlier he had slept rough in a famous Berlin synagogue, planning to creep out just before morning service. Too late, he heard the congregation chanting, and crept down, only to be welcomed as a member of the quorum; the service had not started, and the sounds he had heard has been in his imagination. 'Surely', he claimed, 'a miracle.' A René Clair-like idea, full of character, with a number of interlocking stories, *Miracle in St Anthony's Lane* was another story of exile.[22]

Alternative versions of Pressburger's script provide more expansive detail of the Gozzi family's process of emigration and initially they plotted their journey to New York instead of Canada. In one of Pressburger's later draft versions of the script reset in London, he devotes an entire scene to detailing the Gozzi family's visit to the American Embassy in Grosvenor Square which he describes as 'A small, new, clean, efficient room, divided by a counter [where] Notices inform you that you are on American soil.'[23]

Although I have found no clear explanation for this change of the Gozzi's emigration to Canada instead of the United States, it may have been due to Canada's Commonwealth status and would sit reasonably well within the Rank Organisation's reprioritisation of promotion of its products and stars nationally and throughout Europe.[24]

But it would be several decades before the film impresario J. Arthur Rank would put into motion Pressburger's new version of his portrayal of a cosmopolitan village and its habitués, 'reset among the Italian community in London's Soho', which opens with the sudden and unwelcome invasion of a road gang to replace the asphalt of the fictitious St Anthony's Lane, described by Pressburger as a 'tiny haven in the heart of Cosmopolitan Soho' where 'quietness reigns'.[25] The finalised story for the film is that of the redemption of the self-serving philanderer Michael Morgan through the love of a good woman, Soho local Julia Gozzi, an Italian immigrant who works at the local pet shop. A potential love affair is interrupted by her family's decision to emigrate to Canada. Morgan's redemption is manifested through Julia's prayer for a miracle to stop him leaving Soho after finishing work on the lane, which ultimately results in the water mains flooding the street, causing him to return. However, the doubts vehemently expressed by Julia Gozzi's siblings Mafalda (Rosalie Crutchley) and Filippo (Ian Bannen) on emigrating abroad are never fully developed and their expressed desire to cultivate their own commercial businesses are abruptly dropped by the film. The siblings' desire to remain part of the Soho fabric as opposed to remaining in the family unit with Mama Gozzi (Marie Burke) and Papa Gozzi (Peter Illing) reflect Louis Wirth's argument that the social heterogeneity found within cities reinforces the tendency of the individual to pursue their own interests, leading to a loss of community ties and traditions and an increase in social disorganisation.[26]

Pressburger's decision to spotlight an Italian family living in Soho was wholly unsurprising. As Britain's allies in World War I, the population of Italians in London 'peaked in 1911, at 12,000 but these fell by only a couple of hundred by 1921'.[27] The largest Italian colony in Britain was originally located in London, around the area known as Saffron Hill in Clerkenwell. There, Italian immigrants 'cultivated their own industries [...] catering for their own needs with cafés, delicatessen, restaurants, clubs, a theatre and dance hall'.[28] The 'brilliantly coloured' procession known as 'Our Lady of Mount Carmel', which occurred every July from St Peter's Church located on 136 Clerkenwell Road, was one of several public spectacles organised by the community each summer in London between the wars.[29] Elisabetta Girelli, who has partly examined the representation of the Italian family in *Miracle in Soho*, notes that by the 1920s, 'Italian catering continued to thrive ... Italians in London were entering the exclusive hotel and restaurant industry.'[30] After World War I, the population of Italians in that area moved westwards, largely to Soho. By 1934, according to Jerry White, Soho became known as 'London's Italian quarter'.[31] The area's close proximity to the entertainment centres of Piccadilly Circus and the West End rendered it a dining hub and Italian restaurants prospered. They were run by pre-war immigrants who 'had made their way up the catering trade' and were 'skilled in the demands of display, décor and performance', providing the English public with continental food and taste.[32]

According to Judith Walkowitz, Italian restaurants in Soho were places of hard work and strict regimentation for the immigrants employed there. The Gozzi family's work ethic and value for the Soho community is emphasised by both the community's support of their emigration and their hierarchical positions within various commercial businesses around the Soho lane. The eldest Gozzi daughter, Mafalda (Rosalie Crutchley), manages the Anacapri restaurant, her brother Filippo co-manages Ferrari's Wine Shop and the youngest, Julia, is a shop assistant at Mrs Coleman's pet shop. The Anacapri restaurant is the film's second most used location after St Anthony's Church. Inter- and post-war Soho's catering establishments 'provided stage sets for English fantasies of travel and escape'.[33] The interiors of the Anacapri restaurant are plastered with aspirational travel posters depicting Sardinian coastlines.

Walkowitz has also highlighted how Italian restaurants were stages for political drama, for 'Fascists used the portable food culture of Italy as a vehicle to solidify fiercely nationalistic patriotism at home and abroad. Beginning in 1921, they especially targeted the West End and Soho catering industry as the focal point for fascist takeover of the "Italian colony."'[34] Conflicts between fascist and anti-fascist Italians in Soho existed but the outbreak of World War II and Mussolini's subsequent declaration of war on Britain and its allies in 1940 further intensified racial hostility towards Italian émigrés. Anti-Italian demonstrations took place throughout the country. In Soho, there was an anti-fascist riot prompted by Mussolini's speech in the summer of 1940, which saw the smashing of windows of local Italian businesses, later named by the press as 'The Battle of Soho'.[35] Although *Miracle in Soho* does arguably contain stereotypical representations of émigrés (e.g. the Gozzi family regularly use exaggerated hand gestures during tense exchanges), it is still an example of a sympathetic portrayal (perhaps even acting as a type of anti-fascist protest) of the hardworking Italian family who are respected members of the Soho community. The other commercial/trade spaces are owned and run by the immigrant community: Ferrari's Wine Shop and Mr Swoboda's Continental Bakery. The bakery shop window, which is deliberately kept in shot during the arrival of the road gang to the street in the opening sequence, contains a sign which assures us that this shop is *entirely* British. This may refer to the end of food rationing in Britain in 1954. However, when Michael defends his skirt-chasing habits to the postman Sam Bishop, he pointedly responds that women *aren't* on the ration, suggesting the film takes place in the years of de-rationing.

Production and 1950s Britain

There is a peculiar irony to the ultimate cinematic realisation of Pressburger's script in mid-1950s Britain. Christopher Booker, one of the founding members of *Private Eye* (1961–63) and resident scriptwriter for the satirical television series *That Was the Week That Was* (1962–63), has described in enigmatic detail the 'Never Had It So Good' prosperity of mid-1950s Britain, where 'Increasing personal incomes and homeownership caused a boom in consumer goods, American-style supermarkets and striptease clubs swiftly spread throughout Soho and the cities of the North. Commercial television entered a golden age.'[36]

The income boom in 1950s Britain created novel forms of popular leisure, and the increase in television ownership inevitably led to the decline of cinema-going. In 1956, cinema attendance numbered 1,101 million (down from 1,635 million in 1946). One year later, the Rank Organisation, one of the most dominant forces in UK film production during and following the war, was forced to amalgamate its Gaumont and Odeon cinema circuits resulting in eighty of the Rank Organisation's cinemas closing over the next three years. Chibnall discusses how Rank's expansion of 'contract artists' during the 1950s was 'met with a cautious welcome by a press that was suspicious of publicist hype'.[37] Concurrently, Rank and other British studios were struggling to option films that would appeal to younger audiences who dominated nearly half of their cinema's regular weekly audience. But this did not deter its leader, J. Arthur Rank, whose ferocious promotional strategies for its stars and films in this period, including 'a drive to popularise its contract artists on a scale never before attempted', render *Miracle in Soho* a worthy film to discuss in relation to the history of the post-war British film industry and its relationship to television.[38]

The film's director, Julian Amyes, began his feature film career with a 'competent, if unadventurous, Korean war-story' and joined the BBC in 1951 as a producer.[39] His engagement as director on *Miracle in Soho* was most likely a strategic move on behalf of the studio to employ a technically competent and knowledgeable individual who saw the potential of strengthening the relationship between cinema and television. According to an article published in *Sight and Sound* (1958), Amyes was 'one of the most accomplished directors working in British television', which certainly appears to accord with the Rank Organisation's measured initiatives to collaborate with television. Interestingly, Amyes would only work as a director with the Rank Organisation on *Miracle in Soho*, a film 'less realistic in style and perhaps for that reason less successful'.[40]

The film was shot in Eastmancolor on a mammoth studio set located at Pinewood Studios in Buckinghamshire. The film's director of photography was Christopher Challis, a British cinematographer with a career spanning over seventy British feature films. He was also a long-time collaborator of Pressburger and Powell on films such as *The Small Back Room* (1949), *The Tales of Hoffmann* (1951) and *Ill Met by Moonlight* (1957), the latter being the final Powell and Pressburger 'Archers' film. One black-and-white photograph found within the Moviestore Collection taken during production displays the complexity of art director Carmen Dillon's design and reconstruction of this neighbourhood, albeit fictional, of Soho. In the photograph, we see Challis, cameramen, supporting actors and lighting rigs positioned within close proximity of one another.[41] The facades of the diverse array of shops, schools, flats and restaurants operated by residents of the street, which are specifically dictated by Pressburger's screenplay, highlight the imagined-authentic sphere of commercial Soho but also one that is utilised by guidebook-style filmmaking.[42]

The film is also an important artefact in our examination of technological transformations in the British film industry. Sarah Street has discussed the film in relation to the history of Eastmancolor, a 'relatively cheap widely available film stock' which revolutionised British film from the end of the 1950s onwards. In the article, she examines the ways colour films from the period such as *Miracle in Soho* and Mankowitz's *A Kid for Two Farthings* 'provided an opportunity for greater realism'.[43] Whilst both films were more 'magical realist than hard-hitting social realist films, their vibrant, multicultural settings invested them with a quasi-documentary imperative to deliver "authenticity" at a time when colour was still a relative novelty'.[44] Street states that, for *Miracle in Soho*, Dillon created a particularly 'muted' palette in her recreation of the cosmopolitan locus. The only visibly vibrant or bright colours used in the film are on the scarlet-coloured road closure sign used by the road gang, for 'Chris Challis's cinematography was designed to convey a gritty, realist palette that was supported by art director Carmen Dillon's "restrained" vision'; she later said, 'We decided that all the colours should be as muted as possible, with no strong blacks, whites or primaries. The only patch of sky to be seen was through a narrow alley.'[45] This choice to evoke a muted realism was perhaps employed to assist in the dilution of the film's magical realist elements, embodied by Julia's miracles.

Upon release of the film, critics were disappointed with what they saw as an artificially rendered Soho. *Monthly Film Bulletin* declared, 'This depressing production, with its synthetic Soho setting, has characters conceived strictly within the less happy conventions of British comedy.' *Variety* said, 'A rather slow-moving sentimental yarn', and *Picturegoer* condemned its 'wispy plot, set in a studio-built Soho street', though considering it hopeful in its introduction to a 'peaceful mixture of people, far removed from the gangsters and floozies that usually people the screen Soho'.[46] Critics in recent years have taken a similar view. The British Film Institute's Fiction Curator Dylan Cave said, 'The huge sets [which although they] complemented Pressburger's view of the magic that appears in everyday life ... in a climate increasingly dominated by social realism ... looked stilted and fake.'[47] The announcement for the film's premiere in London was splashed on the front page of *What's On in London* in 1957. The film was described as a 'sentimental little fairy story' which failed in its cinematic representation of Soho. However, they also jokingly added in their review, 'Of course, this isn't really Soho at all, but I don't suppose that's going to worry anyone except a few fussy Sohoians.'[48]

According to Steve Chibnall, during this period, J. Arthur Rank had 'supped with the devil' in extending his efforts to promote films by advertising on new platforms, which included purchasing advertising slots on commercial television and in popular women's magazines. For the film's publicity, Rank even produced a twenty-minute film entitled *Full Screen Ahead* which was screened in Rank's cinemas in April 1957, several months before the film was released in cinemas.[49] The film takes its audience on a day out at Pinewood Studios led by Belinda Lee, with a visit to the set of *Miracle in Soho*. In the year of the film's release, Lee endorsed cosmetics such as Vitapointe of Paris in the *Daily Express*. Marketing for the product even managed to incorporate Pressburger's film, for the tagline reads: 'I want to tell the world! I've found a hair dressing cream that works miracles!'[50] Simultaneously, the movie fan magazine *Picturegoer* ran several profiles of the then twenty-one-year-old Belinda Lee in a partial attempt to reinvent her public persona from pin-up to 'serious' actor.[51] This emphasises the painstaking efforts by studios in this period, including the Rank Organisation's big idea of 1955–57 which involved forgoing the American film market for Europe: 'When Rank had a star such as Belinda Lee, who they believed would appeal to the Italian market, they used the most talented of Studio Favalli's illustrators to promote her films ... Cesselon depicted her as an Anglo-Italian girl in *Miracle in Soho*.'[52] On paper, the film was seemingly the perfect vehicle for Lee's rise to stardom and Rank's move to colonise the European marketplace. Unfortunately, their respective efforts did little to increase the film's appeal at home or abroad.[53] I believe the negative position of critics on the superficial 'authenticity' of the film's Soho could not have been wholly satisfied due to the technological constraints of the period alongside the filmmakers' and Rank studio's desire for control as opposed to the potential risks and great costs of on-location shooting. However, the particular reconstruction of Soho and its community was no doubt driven by Pressburger's imagining of Soho as an area of romantic mysticism and religious faith. His representation succeeds only partially, specifically in the depiction of the convergence of cultural diversity in Soho, but the film's refusal to delve deeper into its history, cultural legacy and development produces an arguably one-dimensional, superficial product.

St Anthony's Lane

In many respects, Soho can be likened to a cultural experiment where large-scale movements of capital and culture are played out in intensely local settings.[54] The localised spaces of the pub and church located at opposite ends of St Anthony's Lane act as metaphor for the conflicting lives of immigrants and natives. This is demonstrated by the Pig & Pot pub, a working-class space which is patronised by predominantly English labourers and tradesmen. In the film, this space is not frequented by the lane's migrant populations; even the pub's landlord, Old Bill (Douglas Ives), warns Michael to beware of foreigners who 'carry knives' (perhaps another signalling of racial discrimination against Italians in the period). The film also plays on existing archetypal representations of Britishness. Charlotte Brunsdon's identification of the pub as a 'low-life landmark' rings true in the case of *Miracle in Soho*. The Pig & Pot's dark and smoky interior 'permit[s] chance interactions and can easily be produced in the studio' and makes the distinction between public and private spaces.[55] This designation aligns with other British films of the period, providing familiar markers for national audiences.

Two miracles actually take place within St Anthony's Church. Shortly after Filippo's discovery of Morgan and Gwladys's affair causes a further rift within the Gozzi family, the Gozzis have been to a concert at the Royal Albert Hall, as relayed to us by the previous scene where Michael listens to the concert and yearns for Julia inside the cramped flat he shares with his father. The Gozzis then attend Sunday mass with other members of the migrant community. Whilst the congregation prays, Julia stands and lights a candle. The camera closes in on her face and we hear her internal thoughts. She prays for her brother to 'do the right thing' by her father. Her prayers are soon answered when Filippo agrees to emigrate with the family, shown as he enters the church and joins in with the choir.[56]

Kevin Gough-Yates has suggested that Julia's answered 'miracles' are in fact a reflection of the changes Pressburger made within his scripts from the 1930s and 1940s: 'The question is less whether the "miracle" is actually a miracle, conjured up by a prayer in the church, but more whether it exists in the imagination of a lovesick girl.'[57] This may relate to Michael Powell's rejection of working on the film. Gough-Yates suggests the filmmaker believed the script 'lacked "substance" [... and] recognised it as too close to [their 1946 film] *A Matter of Life and Death* and didn't want to tread old ground'.[58] The film arguably draws upon the 'rich and strange' magical realism that Raymond Durgnat claims pervades Powell and Pressburger's films released during and shortly after the Second World War.[59] In addition, Powell and Pressburger's films hold an equal fascination for the cinematic relationship between character and place. He states, 'The impact of place on character is explored [by Powell and Pressburger], as landscapes imprint their effect on protagonists, or as concrete places become externally projected renditions of subjective states. These new worlds are given a sense of magic – sometimes utopian, sometimes threatening, sometimes surreal.'[60]

As one body, St Anthony's Lane is a device employed by Pressburger to emphasise his predominant themes of community-under-threat and faith-in-doubt. They wholly manifest themselves during the climactic moments of the film when Julia proves her moral fortitude, embodied by her final prayer to Saint Anthony. The concluding sequence is not simply a demonstration of the magical. It is also a selfless act of redemption. Julia, the daughter of Italian immigrants, has sacrificed the promise of a new life with her family in Canada for Michael, a self-proclaimed lothario who does little to prove he is worthy of her love. We can reapply Wirth to Julia's journey, for 'The city is the product of growth rather than of instantaneous creation ... [the] great expansion of the modern city must acknowledge its rural origins for our social life bears the imprint of an earlier folk society'.[61] Julia's long-standing devotion to her adopted home of St Anthony's Lane and belief in a man she has barely known a week represent her unconscious desire for romantic and urban entanglement. She returns to the lane against the demands of her family to be with the man that she loves and the city to fulfil her potential. Julia's miracles echo the critical reception of the film's 'peaceful' objective to paint Soho as a surreal place, where dreams come true despite the odds. But this relegates the perhaps more interesting and relevant story of a family's immigration and replaces it with a conventional trope of fairy tale romance. The miracles, which begin as a signalled action of Julia's self-sacrifice (forgoing emigration to Canada for an uncertain life in Soho), become obstructed within the film's negotiation of an alleged utopian, cosmopolitan landscape.

Conclusion

Miracle in Soho provides an underlying criticism for the disorganisation of urban life but through the prism of an isolated locality and its engagement with the city. It is also a highly commercial product, competing within a marketplace which saw the dramatic decline of cinema-going and the rapidly growing popularity of commercial television in a decade described by Sue Harper and Vincent Porter as a 'largely unknown country, regarded by critics as dull'.[62] The film was a lost opportunity to convey the real-life evolving migrant ethnography and the tensions found within late 1950s Soho. Perhaps the potentially more powerful transformative story was obstructed by Pressburger's love for magical realism, embodied by the symbolic existence of the damaged St Anthony's Lane and the Gozzi family, who represented his own voyage to Britain. Along with the aggressive commercial strategies for the film employed by J. Arthur Rank, it would appear the filmmakers involved in the production failed to successfully negotiate their own imagined Soho.

Regardless, the film remains a welcome addition to a post-war world massively riven by discord and is a great contribution to a filmography of post-war Soho films that contains an exhaustive array of narratives involving strippers, pornographers and prostitutes. This film provides a rare cinematic representation of Soho as a moral space for the native Englishman. Michael is the sinner who learns the errors of his ways as a result of immigrant Julia's love, personified by her loyalty, devotion and imagination. Like so many of Pressburger's films with Powell, this is a fairy tale that explores the morality of the native and immigrant, positioned within the localised urban and cosmopolitan centre of Soho.

Notes

1 For Italian immigrants in post-World War II Toronto, Saint Anthony of Padua held special meaning. The story of the saint's shipwrecked arrival in Sicily resonated with thousands finding their ways from the docks of Halifax to Toronto's Little Italy. The film's religious themes further contribute towards producer J. Arthur Rank's 'big idea' of the 1950s for films to appeal to the predominantly Catholic, Italian marketplace. See Jordan Stranger-Ross, *Staying Italian: Urban Change and Ethnic Life in Postwar Toronto and Philadelphia* (Chicago: University of Chicago Press, 2009), p. 76. For more on Rank's 'big ideas' see Steve Chibnall, 'Banging the Gong: The Promotional Strategies of Britain's J. Arthur Rank Organisation in the 1950s', *Historical Journal of Film, Radio and Television* (2016), pp. 1–30.

2 In his script, Emeric Pressburger gives his character Michael Morgan a motto for living: 'Never go back ... there will be another street, another set of women to woo'. See Emeric Pressburger, '*Miracle in Soho* Post-Production Script' (Domestic Version)', 27 June 1957. J. Arthur Rank Productions Ltd. Donated by BAFTA (London: BFI National Archive), p. 1.
3 Wardour Street in Soho was once referred to as 'film row'. In 1927, the street had become the primary location for the headquarters of film production, post-production facilities and film distribution companies. See more in Judith Summers, *Soho: A History of London's Most Colourful Neighbourhood* (London: Bloomsbury, 1991), p. 180.
4 See Frank Mort, *Capital Affairs: London and the Making of the Permissive Society* (New Haven, CT: Yale University Press, 2010), p. 201.
5 Ibid., p. 230.
6 John Eade, *Placing London: From Imperial Capital to Global City* (New York; Oxford: Berghahn Books, 2000), p. 61.
7 Ibid., p. 1.
8 Ibid., p. 11.
9 Ann Ogidi, 'Black British Film', *BFI Screenonline*, www.screenonline.org.uk/film/id/1144245/index.html (accessed 11 October 2019).
10 Ibid.
11 This forgotten film remains unavailable for general release but is available to view on request at the BFI National Archive in London.
12 Although 'prostitution in Soho was reputedly as old as the area itself', the popular press exploited the sex industry in a 'sensational vein', regardless of empirical truth, in order to sell papers. See Stefan Anthony Slater, 'Containment: Managing Street Prostitution in London, 1918–1959', *The Journal of British Studies*, 49 (2010), p. 332. See also Mort, *Capital Affairs*, p. 214. The reported increase in prostitution led to the Wolfenden Committee's investigation of homosexuality and sexual behaviours culminating in a report published in September 1957. See also the full report, John Wolfenden and Great Britain. Scottish Home Department, *Report of the Committee on Homosexual Offences and Prostitution*, Cmnd 247 (London: HMSO, 1957).
13 See Frank Mort, 'Scandalous Events: Metropolitan Culture and Moral Change in Post-Second World War London', *Representations*, 93 (2006), p. 122.
14 Ibid., pp. 96–7.
15 'Miracle in Soho', *What's On in London* (12 July 1957), page unknown. Pamphlet scan courtesy of Steve Crook.
16 See Pressburger, '*Miracle in Soho* Post-Production Script', pp. 1–2.
17 Ibid., pp. 1–3.
18 Kevin Macdonald's published biography of his grandfather describes the various obstacles for the production of *Miracle in Soho* before the Second World War. See *Emeric Pressburger: Life and Death of a Screenwriter* (London: Faber and Faber, 1996), p. 107. See also Raymond Durgnat's 'The Powell and Pressburger Mystery', which further describes the ironies of the Powell/Pressburger relationship in terms of national and foreign identity, in *Cineaste*, 23.2 (1997), pp. 16–19.

19 See Macdonald, *Emeric Pressburger*, p. 122.
20 Pressburger is often miscredited as working solely as writer/producer with Powell as director/producer though in recent decades this simplification of his role has been rectified by figures such as Kevin Gough-Yates and Ian Christie who argue Pressburger held a far more complex role in their filmmaking partnership. Ian Christie states that Pressburger was 'far more than the scenarist whose work Powell rewrote [and] created most of their stories, was responsible for most of the producing, collaborated (but never on the floor) in the directing, and worked patiently in the editing room'. Powell and Pressburger parted ways following the release of *Ill Met by Moonlight* in 1956. See Ian Christie, 'Alienation Effects: Emeric Pressburger and British Cinema', *Monthly Film Bulletin*, 51.600 (1984), p. 318. Kevin Gough-Yates reviews Macdonald's biography of his grandfather, shedding light on Powell's other-half, in 'Pressburger: England and Exile', *Sight and Sound*, 15.12 (1995), p. 30.
21 The other writer was Wolfgang Wilhelm, German-born, who emigrated to Britain after the Nazis took power. He co-wrote several films which differed in genre, such as *Farewell Again* (Tim Whelan, 1937) and the spy-comedy *I See a Dark Stranger* (Frank Launder, 1946) starring Deborah Kerr and Trevor Howard. He also co-wrote some of The Saint film series with RKO. He wrote the Powell/Pressburger-produced *The End of the River* (Derek Twist, 1947). See Andrew Moor, *Powell & Pressburger: A Cinema of Magic Spaces* (London; New York: I.B. Tauris; Palgrave Macmillan, 2005), p. 2. See also Gough-Yates, 'Pressburger: England and Exile', pp. 31–2.
22 Gough-Yates, 'Pressburger: England and Exile', p. 35.
23 See Emeric Pressburger, *Miracle in St Anthony's Lane*. An original story by Emeric Pressburger. Script written by Emeric Pressburger in collaboration with Michael Powell. n.d. (With special permission by the Michael Powell Estate, London), p. 37. For Pinewood's twenty-first birthday in 1957, it ran a series of promotional 'guides' for cinema audiences including in fan magazine *Picturegoer* regular 'Stepping Out Tonight?' written by Margaret Hinxman. *Miracle in Soho* stands out as the only romance film. See Hinxman, 'Stepping Out Tonight?', *Picturegoer* (28 September 1957), p. 5.
24 The Rank Organisation's other top promoted films released in 1957 included the Dirk Bogarde vehicle *Campbell's Kingdom* (Ralph Thomas), a 'large-scale adventure story set in Canada', and *Hell Drivers* (C. Baker Endfield), 'a tough tale about short-haul lorry drivers' starring Stanley Baker as an ex-con and Herbert Lom who plays an Italian driver called Gino Rossi. See Chibnall, 'Banging the Gong', p. 25.
25 Pressburger, '*Miracle in Soho* Post-Production Script', p. 1.
26 Wirth was a member of the Chicago School which focused on Chicago, developing their work during an era of extreme and rapid social change as the 'influx of millions of immigrants at the turn of the century' settled primarily in urban areas. Comparably, Britain in the 1950s was extremely crowded by comparison with its neighbours in Europe and was easily the most urbanised country in Europe. In 1956, the United Kingdom of Great Britain and Northern Ireland

was home to just over fifty million people. Historian Dominic Sandbrook's *Never Had It So Good: A History of Britain from Suez to The Beatles* (London: Abacus, 2005) provides a wonderfully engaging and thorough history of post-war Britain; see 'Britain in 1956', pp. 31–66. The urban sociologists of the Chicago School 'reinvented modern sociology by using the city of Chicago as a "living laboratory"'. See Earl Smith for a more comprehensive overview of the School in 'Louis Wirth and the Chicago School of Urban Sociology: An Assessment and Critique', *Humanity and Society*, 9 (1985), p. 1.

27 Jerry White, *London in the Twentieth Century: A City and Its People* (London: Vintage Books, 2008), p. 107.
28 For a fuller history of Italians in London, see James Strang, 'The Italian Colony in London', *Good Words*, 40 (1899), pp. 119–25 and White, *London in the Twentieth Century*, p. 107.
29 Ibid., p. 108.
30 In her commentary on the film's 'open racism', Elisabetta Girelli explores its use of Italian stereotypes and rightly claims that the character of Julia is more of a 'sketch' than a character. See *Beauty and the Beast: Italianness in British Cinema* (Bristol: Intellect Books, 2009), p. 110.
31 Ibid.
32 Judith Walkowitz, *Nights Out: Life in Cosmopolitan London* (New Haven, CT: Yale University Press, 2012), p. 94.
33 Ibid.
34 Ibid.
35 Ibid., p. 132.
36 The phrase 'Never Had It So Good' first appeared in a speech made by the British Prime Minister Harold Macmillan in 1957. The term has, according to Booker, 'never been so damagingly distorted'. Macmillan's actual words were 'Let's be frank about it; some of our people had never had it so good.' See Christopher Booker, *The Neophiliacs: Revolution in English Life in the Fifties and Sixties*, 2nd ed. (London: Pimlico, 1992), pp. 132–5.
37 Chibnall, 'Banging the Gong', p. 251.
38 In 1957, the J. Arthur Rank Organisation was forced to amalgamate their Gaumont and Odeon cinema circuits which resulted in three hundred workers being made redundant alongside the postponement of four productions at Pinewood Studios. See Chibnall, 'Banging the Gong', p. 253.
39 See 'British Feature Directors: An Index to their Work', *Sight and Sound* (Fall 1958), p. 289.
40 Born Cambridge in 1917, Amyes produced and acted in repertory before the war and after army service joined the Stratford Memorial Theatre company. He joined the BBC as a television producer in 1951 and was responsible for such TV productions as *Dial M for Murder*. See ibid., p. 289.
41 There are several uncredited photographs which are currently owned by the British-based Moviestore Collection, including on-set photographs taken during the filming of *Miracle in Soho*. See www.moviestorecollection.com/ (accessed 2 February 2019).

42 See Jingan Young, 'Belinda Lee and the Soho Fair', *IAMHIST* (3 October 2017), http://iamhist.net/tag/cosmopolitanism/ (accessed 2 February 2019).

43 Sarah Street's article is part of the seminal research she is leading on the Eastmancolor Revolution and British Cinema 1955–85 Project based at the universities of Bristol and East Anglia. The project's website includes a wonderful blog, information on upcoming conferences and updates on the project: https://eastmancolor.info/. See Sarah Street, 'The Colour of Social Realism', *Journal of British Cinema and Television*, 15.4 (2018), p. 470.

44 Ibid.

45 Ibid., pp. 473–4. See also Carmen Dillon, 'Building Soho at Pinewood', *Kinematograph Weekly*, Studio Review (28 March 1957), p. ix.

46 Films released that year include the Oscar-winning David Lean's epic prisoner-of-war film *The Bridge on the River Kwai*. See Clem, 'Review: Miracle in Soho', *Variety* (24 July 1957), p. 26. See also 'Review: Miracle in Soho', *Monthly Film Bulletin*, 24.276 (1957), p. 104. Lastly, see 'Miracle in Soho', *Picturegoer* (3 August 1957), p. 14.

47 See Dylan Cave, 'Miracle in Soho (1957)', *BFI Screenonline*, www.screenonline.org.uk/film/id/712912/ (accessed 2 February 2017).

48 'Miracle in Soho', *What's On in London* (12 July 1957). Courtesy of Steve Crook, *The Powell & Pressburger Pages Online*, https://powell-pressburger.org/ (accessed 21 January 2020).

49 The documentary also featured 'scenes from *Across the Bridge* and *Doctor at Large*; and interviews with Peggy Cummins about *Hell Drivers*, and with Flora Robson about *High Tide at Noon*'. In the following January, the Rank Organisation divided the UK provincial press into six regions and appointed corresponding press officers to work from branch offices in Manchester, Birmingham, Glasgow, Leeds, Cardiff and London. They provided a service to 'provincial editors, news, art and feature editors, film and gossip columnists, women's writers and special writers'. See Chibnall, 'Banging the Gong', p. 253.

50 The black-and-white advertisement uses a large photograph of Lee to promote Vitapointe of Paris with a tagline below that reads 'Just 1-minute brushing – and my hair is shining! By Belinda Lee'. See *Daily Express* (26 September 1957), p. 13.

51 These profile articles were written by journalist Derek Walker for *Picturegoer* on the actor entitled 'Belinda Lee Covers Up Her Past'. In part two of the series, we are provided with the 'exclusive' story of how Lee landed the role of Julia Gozzi. The story goes that Pressburger saw her photograph outside his offices at Pinewood and there and then decided '*that* is just what I want for Miracle in Soho'. Derek Walker's profile is accompanied by several images of Lee as a 'pin-up' who wished to change her image into a more dramatic actor. See 'Belinda Lee Covers Up Her Past', *Picturegoer* (16 March 1967), p. 5.

52 See Chibnall, 'Banging the Gong', p. 12.

53 After Rank signed Lee, she told a reporter called Tom Hutchinson, 'I don't suppose I am going to learn all that much about acting with the Rank

Organisation, but I am going to learn about being a personality.' See Tom Hutchinson, *Screen Goddesses* (London: Deans International, 1984), p. 147.
54 Frank Mort, 'Cityscapes: Consumption, Masculinities and the Mapping of London since 1950', *Urban Studies*, 35.5/6 (1998), p. 894.
55 See Charlotte Brunsdon, *London in Cinema: The Cinematic City since 1945* (London: BFI Publishing, 2007), pp. 43–5.
56 As the world is set right again, the camera moves around the church as we hear the hymn being sung, 'Praise, My Soul, the King of Heaven' written by Henry Francis Lyte (1793–1847) in 1834 and set to the tune LAUDA ANIMA by John Goss in 1869, in various languages. The hymn is a paraphrase of Psalm 103 and it appeared in the *Spirit of the Psalms*, published in 1834. See Malcolm C. Doubles, *The Seduction of the Church: How the Concern to Create Gender-Neutral Language in Bible and Song Is Being Misused to Betray Members' Faith* (Eugene, OR: Wipf & Stock, 2010), p. 125.
57 See Gough-Yates, 'Pressburger: England and Exile', p. 35.
58 Ibid., pp. 30–2.
59 See Durgnat, 'The Powell and Pressburger Mystery', p. 16.
60 See Andrew Moor, *Powell & Pressburger: A Cinema of Magic Spaces* (New York: I.B. Tauris, 2005), p. 3.
61 Ibid.
62 See Sue Harper and Vincent Porter, *British Cinema of the 1950s: The Decline of Deference* (Oxford: Oxford University Press, 2003), p. 1.

2

Dropping out: interiority, claustrophobia and decadence in cosmopolitan London cinema of the 1960s and 1970s

Kevin M. Flanagan

Simultaneous to London's swinging period in the mid-to-late 1960s, and its flowering on the world stage as a city of and for the youthful jet set, it was a place that was at times both literally and figuratively removed from the world. The flipside to the London of public exuberance of the late 1960s, as *the* city of pop, op and psychedelic happenings, was a shunning of the scene in favour of quiet contemplation, sheltering in place and a repose from sociability.[1]

This chapter identifies and surveys a counterintuitive strand of London films made by non-native filmmakers whose thematic and spatial focus is not on the breadth, freedom and possibility of the public city but rather on its private spaces. These 'inner space' films, a trend arguably kicked off by *The Servant* (Joseph Losey, 1963), dwell on issues that arise from the obsessive over-identification with interior spaces (apartments, flats, studios, workspaces), often to the extent that the central characters in these films forsake the city streets in favour of the private worlds of their own making. The genius of this conceit is that filmmakers from abroad (mainly the United States and Poland) use London interiority as a means of intensifying any number of psychosocial issues, ranging from PTSD (*Repulsion*, Roman Polanski, 1965) to voyeurism (*Wonderwall*, Joe Massot, 1968) to exploitative labour (*Death Line*, Gary Sherman, 1972). In particular, this chapter will trace a cosmopolitan strand of inner space cinema that at once gels with issues explored by key British writers of the moment (among them V. S. Pritchett, Michael Moorcock and J. G. Ballard) but that very deliberately and distinctively defines the city from the position of the outsider looking inward.

The key collaboration is between the American director Joseph Losey (who fled to Europe in advance of being asked to testify to the House Un-American Activities Committee) and the Hungarian writer George Tabori. Their film *Secret Ceremony* (1968, adapted from a novella by Argentine writer Marco Denevi) explores an obsessive, codependent relationship between mother and surrogate daughter that largely plays out inside of Debenham House in Holland Park, London W14. Like *The Servant*, it foregrounds a baroque, idiosyncratic kind of *mise-en-scène* that comments expertly on the psychological states of the characters. The other film that will be explored in depth began as a collaboration between Tabori and Losey, before being dropped and completed, and inevitably changed, by John Boorman.[2] *Leo the Last* (1970) is about the coming-to-political-consciousness of a deposed European aristocrat (Marcello Mastroianni) who is exiled to a West London home (which evinces a kind of faded grandeur) and who undergoes a personal transformation based on his gradual engagement with the outside world. Taken together, the films explored in this chapter advance an unconventional notion: the inner spaces of London, as represented and explored by those who look at the city from without, are key sites for dramatising and defining a full understanding of the metropolis. With their attention to issues typically outside the remit of urban experience such as small-scale observation and confinement, they provide new windows on a frequently studied moment.

As a social, historical and financial centre, London contains an enviable mix of cultural cachet rooted in traditions of Englishness and a rare status as the crossroads of global cultures, as a sort of signal beacon for empire turned into an agglomeration of the world in miniature. Pam Hirsch and Chris O'Rourke have characterised London as a 'destination for foreign filmmakers' that goes beyond just setting, instead also serving as a production base, an adopted home and a source of inspiration.[3] Roland-François Lack regards London as a central stop for European directors like Michelangelo Antonioni or Polanski, who inevitably brought their own expectations to bear on the place: 'Each in turn documented an outsider's gaze upon the unhomely city, constituting a corpus of London films on the premise of an initial dislocation.'[4] Some filmmakers only stopped in London for specific projects, while others embraced the city on a more permanent basis. A key aspect of films made in and about London at mid-century and up to the mid-1970s is the participation of the exile community brought to England by dictatorial regimes purging its populations of dissidents, Stalinist regimes too repressive to bear, or some avoiding military conscription or just no longer comfortable in their birth country. British film culture was first enriched by exiles from Europe (many fleeing Germany and central Europe from encroaching fascism), including Alexander Korda, Emeric Pressburger, René Clair and Conrad Veidt, and North America, including, most famously, Stanley Kubrick.[5] Another key source of labour arrived in England after the war as a result of blacklisting, actual or threatened, by the House Un-American Activities Committee. Rebecca Prime has exhaustively detailed the migration of industry professionals who left to work in Europe during the late 1940s and 1950s. Among the Leftist filmmakers who had been working in Hollywood and decamped to England were Cy Enfield and Joseph Losey, both of whom made key films about English national identity (though Enfield's *Zulu* (1964) and Losey's *The Servant* could hardly be more different!).⁶ While the filmmakers who came to England during this period were clearly bringing modes of looking related to their home countries (Losey, for example, brought a kind of urban-crime cynicism to a string of early British films such as *The Sleeping Tiger* (1954), *The Intimate Stranger* (1956) and *The Criminal* (1960) that feels more hard-nosed than native productions), these filmmakers also injected a sense of outsider awareness to even the most hyper-local of subjects.

'Walls have feelings': interiority and London-based cinema

Much of the writing on cinematic cities, and about London in particular, examines the city from street level, noting public parks, monuments and modes of transport. Films that emphasise cityscape and interconnecting urban systems are often privileged over those focused on private space. As such, my argument here is that the inner spaces of life in London during these periods gives us a more complete picture of voguish themes, emerging social positions and anxieties to do with urban life than just those films whose key scenes happen in public space.

My focus is on London life during the long 1960s (1963–74), a period roughly coinciding with the ascendancy of what Alexander Walker characterised as 'Hollywood UK', a boom time in British cinema production that tapers off along with the fortunes of the economy.⁷ I am certainly not the first to argue for the importance of interior space as a key component in the study of architecture and urban environments in cinema. Katherine Shonfield's staggeringly original book *Walls Have Feelings: Architecture, Film and the City* (2000) broadly works from ideas first presented by Mary Douglas,⁸ and discusses private spaces as a literalisation of cultural desires to demarcate between outside danger and interior safety (the key phrase for both is 'defence of the border'). Shonfield examines inside spaces as an occasion to meditate on permeability and pollution motifs, both of which are relevant to each of the films discussed below.⁹ Working from an American context, Pamela Robertson Wojcik's *The Apartment Plot* (2010) argues for the distinctive features of apartment-centric narratives and shows how they engage with differently racialised, gendered and classed variations (the genre can accommodate everything from slums to bachelor pads).¹⁰ Wojcik's assessments of design and technology are particularly inspiring. Further departing from Wojcik and of central concern is Hugo Frey's essay 'Shutting Out the City: Reflections on the Portrayal of London in 1960s

Auteur Cinema', which examines how key London films envision 'atomization and alienation' through their focus on private spaces[11] (not famous landmarks in the vein of Charlotte Brunsdon's 'tourist London' paradigm so much as 'detailed and elaborate interior and exterior images of town house apartment blocks and shared Victorian dwellings').[12] Frey makes crucial connections between a corpus of films about violence and dislocation (*Repulsion, Performance*), the centrality of outsider perceptions of the city (expatriate filmmakers or filmmakers new to London) and themes that recur frequently (a bunker-like reliance on the home, conservative tropes to do with the fear in the interloper or the crowd, fears of entrapment).

There is a comparable discourse focused on inner spaces from British writers of the time, a trend that illustrates how the outside version of private space coincides with observations by long-time Londoners. In a somewhat traditionalist vein, V. S. Pritchett contrasts cities elsewhere in Europe and the world with London, which he characterises as being inclined to private life:

> London is millions of small chimneys, millions of Victorian door-pillars displaying the essence of private consequence. It is millions of windows and walls – what goes on inside them is not your business or mine. The feeling of seclusion goes very deep in the London character and is responsible for the intimacy of London life and for a system of abrupt protective manners that makes life very livable.[13]

While Pritchett is certainly viewing the city in terms legible to a professional writer, where privacy and intimacy are important for the labour of literary production, he hits on a larger point about the city's reliance on zones of exclusion and limited access as a counterpoint to the street-level experience of public navigation.

Michael Moorcock captures some of this interiority in his contemporaneous Elric and Jerry Cornelius stories, in which the legacy of decadent art movements of the *fin de siècle* meet the possibilities of science fiction. Mark Scroggins has demonstrated how Moorcock wed an interest in psychology and the internal realms of the self to an abiding interest in entropy, that inevitable tumble towards chaos.[14] For example, Elric is himself introduced in a story called 'The Dreaming City' (first published in 1961), in which he arrives at the Melnibonean city of Imrryr, a place where the inhabitants 'spend many of their days in drugged slumber; in study'.[15] This is an interiority romanticised by a nascent counterculture, of which Moorcock was a part: 'But there was no life-sound emanating from Imrryr the Beautiful, only a sense of soporific desolation. The city slept – and the Dragon Masters and their ladies and their special slaves dreamed drug-induced dreams of grandeur and incredible horror ...'.[16] Fellow *New Worlds* writer J. G. Ballard uses the space of the post-war tower block, and its attenuate social class and taste distinctions that stratify along hierarchical terms, to diabolical effect in his appropriately named novel *High-Rise* (1975). Here, the space of the building and the modes of living that it engineers drive its inhabitants not to languid inactivity but rather to madness and clinical violence, to acts dispassionately narrated but fraught with irrational passion.[17]

It should also be noted that London films about inner space during the period in focus are not the exclusive preserve of exiled or outsider filmmakers. Michael Klinger – whose outfit Compton Films made Polanski's UK work possible – produced English director Peter Collinson's *The Penthouse* (1967), a home invasion thriller based on C. Scott Forbes's play *The Meter Man* (1964). As befits a film adaptation of a stage work, the majority of the narrative takes place in Barbara's (Suzy Kendall) flat. *The Penthouse* is useful for thinking about the connection between the public city and the private. The exterior world is present at the beginning of the film, as the credits play over an ominous shot of Centre Point in Bloomsbury, a brutalist tower completed in 1963 which served as a kind of shorthand for opulent modernity and chic city living. The narrative proper begins as Tom (Tony Beckley) and Dick (Norman Rodway) enter frame, regard each other with a smile and set off towards the building. The remainder of the story takes place inside.

Donald Cammell and Nic Roeg's magistral film *Performance* (shot in 1968, reluctantly released by a baffled Warner Bros in 1970) marks a London-centric response to the countercultural practice of 'dropping out'. In the film, East End gangster Chas (James Fox) goes on the run and overhears about a lodging opportunity in Notting Hill Gate (the exterior to the house is filmed in Powis Square). He bluffs his way into this luxuriant, decaying pile, which houses the mysterious musician Turner (Mick Jagger) and his female retinue of Pherber (Anita Pallenberg) and Lucy (Michele Breton). As he hides out from the associates who want him dead, he becomes enmeshed in the drugs, mysticism and sexual intrigues of his new housemates. While the film is key to so many discourses – it is a baroque crime film, a countercultural document and houses a proto-music video in its 'Memo from Turner' sequence – and an epoch-defining moment that relates to key philosophical and cultural debates of the 1960s, what makes it noteworthy here is that the narrative is designed around shutting out the city. By going into hiding, Chas removes himself from the public spaces of commonplace social life, shuns the precise cultural habitus of the East End gangster and instead redefines himself through his porous relationship with others, going so far as to embrace his femininity (by cross-dressing) and potentially even merging with Turner, such that the two become insoluble by film's end. The justifiably famous final sequence, in which Chas is led from the house to a waiting car to face his former friend Flowers (Johnny Shannon), reveals, in a shot of the car pulling away, that Turner has switched bodies with Chas, even though we seemingly just witnessed Chas shooting Turner in the head. The journey undertaken by Chas within this house goes beyond a simple narrative of personal growth through a physical journey. Rather, the deep dive within redefines even the most obstinate self.

The expatriate experience: inside London as seen from without

American directors have produced some of the strangest versions of interior London but have done so by working with UK-based collaborators and through actors whose work epitomises English eccentricity. Joe Massot's *Wonderwall* fits the bill in that it features a mixture of nineteenth-century English poetry, flourishes of pop art, decadent pantomime and a Ravi Shankar-inflected soundtrack by George Harrison (composed at the twilight of the Beatles' reign as the world's most famous pop act). *Wonderwall* is a timely film for showing what Shonfield calls the 'alienness of walls'.[18] Eccentric scientist and antiquarian Oscar Collins (Jack MacGowran, fresh off of Polanski's *Cul-de-Sac* two years earlier) becomes obsessed with the younger woman Penny Lane (Jane Birkin, at the cusp of world fame) whose flat shares a wall with his; in order to feed this obsession, he strips the wall and fashions himself some voyeur vantages from which to watch her and her friends/lovers. Part of Collins's narrative of self-liberation, from old and stuffy to reinvigorated (though disturbingly scopophilic) is told through Assheton Gorton's production design. At the beginning of the film, Collins's apartment is a monument to nineteenth-century eccentricity. It is stuffed with near-hoarder levels of bric-a-brac, including insect specimens, ageing books and bulky furniture. Its walls are decorated at the top with quotations from two thematically appropriate poems, Tennyson's 'The Day-Dream' (1842) and Christina Rossetti's 'An End' (1850), both suggesting Collins's penchant for chivalry, romanticisation and fatalism.[19] As Collins becomes more smitten and spends more time gazing through the wall at Lane, he strips it of its ornamentation, slowly breaking down the barrier between him and her (and, in the process, trashing some of the 'stuff' that characterises his isolation).

The key visualisation in the film is the suggestion that marvels lie in miniature, interior worlds. This is first offered through Collins's job, as he gazes with fascination into a microscope. It is visualised throughout by the 'magical' property of Collins's looks through the wall: Lane's apartment changes drastically with different days, sometimes showing elaborate fashion shoots, other times Orientalist blissing out. A crucial element is that the angle and point of view of Collins's gaze rarely corresponds to the angles from which we view what is going on in Lane's apartment. In other words, there is a dissonance, or a breakdown, between the two, as though the wall can refract what is on the other side.

A different kind of interiority, this one giving post-war credence to Churchill's fears of a 'deep shelter mentality' of what happens to humankind when it shuts itself out from the world, or Henry Moore's haunting Tube etchings of Londoners sheltering underground during the Blitz, comes across in Gary Sherman's *Deathline* (also known as *Raw Meat*).[20] While the government famously worried about what would happen to Londoners if they permanently took to the Underground, out of necessity or subterranean curiosity, Sherman's film goes back further, looking at unfortunates that were entombed along with the construction of the Victorian metro system in the first place. *Death Line* is about the return of the repressed horrors that were a by-product of industrialisation. A miner and some of his family have been trapped underground and reduced to an animalistic, monstrous state; eventually, they enact revenge on users of the Underground circa the early 1970s through brutal killings. This truth is eventually dredged up via a competitive investigation, between establishment figure Inspector Calhoun (Donald Pleasance) and students Alex (David Ladd) and Patricia (Sharon Gurney). Director Sherman conceived of the project primarily as a comment on the English class system and its inequalities.[21] In *Death Line*, the Underground is an uncanny space, at once part of the fabric of the quotidian city, yet capable of housing elements that have been excluded from society at large.

Polish directors have used this isolation thematic frequently. Jerzy Skolimowksi's work, which Ewa Mazierska describes as embodying 'a balance between realisms and non-realisms', has used interior London to explore both coming-of-age narratives (*Deep End*, 1970) and issues of migration and class exploitation (*Moonlighting*, 1982).[22] In *Deep End*, a British–German co-production that uses some London locations like Angel Street in Stratford and Green Court near Peter Street in London W1, but whose interiors were largely filmed in Munich, the space of a public baths and swimming pool becomes the site of escalating sexual fantasies, culminating with young Mike (John Moulder-Brown) causing older love interest Susan (Jane Asher) to drown.[23] The baths of *Deep End* are a mundane space, first representing Mike's reluctant learning of a work ethic on the path to adulthood, but then a mixture of sexual fear (his encounter with a voracious older woman, played by Diane Dors) and fantasy (his budding love of Susan, who is slightly older than him, though still young and seemingly interested). *Moonlighting* strips romance and sex out of interior London, instead focusing on exploited labour. Nowak (Jeremy Irons) and a crew of Polish builders travel to London to illegally renovate a house, as contractors, and while they slog away to refurbish the space (much to the confusion and consternation of the neighbours), massive political change happens back in Eastern Europe (the Polish Solidarity Movement and nascent challenges to communism), a fact that Nowak keeps from the rest of his men. As with so many of the films under consideration here, the interior space reflects the mood of the narrative and the temperature of the characters: while the men initially gut the house and begin to make improvements, their anger and frustration later damages the house to an extent. In some ways, the film presages themes found in *Dirty Pretty Things* (Stephen Frears, 2002), which also looks at how illegal precariats provide the conditions for London luxury and the invisibility of said labour to ensure the smooth functioning of such experiences.

The most famous Polish director to work in England is Roman Polanski, and two of his films, *Repulsion* and *Cul-de-Sac*, use confinement narratives to explore psychological tensions. *Cul-de-Sac*, set and filmed on Lindisfarne, is outside of the remit of this book proper but deserves mention for its isolation framing device and for its connections to other films in terms of themes and personnel. Lindisfarne is isolated because it is an island and because the only way in by road disappears with the tides. The movie opens on gangsters Richard (Lionel Stander) and Albie (Jack MacGowran) stuck on the causeway. Richard is able to terrorise George (Donald Pleasance) and Theresa (Françoise Dorléac) for as long as he does because they are cut off from the world at large. *Cul-de-Sac* becomes a Pinteresque comedy of role-shifts as it plays out, with issues like symbolic power relations and gender performance characterising an otherwise sparse narrative.

Repulsion, by contrast, evinces just about every thematic and conceptual issue explored in this chapter. Fitting Frey's observations, it is a London film that eschews the monumental city in favour of a curated alternative: 'On the one hand, [these] films are clearly located in the capital and speak to that location; on the other hand, the London setting is rigorously manipulated to support narrative and psychological tension, irrespective of the urban reality.'[24] The movie concerns trauma and the gradual withdrawal from the world of Carol (Catherine Deneuve, real-life sister of Dorléac), as she avoids sexual and emotional contact. Instead, for unspecified reasons (anomie? The suggestion of past abuse?) Carol retreats into her flat, which becomes both a safe haven from the perceived threats of the outside world and a prison cell that keeps her trapped with her projected psychoses. With exteriors filmed in Kensington, and funding from Compton Films, whose production and distribution slate always straddled the line between art and sexploitation, this is an iconic outsider vision of London for the 1960s.

Considering it in concert with Polanski's later *Rosemary's Baby*, Shonfield uses ideas from Mary Douglas to think about how this mode of isolated interiority is used as a kind of defence mechanism against the perceived pollutants of culture:

> Both *Repulsion* and *Rosemary's Baby* implicate the primal fear of smearing, explored through an analogy between the interior space of their heroine's bodies, and the interiors of the apartments where they live. In both, the transgression of the architectural edge – the wall, the floor, the way – holds the threat of the violation of the edge of their bodies. The films deal with fear of penetration writ large: written on the architecture of the interior and the architecture of the cities in which the films' action takes place: London and New York.[25]

Because we spend comparably little time in the streets of Kensington and much in the flat with Carol, our perceptual regime changes along with the protagonist. What counts are the subtle shifts in shadow, the changing texture to walls and how quality of life changes along with these moves. This sense of sight even projects outside of the apartment, such as with Carol's encounters with cracks on the sidewalk. For Veronica Fitzpatrick, the film 'typifies a mode of film that's expressly concerned with the futility of boundaries', and that furthermore embodies 'domestic horror', a mode that features 'the gradual mutation of an ostensibly safe space into something not only potentially gruesome but ontologically unstable'.[26] In Polanski's *Repulsion*, all spaces are compromised, and ideas about home are invaded by contagion that is neither exclusively from without nor expressly from within. The true horror of the film is that Carol cannot or will not seek solace in the outside world, but instead confines herself to a claustrophobic experience from which she cannot escape.

Joseph Losey, the exiled American director who had worked with Brecht and who scraped together a living in the British film industry throughout the 1950s, was, by the early 1960s, a success in Europe, directing films with larger budgets, using his name on productions despite the lingering vestiges of the Blacklist and working in a series of collaborative partnerships that were to bring about some of his most challenging work.[27] In *Secret Ceremony*, covered at length further on, it is his working from a scenario by the playwright George Tabori, his nascent collaboration with Elizabeth Taylor (then a massive star), his continued work with director of photography Gerry Fisher (who, beginning with *Accident*, 1967, was a favoured cinematographer) and production designer Richard MacDonald. For *The Servant*, his famous partnership with Harold Pinter, his continued work with Dirk Bogarde and the work of MacDonald yield another landmark in London's cinema of interiors.

The Servant is a key film, presaging as it does the transference themes of *Performance* and *Secret Ceremony*, while engaging the sense of class struggle so central to *Cul-de-Sac* and *Leo the Last*. The status of the house's representation matches the relationship between servant and master. There is a progressive move towards darkening, gilding and reflection within the interiors of the house, just as the barriers separating posh Tony (James Fox) from the mercurial, resourceful and sinister Barrett (Dirk Bogarde) break down and intermingle. The film charts a shift from 'out there' (talk of a colonial project in Brazil, or scenes of happiness frolicking in the gardens of Chiswick House) to the inner world of Barrett's manipulative decoration (mirrors, photography, perverse bohemianism).[28] Losey is particularly keen on mirrors, and James Palmer and Michael Riley observe that 'these mirrors hang in houses whose decor intimately expresses the narcissism, the preoccupation with self and identity that consumes their inhabitants'.[29] Tony's ultimate humiliation comes when Susan visits him when he is fully in his manservant's thrall, an alcoholic shell of his former self reduced to incoherence. Within the laboratory-like space of Tony's house, Losey and Pinter's experiment with London's classed history takes us from Victorian dutifulness to Soho's hip coffee bars in under two hours. In anticipation of *Repulsion* and *Wonderwall*, the space of the house wordlessly keys the viewer into thematic, ideological and character-based shifts.

The Tabori connection: Losey, Boorman and the politics of the home

Joseph Losey's relationship with George Tabori, Hungarian playwright and fellow interpreter of Brecht, informs *Secret Ceremony* and eventually leads to John Boorman's filming of *Leo the Last*. Tabori was married to Viveca Lindfors, who stars in Losey's *These Are the Damned* (1963). Tabori adapted *Secret Ceremony*'s screenplay from a short story by Marco Denevi. According to Anat Feinberg, it was the only one of Tabori's screenplays with which he was pleased.[30] Colin Gardner notes that Tabori's adaptation gives the film a shifted emphasis, from anguish over issues around guilt and absolution that feature in Denevi's short story to mechanisms 'rooted specifically in Marx (the political economy of surplus value) and Freud (the libidinal economy of desire)'.[31] To use Freudian language, the film explores a transference narrative, as a small-time sex worker Leonora (Taylor) becomes a surrogate mother to Cenci (Mia Farrow). Leonora has lost a child of her own, while Cenci's parents are out of the picture. Their new relationship, forged out of initial loneliness and desperation, takes on sinister implications as it solidifies in Cenci's isolated mansion, and their relationship to figures in the outside world changes as a result. Leonora appears to be continuously sedated and in a kind of trance. The audience is unsure to what extent she is a willing participant in Cenci's game, given the modesty of her means suggested by the beginning of the film. Will playing house in these circumstances allow Leonora to move beyond the squalor to which she has grown accustomed?

At first, the interior space of Cenci's mansion is alluring. Leonora is seduced by the finery of the place (she tries on a fur coat) and seems bizarrely at peace with entering a previously inhabited world. Debenham House (8 Addison Road, Kensington), where the interiors were shot, was designed by Halsey Ricardo (1854–1928), an architect and designer who advocated for tilework as decoration.[32] According to James Stevens Curl and Susan Wilson, 'Ricardo advocated the use of faïence and other glazed materials to resist the depredations of polluted atmospheres of the C19 city, suggesting that coloured materials would supply the equivalents of shadows and half-tones provided by cornices, pilasters and mouldings.'[33] We see that tilework in full array as Leonora first explores the house, its colours and patterns suggesting a mixture of pre-modern terra cotta decoration, Arts and Crafts idiosyncrasy and pre-Art Deco glamour. Ricardo's ideas hold up wonderfully on the screen.

As with so many of the films analysed in this chapter, we intuit characterisation through a simple contrast between spaces: Leonora's flat is barren and bland, whereas Cenci's home initially promises plenty and has an air of forbidden romanticisation about it. Leonora and Cenci's bonding is defined by scattered interactions within the mansion, with Cenci demanding infantilised treatment (to Leonora's initial bemusement and then acceptance). Losey and Fisher add value to the mostly dislocated and ambiguous script by using the camera to redirect attention. Interactions end with the camera tracking away from Leonora and Cenci and onto objects in the *mise-en-scène* such as paintings, thus giving the audience time to focus on the sorts of details that other films would ignore or quickly move away from.

Throughout, the film takes advantage of Holland House's bizarre design. One shot captures Farrow from a low angle, such that her face looms large in the foreground, as Taylor looks on from the gilded balcony above. The mansion is weighed down by bric-a-brac and ornamentation (statues, large musical instruments, artworks). The walls have Orientalist motifs, emphasising patterns, pastel tiles and floral imagery. Virtually every room has a distinctive look. This is complemented by Leonora's increasingly outlandish fashion, supplied to the film by Marc Bohan and Dior.

The film moves beyond its initial stage as a drama about the isolated bonding of Leonora and Cenci as others enter the space of the mansion. Cenci's sinister aunts (played by Peggy Ashcroft and Pamela Brown) have designs on the young girl's future and give scattered references to the lives of her parents; the loutish Albert (Robert Mitchum), university lecturer and frequent drunk, represents a kind of symbolic patriarchal authority who enters and further disrupts the fiction that Leonora and Cenci have created, even going so far as to 'marry' Cenci in a mock ceremony. Tabori and Losey mine Pinteresque elements in all this, with characters constantly bullying one another and speaking in stylised, oblique ways. The film is a sort of pantomime of family relationships, with characters playing at heightened versions of relatedness, with bigger swings towards love, hatred, affection and reconciliation than are seen in life.

The film ends with these people unable to move beyond the grip of the mansion and the scenario they have constructed. Ultimately, Cenci succumbs to the crumbling relationship with Albert (who has raped her) and Leonora (on whom she is now fully codependent). She tries to overdose on pills but then has one more interaction with Leonora before she dies on the balcony. The fiction has ended. At the funeral, Leonora stabs Albert. By the end, Leonora is back in her dingy flat, wordlessly lying in bed. *Secret Ceremony* opened to 'derisive' reviews and minuscule box office in the UK (gross of only $35,989), but slightly better prospects in the United States, where Americans playing at being British is more acceptable.[34]

If *Secret Ceremony* presents an interior scenario in which the characters remain in the thrall of an interior space until their worlds come crashing down, then *Leo the Last* represents a potentially more optimistic transcendence of interiority in that it gives a narrative in which a character moves from isolation and aloofness to engagement and integration into the community. As mentioned above, *Leo the Last* began as a potential collaboration between Losey and Tabori. It was in the works in the mid- to-late 1960s, just before the production of *Secret Ceremony*. Brian Hoyle reports that the film is not based on a Tabori work called *The Prince* (a story repeated by John Boorman himself); rather, it began 'as an original film script called *Black Comedy* that Tabori had written for Joseph Losey', and which the two had spent the better part of three years trying to get made, with eventual lead Marcello Mastroianni considered even then.[35] Once their version of the project collapsed, Tabori and Losey moved on to *Secret Ceremony*. Boorman was alerted to the project by Robert Chartoff, who had produced *Point Blank* (1967), and Boorman and Bill Stair rewrote Tabori's screenplay, removing Brechtian elements and adding a hopeful inflection on the revolutionary ending.[36]

Complicated production history aside, the film provides a near summation of the London films about isolation and interiority from the 1960s in that it has a definite through-line, with the aristocratic Leo (Mastroianni) returning to his father's West London home to find that his sycophantic retinue are trying to get on his good side so that they are considered in the will (his father just died, so the estate is in disorder) and to discover that the neighbourhood surrounding the mansion has become a slum. Famously, Boorman and his crew painted the block around what was Testerton Street, London W11 to suit their vision: 'I decided to exclude all colour from the sets, the street and mansion – flesh tones being the exception. We painted the street black and eliminated all colour from the props, clothes, furniture. I wanted to give the impression that the audience had entered a parallel world where the rules and behaviour were slightly skewed.'[37] Hoyle reports that 'this concept was not in the original scripts, and both Tabori's original version and Boorman's rewrites specifically refer to primary colors', such that 'in the end, the only colors that appear in the sets, props and costumes are black, white, grey, silver and brown, making it, in effect, a black-and-white film in color'.[38] With action restrained to a narrow geographic area – essentially, just Leo's house and the street outside, with occasional forays into spaces that are implied to be close by – the film makes expected and inevitable nods to Alfred Hitchcock's *Rear Window* (1959), as Leo spends much of the film watching life happen around him, only engaging with his community after a long period of indecision. The vignettes that Leo witnesses are like short silent film parables: Chaplinesque snippets of graft, survival and community tensions, often without sound, and viewed through the iris of a spyglass, set amidst an almost colourless world.

Leo is torn between two impulses. To the one side are his father's old retainers and cronies, exemplified by lawyer Max (Graham Crowden, playing to his eccentric best), butler and reactionary militant Laszlo (Vladek Sheybal) and gold-digging fiancée Margaret (Billie Whitelaw); to the other are the members of the community outside, most of whom are Afro-Caribbean, and whom Leo begins to sympathise with and root for – in particular, Roscoe (Calvin Lockhart), a Robin Hood-like figure who liberates food from the grocer to feed his starving family and fights back against Kowalski (Kenneth J. Warren) who sexually assaults his wife Salambo (Glenna Forster-Jones), and Salambo herself, who is tough-minded but turns to prostitution after Roscoe's arrest. The film is good at showing how Leo's benevolent paternalism can misfire, as when he feeds Roscoe and Salambo's family to the point where the bedridden grandfather dies of shock. While some moments overly reward Leo for his white-saviour impulses (his 'buying' of Salambo out of prostitution), there are other moments of genuine community-mindedness, such as Leo's function in the final sequence.

What sets *Leo the Last* apart from the other films treated in this chapter is that the sense of isolation and interiority explored in the film does not ultimately win out. In *The Servant*, *Repulsion* and *Secret Ceremony*, for instance, the 'pull' of the home is so great that it consumes the characters and relationships to a point of no return. By contrast, in *Leo the Last*, Leo joins the community that he once watched from afar, forsaking his birthright and other members of his class and leading a march to destroy the very mansion that represents his largesse. Leo, Roscoe and the rest of the working people remove Laszlo and his reactionaries who, by film's end, have joined with the area's pimps in an oppressive alliance. The film ends not only with the destruction of the mansion – throughout, the symbol of the 'old' world and its values, most of which are indefensible post-1968 – but, in a curious reversal of the norm, a happy ending predicated on ruin and destruction. Leo smiles as he regards the pile of rubble that once was his home and cautiously troops off to the pub to celebrate with his neighbours.

In financial terms, Tino Balio describes *Leo the Last* as 'disastrous', and as being among the films 'written off' during a period of financial crisis by Arthur B. Krim to satisfy United Artists' auditors and the SEC.[39] Even though Boorman was given 'Best Director' at Cannes for the film, it had a disastrous showing elsewhere in the world and quickly disappeared from screens.[40]

The films treated above show how London cinema can accommodate interiors, process their psychological implications and connect (or disconnect) them from the fabric of the city as a whole. A comparison can be made to the discourse of freedom and movement around some other London films during this period. Titles as diverse as *You Must Be Joking!* (Michael Winner, 1964), *The Sandwich Man* (Robert Hartford-Davis, 1966), *Smashing Time* (Desmond Davis, 1967) and *The Optimists of Nine Elms* (Anthony Simmons, 1973), whatever their larger differences, use London as a place for public engagement. *You Must Be Joking!* and *Smashing Time*, for instance, regard London as a giant playground, to be traversed, trodden and pranked. By contrast, most of the London films by exiled or expatriate filmmakers hold true to Hugo Frey's observation about reproducing cautious, conservative themes around the city, focusing on the bunker-like possibilities of private spaces, but almost always showing how people are broken by this sense of isolation.[41] The isolation can be transformative, though, as *Leo the Last* demonstrates. Privacy, privilege and comfort mean nothing if the community crumbles.

Notes

1 I have previous written about the public, outdoor, architectural and documentary experience of the period. See Kevin M. Flanagan, 'Whitehead's London: Pop and the Ascendant Celebrity', *Framework*, 52.1 (2011), pp. 278–98.

2 Brian Hoyle explains that *Leo the Last* began not as an adaptation of a short story or play called *The Prince*, as is often claimed, but rather as an original screenplay by Tabori called *Black Comedy*. See Brian Hoyle, *The Cinema of John Boorman* (London: Scarecrow Press, 2012), pp. 59–60.
3 Pam Hirsch and Chris O'Rourke, 'Introduction: Film Londons' in *London in Film*, ed. Pam Hirsch and Chris O'Rourke (London: Palgrave, 2017), p. 3.
4 Roland-François Lack, 'London circa Sixty-Six: The Map of the Film', in *London Eyes: Reflections on Text and Image*, ed. Gail Cunningham and Stephen Barber (London: Berghahn Books, 2007), p. 151.
5 Kevin Gough-Yates, 'The European Filmmaker in Exile in Britain 1933–45' (PhD thesis, Open University, 1991), p. v.
6 Rebecca Prime, *Hollywood Exiles in Europe: The Blacklist and Cold War Film Culture* (New Brunswick, NJ: Rutgers University Press, 2014), p. 5.
7 For Walker's take on the time, see Alexander Walker, *Hollywood, England: The British Film Industry in the Sixties* (London: Orion Books, 2005 [1974]). Keynesian capitalism began to stagnate during this period, which also coincides with England's referendum to integrate economically with Europe in 1975. For more on the abandonment of Keynesian policies because of inflationary worries and an embrace of Chicago School free marketeering under Thatcher, see Dominic Sandbrook, *Who Dares Wins: Britain, 1979–1982* (London: Penguin, 2019), pp. 94–5.
8 Mary Douglas, *Purity and Danger: An Analysis of the Concepts of Pollution and Taboo* (New York: Routledge, 2001 [1966]).
9 Katherine Shonfield, *Walls Have Feelings: Architecture, Film and the City* (London: Routledge, 2000), pp. 3–4.
10 Pamela Robertson Wojcik, *The Apartment Plot: Urban Living in American Film and Popular Culture, 1945–1975* (Durham, NC: Duke University Press, 2010).
11 Hugo Frey, 'Shutting Out the City: Reflections on the Portrayal of London in 1960s *Auteur* Cinema', in *London Eyes: Reflections on Text and Image*, ed. Gail Cunningham and Stephen Barber (London: Berghahn Books, 2007), p. 142.
12 Charlotte Brunsdon, *London in Cinema: The Cinematic City since 1945* (London: BFI Publishing, 2007), p. 104; Frey, 'Shutting Out the City', p. 138.
13 V. S. Pritchett, *London Perceived* (Jaffrey, NH: David R. Godine, 1990 [1962]), p. 22.
14 Mark Scroggins, *Michael Moorcock: Fiction, Fantasy, and the World's Pain* (Jefferson, NC: McFarland, 2016), pp. 39–40.
15 Michael Moorcock, *Elric: The Stealer of Souls* (New York: Ballantine/Del Rey, 2008), p. 20.
16 Ibid.
17 I have explored these themes in Kevin M. Flanagan, 'Wheatley's Progress: *High-Rise* (2015) and the Burden of Ballard', *Adaptation*, 9.3 (2016), pp. 434–8.
18 Shonfield, *Walls Have Feelings*, p. 57.
19 The visible part of 'The Day Dream' is from the section called 'The Departure': And on her lover's arm she leant,/And round her waist she felt it fold/And far

across the hills they went/In that new world which is the old;/Across the hills, and far away/Beyond their utmost purple rim,/And deep into the dying day/The happy princess follow'd him'; A. Tennyson, 'The Day Dream', in *The Poetical and Dramatic Works of Alfred Lord Tennyson*, ed. W. J. Rolfe (Boston, MA: Houghton, Mifflin and Company, 1898). The Rossetti poem reinforces key themes: 'Love, strong as death, is dead./Come, let us make his bed/Among the dying flowers:/A green turf at his head;/And a stone at his feet,/Whereon we may sit/In the quiet evening hours'; Christina Rossetti, 'An End', *The Germ: Thoughts towards Nature*, 1 (1850), p. 48.

20 For a look at the psychological and policy issues around sheltering, see Davide Deriu, 'Managing the Body and the City: The Contested Re-appropriation of London Underground in Wartime', in *Organizing Metropolitan Space and Discourse*, ed. Rolf Solli and Barbara Czarniawska (Malmo: Sweden Liber, 2001), pp. 47–66.
21 Sean Hogan, *Midnight Movie Monographs: Death Line* (Hornsea: Electric Dreamhouse/PS Publishing, 2017), p. 88.
22 Ewa Mazierska, *Jerzy Skolimowski: The Cinema of a Nonconformist* (London: Berghahn Books, 2010), p. 172.
23 Ryan Gilbey, '*Deep End*: Pulled from the Water', *Guardian* (1 May 2011), www.theguardian.com/film/2011/may/01/deep-end (accessed 12 May 2021). For locations, see 'Deep End', *Reel Streets*, www.reelstreets.com/films/deep-end/ (accessed 12 May 2021).
24 Frey, 'Shutting Out the City', p. 139.
25 Shonfield, *Walls Have Feelings*, p. 55.
26 Veronica Fitzpatrick, 'Home's Invasion: *Repulsion* and the Horror of Apartments', in *The Apartment Complex: Urban Living and Global Screen Cultures*, ed. Pam Wojick (Durham, NC: Duke University Press, 2018), pp. 126, 129.
27 For a career overview, see David Caute, *Joseph Losey: A Revenge on Life* (London: Faber and Faber, 1994).
28 See Adam Scovell, 'In Search of the Locations for Joseph Losey's Classic *The Servant*', BFI (30 June 2017), www.bfi.org.uk/features/servant-locations-joseph-losey-dirk-bogarde (accessed 12 May 2021).
29 James Palmer and Michael Riley, *The Films of Joseph Losey* (New York: Cambridge University Press, 1993), p. 12.
30 Anat Feinberg, *Embodied Memory: The Theatre of George Tabori* (Iowa City: University of Iowa Press, 1999), p. 20.
31 Colin Gardner, *Joseph Losey* (Manchester: Manchester University Press, 2004), p. 183.
32 'Secret Ceremony', *Reel Streets*, www.reelstreets.com/films/secret-ceremony/ (accessed 12 May 2021).
33 James Stevens Curl and Susan Wilson, 'Ricardo, Halsey Ralph', in *A Dictionary of Architecture and Landscape Architecture* (Oxford: Oxford University Press, 2015).
34 Caute, *Joseph Losey*, pp. 224–5.

35 See John Boorman, *Adventures of a Suburban Boy* (London: Faber & Faber, 2003), p. 169; Hoyle, *The Cinema of John Boorman*, pp. 59–60.
36 Boorman, *Adventures of a Suburban Boy*, p. 169; Hoyle, *The Cinema of John Boorman*, pp. 60–2, 63.
37 Boorman, *Adventures of a Suburban Boy*, p. 171. For images and more exact addresses for filming, see the *Reel Streets* website at: 'Leo the Last', *Reel Streets*, www.reelstreets.com/films/leo-the-last/ (accessed 12 May 2021).
38 Hoyle, *The Cinema of John Boorman*, p. 67.
39 Tino Balio, *United Artists: The Company That Changed the Film Industry* (Madison, WI: University of Wisconsin Press, 1987), pp. 329, 313.
40 Boorman, *Adventures of a Suburban Boy*, p. 180.
41 Frey, 'Shutting Out the City', pp. 135–47.

3

On location in 1970s London: an interview with Gavrik Losey

Paul Newland

Gavrik Losey was born in New York in 1938. His father was Joseph Losey. He grew up in Hollywood during the late 1940s, where he witnessed first-hand the effects of the McCarthy witch hunts which forced his father to flee the United States in 1951 to avoid testifying before the House Un-American Activities Committee. Losey eventually followed his father to England in 1956. He enrolled at University College London and entered the British film industry as a full-time professional in 1959.

Before moving into film production, Losey gained practical experience of the creative side of the industry while training as a film editor, cameraman and assistant director. He was a camera assistant on *Tom Jones* (Tony Richardson, 1963) and *Girl with Green Eyes* (Desmond Davis, 1964) and worked as a news cameraman for the first series of Granada Television's *World in Action*. He was asked to become an assistant director on *Modesty Blaise* (Joseph Losey, 1966) and *Dare I Weep, Dare I Mourn* (Ted Kotcheff, 1966).

Losey then moved into production management. He was to work on more than twenty films in this capacity, including Peter Yates's *Robbery* (1967), Joseph McGrath's *30 Is a Dangerous Age, Cynthia* (1968) and Lindsay Anderson's *If ...* (1968). During this period he was also approached to work on the television film *Magical Mystery Tour* (1967) by the Beatles. In 1968 Losey became an in-house production supervisor for Woodfall Films, where his projects included *Hamlet* (1969), *Laughter in the Dark* (1969) and *Ned Kelly* (1970), all directed by Tony Richardson.

Losey remained busy during the early 1970s. He worked on two films for director Michael Tuchner – *Villain* (1971), as assistant producer, and *Fear is the Key* (1972), as associate producer. He joined David Puttnam and Sandy Lieberson at Goodtimes Films as an associate producer/producer, working on *Melody* (Waris Hussein, 1971), *The Pied Piper* (Jacques Demy, 1971), *That'll Be the Day* (Claude Whatham, 1973), *Stardust* (Michael Apted, 1974) and *Flame* (Richard Loncraine, 1975).

Losey produced some of his best work as a freelance producer during the 1970s. Stuart Cooper's *Little Malcolm* (1974) was the winner of a Silver Bear at the Berlin Film Festival. Losey was installed on J. Lee Thompson's *The Greek Tycoon* (1978) as production consultant. He helped to produce *Agatha* (1979), another Michael Apted film starring Dustin Hoffman and Vanessa Redgrave. He remains especially proud of his work on Franco Rosso's *Babylon* (1980). Working with Stuart Cooper he also completed the first Anglo-Canadian co-production treaty film, *The Disappearance* (David Hemmings, 1977), starring Donald Sutherland.

During the 1980s Losey became the Deputy Managing Director (Production) for the Legion multi-media group, which made films, records and TV commercials. At Legion he produced the Charles Gormley feature film *Living Apart Together* (1982) and a two-hour documentary for the BBC, *The Foreign Legion*. Between 1989 and 1991 he worked on the production of the television film *A Child from the South* (Sergio Rezende, 1991), which was shot towards the end of the civil war in Mozambique.

Since the late 1990s Losey has acted as a freelance production adviser on projects for Paramount and Warner Bros. More recently he has also been employed as a freelance lecturer, delivering industry seminars on budgeting and scheduling for HTV and teaching in a variety of educational settings, including the London Film School, Bath Media College and the University of Bristol. Gavrik donated his archive to the Bill Douglas Centre (now the Bill Douglas Cinema Museum) at the University of Exeter. He became an Honorary Fellow of the University of Exeter in 2003.

PN: I would like to begin by talking about *Villain* (Michael Tuchner, 1971), a very interesting film in terms of location shooting. Can you tell me about your memories of what happened on location and, indeed, which locations were chosen and why?

GL: The decision to shoot *Villain* entirely on location was based on problems related to cost. There is a point at which, if you are going to be on a film set, or in a location, is it cheaper to build it in the studio, where you don't have the transport costs but you have the studio costs, or you don't have the catering costs because everyone gets their own lunch, but you do have the restricted time spaces – the union requirements for the studio, and the overheads – lighting and certain things like that – and the costs of actually building the sets and decorating. So you sit down and in the usual way of things there is a decision about whether it is actually better to do the locations and then to go into the studio to build the sets or whether it is better to use real locations.

One of the things that problematised location shooting was actually the BBC, who were very arrogant. They never cleaned up after themselves, and they made location shooting much more difficult. People had initially been very receptive and loved the idea. Then people began to realise that there was money in it, and there was a hell of a lot of aggravation that went with it. In *Villain*, the robberies, the chases, all those things – one went to the local police station; one saw the sergeant; one told the sergeant. It was a bit lackadaisical. The duty officer would turn up.

PN: So working on a film like *Villain* in the early seventies you didn't have to approach a body to get permission to film?

GL: No. You didn't need shooting permits. You never needed them in England. I mean you needed shooting permits in France and other places because it was sort of left over from the war – a security thing. But you never needed a governmental shooting permit. You just went and shot. You had a location manager and you did it yourself and you chatted up the local residents and you threw five pound notes about. That changed. It became a commercial business. Now you are looking at £1,000 a day to let somebody's property. In those days you would be happy to have twenty-five quid in the hand. Now if you give them £1,000 a day they have got to sign for it. It goes on a tax bill. On the other hand now it's much more professional. You can have a policeman – you buy an off-duty cop and pay his off-duty hourly rate. The Film Office will help you set all that stuff up.[1] Now, before that it was all ad hoc. You would go to see the duty sergeant. If the bung was good enough you got a lot of help. Very often you would put fifty quid across the desk to buy the boys a drink which, without wishing to say the police were corrupt, went into somebody's pocket – but, lo and behold, you know, a lot of assistance came your way. Now you get it professionally. It's a much better system.

PN: What other problems did you face shooting on location in London for *Villain*?

GL: *Villain* was actually, interestingly enough, very straightforward. The initial preparation work which I wasn't involved with – because I was doing *Fear Is the Key* (Michael Tuchner, 1972) for the same company[2] – had been very well set out, and the whole thing had been organised and laid out so it worked extremely well. I think it also worked extremely well because it was done more in the suburbs. Not much of it was done in central London.

PN: Can you remember where you filmed parts of *Villain*?

GL: Well, the bank is actually in Twickenham. The Westminster Bank in Twickenham town centre – we used the exterior there, and the interior was an abandoned bank which we hired.

PN: There is a very interesting scene where Burton's gang chases a car into some kind of new business park or industrial area – a very interesting location – by a big Clark Eaton factory.

GL: That was out in Bracknell. There were also lots of shots by railway arches. In the seventies there were a vast amount of abandoned areas – brownfield sites, I think they would call them now. The end of *Melody* is shot in abandoned railway yards at Waterloo. *Villain* uses a series of railway arches which I think are in Lambeth and areas around Clapham.

PN: The final sequence – in which Vic (Richard Burton) shoots Joss Acland – that looks like it was filmed under railway arches in Battersea.

GL: I think so, yes.

Look, the pressure is immense. Shooting a film, on the production side and on the acting side, is a minimum twelve to fourteen hours a day. On the production side it is seven days a week because if you work five you prepare on the sixth day, and on the seventh day you pick up on the mistakes that you've made in the week before and in the advance. So most production teams work seven days a week. Now the big advantage of being in the studios was that at Friday at five o'clock they locked the doors, and there was very little you could do. When you are on location things are shifting all the time. The woman who owns the house's mother has just died. What do you do? You haven't got a location until Monday. Everybody gets turned out of bed to go and find an alternative. On the Sunday afternoon the director is dragged out of bed to approve the place so that the prop department can get in much earlier than they had planned it to re-dress the damn set because they're in the wrong place. Those kinds of working-on-your-feet constant changes are exciting and interesting and gave a dynamic to film-making that the studio doesn't have. The studio is much more rigid and formulated.

PN: *Robbery* (Peter Yates, 1967) was filmed in the centre of London without permissions, was it not?

GL: Without permissions, but with a very basic kind of clearance. You couldn't do what we did on *Robbery* today, except with a very large police presence and a lot of people knowing what you were doing.

PN: The car chase is extraordinary. It looks very dangerous.

GL: It was very dangerous!

PN: Was it fully planned?

GL: Totally planned. Every single inch of that thing was planned and plotted.

PN: Were streets closed for filming?

GL: Streets were closed off by the police. We had quite a good police presence. But in the areas we were shooting in there wasn't an overall film bureau that assisted us. The police presence didn't come from the Met, but was local.

PN: That car chase is, of course, a precursor to the famous Steve McQueen chase in Peter Yates's *Bullitt*.

GL: The car chase *got* Peter Yates *Bullitt*.

PN: According to the cross plot in your file, the chase scenes were filmed in Marble Arch and elsewhere across West London. You also shot footage in Hatton Garden, London Airport, Battersea Park (Jacko's garage) and on Carnaby Street.

GL: And we filmed in Northumberland Avenue, around Trafalgar Square and in the Strand. We filmed around Notting Hill Gate, around Little Venice. We filmed in Roehampton. The end of the chase is in Roehampton – the new tower blocks were just by the edge of Wimbledon Common there. The beginning of the chase and the gassing takes place in Northumberland Avenue, where the diamond car crashes.

The scene in *Robbery* where you see one of the cars shooting down the road and you'll see a figure appear from roughly the camera position and run across the road and grab a little old lady and have some kind of a tussle with this little old lady, and the police car and the Jaguar go by, and that is actually me rushing across the road because the little old lady is deaf and not paying any attention, to stop her from crossing the road. She tells me that she's crossed this road on this day every day at this time, and she's not going to stop for any film unit. We would have had sort of a pressed little old lady if somebody hadn't rushed across her – being me – and stopped her [laughs].

Those were the kind of things that you did encounter – that people have fixed routines.

The other thing that was interesting about both *Villain* and *Robbery* was that we had to get location clearance; that the owners recognised that the property was being shown as the property belonging to somebody who was a criminal. Now, the litigious end of that was beginning to evolve when we reached *Villain*. I mean, the owners of property would suddenly welcome you in and turn nasty. They would realise there was money behind it. The insurance companies wanted the most elaborate clearances. The clearances on *Villain* and *Robbery* were about six pages. Nobody could actually get out of saying they didn't know what was being used and what for.

PN: Moving through the seventies, did you detect any differences in the ways in which you were treated when filming on location in London? It became more difficult for you, did it not?

GL: The whole attitude towards everything changed. In practical production terms, to begin with everybody is very helpful. Then they begin to realise you are actually breaking the law, working on the fringes of the law, and it isn't a good thing. Now, that changed gradually. Then the London Film Commission arrived in the early nineties. It then became more professional. The ground shifted. London realised – like New York had done, with *Fame*, etc. – films could be made there. Before, there were a lot of cowboys out there, and I was one of them, in the sense that there was no structure, no way of doing it, and the business was to get the job done so you moved things around; you manipulated; you bought people; you did bits, to make things happen. If you had some kind of integrity you cleaned up after yourself and you made sure nobody got hurt, and you made sure you were properly insured. Then people like the Film Producers' Association tried to establish a professional way of actually going about making films in London. In a way it's now less interesting because it's much more restricted. You now get all the police cover you want if you pay for it, in almost any place you want, provided that it works within the whole. The result is you are much more restricted by health and safety, by all the things that go with it, reasonably or unreasonably. Through until the eighties you could do what you want.

PN: Perhaps we could now talk a bit about your experiences filming *Laughter in the Dark* (Tony Richardson, 1969) in London?

GL: *Laughter in the Dark* was a disaster. Tony Richardson wanted to use Nicol Williamson to play the leading part. United Artists said they would back it if it starred Burton. And Burton said he would do it. So we started to make the film with Anna Karina and Burton and a number of other quite good actors. I set up to close Bond Street on a Sunday completely – this is before Sunday opening, so it wasn't that big a problem – so that we could take a real Goya painting and put it in the window of Wildenstein galleries. We had already filmed the picture at auction at Sotheby's. And the auctioneer had actually given the actor's name. He had been slipped £500 and when it came to the final bid he said 'sold to Mr ...' So we had the cut. We had the auctioneer in Sotheby's actually auctioning this picture to Richard Burton.

PN: According to files now in your archive, *Laughter in the Dark* had sequences shot in the Mayflower Coffee Bar, Hogarth Place, Earl's Court; Shepherd's Market; a flat in Prince Albert Court, north-west London; Farringdon House; Crockford's casino in Carlton House Terrace; the National Portrait Gallery; offices in the Courtauld Institute of Art; and, of course, as you say, Sotheby's in New Bond Street. This filming took place in the summer of 1968. You received letters of complaint from the Royal Borough of Kensington and Chelsea regarding filming in Addison Road – your trucks caused a certain amount of disruption! But you did receive a letter from the Ministry of Public Building and Works saying that they had no problem with you filming in and around Hyde Park and St James's Park in June '68.

So then you went to work with Puttnam and Goodtimes. You filmed *Melody* in London, too?

GL: David [Puttnam] called me up one day and said, 'I'd like to meet you. I want to make a film. I don't know anything about it'. So he came up to the Roundhouse where I was doing *Hamlet* with Tony Richardson, and he took me across the road to the café where we ate egg and chips.

PN: You remember what you had for lunch!

GL: That was it. He bought me egg and chips and a cup of bad tea in a greasy spoon on Camden High Road and said, 'I've got the money, I've got the people, I've got the script and I don't know what to do'. And I said to him, 'All the hard work is done. The rest is easy. All you have to do is make it, and there are plenty of people like me who can do it' and he said 'Well, do you want to do it?' and I said 'Yes, I'd love to do it'. So when I finished *Hamlet* I went to work for Goodtimes setting up *Melody*. *Melody* had one interesting aspect to it. A month before we were going to shoot in Lambeth, the construction manager rang me up and said, 'There is an abandoned school which is the St Paul's School, which is empty in Olympia'. And we just upped and moved the entire production into a ready-made school building. And that was perfect. And after it worked extremely well because most of it was done in a confined area. We were able to control it. It was called Collett Gardens, near Hammersmith and Olympia. It worked really well. And then we went out to Waterloo and did some stuff in the grounds and things like that. That would have been a lot harder production if that particular thing hadn't turned up. And we moved in there, and it all worked extremely well.

PN: How about *Babylon*? That's a terrific London film. What was it like working on location in the late 1970s?

GL: *Babylon* was fairly restricted. I mean, we didn't have to have Piccadilly Circus. We didn't have to have Northumberland Avenue. We didn't have a huge car chase that we had to deal with. We had a duty cop with us throughout all the external shooting. The interesting thing about the particular moment we were making *Babylon* was that there was a lot of money being pushed into trying to regenerate that whole area. Therefore there was a tremendous amount of community support, which enabled us not to be restricted. A lot of what you have to do, if people don't interfere with it, you just get on with it and it gets done and it's over.

Babylon is, in a cultural sense, a creative sense, an attempt to tell it as it was: to actually show on screen with language, with lighting, with text, with locations, an actual segment of society which had a separate life; enjoys a separate life; fundamentally didn't interfere with the rest of society until the rest of society started to interfere with it. The making of it was absolutely horrendously great fun – it was awful and yet absolutely amazing. The crew was handpicked because they were going into a community which was completely alien to all the people who worked on the film. The Black community totally accepted us. I think that that's largely because Franco [Rosso] and Martin [Stellman] had a relationship with the Black community where they were trusted. Therefore they were allowed to be a part of it in a way that other people might not.

PN: What was the response of the community to what you were doing?

GL: I think the Black community understood from Franco and Martin that the people who were involved in making this film were genuine people – they weren't there to actually send up the Blacks or to create a problem with this section or that section of the community. Except for the actors, who are named on the screen – of which there are probably twenty – all the crowds and the ancillary people, all the people around it are real. It's all real location, all shot in the real place.

PN: South London

GL: Yes, South London. We took over the second floor of the Methodist Mission in Deptford High Street. They were very pleased to have us because we were paying them rent and they were very broke. We used this as our production base. And then there were various Black community projects that were going on which enabled us to draw on potential actors and bit-part players and people like that. The band Aswad came complete. Brinsley Ford was a child actor. It was very tight budget. It was held very close to the budget.

PN: The budget was approximately £350,000.

GL: That's right. I don't think under modern health and safety laws we would have been able to do what we did because we were working in halls without licences and all sorts of things like that, but that was just the nature of filmmaking then. Now, you know, you have to have all kinds of things. It wasn't that we were uninsured or we did anything illegal. But now, rightly or wrongly, that kind of filmmaking is not really practical because of the constraints that are added by the new legislation. Shooting in the real community, that real community is poor, that real community lives in that condition. Deptford is a deprived area – it certainly was then, I don't know what it's like now – so you just wouldn't have gotten away with it. We shot in the West End without permissions. The whole ability to do this kind of filming of almost reportage photography of shooting in the West End to a large extent was down to Chris's [Menges] ability to just light with a single handlight and to give it a quality which looks very real. He built a whole range of lights for the garage where they store their equipment with incandescent fluorescent tubes to give it a cold light effect. His contribution was really extraordinary. Franco handled the actors extremely well. A guy called Tom Schwalm cut it but largely under Franco's direction. And I think Franco shot it within his own idea of editing so there wasn't a lot of choice within it. I mean, that's the old-fashioned way. You can't mess it about if you haven't got the material [laughs].

We were incredibly lucky with the weather. We were very lucky with almost everything. Overall, it was actually a very, very good shoot.

PN: How well planned was the shoot? Was it always important for you to have everything pre-arranged?

GL: In the structuring of the film, obviously you break it down and you schedule it as best you can within the confines of continuity, within the confines of money available, within the confines of locations and things like that. And you then budget to that requirement. If you get serious changes it can throw the whole thing out. Also, when you are working in the street you have the advantage of being slightly flexible. If you are working to a studio situation and you have to go out and come in, it is much more difficult because you are a compact unit which is mobile. So if the weather changes you always try and get weather cover so that you have somewhere to go. You know, if the light goes … It's a fixed moveable feast. But luckily in this particular production there wasn't any real need for that.

PN: Was it all shot on location?

GL: There was no studio shoot at all. We did dress and convert – the pool hall scene is done in a disused shop. The location guy got the permission. We went in, dressed it. It was convenient not to move. We had an exterior and an interior.

PN: Was it was still much cheaper than using a studio, dressing this shop?

GL: Yes, within the confines, if you can do it. I mean, there is a point where, if you can rid yourself of your tail … Look, in the studio you don't need transport, you don't pay for meals, you don't carry a whole range of things which you would carry on location. So you don't have a whole range of costs. But you have the studio costs. So there's a balance. It used to be that you had three days' work on a set, which was a simple set or a location, it was almost cheaper to build it. But it was only cheaper to build it if you can divest yourself of your tail. If you can get rid of the trucks, if you can get rid of the catering, if you can get rid of all that stuff, then you are not spending that money. But if you stick in a studio shot in a location shot, then it is a matter of cost. I mean, a simple, dirty old room which has a pool table in it – it's cheaper to do it on location and build it. Also, you could put your sets near to your locations, so if the weather changed you could go inside – what is called 'weather cover'. You would set up your schedule on a weekly basis, with potential weather cover days set at the end of the week, so if on Monday it rains you call Friday's work. And on the call sheet you will 'stand by' the actors for Friday as well as calling the actors for Monday – so you can shift it. And if on Tuesday it rains you go to Friday's work – and so it goes – and if you get to the end of the week, you may move your weather cover into the next week and keep shooting while the weather holds. It's a mental trick. Those big crowd scenes, the toasting scenes, took an enormous amount of time, because you are dealing with a huge crowd of very relaxed, very stoned people. They don't want no aggro; they are here to hear the music; they are nice people. But they are not easy to move around. They are not like professional crowds. Overall the crowd was really good, too. They responded well to it. Mikey Dread was an important pillar of the community in the Rasta community, and the Rasta community gave the production the OK. So we have several scenes in Rasta churches where Blue (Brinsley Forde) walks in – he has sort of lost his way in life – and walks into a Rasta service. All that is real people doing the real thing. In those respects, visually it is quite amazing.

Notes

1 The London Film Commission (LFC) became Film London along with the London Film Video and Development Agency (LFVDA). Film London was founded in March 2003 under the aegis of the UK Film Council and the London Development Agency. Sandy Lieberson was appointed Chairman of the Board. See www.filmlondon.org.
2 Kastner – Ladd – Kanter Productions. While financed by Nat Cohen at Anglo-EMI, *Fear is the Key*, starring Barry Newman and Suzy Kendall, was shot mostly on location in the southern United States. But the large house which features in the film was shot in Surrey.

4

Outside in: *Twilight City* and the birth of global London

Malini Guha

There is little doubt that the withdrawal of the UK from the fold of the European Union threatens London's status as a top-tier global city. After all, as former Prime Minister Theresa May odiously declared shortly after the leave vote, 'If you believe you are a citizen of the world, you are a citizen of nowhere'.[1] While a number of right-wing factions have both seized upon and reduced 'the global' in recent years to a form of shorthand for racism, economic crises, terrorism and cyberwarfare, early on others expressed concerns that Brexit would send London hurtling backwards, to a past steeped in imperial nostalgia and maligned by race riots, bad infrastructure and other 'British' ills.[2] While most London boroughs voted to remain, such an outcome does not entirely diminish these anxieties given broader regional as well as global circumstances.[3] The onset of the COVID-19 pandemic in late 2019 has only heightened the increasingly fraught tenor of neoliberal globalisation, as battles over the procurement of personal protective equipment, the complexities of maintaining global supply chains in a time of restricted borders and large-scale inequities concerning the sharing of vaccines seem to all lead in the direction of 'nation first', a trend reignited by former American President Donald Trump's notorious 'America first' slogan. What happens to the 'global city paradigm' and to London's designation as one of its prime examples within the context of a rapid and potentially radical reconfiguration of globalisation in its myriad understandings and formations?[4]

These conditions suggest that the time for sustained reflection has arrived. In his introduction to *Outsider: Films on India 1950–1990* Shanay Jhaveri observes that the 'transformative powers of globalization', marked by a relentless and often ruthless movement forward across the Indian subcontinent, has initiated the opposite tendency, which is a drive towards remembrance.[5] The potential demise of globalisation as we presently know it, the politics of which are unravelling in very particular ways in London, similarly provoke a need to consider anew the origins of neoliberal globalisation. As such, there is perhaps no better time to revisit Black Audio

Film Collective's (BAFC) *Twilight City* (Reece Auguiste, 1989), a film that Kodwo Eshun designates as possibly the first essayistic exploration of global London.[6] Additionally, Jhaveri claims that these calls for reflection and remembrance in an Indian context are oriented towards 'expressions of outsider perspectives' that are 'both material and utopian' in their scope.[7] Outside, in this context, denotes an external relation to contemporary iterations of globalisation while also gesturing towards a 'foreign' perspective, which is the typical characterisation of the outsider film. The eternal promise of the outsider view is that of insight, which cannot be gleaned by those solely residing on the inside.

Twilight City occupies a unique position with respect to both conceptions of the outside that Jhaveri gestures towards. As Eshun observes, this film prefigures what is now a well-established indictment of the deep inequalities sired by neoliberal governance.[8] However, *Twilight City* forges this critique by charting what still remains an uncommon route through the imperial past and its enduring legacies, which includes memories of exploitative labour practices, the oppressive presence of monuments as well as the testimonies of figures belonging to the Black and Asian diaspora in Britain, constituting what David Gilbert and Felix Driver situate as among the most enduring traces of the history of empire.[9] This is how, to draw from Eshun, the film distinguishes itself from a significant strand of scholarly writing on globalisation that involves the language of flow, scapes, differentiation and networks.[10] Building upon Eshun's work, this chapter considers the question of what models of thinking about the global *Twilight City* can be aligned with and why the claims produced by these forms of thinking matter in the present.

Out of time

How does *Twilight City* constitute a cinematic form of thinking, seeing, hearing and feeling about London's transition to global city? One can begin to address this question by turning to claims made by members of BAFC, including *Twilight City*'s director and critics such as Eshun, that the Collective engaged in struggles over the epistemological terrain of Black independent cinema 'through modes of visual articulation and narrative concerns which do not desire to emulate or mimic other cinemas'.[11] BAFC's use of the essay film as a form across much of their oeuvre is fitting, as one of the most explicitly positioned and recognisable intellectual traditions of the cinema. But as former BAFC member John Akomfrah once noted in an interview with Coco Fusco (and retold to Eshun), the Collective was as transfixed by formal questions as they were by emotional ones.[12]

In response to criticisms of 'anti-intellectualism' that followed, Akomfrah tells Eshun the story of watching *Police Five* with his brothers and praying that the mugger on screen would not be Black. As he says, 'there was a certain kind of tyranny which overdetermined our lives, that came via the image, which forced you to have both a theoretical, an emotional and a philosophical approach to images'.[13] Akomfrah suggests that the moving image and images more broadly have historically assumed a catastrophic role in overriding the realities of Black life, ensuring that their making and subsequent deployment cannot be mere exercises in form or theoretical conjecture. As Ben Highmore has observed about Akomfrah and, by extension, BAFC films, the conjuring of an 'elegiac mood' is a signature component of their formal practice so that thinking is entirely bound up with specific modalities of feeling.[14] As will become evident, and in keeping with BAFC's body of work, *Twilight City* develops an essayistic approach that combines theory, emotion and a philosophical attitude to the new London.

Auguiste reworks the epistolary strand of the essay film by structuring *Twilight City* as a response to a letter that triggers an expansive rumination upon the then current state of London. Olivia Levelle, whom we hear in the form of voice-over narration and see writing on a notepad but whose face never appears in its entirety on camera, considers the contents of a letter written by her mother Eugenia. The latter left for Dominica in 1979 but longs to return to London after a ten-year absence. The ensuing film addresses her mother's request for an invitation to come back, moving through the litany of changes that have taken hold of the city in the interim and giving credence to Olivia's claim that 'the London you left behind is disappearing, perhaps forever and I don't know if you will want to return to the new one'. Olivia informs us that she is researching the creation of wealth, a project that takes her across the urban developments of the 1980s, including the gentrification of the Docklands and the Isle of Dogs, while also returning her to the recesses of the imperial past. The film is interspersed with interviews conducted with scholars and writers including Paul Gilroy, Gail Lewis, George Shire, Rosina Visram and Homi Bhabha, among others, who address the city of the past, present and future in different idioms; some offer scholarly analysis while others return to their childhood memories as the basis of their critiques that centre upon spatial segregation and the ensuing politics of dispossession. As Olivia notes in her voice-over, 'each interview begins with a new London'. *Twilight City* provides a variation upon the letter film by incorporating traces of a 'talking heads' documentary aesthetic in these interviews so that the production of knowledge about the city is as personal as it is scholarly. This film, as Eshun puts it, 'use[s] the moving image to portray an emergent public sphere of diasporic intellectuals'.[15]

While the film's formal hybridity is in keeping with a chief attribute of the essay film, this method also enables *Twilight City* to present its myriad Londons in the guise of the metaphoric city. Ben Highmore situates metaphoricity not as a means of representation but as 'the lived reality' of the density of urban spaces as 'ghostly accumulations of past lives, past cities'.[16] The film establishes an intimate connection between Olivia and the many Londons that appear in the film, where she often assumes the voice of the city while images of London are intertwined with her musings, even seeping into her dreams. Visions of the city in this film are as textual as they are geographical, emulating states of mind as much as they function as material sites of being. The film presents Olivia and the Londons she investigates as deeply unsettled, which conforms to an attribute of the essay film more broadly in its rendering of an intellectual response that is stimulated by an 'unsettled subjectivity'.[17]

In her writing on the essay film, Laura Rascaroli returns to one of Theodor Adorno's pronouncements concerning the value of the essay as form, which is its anachronism. As she proclaims, 'the essay film is the future film, the film of tomorrow' because 'the essay is against its time'.[18] The outsider status of the essay film rests in its formal procedures but also in its orientation away from the time of its release. While Rascaroli centres Adorno's claims concerning the hybrid, transgressive and subversive qualities of the essay as the source of its anachronism, Adorno makes other observations in 'The Essay as Form' concerning the temporal nature of the essay that also bear relevance for a film like *Twilight City*.[19] Following Simmel, Lukás, Benjamin and others, Adorno denotes essayistic thinking as a form of speculation on 'specific, culturally pre-formed objects'.[20] In addition to conceptualising the essay as a speculative form, Adorno rejects what he delineates as the Platonic philosophical tradition that repudiates transience and ephemerality as correct subjects for philosophical discourse.[21] For Adorno, the essay focuses precisely on what is transient and ephemeral in an effort 'to render the transient eternal' in opposition to an approach that aims to do the opposite.[22]

Twilight City meets the temporal criteria outlined by Adorno in its outsider presentation of the new London. The film explores the city in a state of transience near the end of Margaret Thatcher's reign or, as Olivia describes it, 'a London that is disappearing and a London that is being born'. To do so constitutes an act of speculative thinking. The title of the film immediately speaks to the temporal character of transition. Twilight is a word that is frequently used to signify an impending end but a cursory examination of its etymology reveals a series of definitions that are also, unsurprisingly, related to vision. Twilight vision, for instance, denotes a state where colours are hardly perceptible due to the dimness of light. While images of the sun setting over the River Thames and the sun rising over a shadowy London are dispersed across the film, twilight vision is a structuring motif that governs key aspects of the film. *Twilight City* develops a series of constellation-like configurations, as is typical of the essay film, where the difficulty of seeing is linked to the question of time and, more precisely, to the notion of forgotten time.

There is a section of the film where Olivia declares that she has read Eugenia's letter four times and each time finds something new to say in response. She notes a hint of fear in Eugenia's longing to return to London and wonders whether a similar fear was present during a childhood trip to Clacton-on-Sea. The images that accompany this recollection are of Black women and children enjoying themselves on the beach. Olivia's personal memories are channelled towards a collective remembrance of Black life in Britain, in the guise of leisure. Her evocation of a sense of fear pervades these images of pleasure through the discomforting nature of Trevor Mathison's electronic score. The music, which, for Eshun, 'simulate[s] wordless vocal wraiths, of the distant refrains of whales singing' is a perfect fit for the archival, silent film footage of Lascars in London (1924) that follows.[23] Lascar was the name given to Indian sailors who were first employed in the seventeenth century by the East India Company to work on merchant ships. The music used in these sequences further amplifies the already spectral quality of these filmed bodies of teenage Lascar boys rowing and of other adults smiling at the camera. As the images of the Lascars appear on screen, Olivia observes, 'We have old fears because we live in an old, flat world and when people and things reach the abyss, they fall in and disappear forever, like the Indian seaman, the Isle of Dogs, The London Mission Society and the East India Company'. This statement can be taken as an instance of meta-commentary about the film as a whole. The Londons conjured by *Twilight City* resist flatness as well as the fate of the abyss in the film's summoning of a host of Londons that have become difficult to see. In this sequence, an imperial London emerges via the archival imagery of the Lascars.

As the sequence progresses and the rhythm of the music builds, Olivia describes learning about a Lascar community that once lived on the Isle of Dogs during the nineteenth century, on the site of her childhood home on Shadwell High Street. They were abandoned by the East India Company and left to fend for themselves on the cold streets of London. Olivia tells us that while they were 'offered Christianity by the London Mission Society', the last Lascar was discovered buried under three feet of snow. The images alternate between footage of a cemetery, which includes shots of monuments and crypts, archival images of a teenage Lascar boy getting his hair cut and, finally, people sleeping rough on the streets in the present. These images are followed by an interview with Rosina Visram, who adds further context to the story of the Lascars. She makes explicit their exploitation as they were used as cheap labour and then discarded on the streets of London when they were no longer useful. And even when they demanded redress and the East India Company did provide lodging, as Visram describes, 'their conditions were appalling'. Visram's words are intertwined with the images of the cemetery, some of which were also used during Olivia's narration, in conjunction with more footage of Lascars who smile at the camera and contemporary footage of sleeping bodies on the streets, flanked by cardboard boxes. This section of the film is summed up in a shot of the nighttime river, where the movement of the black water reinforces the ominous, unsettled nature of the previous shots while also suggesting that these histories have left no visible trace on the waters upon which they transpired.

This sequence is indicative of how *Twilight City* positions Olivia as essayist in Adorno's terms. The laboriousness of the task of the essayist, who 'turns ... the object around, questions it, feels it, tests it, reflects on it, attacks it from different sides', is granted to Olivia as she reviews the contents of Eugenia's letter.[24] She functions as 'an arena for intellectual experience without unraveling it', as Adorno writes.[25] Her voice links facets of past and present together in the absence of explanation. The film's structure conforms to what Adorno refers to as a method of 'reciprocal interaction' that leads to the disassociation of the object in question into 'moments' and thus, the object ceases to be 'mere object'.[26] *Twilight City* turns London from filmed object to 'moments in time' that exemplify the transient nature not only of essayistic thinking but also of the city itself.

This sequence also draws a discomforting affinity between the conditions of the Lascars, as described by Visram, and the images of the homeless. Social anthropologist Athena Athanasiou's phrase 'the distribution of vulnerability' bears relevance to *Twilight City*, which demonstrates how vulnerability is distributed across time, space and circumstance.[27] The homeless are positioned as the casualties of a then gentrifying East End of the city, reinforced by other sections of the film that emphasise the problem of gentrification on a larger scale. George Shire, for example, describes the technocratic nature of Conservative governance and the corresponding imperative to clear areas of Black settlement in the city to make way for industrial and economic development. In *Twilight City*, the birth of a new London is predicated on the production of a range of outsiders who may be dispossessed or may be forced to exist in the absence of communal relations that grew in their earlier sites of habitation. A similar fate was imposed upon the Lascars, as Visram articulates. They belong to the history of imperial wealth as its constitutive cogs but were treated as outsiders upon arrival to London, as the disposable by-products of the British Empire. In a later sequence of the film, Visram proclaims British maritime wealth was built on the backs of Lascars, her words serving as a searing indictment of empire.

Returning to the sequence at hand, Visram's words evoke images of the vulnerable and exposed bodies of the Lascars but the bodies that we see on screen are those of the homeless. The archival footage of the Lascars does not document these harsh realities. Rather, in their smiles and direct looks into the camera, they resemble the shots of the Black children on the beach that we see near the start of this sequence, some of whom also acknowledge the presence of the camera. This similarity appears all the more jarring given that the Black children are dressed in formal clothing and enjoying themselves on the beach while some of the footage of the Lascar youth is of them at work. The music remains the same across both sets of imagery, suggesting a disquieting link that troubles attempts at definitive explanation. While writing about the 'temporal fissures' produced by Mathison's score, Eshun makes an observation than can be extended to the film as a whole; he writes, 'This is more than simply joining new music to an old image; it holds together different audiovisual eras that fail to resolve into a third new form'.[28] This failure of resolution is typical of the essay film, in its refusal to clarify the relations between its various parts. The similarities as well as the discontinuities between the images of the Lascars and the Black children cannot be resolved into a third meaning, which heightens the disturbing mood of the sequence.

If Britain's imperial history and its enduring legacies are generally considered to be an outsider or external experience, a condition articulated by numerous scholars including Stuart Hall and Bill Schwarz, *Twilight City* positions these histories as intrinsic components of the rise of global London, in laying the foundation for the unabashed accumulation of corporate wealth that transpires in the neoliberal age. The film embarks on what Eshun refers to as a process of excavation, where 'a threatened past is unearthed to come to the aid of the endangered present, and in doing so helps to open a previously unglimpsed futurity'.[29] Between these evocations of past and present, brought together by a mutual vulnerability, is where the speculative nature of the film resides. However, the film's engagement with the city's imperial past does not begin and end with the deployment of rare archival footage of the Lascars. BAFC's long-standing preoccupation with what Eshun refers to as 'the malevolent obsolescence of the imperial statue' is also in evidence in *Twilight City*.[30] In the sequence described above, the repeated imagery of tombstones and statues in the cemetery skirts the line between remembrance and forgetting. Certainly, part of the point seems to be to demonstrate that the Lascars are not commemorated in this cemetery, even if they are buried there, and that their claim to official history has long been vanquished. But the stillness and solidity of the statues is also in sharp contrast with moving bodies documented in the archival footage. If the Lascars evoke the spectral quality that, in different times and circumstances, has been associated with the moving image, these statues stand outside of time in a different though related manner.

Why monuments never die but need to be seen

In a conversation between Michael Taussig and W. T. Mitchell that took place at the Dia Art Foundation, the latter details everything that a monument may want, very much in the vein of his previous work on what images may want.[31] The monument, as Mitchell puts it, 'wants to defeat time and history' but is ensnared in a paradox; while monuments want to live forever and thus to be 'alive in the present', they are inanimate, solid, dead matter.[32] Monuments crave human sacrifice and respect but, as Mitchell notes, during key historical moments, they are treated with disgrace.[33] However, as Taussig points out, monuments often remain strangely invisible, even 'playing dead', as he puts it, though they seem to desire so much in the way of attention.[34]

Eshun's description of BAFC's signature preoccupation with the 'malevolent obsolescence' of monuments, amplified during specific historical moments such as the one recounted above, precisely captures what I delineate as BAFC's medium-specific contribution to a discourse on the function of monuments articulated by Mitchell and Taussig, among numerous others across various fields of study.[35] Drawing from Hal Foster and Barbara Johnston, Eshun advances the argument that the 'non-synchronous presence' of monuments contains signals of lost dreams to which they could be made to speak.[36] As he writes, there are moments across BAFC's body of work where the camera 'gaze[s] into the blind eyes of a statue, as if to enlist them in a metropolitan drama against their wishes'.[37] By filming these statues, and thereby rendering them visible for an audience, BAFC reinserts them into the flow of time. Their desire to 'defeat history' is effectively thwarted through such a gesture but they are simultaneously granted the kind of attention that they, in fact, do not seek.[38] Returning to the Lascar sequence, in making monuments as well as crypts visible vis-à-vis moving images of Lascar youth and adults, the film activates a further tension between animation and stasis. The imagery of the Lascars, as they directly address the camera, is a stark reminder that they were once very much alive while adding further poignancy to the story of their horrific treatment. The monuments, when brought into relation with this footage, signify death in a double register. Their solidity, stillness and placement within the cemetery already equates them with the loss of life. However, when these images are alternated with those of the Lascars, the sequence deftly works to expose the death drive of the imperial project, where life was routinely sacrificed to further the accumulation of wealth.

The metropolitan drama of which Eshun speaks is manifested perhaps most directly during a sequence dedicated to the exploration of knowledge and silence. The music used in this sequence elicits strong feelings of dread, as Olivia recalls her mother's words – 'If you really want to know someone, listen to their silences'. Linking her personal recollections to the city, Olivia says, 'I'm beginning to think that in order to understand a city, you have to do the same thing'. The shots accompanying her narration are close-ups of monuments, some of which are of hands while others focus on faces and eyes. She describes speaking to one such statue, who reveals that their silence is the source of their power as they keep secrets that belong to those who claim ownership over the city's future. These guardians of the city revel in 'the power of inheritance', Olivia says. This sequence confers visibility on these monuments, as is true of earlier and later sequences, but in intensified form. The camera forces us to gaze into their eyes and a number of them, including Winston Churchill, appear to look back.

Here, *Twilight City* further advances the thesis that the origins of neoliberal London reside in Britain's imperial past as these monuments to empire, to draw upon Eshun's language, contain signals of dreams. In this instance, these dreams have become a partial reality as the film makes clear the strength of the bond that exists between the city's past and its global future in an imagined dialogue between Olivia and these long-silenced statues that now begin to speak. This bond is based in what scholars across disciplines have identified as a long-standing desire, often though not exclusively held by members of the political class, to restore Britain to the so-called glory of its former imperial identity without actually returning to an age of empire.[39] A similar sense of dread, cultivated through music, slow camera movements and a grey colour palette, is linked to a shot of the Bank of England that appears twice in the film. The camera moves laterally behind a series of columns, gradually unveiling the City of London with its bustling streets. By filming this area of the city in ways that bear direct resemblance to how monuments are filmed throughout, *Twilight City* confers a sense of monumentality upon the financial district that subtly activates its imperial legacies in the guise of malice. The film also contains a sequence dedicated to the statue of Mahatma Gandhi in Parliament Square; the editing fragments the statue into hands and a face and is then followed by archival footage of Jawaharlal Nehru, the first prime minister of an independent India, visiting the monument in 1963. The music does not inspire dread but rather feeds into the elegiac mood of the entire section, which also includes archival footage of Gandhi's dead body accompanied by thousands

Twilight City *and the birth of global London* 81

of mourners on his final journey through the city. The statue of Gandhi in London signifies a different kind of post-imperial trace, one that implicitly references the history of anti-colonial movements that participated in bringing about the end of the British Empire. In linking Gandhi's monument to archival footage, *Twilight City* grants this statue the presence of history as well as visibility and, as such, differentiates this form of remembrance from the other monuments in the film that, to borrow Taussig's phrase, are used to 'playing dead'.[40] And yet I am still reminded that is it the Lascars, the figures who were indispensable to the consolidation and perpetuation of the British Empire, who remain almost entirely forgotten.

To return to Akomfrah's comments regarding BAFC's commitment to formal as well as emotional concerns, the use of music and methods of framing across more one than sequence suggests that these monuments are not simply representations of official history. *Twilight City* aligns these seemingly benign statues with the violence of the colonial past that continues to wield its power and influence over the making of the new London. Global London has its own iconography, one of high-rises and skyscrapers that began to reach a point of culmination during the time of filming. A key event in the history of the gentrification of the city in the 1980s is the redevelopment of the Isle of Dogs into Canary Wharf, a new centre of finance that embodies London's transformation into a global city. As such, Peter Wollen once referred to these high-rises, particularly those located in Canary Wharf, as 'citadels of international capital'.[41] *Twilight City* contains numerous sequences of the city shot from above that feature a topography of skyscrapers and high-rises, many of which are filmed in the East End of the city as well as shots of the river that Eshun associates with the gaze of the 'property developer, the master planner, the urbanist'.[42] These forms of architecture, in their grandeur and opulence, visually embody the promise of global London as a city that will generate wealth on an accelerated and unregulated scale. The film suggests that these forms of architecture will constitute a new form of monumentality for this incarnation of the city.

Do the reoccurring shots of the Thames across the film suggest an alternative to monumental forms of remembrance? The surfaces of the river, as noted previously, are devoid of any visible vestiges of any of these pasts, including those of the transatlantic slave trade. And yet, the river is instrumental in the narrative of imperial expansion that transpired on the basis of dispossession, resource extraction, slavery and later exploitative labour practices. The gentrification of areas alongside the river, such as the Isle of Dogs, was also significant to the birth of the new London. As a living, moving and non-representational entity, the river, at least for now, remains an eternal trace of these histories but one that cannot be reduced to them. *Twilight City*, in fact, implicates the river in one of the possible futures of the city, as figured through Olivia. The sequence in question begins with Olivia's recollection of a message she left on a wall for her mother in 1979. Olivia says, 'Love me and don't forget me' while 'Love me' are the only words we see etched on a wall of a housing estate on the Isle of Dogs where she used to live. This shot is followed by archival footage of the lanes, signs and storefronts of Pennyfields Chinatown (1924) that was destroyed by the Blitz of 1943. While both the housing estate and Pennyfields Chinatown were located in the East End of the city, Olivia's voice-over narration draws a further link between the two as she ponders the question of 'why someone so young thought love could banish forgetting'. Over a shot of the river at twilight, she says, 'My love is still here, like the water. That's all that is left of our life on this estate. Why do you want to return to this?' Near the end of the film, which features one of many sequences of Olivia driving through a nocturnal London, she asks her mother to return and to love her as this love will be needed in the new world. The film ends with an image of the sun slowly rising over the water.

As is also the case with the Lascar sequence, *Twilight City* situates the site of Olivia's home as one of excavation, where myriad historical 'Londons' come into focus through the use of archival footage. This is how the film works against a broader impetus to 'banish forgetting' and, more specifically, the banishing of histories often classified as outsider experiences of London. But the film ends with the promise of love, of impending return and possible reconciliation. All three sentiments are linked to images of the river, which suggests perpetual movement and correspondingly infinite possibilities for transformation and renewal. This is particularly true of the final sequence that features the river at twilight so that the word is no longer associated solely with decline. Monuments, in contrast, are linked to a closed image of the city, where the future is already foretold and thus foreclosed. The river gestures to the time of the past as much as it does towards a time that has not yet arrived. The film ends on a note of speculation, grounded in the possibilities that love and reconciliation may afford as coping mechanisms for what is yet to come.

The twilight model: a reckoning with ambivalence

As noted previously, Eshun argues that *Twilight City* 'prefigures, yet distinguishes itself from, the discourse on globalisation developed by scholars such as Saskia Sassen, Manuel Castells, and Arjun Appadurai'.[43] In its presentation of contrasting imagery of the new London, where skyscrapers rest in marked contrast with homeless people sleeping on the street, the film prefigures a now signature claim made by Sassen in her pioneering work on the global city; as she argues, these urban entities construct 'a new geography of centres and margins'.⁴⁴ And of course, *Twilight City*'s emphasis on high-rise-driven developments is an attribute of the global city that Sassen famously articulates, as these structures are built in order to accommodate as well as represent the city's shifting financial status.⁴⁵ Where *Twilight City* parts ways from some of the canonical literature on the global city and from the work of Castells and Appadurai, in particular, has to do with its refusal to work with movement and liquidity models. Examples of such models include Appadurai's now famed notion of 'scapes' through which global cultural flows can be apprehended and Castell's signature concept, 'the space of flows', which denotes communication, information and transportation infrastructures that facilitate the simultaneity of 'social practices' across disconnected spaces.⁴⁶ As cultural geographer Doreen Massey argues, such models can be inadvertently aligned with market-driven understandings of globalisation where unfettered circulation is taken as a given rather than as a potential problem.⁴⁷ Instead, the film gives us the 'twilight model', where the transition to the global is rendered through historical means, traces of which are often not readily visible. A pertinent example of the 'twilight model' as developed in a scholarly context takes us to the recent work of Homi Bhabha and to his concept of the 'past-present'.⁴⁸

A young Bhabha, titled as a 'writer and critic', is a prominent feature of *Twilight City*. In one interview, he discusses the devastating consequences of economic polarisation in his native Bombay. He describes a common scenario, where the building of a skyscraper leads to the development of shanty towns around it for the workers without whom the skyscrapers would not rise. The images that accompany his narration are not of Bombay but of London, specifically of its high-rise skyline, and later of traders hard at work. The choice of imagery gradually becomes clearer as Bhabha describes the production of black money, specifically as a result of the deregulation of financial markets in places like the UK, that fuel these developments in India. His narration is followed by shots of architectural models and plans of high-rise as well as other examples of modernist and brutalist-style developments in London. While Bhabha does not believe that an exact comparison can be made between the two cities, he does argue that one will begin to see such developments in London appearing on the margins of areas of the city with radically different histories of depression, devastation and migratory settlement. Bhabha's approach to the subject of the new London activates an alternative understanding of globalisation, where his experiences of Bombay emerge as a constitutive component of his critique of the growing inequality and dispossession taking hold of London. The global emerges in its methodological guise through his observations, as a way of doing the work of relationality to garner insight that it is not possible to derive solely from an insider's perspective.

In 'Notes on Globalisation and Ambivalence', an established Bhabha remains as preoccupied with the question of dispossession as he is in *Twilight City*. Though he does not make reference to the film in his essay, many of the questions and observations that it poses seem to stem back not only to the content of his interviews in *Twilight City* but to the film as a whole. The essay begins with a meditation upon a trip to Nuremberg, where Bhabha is confronted with the cultural remnants of the Nazi past. He describes the experience of coming into contact with now 'dis-possessed' cultural monuments, 'the half-life of heritage ... on the other side of which lies the death of culture and the destruction of humanity'.[49] As argued previously, *Twilight City* draws attention to historical narratives of exploitation, neglect and death that similarly lie on the other side of cultural monuments, thereby aligning them with the violence of empire against their standard association with 'cultural heritage'.

Bhabha reflexively asks the reader to consider why his essay on global culture begins with a 'return to the ruins of the past'.[50] The same question can be asked of *Twilight City*. He asserts, following David Held, that any attempt to chart an ethics-based genealogy of the global must begin with relevant histories of brutality and violence.[51] This history returns Bhabha to Nuremberg but, for BAFC, a similar aim returns them to the forgotten vestiges of the British Empire, among other catastrophic events including the Blitz and occasions where fire has decimated areas of the city. Bhabha employs the metaphor of a partially cracked and encrusted mirror to illustrate the processes of cultural memory. As he writes, cultural memory 'sheds its light on the dark places of the present, waking a witness here, quickening a hidden fact there, bringing you face-to-face with that anxious and impossible temporality, the past-present'.[52] The concept of the past-present is akin to the twilight model, one that foregrounds the difficulty of seeing. The 'anxious and impossible' temporality of the past-present is manifested in cinema through the use of montage and, as is clear, the essayistic structure of *Twilight City* activates exactly this temporal register by bringing archival footage of lost or forgotten 'Londons' into a series of configurations with images of the contemporary city, augmented by sound, music and voice-over narration.

Bhabha's interventions within dominant discourses of globalisation are clear; his metaphors and method offer an expanded timeline of the global, a similar argument advanced by *Twilight City*. And still work by others, including scholars such as Timothy Brennan and Etienne Balibar, makes definitive links between the imperial past and the global present.[53] But beyond this aim, Bhabha seeks to position ambivalence as that which emerges from within the midst of all 'One World' projects.[54] He argues that state-driven policies geared towards global integration ensure that no 'free space' remains for the stateless, including the migrant, the refugee, the asylum seeker, minorities and undocumented workers.[55] As he writes, these figures are both inside and outside the parameters of the nation state and even those granted citizenship or the right to remain can suddenly and shockingly find themselves on the wrong side of state policies, as is exactly the case with the Windrush scandal of 2018.[56] The Windrush scandal denotes the wrongful deportation of members of the Windrush generation, who arrived as Commonwealth citizens to the UK. Those who were not deported were often detained and/or denied legal rights as well as access to vital services including medical care. These instances, where the turbulence and violence of post-imperial racisms rise once again to the ranks of state policy, puncture a neutral understanding of London and, by extension, Britain as home to 'superdiversity' or to a much broader range of migrant populations from around the globe without obvious links to the British imperial past since the 1990s.[57]

Twilight City prefigures Bhabha's assertions concerning ambivalence and the global experience as it pertains specifically to London. Bhabha observes that ambivalence is a 'spur to speech, an urge to utterance, a way of working-through what is contradictory and unresolved in order to seek the right to narrate'.[58] In the case of this film, the right to narrate is claimed by BAFC but in essayistic fashion, so that contradictions are not worked through but presented in ways that stimulate critical thinking and a range of emotional responses to London's then present-day condition. The insider/outsider status of the film's diasporic subjects is yet another way the film cultivates a discourse of ambivalence. As noted previously, Eshun argues that the film participates in the articulation of an 'emergent public sphere' of diasporic intellectuals. What most of these scholars and writers share are experiences that are indicative of the complexities of the insider/outsider position or, to put it more directly, the difficulty of being Black in London. Paul Gilroy speaks to his childhood experiences of segregation in the city where he recalls having a firm understanding of precisely where not to go. But he ends this interview on a telling note, when he says that these forms of mapping are 'no longer useful to me'. Soon after, Gail Lewis speaks about her childhood, where she grew up in derelict, rat- and mice-infested housing in the 1950s but derived comfort from 'this difference', as she puts it, because it 'projected a degree of confidence about its own existence'. The content of both interviews gestures towards the past but also to a future time that oscillates between inside and outside, where belonging is fraught but also not necessarily desired and especially not in its compromised iteration.

The film positions Olivia, the fictional essayist and diasporic subject, as part of this emergent public sphere, which pulls us deeper into speculative terrain. Olivia is a fictional figure who engages with the historical realities of the city as well as its then contemporary battles concerning race, class and sexuality. Her narration returns time and again to the difficulty of belonging but one that is staged as a matter of public as well as personal politics, of fiction and reality. Echoing Gilroy, Olivia expresses the difficulty of living in two different worlds and 'in both worlds, belonging is never an easy question'. Through the course of the film, we learn that Eugenia is a former Carnival Queen, a member of the Conservative Party and is deeply committed to Christianity. And we learn that Olivia is gay. This conceit opens up considerations of the new London that move beyond a financial discourse. Footage of a gay pride demonstration in 1988 is accompanied by Olivia's narration, as well as interviews that outline the predicament caused by Section 28, the law that criminalised the 'promotion' of homosexuality on the part of schools and local authorities. Olivia outlines a hypothetical scenario where she sees her mother on the street and wonders if she would join Olivia or stay where she is, amongst her homophobic friends. In an interview that follows, Femi Otitoju describes the constricting ramifications of the legislation, one that will limit the kinds of opportunities queer people will decide to pursue. In effect, it is a piece of legislation that produces yet another outsider experience of the new London and one that is intended to restrict a queer presence within the public domain while simultaneously, as Otitoju puts it, 'legitimizing hate'.

During one of the many sequences shot from the perspective of a car driving through the nighttime streets, and accompanied by the film's signature soundtrack which features a voice that seems to be mourning, Olivia recounts another aspect of her mother's letter where the latter asks if she has joined the city's 'lost souls'. Significantly, Olivia says, 'And as the old London dissolves, your lost souls are becoming more visible'. The images that follow are of naked Black male bodies that re-enact a number of photographs by Rotimi Fani-Kayode (in collaboration with his partner Alex Hirst) as well as shots of the photographs themselves. One of the images from this sequence features a naked man drinking from a jug, as the milk spills out of his mouth and down the length of his body, which is a re-enactment of Fani-Kayode's photograph *The Milk Drinker* (1986). A dream sequence that appears a little later displays a series of Fani-Kayode's photographs, including *The Fish Vendors* (1986), where Olivia refers to the figures in the photographs as 'her friends'. She describes arranging them in a circle, when 'dimly' she could make out a crowd of men who were speaking in a language she could not understand. The image that follows is of a large group of traders. During the tail end of the sequence, *The Fish Vendors* is brought to life through performance as two men arrange the scene and one of them holds the fish above his head.

Eshun refers to these sequences as *tableaux vivants* and, alongside scholars such as Kass Banning, he situates the use of *tableaux* as a signature component of BAFC's aesthetic.[59] The re-enactments can be aligned with other sections of the film that restore presence and movement to forgotten histories. Fani-Kayode can also be enveloped within the emerging diasporic public sphere that Eshun writes about, as he hails from Nigeria but lived in London for a considerable time before his death in 1989, the year of the film's release. As Kobena Mercer puts it, 'Fani-Kayode occupied multiple subject positions as a postmodern African artist, an out Black gay man and a key animateur in the field of Black British photography'.[60] But he also notes that Fani-Kayode's work emancipates these bodies from any 'obligations to identity'.[61] The film similarly does not situate the re-enactments within an identity-based framework but rather as figures in a new cityscape being reinvented for the aims of a neoliberal world order. The point, as was also the case with the Lascars, is to amplify presence rather than identity. Olivia's voice-over narration *repositions* the city as a site for new visibilities to emerge, an assertion that is carried across the film. Some of these narratives shed new light on neglected pasts while others encase future possibilities.

In these instances, twilight vision isn't associated solely with the past but with the present and *for* the future. As Bhabha writes, 'Narrative ... is part of a moral universe that floods the conscious experience of the present with the disruptive ghosts of memory, and draws upon a future *that has not yet taken place* to provide a virtual, yet aspirational locus for the activity of ethical judgement'.[62] Many of the interviews featured throughout the film make space for the possibilities of new forms of becoming in the city that centre upon an increasingly visible diasporic presence, mostly Black British and British Asian in this case, in its intersection with queer and class-based politics.[63] *Twilight City* takes its place among a number of films made during this time period that explore similar terrain through different genres and modalities of filmmaking, including perhaps most famously the narrative features *My Beautiful Laundrette* (Stephen Frears, 1985) and *Sammy and Rosie Get Laid* (Stephen Frears, 1987), both of which centre on the post-imperial Pakistani and Indian diasporas in Britain.

The speculative aspect of the film's politics is given more direct expression in the footage of an abstracted world from space featured multiple times throughout the film. While it is possible to view this footage in relationship to the abundance of high angle shots of the city, which Eshun attributes to view of the urban planner, these images also seem to allude to possible futures that are never visible in views from above. *Twilight City* situates the city itself as the 'locus for the activity of ethical judgement' that spans past, present and future.[64] As Bhabha notes, a global ethics 'demands that we take responsibility – imaginatively and actively – for a world that is caught between a past that refuses to die, and a future that refuses to wait to be born', a statement that almost seems made for *Twilight City*.[65]

In the time of Brexit

A repeated refrain across *Twilight City* and one that makes its way into one of the film's posters is as follows: 'Sacrifice a piece of the past for the whole of the future'. This phrase pertains to the question of gentrification as well as the other pasts that have been sacrificed for the future, which includes a cultural and political reckoning with the imperial past. To return to beginning of this chapter, where I suggested that Brexit, among other global issues, has generated a need for reflection, scholar Priyamvada Gopal's essay in the *Guardian* succinctly charts the return of the imperial past in the present-day discourse on Brexit.[66] One of her examples includes then Prime Minister Boris Johnson himself, who claimed that Britain occupies the status of colony within the empire that is the EU, in addition to a general sentiment that British national pride rests once again upon mythical versions of its imperial history.[67] Gopal argues that a true reckoning with the histories of British imperialism on the shores of the nation can offer 'common ground' to begin to fully address the question of British identity and what that identity signifies in the present.[68] As she rightly observes, concepts such as race, development and free trade were 'forged in the crucible of empire'.[69]

The global city thesis advanced by *Twilight City* and by other works of scholarship is relevant today in asking the question of when is a city like London and its aspiration towards globality – in metaphorical terms but also in empirical scales à la Sassen's schema – achieved? The film accomplishes this goal by shifting between and across distinct temporal registers while simultaneously presenting a variety of insider/outsider positions that make these reflections possible. London finds itself once again in a transitional period, as Britain stages a messy, uncertain and potentially devastating departure from the European Union. Britain's imperial past makes yet another appearance in this period of crisis and of transition but this time the longing to reclaim Britain's imperial glory is woven into the discourse surrounding the 'leave vote'. In a recent essay on the folly that is Brexit, Bill Schwarz puts it best: 'in England – the geopolitical motor of Brexit – the crisis of the state is accompanied by a pervasive historical forgetfulness'.[70]

For Schwarz, this mode of forgetting is pathological, grounded in a deliberate lack of care.[71]

Twilight City makes clear that the imperial past remains instrumental to considerations of London's rise to global city. The film also suggests that the factors leading to the implosion of globalisation today, including xenophobia, disenfranchisement and dispossession, were inherent features of its origins. As such, Brexit is not returning London to its imperial past; rather, traces of this past have always been present to some degree and are rekindled in moments of transition and crisis. Brexit is one logical outcome of this history, though by no means the only one that could have been imagined. In activating the time of the past-present, *Twilight City* models an ethically driven engagement with a transitional period that brings past Londons and their respective modalities of loss and violence into engagement with contemporary circumstances without closing off possibilities for another kind of future shaped by the city's outsiders. A similar mode of reflection is precisely what might be needed in the post-Brexit period.

Notes

1. Max Bearak, 'Theresa May Criticized the Term Citizen of the World. But Half the World Identifies That Way', *Washington Post* (5 October 2016), http://bit.ly/3lJNx7s (accessed 22 April 2020).
2. Marc Champion, 'What Will Become of London after Brexit?', *Bloomberg* (21 October 2016), https://bit.ly/3NoHhNM (accessed 28 April 2020).
3. See 'EU Referendum: Most London Boroughs Vote to Remain', *BBC News* (24 June 2016), www.bbc.com/news/uk-politics-eu-referendum-36612916 (accessed 2 March 2020).
4. Saskia Sassen, *The Global City: New York, London, Tokyo* (Princeton, NJ: Princeton University Press, 1991).
5. Shanay Jhaveri, 'Wanting to Be a Rememberer', in *Outsider: Films on India 1950–1990*, ed. Shanay Jhaveri (Mumbai: The Shoestring Publisher, 2009), p. 9.
6. Kodwo Eshun, '*Twilight City*: Outline for an Archaeopsychic Geography of New London', *Wasafiri*, 19.43 (2004), p. 7.
7. Jhaveri, 'Wanting to Be a Rememberer', p. 9.
8. For example, Eshun draws our attention to the sharp disparities of the gentrification of the East End of featured in the film, where the glittering high-rise towers in Canary Wharf are matched by a new wave of disenfranchisement and homelessness ('*Twilight City*', p. 9).
9. Felix Driver and David Gilbert, eds, *Imperial Cities: Landscape, Display and Identity* (Manchester: Manchester University Press, 1999), p. 15.
10. Eshun, '*Twilight City*', p. 7.
11. Auguiste, 'Black Cinema, Poetics and New World Aesthetics', p. 152.

12 John Akomfrah and Kodwo Eshun, 'John Akomfrah in Conversation with Kodwo Eshun', in *The Ghost of Songs: The Film Art of the Black Audio Film Collective*, ed. Eshun Kodwo and Anjalika Sagar (Liverpool: Liverpool University Press, 2007), p. 133.
13 Akomfrah and Eshun, 'John Akomfrah in Conversation with Kodwo Eshun', p. 134.
14 Ben Highmore, 'Giving a Damn', *New Formations*, 82 (2014), p. 145.
15 Auguiste, 'Black Cinema, Poetics and New World Aesthetics', p. 9.
16 Ben Highmore, *Cityscapes: Cultural Readings in the Material and Symbolic City* (Basingstoke: Macmillan Education, 2005), p. 5.
17 Timothy Corrigan, *The Essay Film: From Montaigne, After Marker* (New York: Columbia University Press, 2001), p. 55.
18 Laura Rascaroli, *How the Essay Film Thinks* (New York: Oxford University Press, 2017), p. 6.
19 Ibid., p. 6.
20 Theodore Adorno, 'The Essay as Form', in *Notes to Literature: Volume 1*, trans. Shierry Weber Nicholsen (New York: Columbia University Press, 1958), p. 3.
21 Ibid., p. 10.
22 Ibid., p. 11.
23 Eshun, '*Twilight City*', p. 11.
24 Adorno, 'The Essay as Form', p. 17.
25 Ibid., p. 13.
26 Ibid., p. 14.
27 Athena Athanasiou and Judith Butler, *Dispossession: The Performative in the Political* (Cambridge: Polity Press, 2013), p. 2.
28 Eshun, '*Twilight City*', p. 11.
29 Ibid., p. 9.
30 Ibid., p. 12.
31 W. T. Mitchell and Michael Taussig, 'Discussions in Contemporary Culture: Monuments, Monumentality, Monumentalization', DIA Art Institute, 2014, www.youtube.com/embed/caGhHQT9WYY?list=UUillOYNBumCBEgGS3q1QOYA (accessed 29 June 2019).
32 Ibid.
33 Ibid.
34 Ibid.
35 Eshun, '*Twilight City*', p. 12.
36 Ibid.
37 Ibid.
38 Mitchell and Taussig, 'Discussions in Contemporary Culture'.
39 As Stuart Ward and Astrid Rasch note, former prime ministers Theresa May and Boris Johnson have both given speeches laced with imperial undertones for a post-Brexit 'independent future'. See Stuart War and Astrid Rasch, eds, *Embers of Empire in Brexit Britain* (London and New York: Bloomsbury Academic, 2019), p. 2.
40 Mitchell and Taussig, 'Discussions in Contemporary Culture'.

41 Peter Wollen, 'The Last New Wave: Modernism in the British Films of the Thatcher Era', in *Fires were Started: British Cinema and Thatcherism*, ed. Lester Friedman (Minneapolis, MN: University of Minnesota Press, 1993), p. 31.
42 Eshun, 'Twilight City', p. 12.
43 Ibid., p. 7.
44 Quoted in ibid., p. 8.
45 Sassen, *The Global City*, p. 328.
46 For example, see Arjun Appadurai, 'Disjuncture and Difference in the Global Cultural Economy', *Theory, Culture and Society*, 7 (1990), pp. 295–310; Manuel Castells, 'Grassrooting the Space of Flows', *Urban Geography*, 20.4 (1991), pp. 294–302.
47 Doreen Massey, 'Landscape/Space/Politics: An Essay', *The Future of Landscape and the Moving Image* (n.d.), https://thefutureoflandscape.wordpress.com/landscapespacepolitics-an-essay/ (accessed 4 March 2020).
48 I have drawn upon Bhabha's concept of the 'past-present' in some of my previous work on cinema and migration. See Malini Guha, *From Empire to the World: Migrant London and Paris in Cinema* (Edinburgh: Edinburgh University Press, 2015). Homi K. Bhabha, 'Notes on Globalization and Ambivalence', in *Cultural Politics in a Global Age: Uncertainty, Solidarity and Innovation*, ed. David Held and Henrietta L. Moore (Oxford: Oneworld Publications, 2007), p. 43.
49 Bhabha, 'Notes on Globalization and Ambivalence', p. 37.
50 Ibid., p. 37.
51 Ibid., p. 37.
52 Ibid., p. 43.
53 Etienne Balibar, *We, the People of Europe: Reflections on Transnational Citizenship* (Princeton, NJ: Princeton University Press, 2004); Timothy Brennan, 'Postcolonial Studies and Globalization Theory', in *The Postcolonial and the Global*, ed. Revathi Krishnaswamy and John. C. Hawley (Minneapolis, MN: University of Minnesota Press, 2008), pp. 37–53.
54 Bhabha, 'Notes on Globalization and Ambivalence', p. 44.
55 Ibid., pp. 38–9.
56 Ibid., p. 40. These individuals were victims of the 'Hostile Environment' legislation of 2012. Many of these individuals either did not have documentation or their documentation was destroyed by the British Home Office.
57 See Steven Vertovec, 'Super-diversity and Its Implications', *Ethnic and Race Studies*, 30.6 (November 2017), pp. 1024–54.
58 Bhabha, 'Notes on Globalization and Ambivalence', p. 44.
59 See Kass Banning, 'The *Nine Muses*: Recalibrating Migratory Aesthetics', *Black Camera: The New Series*, 6.2 (2015), pp. 135–46; Kodwo Eshun, 'Drawing the Forms of Things Unknown', in *The Ghost of Songs: The Film Art of the Black Audio Film Collective*, ed. Eshun Kodwo and Anjalika Sagar (Liverpool: Liverpool University Press, 2007), p. 91.
60 Kobena Mercer, *Travel and See: Black Diasporic Art Practices since the 1980s* (Durham, NC: Duke University Press, 2016), p. 99.

61 Ibid., p. 99.
62 Bhabha, 'Notes on Globalization and Ambivalence', p. 45.
63 A few sections of the film are dedicated to Somali migrant communities lamenting the lack of day centres and other services, rendering them as another 'forgotten people' from the vantage point of British governance.
64 Bhabha, 'Notes on Globalization and Ambivalence', p. 45.
65 Ibid., p. 47.
66 Priyamvada Gopal, 'Britain's Story of Empire is Based on a Myth. We Need to Know the Truth', *Guardian* (6 July 2019).
67 Ibid.
68 Ibid.
69 Ibid.
70 Bill Schwarz, 'Forgetfulness: England's Discontinuous Histories', in *Embers of Empire in Brexit Britain*, ed. Stuart Ward and Astrid Rasch (London and New York: Bloomsbury Academic, 2019), p. 50.
71 Ibid., p. 51.

5

'Where I come from, we eat places like this for breakfast': Aki Kaurismäki's *I Hired a Contract Killer* as transnational representation of local London

Claire Monk

Leave it to Kaurismäki to make a movie in England with French movie legend Jean-Pierre Léaud in the lead, prompting the exchange ... 'Why did you leave France, Henri?' – 'They didn't like me there'.[1]

Populated by shabby gangsters and ancient cabbies ... Kaurismäki's phantom London is a patchwork Nowhere, a hellhole redeemed only by the chance that you might stumble on Serge Reggiani running a hamburger stand or Joe Strummer playing solo in your local pub.[2]

This chapter considers Aki Kaurismäki's film *I Hired a Contract Killer* (1990) as an iconoclastic (not to say eccentric) addition to the small canon of transnational 'outsider' representations of London by European directors and involving European stars. Its more particular interest, however, is in exploring *Contract Killer*'s London in terms of its cinematic geography and the specifics of its resonant choice of determinedly off-centre locations (drawn from the post-industrial, post-imperial East London docks and old East End, but extending to a wider palette of districts in London EC, N and W), and in the insights that might emerge from detailed attention to these.

As Charlotte Brunsdon explores in the introduction to her book *London in Cinema*, the task of 'thinking about London in the cinema' is fraught with 'difficulty'.[3] Part of this 'difficulty' has to do with the gap between the methodologies and usual concerns of 'legitimate' film studies and the different approaches and preoccupations of both other salient academic disciplines (such as cultural geography or urban history) and other genres of writing engaged in 'thinking about London'. Within non-fiction alone, the latter range from London and local-London histories to the psychogeographic strand – creative, non-immersed in the minutiae and histories of its locales – to what Brunsdon calls 'list-books' documenting London film locations.[4] While, in the psychogeographic cluster, Iain Sinclair's books/writings have become the best known (although his trademark preoccupations have come to assert a prohibitive authorial ownership over his favoured East London territory), such work also extends to self-published (and overtly anarchist) instances such as the Hackney-based artist/writer Laura Oldfield Ford's fanzine *Savage Messiah* (published both in print and online at http://savagemessiahzine.com), a mix of urban theory, intemperate sloganeering ('Today's gated estates = tomorrow's GULAGS!') and psychogeographic 'drifts', across developer and gentrification-threatened north-east London from Dalston to the 2012 Olympics site and beyond

A second area of 'difficulty' arises from the delicacy of the transtextual relationship(s) between films set in London (and hence, at some level, representing it) and the various 'texts' presented by the extra-cinematic London: not just by the material city and its neighbourhoods (the 'texts' of London's geographies, physical environment, architecture) but also by the narratives, myths and histories embedded within these. While I use the term 'transtextual' in the sense proposed by Gérard Genette – 'all that puts one text in relation, whether manifest or secret, with other texts' – I conceive of this relationship as a multi-directional interplay, not a one-way hierarchy in which film representations are relegated to hypertexts of the city itself or its anterior (hi)stories.[5] *I Hired a Contract Killer* presents a fascinating case study, both in the use of location in itself and for practical exploration (if not resolution) of some of the issues surrounding the London–film relationship and its analysis in critical (or creative) writing. Its choices of location are sufficiently idiosyncratic that they can legitimately become a focus of semi-autonomous interest in themselves rather than merely presenting a setting for narrative. One obvious 'difficulty' here is that, for viewers who have the London knowledge to identify them, such locations hold a double fascination which is by definition denied to the majority of viewers who do not. But while this (self-)foregrounding intrusion of setting invites a response to *Contract Killer*'s locations as a parallel pleasure and potential parallel text, this chapter will also illustrate how they work to variously support, enrich and ironise its narrative, themes and outsider perspective. Accordingly, my reading draws upon the extra-textual knowledge of the London 'insider' rather than wholly resisting this.

While much of the critical response to *Contract Killer* (contemporary and retrospective) has noted the effectiveness of its use of locations, most of this discussion has focused on the mood invoked more than their specifics. Within this, opinion has split between those critics for whom the film achieves a specific London atmosphere – Tim Pulleine praised its 'lively response to the London scene, with a constantly recognisable atmosphere that manages completely to avoid familiar landmarks' – and those like Jonathan Romney (quoted at the start of this chapter) for whom its

London is no more than 'a patchwork Nowhere': a placeless analogue for Kaurismäki's equally depressive Helsinki.[6]

Paul Newland's essay on the film steers a path between these two responses, acknowledging its solitary, depressive, jobless French protagonist Henri Boulanger (Jean-Pierre Léaud) as a 'profoundly displaced, rootless figure', adrift and uncomprehending in a 'distinctly liminal' environment, but also arguing for the more specific significance of the film's location in 'marginal' territories 'east of the City of London'.[7] Newland's reading primarily develops a set of general analogies between this socioeconomic and material terrain – post-industrial and post-imperial, 'signify[ing] a vanished fecundity and an uncertain future' – and Henri's position as a victim of 'the spiritual violence of late capitalism', at risk, like East London itself, of being viewed as 'unproductive'.[8]

My goal in this chapter is to explore where a more detailed and less abstract consideration of *Contract Killer*'s specifics of location might take us in enriching our understanding (and enjoyment) of the film. I expressly want to oppose the notion that Kaurismäki presents an unrecognisable, unreadable London or a 'nowhere'. On the contrary, his film is of distinct interest for its potential for a reading in terms of the particular social-historical, mythic and cultural-geographical resonances of its settings, informed by both historical awareness and post-1990 hindsight.

However, the film's locational choices also illustrate the tensions between representation and appropriation, and, within the latter, the co-presence of the evident appropriation of decaying, 'marginal' London sites in the service of Kaurismäki's trademark 'grim vision [and] unsentimental sympathy for the downtrodden'[9] and the more implicit appropriation of the discourses embedded in an East London (and, crucially, in its specific locales) which 'continues to resonate with powerful narratives concerning class politics ethnic "Otherness", degeneration and dark criminality'.[10] While the former mode of appropriation clearly operates transnationally, the latter affirms that *Contract Killer* simultaneously solicits a reading strategy which is attentive, to a greater or lesser degree, to the 'local'. But, in a further twist, *Contract Killer* inhabits an East London terrain where 'the local' itself has been – and continues to be – shaped and inscribed by a profoundly transnational history and economy.

In this context, *Contract Killer*'s locational choices make it a fortuitous (if semi-accidental) document capturing the capital (and indeed Capital) at a moment of transition between Thatcher and the 1990s. What it captures, with some precision, is the juncture after the death of the docks (hub of global trade during London's heyday as an industrial and imperial 'world city'), when builders' cranes still surrounded a half-built Canary Wharf prior to the imminent influx of global big capital and the renascent rhetoric of London as 'global city' (this time founded on the virtual trade of the international financial markets). The film's specifics of setting thus suggest two different modalities of 'thinking about' location which will be evident in my analysis: the one informed by an awareness of the histories embedded or encoded in a location; the other by hindsight (social, economic and political as much as physical and architectural) about what that location has become.

Production context

I Hired a Contract Killer remains Kaurismäki's only 'British' film to date – although, financially and institutionally, it was a Swedish–Finnish co-production and in other respects a complex transnational collaboration. Its main producers were Kaurismäki's own company Villealfa (named in tribute to Godard's 1965 *Alphaville*) and the Swedish Film Institute, co-funded by the Finnish Film Foundation, the French distributor Pyramide and Channel 4 television in the UK. Kaurismäki's exact impetus for making a film in London at that juncture is unclear from contemporary interviews – perhaps precisely because the production dates from the peak of his cult profile in Britain. This stemmed primarily from *Leningrad Cowboys Go America* (1989): a road-movie rockumentary following the absurdly quiffed 'worst rock band in the world', which attracted the attention of Jonathan Ross – leading to Kaurismäki's promotion in the UK as a novelty crazy/hard-drinking/rock 'n' roll Finn – and spawned two sequels. Since the mid-1990s, Kaurismäki has accrued (or perhaps regained) a more serious critical stature through films such as *The Man Without a Past* (2002), which won the Grand Jury Prize at Cannes, although in the same period the UK visibility of his films has narrowed.

If *Contract Killer* dates from a transitional moment in Kaurismäki's career, this is true equally of its place in the uneven career trajectory of its unlikely star Jean-Pierre Léaud and the evolving European co-production context of the time. Kaurismäki's cinephilia – and particular Godard-philia – was presumably a factor in the casting of Léaud: one-time child (and adolescent) star as François Truffaut's troubled double Antoine Doinel in *Les Quatre cents coups* (1959) and its sequels, and an icon of the French New Wave carrying particular associations with Godard (for example, as the Maoist student Guillaume in *La Chinoise* (1967)). But the adult Léaud also became publicly known as a real-life depressive, and it is clear that his role as Henri in *Contract Killer* plays on both this 'real' (depressive) identity and his 'cinematic' one – the latter defined, Australian critic Philippa Hawker has argued, by 'the exploration of inadequacy, failure and despair'.[11] In retrospect, the film also marks a staging post in Léaud's gradual, post-crisis, cinematic comeback since the late 1980s and more substantially since the mid-1990s.

Although *Contract Killer* evidently belongs to the late 1980s–early 1990s trend towards increased British–European co-production, it slightly pre-dates most of the quasi-official UK bodies and initiatives promoting this (the British Film Commission was formed in 1991 and the European Co-Production Fund – with Louis Malle's *Damage* as its first UK production – in 1992) or the use of London and the UK as filming locations (the London Film Commission, promoting the former, arrived in 1995). It was line-produced by David Kelly and Martin Bruce-Clayton of First City, specialists in support for international directors shooting in the UK, who went on to run the (private) European Co-Production Bureau; but with its £1 million budget and rough-and-ready creative genesis, it was a more artisanal project than the widely mocked, higher-budget 'Europuddings' of the period. Its intended tone seems even to have wrong-footed its own line producers: an 'on-location' feature in the trade magazine *The Producer* reported that they were enthused by Kaurismäki's 'different perspective on Britain' and 'excited by his vision of London as a European city' – comments at odds with the decrepit settings and morbid humour of the finished film.[12]

Contract Killer as 'outsider' vision of London

I Hired a Contract Killer views London from a dual 'outsider' perspective: that of its French protagonist Henri – a friendless clerk, made redundant at the start of the film after fifteen years' service to 'Her Majesty's Waterworks' (an invented civil service department about to be privatised), whose twice-failed suicide (first attempt: hanging; second: gas) leads him to the course of action recounted in the film's title – and the famously deadpan, miserabilist-absurdist sensibility of its Finnish director. Its appeal stems from its unlikely blend of evocative but 'unfamiliar' London locations; the persona and intertextual baggage brought by Léaud; a wider array of (often equally ironically intertextual) cameos from its (largely British) supporting cast; and a plot that, as noted by *Variety*'s reviewer 'Strat.', 'has seen service in Hollywood pics of the past'.[13]

While the film notably benefits from the input of British character actors – centrally, Kenneth Colley as the titular Killer – its eclectic casting spans Joe Strummer, former vocalist of The Clash, in a joke cameo as a pub musician; another British ex-punk, Nicky Tesco of The Members (best recalled for their 1979 UK Top 20 hit 'Sound of the Suburbs') as a petty criminal – and, more crucially, as uncredited location consultant;[14] and the 68-year-old Italian French migrant veteran actor, singer and anti-fascist Serge Reggiani in a brief cameo as 'French' burger-seller Vic, operating from a corrugated cabin inside Abney Park Cemetery in Stoke Newington, north-east London.

While this use of Reggiani was condemned by some as 'demeaning',[15] the film's most contentious element was the casting of Liverpool-born actress Margi Clarke (big-hearted peroxide-blonde star of Chris Bernard's 1985 *Letter to Brezhnev*) opposite Léaud as his somewhat Brechtian love interest, pub-to-pub rose-seller Margaret.[16] The encounter with Margaret renews Henri's will to live, and he attempts to cancel the contract he has taken out on his own life – but with no more success than his earlier suicide attempts, since the Killer, himself terminally ill, declares an existentialist as well as financial commitment to completing the task: 'Nobody wants to die, but die they must'.

Contract Killer's sensibility, geography and settings as well as casting strategies set it apart significantly from most other European/co-production cinematic representations of London; indeed, it evades easy comparison with such precursors. First, it deploys British genre tropes, character types and settings associated with the mythology and iconography of London's ('hard' criminal) East End with a rigour and sense of place unexpected in an international co-production. In a further paradox, this immersion in London myths and specifics and British cinematic heritage prove anachronistically well suited to Kaurismäki's style and parodically downbeat mood. On the one hand, *Contract Killer* opens with a dedication to Michael Powell (who had died in February 1990), while *Time Out*'s Nigel Floyd described it as 'an Ealing comedy on downers'.[17] On the other, its visual style and rhetoric show Kaurismäki's characteristic grasp of the codes and clichés of classical Hollywood noir – filtered through the mid-twentieth-century office-interior compositions and isolated human figures of the US painter Edward Hopper, while sharing the working-class focus and (equally Hopperesque) retro colour palette (grey-blues, mahogany browns, deep reds) of his Finnish films – which, in turn, transplanted to London and coupled with the casting of Léaud, reads like a dingy tribute to both Powell's and Godard's mastery of non-naturalistic colour.

Contract Killer has little in common with the post-1980 'British' films of other Scandinavian filmmakers – notably Lars von Trier's *The Element of Crime* (1984) or *Breaking the Waves* (1996) which, with their Scottish locations, imply a northern European affinity of identity, sensibility (and, indeed, light and climate) between Scandinavia and Scotland. As a Finn, rock fan and implicit socialist, Kaurismäki's transcultural compass points in rather different directions: US popular culture and polyglot rock 'n' roll to the west, Finland's Baltic and (former) Soviet neighbours to the east.[18] These orientations suggest at least a loose logic for his choice of East London (linked to the Baltic by a shared maritime trading history) and use of Strummer as a loser pub musician who stands in front of a photo of Elvis Presley wistfully singing 'I've been to California ...' to a handful of inattentive old men.

The film's mood and the derelict, marginal milieu it articulates through location place it in a still stronger oppositional – indeed, bathetic – relationship to the affluent, glamorous, cosmopolitan modernist lineage of a more familiar strand of London films by European or other 'outsider' auteurs, from Polanski's *Repulsion* (1965) or Antonioni's *Blow-Up* (1966) to, more recently and less felicitously, the would-be-erotic melodrama of Louis Malle's *Damage* (1993). While it is tempting to summarise this latter strand of films as 'European', some of the UK films of the US-born Joseph Losey (notably 1959's *Blind Date* and, venturing beyond London to Oxford, 1967's *Accident*) share similar traits, as do the further overlapping cluster of UK-set films in which European casting (usually female, often French) – not necessarily by European directors – stands as a sign for sophistication, exoticism and sexuality.

In marked contrast, *Contract Killer* focuses on a London, and characters, who are strangers to affluence, and shows an accordant (and un-erotic) 'preoccupation with loneliness, physical and spiritual sickness and death'[19] and with neglected, defiantly unmodern(ised) sites and architecture. Its opposition to its EuroLondon precursors is, moreover, encapsulated in its social, economic and symbolic geographies: not just in its preference for East London or its stringent shunning of tourist landmarks and 'swinging London' locales – whether the Chelsea or South Kensington of *Blow-Up* and *Repulsion* (then ostensibly bohemian sites, now home to bankers and the international super-rich) or the West End – but in its more specific, idiosyncratic locational choices.

The latter owed much to Nicky Tesco, who drove Kaurismäki around his favourite decrepit corners of East London and beyond. Although the resulting film draws centrally on both the unmodernised streetscapes, railway arches and liminal sites of the inland East End (Bethnal Green, Whitechapel) and the disused docks on the Isle of Dogs and further east, its locations also extend to parts of the borough of Hackney in northeast London (Shoreditch, Dalston and, at the narrative climax, Stoke Newington), West London (Portobello Road, Westbourne Park Road) and occasionally more central areas. Significantly, however, even the film's 'central' locations avoid the West End or the monumental financial City in favour of the 'City Fringe' (the adjacent EC and SE postcodes), plus one brief scene in the original Victorian Gothic panelled ticket hall of George

Gilbert Scott's 1868 St Pancras station. (Here, Margaret, anticipating by seventeen years the relocation of the Eurostar terminal to St Pancras International from Waterloo, buys rail tickets so that she and Henri can flee the UK and the Killer, declaring later that 'the working class have no Fatherland'.)

While the choice of St Pancras marks *Contract Killer*'s closest brush with the London of 'familiar landmarks', Kaurismäki presents only this one decontextualised interior. This approach fits with a more widely evident strategy of formally excluding 'landmark London' from the frame (rather than avoiding potential 'landmark' locations altogether). The unseen proximity of the vast, long-contested King's Cross railway lands site, coupled with the status of St Pancras station itself at the time of filming as an edifice in disrepair (and, in the case of the attached Midland Grand Hotel, under threat), nevertheless accord with the film's wider preoccupation with sites which, in 1990, seemed to be in a state of perpetual suspension – with hindsight, rendered more clearly comprehensible as a state of redevelopment – or gentrification in waiting.

The London of *I Hired a Contract Killer*

Significantly, even the London-obsessive writer Iain Sinclair – one of *Contract Killer*'s admirers and sufficiently steeped in its screen territory to play 'spot the location' – does not try to claim that its locations are identifiable or readable by the average viewer – but, as I hope to illustrate, this is one of the precise reasons why attention to their resonances is a productive exercise. Indeed, this difficulty is exactly why Sinclair praises it as 'probably the best example of how the imaginative use of locations can benefit a film': 'There are so many unusual buildings and streets that most people will be totally unfamiliar with [including] a great scene in the Monster Doss House in Whitechapel [which] Jack London mentioned in The People of the Abyss.'[20] The film's delight in such quirkily specific sites is, however, coupled with an inconsistent approach to spatio-temporal literalism: its screen geography is in some sequences plausible, in others not. *Contract Killer* thus ultimately constructs a 'London' which is more a sociohistoric and psychogeographic composite than a spatially coherent rendition of the capital or even its east.

The opening credits present a sequence of twelve shots – the first ten static and of deserted locations, initially along the River Thames – under a predominantly grey dawn sky, accompanied by Little Willie John's 1956 US blues track 'I Need Your Love So Bad'. While this juxtaposition may seem calculated to establish mood (both retro and downbeat) more than place, the sequence can be broken down into four blocks, each carrying distinct economic-geographic, as well as narrative, significances.

Shots 1–2 show the London docks: constructed (as their very names indicate) in the mid-Victorian age of empire and once a hub of international trade, abandoned by 1990 but also displaying early hints of an emergent new, and equally transnational, economic role. Both shots are taken from the vast, disused Royal Victoria Dock in Silvertown, east of the Isle of Dogs, constructed on Plaistow Marshes in 1855 and closed in 1981. Shot 1 looks west towards the equally deserted West India Docks; shot 2 reverses the camera position to record the vast, disused Royal Albert Dock to the east. These 'empty' images of 'dead' sites have a narrative-establishing function: the supposed view from Margaret's 1960s tower-block flat, shown later in the film, implies that she lives just south of Victoria Dock. But they carry a further meaning: these are sites now transformed by the vast redevelopment of the docks (steered by the private London Docklands Development Corporation from 1981 to 1988) as a major international financial centre following the City of London's stock market 'Big Bang' of the mid-1980s.[21] Shot 1 shows the site which will shortly become the epicentre of this, Canary Wharf: indeed, construction of the first of the Wharf's corporate towers, One Canada Square (which had begun in 1988 and became the UK's tallest building at just over 235 metres high), is just visible in the distant left of the frame while construction cranes form a distant silhouette to the right, with the bunker of Richard Rogers's 1987 Reuters computer data centre (another early harbinger of the transformation to come) visible between them. Shot 2, by contrast, foregrounds the obsolete cranes of the old docks but, if taken today, would be dominated by London City Airport.

Shots 3–4, to also contrast them, introduce the old financial City and establish more clearly for the inexpert viewer that we are in London. Shot 3 presents an uninspiring vista of the City riverfront across the Thames from the south. The only prominent 'landmarks' are financial/commercial – most obviously the NatWest Tower (London's tallest building prior to Canary Wharf, now renamed Tower 42) – and omnipresent cranes show that even the old City is in a constant flux of redevelopment. Shot 4, taken from a position very nearby, further undermines the City's putative grandeur by rotating the camera to point across an 'empty' site on the south bank (since 2002 filled by Norman Foster's bulbous glass Greater London Authority building) towards the concrete brutalist towers of Guy's Hospital.

Perhaps more significantly, however, the framing of shots 3–4 pointedly excludes two famous tourist landmarks just to the east. Both are taken from a point on, or very close to, the southern approach to Tower Bridge – the most internationally recognisable of the Thames bridges (routinely mistaken for London Bridge by tourists) – yet exclude both this and the Tower of London on the north bank opposite (just visible inside the right margin of shot 3). Shots 5–10 shift to a very different milieu central to *Contract Killer*'s narrative, the parodically mythic old East End: long projected as marginal and profoundly 'other' from the perspective of the financial City or 'respectable' London, yet geographically sandwiched between the City and the old zone of imperial trade (the docks). Narratively, Kaurismäki is strong on the myths and genre clichés ingrained in the area; locationally, his choices and uses of its built (or, often, demolished) environment imbue it with a surreal otherness while making visible its proximity to the City. This is the domain of the preposterous Honolulu Bar – indicated externally only by a neon basement sign on a spookily roofless Victorian board school surrounded by dereliction – where Henri travels to meet the Killer's boss (Michael O'Hagan) and his intermediaries (Nicky Tesco and Charles Cork) to arrange the contract, only to find it demolished when he changes his mind – and the equally misnamed Hotel Splendide, where Henri and Margaret later hide from the Killer. But in a prime example of the film's construction of a mythic rather than literal geography, while its East End centres narratively on Whitechapel, its 'East End' locations are rather more wide-ranging. When the intermediaries are arrested for shooting a jeweller dead during a botched raid – for which Henri, caught accidentally on camera holding the gun, is initially framed – a newspaper headline calls them the 'Whitechapel Murderers' in a joke allusion to Jack the Ripper. The raid itself, however, was filmed at a shop (presumably chosen for its aura of near-obsolescence) on Kingsland Road, Dalston, some miles north-west of Whitechapel.

The first of the film's 'East End' establishing shots shows a specialist taxi-wash and garage (in Dunbridge Street, Bethnal Green) in a railway arch beneath the main line running out of Liverpool Street from the City. This detail anticipates, both thematically and geographically, Henri's encounter with the cliché East End cabbie who directs him to the Honolulu Bar. The spectacularly dank railway arch where the cabbie drops Henri ('I shan't be coming any further, guv' … That'll be six quid for the ride, and ten for the information') is barely five minutes' walk away, west along (and across) the same railway line: a route punctuated by a concentration of sites linked with 1960s gangsters the Kray twins sufficient to (extra-textually) justify the cabbie's foreboding. The subsequent shots (6–10) show a variety of derelict or neglected backstreet sites, some chosen for abstract qualities more than a sense of place. A warehouse stands half-demolished next to a huge pile of rubble; a symmetrical duo of run-down, deserted 1950s or 1960s business units with filthy curtains are superimposed with the credit for line producers First City.

Shots 11–12 end the credits sequence, introduce the first significant camera movement and diegetic sound, and take us jarringly and briefly to Henri's workplace just inside the perimeter of the City proper (where he will shortly be made redundant). But behind the solidity of the marble door surround and brass signage (on Farringdon Street, EC4) lies a non-matching Hopperesque office interior as run-down and obsolete as the film's East End: the ancient equipment, institutional paint scheme, strip-lighting and noirish low-angled shots invoke post-war austerity more than 1990 London.

Kaurismäki's location choices in this opening sequence illustrate perfectly the tensions between three critical apprehensions of 'his' London: the 'unrecognisable', the abstractly evocative and the highly specific local London. While the last may be fully intelligible only to the reader/viewer possessing (or possessed by) Sinclairesque expertise, it is also the source of the film's richer economic and transnational resonances, and of the histories and myths which both provide its allusive humour and connect it with Kaurismäki's signature social concerns. Thus while the aura of the East End shots sets the scene for Henri's (double) isolation and disorientation as an economically redundant cultural outsider and establishes the contrast between Kaurismäki's London and the wealthy, swinging or landmark London, awareness of their locational specifics – whether their startling proximity to the wealthy City or the working-class and criminal (hi)stories ingrained within them – enriches and solidifies the film's narrative and thematic meanings.

Two further significant locales are not previewed in the opening sequence. First, Westbourne Park Road and Portobello Road in West London: Henri lives in a small corner flat over a shop on the former (again furnished in a drab retro style that owes more to the 1950s than 1990) and first encounters Margaret in the Warwick Castle pub a block or so away on the latter. Second, Stoke Newington – a settlement with seventeenth- and eighteenth-century origins and its own distinct resonances – site of the film's denouement in (the fictitious) Vic's café and (the real) Dr Watts' Chapel in Abney Park Cemetery. Just as *Contract Killer* fuses disparate locations to construct an imaginary 'East End', so it also links these two locales through creative cinematic geography, suggesting an alertness to affinities which transcend their geographical separation, producing an East–West fusion which is also metaphorically suggestive in relation to the film's politics and Kaurismäki's cultural allegiances. Both places share significant histories of dissent and political resistance (manifested by the 1970s–1980s in a shared concentration of punk, squatter and broader anti-capitalist activity), and the film fuses them via an emphasis on two distinctive shopfronts, which its editing implies to be proximate: the 1970s-style Nu-Line plumber's merchants, shown in point-of-view from Henri's flat window (and genuinely on Westbourne Park Road), and the appealingly old-fashioned General Woodwork hardware shop, where Henri buys the rope to hang himself (in reality several miles north-east on Stoke Newington High Street). This dual emphasis suggests an aesthetic and ethical valuing of the kinds of practical businesses valued by local communities and explicitly serving working-class trades, but which – in an advanced-capitalist metropolis with 'global city' pretensions – are placed under increasing threat.

In a further creative spatial leap, when Henri flees the flat because the Killer is inside, the very next shot shows him on a distinctive fenced-in metal bridge across the District line of the London Underground or Tube – east across town, back in Whitechapel and expressly in Jack the Ripper territory. This bridge funnels in one direction into a truly Dickensian narrow alley and in the other to Durward Street, formerly known as Buck's Row: the site in 1888 of the first recorded Ripper murder but also of the disturbingly ruined school which serves as the film's Honolulu Bar.

The film's 'Hotel Splendide', also in Whitechapel (Fieldgate Street, southwest of the Tube bridge and the Krays' childhood home, Vallance Road) similarly interjects its own intertextual history. The building's real name is Tower House – or, for Jack London, writing in 1903, the 'monster dosshouse'; its subsequent guests included George Orwell (as recorded in 1933's *Down and Out in Paris and London*) and Joseph Stalin. This thoroughly intimidating turreted red-brick edifice with its arrowslit windows opened in 1902 as one of the 'Rowton Houses': hostels for homeless or transient men, most with similar architecture, boasting as many as 800 bedrooms or 'cubicles' but also offering impressive facilities from baths and laundries to barbers and libraries.

Similarly, the film's closing showdown in the chapel at Abney Park Cemetery – in which the Killer shoots himself rather than Henri – gains a redemptive tone not merely from taking place in a cemetery but from the specific historical and ideological resonances of this one. Stoke Newington's association with political and religious dissenters stretches back long before the late-twentieth-century punk, squatter, anarchist and psychographic traditions already noted (via the 1971 arrest of the Angry Brigade, synonymously the 'Stoke Newington Eight') to such residents as the nineteenth-century Gothic writer Edgar Allan Poe and the seventeenth-to-eighteenth-century writer and pamphleteer Daniel Defoe. Abney Park itself opened in 1840 as Europe's first non-denominational 'garden cemetery'; its site had previously housed a non-conformist religious academy attended by Defoe and the hymnwriter Isaac Watts. Although by 1990 it had been secularised as a 'nature park', the shell of the commemorative Dr Watts' Chapel at its centre – site of the film's final confrontation – remains.

Conclusion

As such examples demonstrate, *I Hired a Contract Killer*'s locations signify not just atmospherically and narratively but historically, and often carry provocative social or political-economic resonances – whether in relation to their industrial past, present emptiness or future destiny. But while many of the film's locations gain meaning from the histories they embody, their resonances are also shaped or sharpened by retrospective awareness of the drastic transformation or obliteration of many of these sites since the film was made – placing them indeed beyond recognition and transforming Kaurismäki's film into an unwitting historical document of the traces, places (and potentially memories) lost in the process of accelerating redevelopment and gentrification in London as an advanced-capitalist 'global city'. Where the once-empty docks are now 'Docklands', Tower House and the Durward Street school are now 'luxury apartments', marketed in terms which erase their history. Moreover, the changes such sites have witnessed – which Kaurismäki captures either in process or in waiting – exemplify precisely the material impacts of transnational economic forces on the fabric of the very local.

The question of the relation of this parallel locational 'text' to the narrative text of the film remains a delicate one. Nevertheless, as this chapter has sought to illustrate, the resonances of *Contract Killer*'s locational specifics operate in a variety of ways to amplify, concretise or enrich the narrative meanings and mood already available to the 'general' viewer. While, when read merely as 'evocative', Kaurismäki's use of Durward Street and Tower House exploits the power of intimidating architecture, 'unfamiliar' place and manifest or imminent dereliction to invoke foreboding and, for the outsider (Henri, and the majority of viewers), disorientation, attention to the specifics of place reveals transtextualities which are both more particular and more varied. On the one hand, Durward Street's disturbing aura (and Henri's terrified assumption nearby that a harmless tramp is his Killer) gains a concrete motivation from its actual association with Jack the Ripper. On the other, the history inscribed in the 'monster doss-house' both amplifies the irony of its appropriation as the 'Hotel Splendide' and references a tradition of philanthropy and social concern valued by Kaurismäki but wilfully lost under the ruthless march of advanced capitalism that has cast aside both Henri and Tower House.

Notes

1 J. Anderson, 'Cold Comforts', *Eye Weekly* (12 June 2003), www.eyeweekly.com/eye/issue/issue_06.12.03/film/kaurismaki.php (accessed 20 April 2020).

2 J. Romney, 'Last Exit to Helsinki', *Film Comment*, 39.2 (March 2003), p. 44.
3 Charlotte Brunsdon, *London in Cinema: The Cinematic City since 1945* (London: British Film Institute, 2007), p. 11.
4 For a fuller analysis of the psychogeographic strand, see C. Geraghty, 'The Woman between: The European Woman in Post-war British Cinema', *European Journal of Cultural Studies*, 2 (1999), pp. 147–62. For 'list-books', see Brunsdon, *London in Cinema*, p. 6.
5 Robert Stam, *Film Theory: An Introduction* (Malden, MA and Oxford: Blackwell, 2000), p. 207.
6 T. Pulleine, 'I Hired a Contract Killer', *Monthly Film Bulletin*, 58.685 (1991); Romney, 'Last Exit to Helsinki', p. 44.
7 Paul Newland, 'A Place to Go? Exploring Liminal Space in Aki Kaurismäki's *I Hired a Contract Killer* (1990)', *Wider Screen*, 10.2 (2007), www.widerscreen.fi/2007/2/place_to_go.htm (accessed 20 April 2020).
8 Newland, 'A Place to Go?'.
9 Anderson, 'Cold Comforts'.
10 Newland, 'A Place to Go?'.
11 Philippa Hawker, 'Unbearable Lightness', *Senses of Cinema* (August 2000), p. 2, www.sensesofcinema.com/2000/jean-pierre-leaud/lightness/ (accessed 20 April 2020).
12 R. Malik, 'On Location with *I Hired a Contract Killer*', *The Producer*, 13 (Autumn, 1990), p. 28.
13 Strat., 'I Hired a Contract Killer', *Variety* (24 September 1990).
14 Malik, 'On Location'.
15 Pulleine, 'I Hired a Contract Killer', p. 4.
16 Clarke's performance was seen as the film's weak link by some of its admirers as well as its detractors.
17 Nigel Floyd, 'I Hired a Contract Killer', in *Time Out Film Guide 13*, ed. J. Pym (London: Time Out, 2004), www.timeout.com/film/75836.html.
18 These cultural reference points are fused in Kaurismäki's 1994 film *Take Care of Your Scarf, Tatjana*, summarised by Romney as 'a Sixties road comedy' in which two Finnish 'middle-aged rockers in a vintage American car' give two young women, Estonian and Russian respectively, a lift to the Helsinki–Tallinn ferry. Romney, 'Last Exit to Helsinki'.
19 Newland, 'A Place to Go?'.
20 Iain Sinclair, 'Jack the Rip-Off', *Observer* (27 January 2002).
21 The LDDC was the second of several 'urban development corporations' (UDCs) formed by the Thatcher Conservative government under the 1980 Local Government, Planning and Land Act and granted extensive powers unconstrained by the planning system.

6

Bollywood's London: the moral-political undertow of London's Hindi cinema presence

Shakuntala Banaji and Rahoul Masrani

From the now famously conservative culture-clash blockbuster *Purab aur Paschim* (East and west; Manoj Kumar, 1970), which pits supposedly authentic and patriotic Indians against the deracinated diaspora, to the 2018 patriotic romance *Namaste England* (Shah, 2018), London has appeared in hundreds of Hindi films. In 2007 alone more than forty films were shot in London, either partially on location or in other parts of the UK masquerading as London.[1] Since then, it has appeared in hundreds more, and been the key locational backdrop to blockbuster romances such as *Cocktail* (Homi Adajania, 2012) and *Jab Tak Hain Jaan* (Yash Chopra, 2012) as well as comedies such as *Housefull 3* (Sajjid-Farhad, 2016) and action thrillers like *Aiyaary* (Neeraj Pandey, 2018). Sometimes London is filmed sparsely and with such banality that it is a clichéd backdrop to heartbreak or consumption and romance (as in the song 'Heer' in *Jab Tak Hain Jaan*, which starts with the central female character alone on a London Underground platform, or the Camden sequences of *Mujse Dosti Karoge?* which could be set in any global city). With increasing frequency, however, London appears as a metaphor epitomising the tensions of secular, globalised modernity, longing for an idealised home nation (India) and (Hindu) nationalist identity, both for those in the diaspora and, as our chapter will argue, for those already identified with a powerful Hindutva nationalism in India.

In the wake of Aditya Chopra's phenomenally successful *Dilwale Dulhaniya Le Jayenge* or *DDLJ* (The one with the heart will win the bride; Chopra, 1995), in which the young lovers Raj and Simran, played by Shah Rukh Khan and Kajol, walk, run, sing and dance their way from Trafalgar Square, Angel station and King's Cross to Richmond and back, a significant change began to take place in a number of Hindi films set in London. This change was unconnected to Film London's explicit policy of inviting investment from Bollywood producers through the development of London as a location. In terms of the narrative, the city began to figure as an ambivalent semiotic marker of personal choice, anonymity and modernity which ultimately sours and leaves the protagonists ashamed of themselves and longing to return to their roots, homeland and supposedly Indian traditions – but which also, at times, provides space to explore unconstrained love and sexuality. In the hit *Namastey London* (Shah, 2007), for instance, which we will compare to *Guest iin London* (Dhar, 2018), London's Docklands is the iconic and spectacular backdrop for a series of white racist comments and an equally racist 'Indian' nationalist speech about thousands of years of Indian history and culture. In *Patiala House* (Advani, 2011), a film set in the past, Southall appears as the home to young ambition, cricket and also the burning white racism of the 1970s. Meanwhile, in *Guest iin London*, the film on which we dwell considerably in this chapter, the Shard skyscraper, Tower Bridge, the Millennium Bridge, Piccadilly Circus, Southall and other recognisable London locations play a complicated role in the courtship, misunderstandings and moral realisations of the awkward young protagonists.

At the heart of these films, which we analyse in this chapter using a modified ideological analysis and audio-visual discourse analysis, both drawing on Barthian semiotics, lies a desire to attract viewers to London for its history and economic potential but also to guard against and reject its supposedly ephemeral Western allure by emphasising the moral superiority of simply *being Indian*. The narratives of several of the films we've mentioned end by putting London firmly back in its place – somewhere superficial, where it is fun to shop and party, energising to walk, but which has, apparently, no heart and no soul. They end with a re-entrenchment of invented Hindu chauvinist traditions and characteristics posited as *essentially* and *exclusively* Indian. In this sense, Bollywood's London, although considerably different from that of UK/Hollywood productions like Sharon Maguire's *Bridget Jones's Diary* (2001) or Roger Michell's *Notting Hill* (1999), also use the city to portray a particularly conservative and patriarchal construction of diaspora, ethnicity and nation.

If the English-language productions centre a depoliticised, deracinated and equally fabricated Britishness by focusing on a version of unthreatening but steely English identity (through representations that erase or disavow British colonialism, class, race and gendered politics), the Indian ones cannot be seen as a simple postcolonial riposte or counterpoint. It is crucial that we read them, and their audiences, within their own hegemonic context of Hindutva fascist politics which pushes for global acceptance of an Indian citizenship discourse that is overtly discriminatory against Muslims, Dalits and other non-upper-caste Hindu groups, privileges the upper classes and castes through neoliberalism and private business, and wreaks unbearable violence on those who are poor or do not conform to and fit the global Hindu nationalist vision.[2] Bollywood's London in the first two decades of the twenty-first century emerges, therefore, as a contested space while leaving little space for political contestation of what Indian identity is or could be, a place where the economic benefits and multicultural mixing of different races, religions and genders are judged as an abject failure in order to highlight the supposed strengths of the Hindutva vision while offering diasporic caste Hindus a do-it-yourself version of moral capital as they move between economic prosperity, modernity and nostalgia for the comforting hierarchies of homeland.

Symbolic power

London's complex material and symbolic identity as the former capital of the British Empire and now an important global financial centre, in both Bollywood and English-language films, is often reduced to a screen identity centred upon consumption in late capitalism.[3] In her discussion of the Hollywood-made, London-based romantic comedies released in the late 1990s for example, Church Gibson notes that these films were commercially successful partly due to London's key role as a hub for global capitalism.[4] Similarly, in his exploration of London's cinematic identity in the late 1990s and early 2000s, Masrani posits that mainstream films in this period communicate the city's symbolic power through 'the visual focus on the city's expensive retail, dining and entertainment offerings, and indeed the visual construction of the city as one of iconic spaces and monuments'.[5] Georgiou echoes this assertion in her discussion of London's post-EU referendum screen image. She notes that London's on-screen identity contributes to the 'commodification of a cosmopolitanism that is accessible and consumable among global audiences'.[6] The glossy, tourist-friendly side of London, with its well-known sights and plentiful opportunities to engage in consumptive experiences, solidifies this metropole's position as a global city.[7]

Whilst the signs of modernity such as offices in the Shard at London Bridge are also convenient visual signifiers of late capitalism, we need to understand the city's role throughout recent history, first as a hub for migrants from other parts of the UK, from the former British colonies and, more recently, as a magnet for workers from other European Union nations. London's kaleidoscopic population is evident both materially and on screen, with Bollywood providing particularly rich examples of the city's multifaceted identity. From a cinematic point of view, London's cosmopolitan qualities are simultaneously a cause for celebration and despair, where the city functions both as a space of liberation and refuge for the marginalised and as a space of exploitation for those in the lower echelons of society. Whereas the glossy and glamorous portrayals of the city in the romantic comedies and romantic dramas of the late 1990s and early 2000s avoid obvious indicators of London's ethnic diversity, the London-set English-language melodramas of the period tackle hard-hitting issues like illegal immigration, racism and the exploitation of the migrant working classes. Examples of films that tackle these more hard-hitting issues include *Dirty Pretty Things* (Frears, 2002) and *Breaking and Entering* (Minghella, 2006).

Indeed, Masrani, in his discussion of the hybrid nature of the city itself and of cinematic representations of the city in this period, notes that the 'representations of the cinematic city across the two thematic categories [glamorous and multicultural] paint a diverse picture, in many ways mirroring the diversity in the "real" city'.[8] Furthermore, London's multifaceted screen identity creates an allure that is linked to the city's symbolic power. Branding expert Thomas Sevcik believes that the idea of creating a believable urban 'narrative' is key in advancing a city's symbolic power on the global stage.[9] Films promote the city whilst the city promotes films. Hindi films set in London are particularly rich sites for exploration, precisely because of their pervasiveness and the complex combination of the postcolonial undertones that undeniably underpin these films' narratives, with neoliberalism and the distinctive Indian paradigm of Hindutva, discussed briefly above. The frequent use of the English language interspersed with Hindi or Urdu plus the overall ease and familiarity with which the characters in many London-set Bollywood films use the city space are indicative of the historical migration ties between the UK and India while also speaking of a particular class paradigm, where the protagonists engage in international air travel as an unremarkable, naturalised activity.

In many instances, it is evident that Hindi films set in London are tools in a wider effort to market the city to South Asian audiences who could become tourist consumers. In their work on place marketing, Josiam et al. suggest that many Indian tourists visit the UK because the country is 'prominently featured in many Bollywood films'.[10] In 2007, the agency tasked with promoting London as a film destination both for filmmakers and visitors, Film London, released a 'Bollywood Movie Map', guiding tourists as they visit locations featured in their favourite London-set Hindi films. This conceptualisation of the city, one that is both filmic and 'real', is rooted in the blurring of the distinction between the city as a lived space and as a cinematic fantasy. Jansson calls this 'mediatised spatial phantasmagoria', where tourists will attempt to live out their cinematic experiences of the city during their visits.[11] Taking this idea further, Reijnders theorises this type of visit as a 'media pilgrimage', citing the tourists who attempt to recreate an iconic shot from a James Bond film at Westminster Bridge in central London.[12] Given London's pervasive screen image, in both English-language and Hindi films, it is unsurprising that the city is an important global destination in which such media pilgrimages take place. London is full of 'readymade historical and iconic spaces' but equally some lesser-known spots that inspire film-induced tourism.[13]

Locating the diaspora

Creating filmic content in a city like London demonstrates both the wide appeal of Hindi cinema for an array of audiences and the importance of London as a global city with international appeal. Whilst the domestic Indian cinema market is buoyant, the overseas market has recently grown considerably. For example, in 2017, 'box office collections for Indian films overseas took $367 million – up almost three times from $125 million the year before'.[14] This astounding statistic suggests two things: firstly, that Hindi films are increasingly appealing to global audiences; and, secondly, that members of the Indian diaspora, with high numbers in the UK and USA (1.5 and 2.5 million respectively), are helping to augment the success of Hindi films outside India.[15] It is precisely this combination of factors that has contributed to Hindi films being screened in mainstream movie theatres outside India, such as those belonging to the Regal Cinemas chain in the USA[16] and the Odeon, UCI and Vue chains in the UK.[17]

Whilst mainstream, foreign interest in Bollywood films is certainly growing, the role of Indian diasporic audiences in countries such as the UK and USA is also significant. Takhar et al., in their study of the viewing habits of members of the British Sikh community, call Hindi films 'an international obsession with the Indian diaspora', whereby these films simultaneously provide viewing pleasure and a connection to a South Asian cultural identity.[18] Given the complexities of this identity, with a combination of a sense of rootedness in their adopted home and a putative longing to return to their country of origin even if they have come to the UK via several generations in Uganda or Kenya, plot lines in Hindi films set in non-Indian locations such as London often focus on 'clichés such as the return to the motherland'.[19] These complexities, in conjunction with the wide appeal of Bollywood films amongst the Indian diaspora, are framed in the context of a modified version of the hate-fuelled Islamophobic rhetoric of the Hindutva nationalist Bharatiya Janata Party (BJP), led by Narendra Modi. Although the BJP has only been in power since 2014, 'its sister militant nationalist organisations, the Vishwa Hindu Parishad and the Rashtriya Swayamsevak Sangh (RSS), have been seeping into the diaspora since the 1970s'.[20] Indeed, the myth of the 'pure' Hindu nation coupled with nostalgia for the 'motherland' suggest that the representation of Indianness in Bollywood films that take place outside India form part of a wider effort to construct a particular ethnocentric vision of Indian identity.[21]

Analytic lens and methods

Taking up this theme, Harveen Sachdeva Mann compares the delicate critiques of racialised patriarchy to which London is subjected by British Asian writer Hanif Kureishi's *Sammy and Rosie Get Laid* (1987), directed by Stephen Frears, with its increasingly central representation as a hub for supposedly British Indian cultural values in Bollywood films of the 2000s:

> *DDLJ* and *K3G* globalize London, occidentalizing the city and strategically containing it within an 'alien', postcolonial script. The import of this is twofold: to underwrite narratives of resistance in these Bollywood films, which interrupt mainstream western cultural values and dominant literary and media images of both east and west; and, paradoxically, to reinforce the traditional, immigrant discourse of ethnicity and religion-, caste-, and nation-based identity, but to do so within the heart of the western metropolis.[22]

Mann's points are well made but have not been pursued in any depth by subsequent scholarship. In what follows, we offer insights based on a combination of audio-visual discourse and ideological analysis, both reliant on an occasional pursuit of semiotic clues.

In a classic ideological analysis, stereotyping plays into, maintains and reinforces social structures of power from multiple spheres, setting the tone of the dominant discourses within which knowledge about 'Others' circulates. In his work on 'The Spectacle of the "Other"', Stuart Hall defines stereotyping as a representational practice which 'reduces people to a few, simple, essential characteristics, which are represented as fixed by Nature'.[23] Fetishisation, another strategic representational practice that Hall invokes in this superlative essay, involves a strategy wherein desire for and fascination with the 'Other' are simultaneously indulged and disavowed.[24] All of these strategies are apparent in the aesthetics and narrative of the two London-set Hindi films discussed below. In this context, the task of analysis is a political one – the uncovering and denaturalisation of the ideologically weighted stereotypes and fetishes found in contemporary visual culture, with a concomitant attempt to unpick and address the tensions and power relations sustained by these representations.

Drawing together Roland Barthes's simple work on connotation from *Mythologies* and insights from linguists-turned-discourse analysts like Norman Fairclough, audio-visual discourse analysis provides a way of operationalising ideological analyses of texts by providing a framework for evidencing ideological claims.[25] If we understand Gillian Rose's assertion that 'discourses are articulated through all sorts of visual and verbal images and texts' to mean that ideology too is articulated in this manner, and permeates the discourses so articulated, it is possible to see how a systematic reading of audio-visual signs in Hindi films, connecting these signs to the contexts that produced them and in which audiences reside, will lead to a better understanding of the workings of ideology on and off screen.[26] Sidestepping the sometimes myopic focus of pure semiotic analysis while nevertheless availing itself of insights about connotative meaning, audio-visual discourse analysis thus never loses sight of the bigger picture – the historical and geopolitical tensions, the visual and structural power relations, the intertextual repetitions, layering and intertwining of particular iconic images within and across genres, as well as between different eras and viewers. Understanding and foregrounding the bigger picture is essential in an analysis such as the one we provide in this chapter, particularly given London's complex identity and its central role as a global, cinematic city. Acknowledging and highlighting the sociological elements helps us provide a critical analysis that denaturalises the aspects of the films that are presented as 'normal' and taken for granted.

In the coming section we will analyse key moments in the narratives of two films produced a decade apart, *Namastey London* and *Guest iin London*. These sequences have been selected based on their typicality with respect to the narratives of the whole films and also their typicality with respect to the entire subset of Hindi romantic comedies and dramas set in London.

London: epicentre of romance, false promise of diversity and modernity

While a spotlight has been shone multiple times on the mega-blockbusters *DDLJ* (Aditya Chopra, 1995) and *K3G* (Karan Johar, 2001), our focus on these two slightly less widely circulated and analysed films is linked to the powerful typicality of their ideological and discursive terrain, and of their visual rendering of the British Asian cultural encounter with apparently authentic Indianness, embedded as it is in London and set amidst an ambivalent critique of London's multicultural streets, its melting pot reputation and its Asian cuisines. Both films make snide, adulatory and jokey intertextual references to dozens of other films such as *Hum Dil De Chuke Sanam* (Sanjay Leela Bhansali, 1999), *K3G* and *DDLJ*. Of course, these throwback references to iconic plot moments are relevant for an understanding of how discourses of nation, loyalty, duty and tradition are constructed through the boundaries of acceptable masculinity and chaste femininity. The use of the cityscape in all these films is facile and retrograde, at once a neoliberal spectacle of consumption and a product to be consumed. It is also, however, potentially polysemic, offering the promise of privacy, the possibility of sex before marriage, a loosening of parental surveillance, cross-racial friendship and refuge from arranged marriage. Like most Hindi mainstream romantic comedy-dramas, both films are awash with snide racist tropes and jokes aimed primarily at Pakistanis and Muslims, but also at Chinese and Black British characters. Both films specialise in the disavowal of their own racist stereotyping of South Asian 'desi' migrants as somehow being only a projection and rejection of what deracinated British Asians and colonial white people think. Notwithstanding some critical rejections, both films must be read in the context of an audience to whom the jaw-dropping racism and sexism of the scripts is familiar and welcome.[27] This assertion is supported by hundreds of positive user reviews online and genuine ripples of laughter and cheering in the Indian and diasporic movie theatres where we viewed the films.

Namastey London

Namastey London attempts to recreate the jingoism of 1970's *Purab aur Paschim*. Set against the backdrop of the Blairite Labour Party's rhetoric of 'cool Britannia' yet enacted in an uber wealthy milieu of penthouse offices, snobbish aristocrats and palatial mansions, *Namastey London* tells the story of a bratty British Asian wild child Jazz (short for Jasmeet), played by mixed-race superstar Katrina Kaif, who despises 'Indian men', drinks, flirts with white men and dresses in revealing supposedly Western clothes as she discovers that her true love is not her promiscuous boss Charlie Brown but rather the Indian village hunk Arjun, played by megastar Akshay Kumar, to whom her parents marry her off halfway through the film. Although the marriage itself takes place in an apocryphal Punjabi village, approximately 80 per cent of the film is set in London and iconic London locations feature as both a backdrop to Jazz and Arjun's growing intimacy and a clunky metaphor for Arjun's attempt to 'bridge' the gap between Jasmeet/Jazz's London life and her supposedly authentic desires.

The title soundtrack and visuals establish that South Asian masculinity and London will be the twin focal points of the narrative, with rapid cuts between aerial views of the Thames, different London tourist landmarks and the faces and upper bodies of the only ordinary South Asian men to feature in the film as they walk along streets of ghetto neighbourhoods. The London Eye, featured in this sequence, is revisited at least nine other times in film, and Tower Bridge also appears repeatedly. This sequence ends on a teaser for the plot: a suited Akshay Kumar leading a brooding Katrina Kaif down the aisle at a posh British cathedral, filled with white folk and a few brown faces, to hand her over to her white husband-to-be.

A quick succession of shots of iconic London tropes – a retro bar, a black cab and Tower Bridge – are used to establish Jazz's character: she's witty, she's modern, she's sexy, she finagles her way out of a parentally mandated date by downing vodka shots and dropping hints about her sex life and she scolds the cab driver for leering at her when she boldly changes out of a traditional Indian garment into a minidress and boots en route to her office in the Shard. The script is unsubtle: lounging at Tower Bridge, a friend asks her, 'What's your problem with Indian guys? You're Indian too' and she quips back, 'That he's Indian. I am British … . My thinking, my attitudes, my likes are all British – so how can I be Indian?' The film's insistence on the incompatibility of the two identities, Indian and British, is further explored in the awkward encounter between the Malhotras and the Browns. Relying on colonial-era stereotypes of race, class and cultural norms, the scene culminates with Jazz's father quipping that 'although their name is Brown, they are pristine white'.

The film's obtrusively touristic gaze fetishises both Jazz's body and a number of large stone British buildings and monuments to the point of absurdity. That is to say, a psychoanalytic reading of the positioning of the buildings and of Jazz's face and body would yield excruciating results. The sequence when Jazz's boss attempts to impress her by stopping off at Buckingham Palace for 'a quick conversation' with Prince Charles as Jazz looks on from his luxury car in awe is both laughable and revealing of the director's occidentalism and imperial imaginary, shared by at least some of the Indian audience. There are no ordinary white people in the London of this film, just as there are no middle-class houses, flats or working-class neighbourhoods after the opening credits. There are no working-class Londoners at all, no university students, no cleaners and certainly none who are not represented as at least partly racist. There are, however, a great number of plummy and offensively aristocratic white people who live in palatial country estates surrounded by acres of lawn and party in yachts and tea gardens. Even Jasmeet/Jazz's family, supposedly the owners of a store selling branded jeans, lives in a house so enormous that it has eight bedrooms, a stone terrace all of its own and no houses nearby. Apart from the initial black cab ride and the couple of times we see one of the characters in a car, one moves instantaneously and seamlessly between the Thames at Tower Bridge, a pod in the London Eye, Greenwich Park and these palatial homes as if traversing these spaces happens invisibly. Only once in the film, at a moment of extremely heightened emotion during a song sequence when married-but-rejected Arjun is silently shadowing and courting Jazz, but not overtly telling her to give up her engagement to her posh boss Charlie Brown, do we see either of the main characters on London transport: in this case, a mainline train which appears to be pulling into one of London's main train stations.[28]

The music that accompanies all of these locations changes depending on the mood of the protagonists: at the outset when Jazz is having fun or arguments, it is upbeat and commercial; in the middle when she is conflicted it becomes soulful and Indian; and when she is in India it becomes a medley of Hindi film, soap and Indian pop, something that would be recognisably familiar to anyone who watches serials or listens to Asian radio stations in the diaspora but that has little traditional Indian melody to it. If London is a tourists' London, so is the India that Jazz visits forty minutes into the film.

One final sequence that deserves close attention for its gross revelation of the jingoistic nationalism of the BJP, which was already very much in evidence in India in the early 2000s and which has now become the standard form of discourse, is Jazz's engagement to Charlie Brown on a yacht on the Thames. Here, in what could be deemed a uniquely romantic tourist location, and with different parts of London on either side, 'white folk' are constructed as unregenerated colonial racists, first insulting Jazz as the fourth-wife-to-be and then reducing India to a land of 'snake charmers', 'Indian rope tricks', 'elephants', 'chicken tandoori' and 'call centres'. This familiar but also parodic rendering of the mundane racism experienced by so many migrant workers and students from South Asia during their everyday lives in the UK is a turning point in the film's narrative as it marks the 'awakening' of Jazz to the wonders of India and the meanness of her fiancé and his set. The hero, Arjun, folds his hands in traditional Indian greeting (the eponymous Namastey) and orates about India's tolerance of all religions, its acceptance of outsiders, its military and economic prowess and its courtesy to strangers. The subsequent challenge of an India (brown) versus England (white) rugby match ends in defeat for the racist Brits, parodying nationalistic sports films such as *Lagaan* (which is openly mentioned), and further undermines the claims to masculinity of Jazz's white fiancé, who has to add 'sore loser' to his repertoire of racist and juvenile behaviours.

Namastey London's closing sequence depicts a now happy and presumably psychologically healed Jasmeet dressed in Indian clothes riding pillion on Arjun's motorbike in India, having discovered her soulmate and run (literally) down the aisle away from London and away from her white husband-to-be and her false self. As they ride, Jasmeet asks Arjun why he pretended not to know English and Arjun taunts her that his English is better than hers, even though she assumed he couldn't speak it because of her stereotyped expectations about Indian villagers. The connotations of the sequence are clear: India is best in every way and is always willing to accept its 'desi British' sons and daughters back into the fold. All they have to do is to renounce their Western lovers, assume Indian (read, upper caste and Hindu nationalist) values and recognise the superiority of Indian traditions. Opening sequence: London. Closing sequence: Punjab. Irony: zero.

Guest iin London

Guest iin London is a lower budget and less successful film than *Namastey London*. Consequently it boasts few big-name stars apart from Paresh Rawal as Chachaji and a cameo from Ajay Devgan as his (dead) son. It tells the story of Aryan (Kartik Aaryan) and Anaya (Kriti Karbanda), young Londoners who are planning a marriage of convenience so that Aryan, a Non-Resident Indian (NRI) who loves his job at a software company ('SoftDog') in the Shard, can obtain leave to remain and work in the UK and so that Anaya, open-minded British Asian taxi driver and party animal, can finance her accommodation. Apparently her divorced parents do not support her and she sleeps in her taxi. The *deus ex machina* is 'Chachaji', bumbling tenant of a neighbour of Aryan's uncle back home in Punjab who, alongside his plumply nurturing, racist and – as it turns out – Muslim wife, Guddi (the generally sophisticated actor Tanvi Azmi), becomes an uninvited guest in Aryan's Southall home in the run-up to his fake wedding. In the process he plays havoc with the couple's incipient love life and with their scamster plans, upending jobs and neighbours, and 'teaching' the young couple the apparently intrinsically Indian meaning of love, sacrifice and family. Less overtly nationalistic with a big N than *Namastey London*, *Guest iin London* at first appears more attuned to British Asian middle-class sensibilities in its references to and construction of ethnically diverse residential neighbourhoods and issues such as visas, jobs and police permission for noisy public displays. This facade, however, conceals as much as it reveals.

Guest iin London opens to a panoramic aerial shot of central London – with the London Eye in pride of place – and a glass-windowed office in the Shard where Aryan is explaining to his extremely assertive British Asian boss 'K' that he's about to have an unexpected guest. Within a few frames, we have also been introduced to Chachaji – the uninvited guest – who is on a flight from India, the epitome of a stereotype of an uneducated, unrefined Indian, taking more alcohol from the flight attendant than he's allowed, distributing home-cooked food, farting loudly in public and generally causing confusion.

We cut straight to a very British courtroom, with a magistrate who speaks in a posh English accent (like most of the few other white characters). The accents, mainly BBC and Eton though with the occasional cockney one, as much as any other semiotic cue in the film are intended to display the proximity of characters to authentic British or Indian culture. The two protagonists, Anaya and Aryan, are trying to get a date for their 'fake' marriage and a caricatured Pakistani British police officer, Mr Habibi – who turns out to be their neighbour, wears a skull cap and has henna in his hair – doubts the authenticity of their union only to be told by the magistrate: 'You Pakistanis always have a problem with Indians'. This sort of remark about Pakistanis is repeated several times during the film, particularly by Chachaji when he first meets Habibi, and relentlessly used to gain laughs from a xenophobic audience, while being positioned next to an apparently warm and glowing friendliness extended by the authentic Indian couple to everyone, including Pakistanis. In an intertextual parody of the intense and moving Andie MacDowell–Gérard Depardieu cross-questioning sequence in the Hollywood film *Green Card* (Peter Weir, 1990), Anaya and Arjun answer quick-fire questions about each other in separate rooms and are subsequently granted permission to marry in a fortnight. A few sequences later, after we have seen Mr Habibi trying to spy on Anaya and Arjun in their quaint Southall terrace, and Anaya's character has been established as shrewd and bossy, with Indian wedding music in the background, we hear Arjun explaining to a turbaned Sikh colleague: 'I had no choice. I've been in this country for four years on a working visa. As soon as my visa expires, the whites will send me back. I had no other option but to marry in order to settle here … . But … how can I bring real guests to a fake wedding?' Meanwhile Anaya, whom we never once see driving or doing her job, even though she is a taxi driver, meets her friends at Piccadilly Circus (they later picnic at Trafalgar Square) and they persuade her that she needs to go ahead with the fake wedding.

From this point onwards the director milks the 'uncouth South Asians in London' trope for apparently comic effect, producing every stereotype of 'simplicity' from Guddi Chachi, who can't climb onto an escalator in the Shard, triggering a security breach, and claims that Indian massage can turn a Black baby fair, to Chachaji, who lectures Anaya about unchaste clothing and calls every neighbour into the house, thus introducing a sense of community to the residential London street which had, apparently, none before he arrived. The community thus created is superficially diverse, with older Indians, Mr Habibi, his Black wife and baby and a white couple who rarely speak. Indeed, both at Aryan's Shard software development firm and in their street, visual diversity and multiculturalism are stressed repeatedly. There are South and East Asians, mostly silent Black characters and white British police officers. London is resplendent as a tourist city – and is on full display during the sequence when Anaya and Aryan take Chachaji and Guddi Chachi to see Buckingham Palace, the changing of the guard and St Paul's Cathedral, as well as when Anaya admits her love for Aryan and they sing against a backdrop of Tower Bridge, the Thames and City of London School.

A creeping misogyny intersects the racist representation of every one of the women characters apart from that of Guddi Chachi – although there is a distinct and deliberate moment of tension when she is 'revealed' to be a Muslim. Brash and independent British Asian Anaya is taught a lesson about humility and humanity when she discovers that the unwanted guests lost their only son in the 9/11 attacks; Habibi's Black wife apparently goes out to work and leaves her baby unattended so that it ends up with Guddi Chachi; and, vying for the worst script line in the film, having 'saved' Aryan's Chinese colleague Lui from molestation by their slimy boss K during an office party, Chachaji comments, 'I won't let you rape her – It's so easy for a woman to lose her honour and get spoiled – especially as she's already Chinese and Chinese women are already prone to getting corrupted'. Of course, there are semiotic possibilities which might erode the unrelenting racism and sexism of the main plot for certain audience members. There are moments of fellow feeling between the two awkward lead characters and some genuine nostalgia for the loving parents and relatives back home, when it comes to NRIs.

Ideology, agency and meaning

Both Paresh Rawal, the big-name star in *Guest iin London*, and Akshay Kumar, the star of *Namastey London*, have played a singularly repellent role through supporting the rise of the BJP and of Hindutva fascist politics in India and the diaspora. Akshay Kumar's films have become increasingly propagandist not just for Hindu chauvinism and nationalism but directly aimed at endorsing Modi's regime, from his championing of the Modi government's supposed flagship 'clean India' programme in the film *Toilet* (Shree Narayan Singh, 2017) to his obscenely sycophantic interview with Modi in the run-up to the 2019 elections.[29] Twitter handles persistently deride anyone who is critical of Modi and spew out the standard jingoistic propaganda at moments of heightened tension in India or with Pakistan. In the years between the making of *Namastey London* and *Guest iin London*, Modi has had his image massaged and managed by a team of propagandists, many of whom are located in London and Washington, became the Prime Minister of India at the 2014 election, had his travel ban for links to the 2002 Gujarat genocide withdrawn and held a rally at Wembley in London which attracted over 60,000 followers.

Engaging this sociopolitical backdrop, but also departing from it, this chapter has posited London as an ambivalent and shifting signifier in Hindi cinema. It has to function, simultaneously, as a dream (of women's liberation, privacy, romance and escape) that fuels the plot, and an illusion (of progressive or racist Westernisation) to be debunked and rejected by 'true' patriotic Indians in favour of an assemblage of invented and decontextualised caste Hindu traditions which function as markers of the Indian nation and an essentialised Indianness. Given the ubiquity of this trope in recent Hindi films and the role it has come to play in the discourses that make the current Hindutva fascist government in India a worthy cause for celebration and funding by troubling numbers in the diaspora, it is surprising that there has not been more written on this topic.[30]

The romantic comedy genre of the films we've examined both deploys and disavows a plethora of damaging stereotypes about London as a city and about life in London: it is a city of wealth and desire, but one which will trap young British Asians and corrupt their true values. It retains its links to empire. Migrant workers in London work in high-tech jobs and offices – or as taxi drivers. Tech firms win contracts from China. Whites are colonial racists. White women and Chinese women are sexy and easy. Black women are ugly, not worthy of dancing with and bad mothers. People of colour who have lived side by side on a street come together only when an authentic Indian catalyses their community. British Asian women wear skimpy clothes, can't cook and go to clubs all the time; British Asian parents need to control their children better. Authentic Indians are loyal and forgiving. There is no way to break the bond of the seven *pheras* of a Hindu marriage ritual. There are no moments of irony or reflection on these tropes in either of the films we've analysed in this chapter – only a poor attempt to pretend that they were actually trying to critique the audience's inherent racism and tendency to accept stereotypes by introducing a tragic twist in the narrative some way through. Meanwhile, the connotations of London as a melting pot city which is ripe for romance, economic betterment and tourism are repeatedly and insistently undercut by dialogues about retaining one's heritage, traditions, roots and respect for elders.

Our analysis in this chapter both acknowledges and takes issue with the notion of 'mainstream Western cultural values' and 'resistance', noting that each of these concepts contains within it a plethora of conflicts over their meaning and essence. Each term is only a reflection of what different groups claim to be the case. As Masrani noted of London as a signifier in *Dirty Pretty Things*, which tried to represent the grim reality of London's hostility to low paid migrants, 'viewers are presented with the city as a site of hope ... and even seemingly negative portrayals of London contribute to its symbolic power as a global city'.[31] The director of *Dirty Pretty Things* urges a consideration of the notion of 'Western values' as complicated and ambivalent, comprising compassion for refugees and migrants as well as a disavowal and exploitation of their suffering, a democratic tradition of solidarity between the underdogs and a colonial revulsion for the other; the directors of *Guest iin London* and *Namastey London* disavow historical and emotional complexity and any cross-racial solidarity while milking London's charms as a backdrop for 'desi' romance.

The underlying ideological assertion is clear: live in the West (represented by London), consume, succeed, build families and businesses but reject all values that stem from London. While attempting to explore the meaning of a culture clash for young British Asians, these directors claim a homogeneous authentic Indianness as the epitome of good and, unlike the white population, the diaspora is blessed because it still has the capacity to learn and be led by Indian magnanimity and sacrifice. Banaji's work on ways of reading and interpreting closure in Hindi films and her argument connecting agency and co-option in relation to tech use and media consumption, which posits that agency is not pure and absolute but can be contaminated by structural inequalities, suggests that viewers' agency in delimiting the meanings of cinematic London in Hindi films such as the ones analysed here is implicated both in the hopeful multiculturalism and in the obscenely sexist and racist Hindutva politics.[32] To understand how, why and to what extent one can still call contaminated meaning-making that appears to be part of hegemonic ideological processes agentic, and the role such contaminated audience agency around depictions of London and India may play in sustaining authoritarian diasporic and Indian politics, a full-fledged audience study comparing those who cheer for Akshay Kumar and Paresh Rawal in these films with those who leave disappointed and even angry reviews is now overdue.

Notes

1 Film London (https://filmlondon.org.uk/).
2 See, for example, S. Banaji, 'Vigilante Publics: Orientalism, Modernity and Hindutva Fascism in India', *Javnost – The Public*, 25.4 (2018), pp. 333–50. Christophe Jaffrelot and Ingrid Therwath, 'The Sangh Parivar and the Hindu Diaspora in the West: What Kind of "Long-Distance Nationalism"?', *International Political Sociology*, 1.3 (2007), pp. 278–95. G. Osuri, 'Transnational Bio/Necropolitics: Hindutva and Its Avatars', *Australia: Somatechnics*, 8.1 (2011), pp. 138–60. S. Thobani, 'Alt-Right with the Hindu-Right: Long-Distance Nationalism and the Perfection of Hindutva', *Ethnic and Racial Studies*, 42.5 (2019), pp. 745–62.
3 See, for example, P. Church Gibson, 'Imaginary Landscapes, Jumbled Topographies: Cinematic London', in *London: From Punk to Blair*, ed. J. Kerr and A. Gibson (London: Reaktion Books, 2003), pp. 363–9. R. Murphy, 'Citylife: Urban Fairy-tales in Late 90s British Cinema', in *The British Cinema Book*,

ed. R. Murphy, 3rd ed. (London: British Film Institute, 2009), pp. 357–65. R. Masrani, 'The Reel City: London, Symbolic Power and Cinema' (PhD thesis, London School of Economics, 2016), http://etheses.lse.ac.uk/3342/1/Masrani_The_Reel_City.pdf. Charlotte Brunsdon, *London in Cinema: The Cinematic City since 1945* (London: The British Film Institute, 2007).

4 Gibson, 'Imaginary Landscapes, Jumbled Topographies', p. 365.
5 Masrani, 'The Reel City', pp. 234–5.
6 M. Georgiou, 'Is London Open? Mediating and Ordering Cosmopolitanism in Crisis', *International Communication Gazette*, 79 (2017), p. 223.
7 S. Sassen, *The Global City* (Princeton, NJ: Princeton University Press, 1991).
8 Masrani, 'The Reel City', p. 237.
9 T. Sevcik, 'Strategic Urban Narratives: Beyond Conventional City Branding', *Development*, 54 (2011), p. 344.
10 B. M. Josiam et al., 'Namastey London: Bollywood Movies and Their Impact on How Indians Perceive European Destinations', *Hospitality Review*, 31.3 (2014), p. 6.
11 A. Jansson, 'Spatial Phantasmagoria: The Mediatization of Tourism Experience', *European Journal of Communication*, 17.4 (2002), DOI:10.1177/02673231020170040201.
12 S. Reijnders, 'On the Trail of 007: Media Pilgrimages into the World of James Bond', *Area 42*, 3 (2010), p. 371.
13 Masrani, 'The Reel City', p. 232.
14 P. Vohra, 'Indian Movies Attract Millions around the World – and That Number Looks Set to Grow', *CNBC.com* (3 August 2018), https://bit.ly/3oOtIxf (accessed 4 February 2020).
15 Ibid.
16 Ibid.
17 A. Takhar, P. Mclaran and L. Stevens, 'Bollywood Cinema's Global Reach: Consuming the "Diasporic Consciousness"', *Journal of Macromarketing*, 32.3 (2012), p. 267.
18 Takhar et al., 'Bollywood Cinema's Global Reach', pp. 267, 277.
19 Dudrah, p. 82.
20 S. Shankar, 'India's Liberal Expats Are Modi's Biggest Fans', *Foreign Policy* (7 May 2019), https://foreignpolicy.com/2019/05/07/indias-liberal-expats-are-modis-biggest-fans/ (accessed 14 April 2020).
21 S. Banaji, *Children and Media in India: Narratives of Class, Agency and Social Change* (London and New York: Routledge, 2017). S. Banaji, *Reading 'Bollywood': The Young Audience and Hindi Films* (Basingstoke: Palgrave, 2006). Banaji, 'Vigilante Publics'.
22 H. S. Mann, 'Cultural Representations of London in British-Asian and Bollywood Films', *Quarterly Review of Film and Video*, 31.5 (2014), p. 488.
23 S. Hall, 'The Spectacle of the "Other"', in *Representation: Cultural Representations and Signifying Practices* (London: Sage, 1997), p. 257.
24 Ibid.

25 R. Barthes, trans. Annette Lavers, *Mythologies* (London: Vintage, 2009 [1957]). N. Fairclough, *Language and Power*, 3rd ed. (London and New York: Routledge, 2015).
26 G. Rose, *Visual Methodologies: An Introduction to Researching with Visual Methods* (London: Sage, 2007), p. 142.
27 S. Chatterji, 'Guest Iin London Movie Review: Paresh Rawal and Kartik Aaryan's Film Is Beyond Redemption', *NDTV* (20 March 2019), http://bit.ly/3K9jwYf; londonalice, 'Londonist Film Club: Namastey London', *Londonist* (26 April 2009), https://londonist.com/2009/04/londonist_film_club_namastey_london (accessed 3 May 2020).
28 The sequence was actually shot at Brighton station.
29 www.youtube.com/watch?v=yYdmRnGbNPw (accessed 20 May 2020).
30 See N. Sud, 'Tracing the Links between Hindu Nationalism and the Indian Diaspora', *St Antony's International Review*, 3.2 (2008), pp. 50–65. S. Daniyal, 'BJP Is Leveraging Its Impressive Hindu Diaspora Network to Influence Politics in UK, US and Canada', *Scroll.in* (16 November 2019), http://bit.ly/3ndXn1N (accessed 4 June 2020).
31 Masrani, 'The Reel City', p. 123.
32 Banaji, *Children and Media in India* and Banaji, *Reading 'Bollywood'*.

7

Brazucas on screen: the Brazilian diaspora in London as depicted in Henrique Goldman's *Jean Charles*

Stephanie Dennison

Brazil, as a former colony in South America and part of the New World, has always been identified as a place that people emigrate to, rather than emigrate from: a 'country of destination' in the eyes of the Organisation for Economic and Co-operative Development.[1] Yet Brazil's most recent census (2011) counted more than 670,000 Brazilians living abroad, while figures from the Brazilian Ministry of Foreign Affairs in 2008 estimated the true number to be more than two million.[2] A total of 99,000 Brazilians emigrated to OECD countries in 2017 alone, and in 2018 the number of Brazilians leaving Brazil to live abroad was double the number of immigrants into the country.[3]

Despite an exponential increase in the number of Brazilians leaving their country of origin to seek employment and study opportunities abroad since the 1980s, there are very few fictional representations of this emerging Brazilian diaspora, either in print or in audio-visual media. The lack of audio-visual representation of Brazilians abroad can only partly be explained by the challenges facing Brazilian filmmakers who wish to film outside of Brazil. Making international co-productions without the support of a formal audio-visual co-production treaty is challenging, to say the least, and director Henrique Goldman has acknowledged these challenges in relation to the production of his London-based movie *Jean Charles*. The UK–Brazil audio-visual co-production treaty was signed in 2012 as part of a series of Olympic handover activities but it was only ratified in 2017. This explains why the one other Brazil–UK fictional feature film of note, *Trash: A Esperança Vem do Lixo* (*Trash*, dir. Stephen Daldry and Christian Duurvoort, 2014) brought on board a German producer to facilitate with bureaucracy.[4] Even where formal co-production treaties exist, film business can be hard to conduct because of bureaucratic constraints.[5]

One might assume, then, that it is only movements of peoples *into* Brazil, whether forced via the Atlantic slave trade (until as late as 1850) or as part of sizeable emigratory waves in the nineteenth century (mostly from Europe) and the twentieth (with notable communities of Syrians, Lebanese, Japanese and Koreans making their mark on cities like São Paulo, for example), that have impacted on questions relating to Brazil's national identity within audio-visual culture. But even here the numbers of filmic representations are not considerable.[6] In contrast, there has been a sustained interest on the part of Brazilian filmmakers in depicting the considerable *internal* migration from the rural, drought-ridden and under-resourced north-east and north of the country to the more urban and economically well-off south-eastern region (Rio, São Paulo and surrounding areas) that has characterised Brazilian society since at least the 1940s.

Even with increasing investment on the part of the Brazilian film industry in international co-productions, which are by their nature more likely to support storylines involving more than one country, one can count on the fingers of one hand the significant films that have emerged in which Brazilian characters engage meaningfully with and reflect on life beyond Brazil's borders. By far the most cited of these films is Walter Salles and Daniela Thomas's Brazil–Portugal co-production *Terra Estrangeira* (*Foreign Land*, 1996) a film whose main focus is the lives of Brazilians forced by economic necessity to flee to Portugal in the early 1990s, where they swap the dream of a life beyond Brazil for one of 'underemployed immigrant existing on the margins in an inglorious adventure'.[7] The second most cited of these fictional interpretations of the Brazilian experience abroad is José Joffily's *Dois Perdidos Numa Noite Suja* (*Two Lost in a Dirty Night*, 2002), the adaptation of a play originally set in Brazil but transposed on screen to New York's underworld. While it is a fascinating exploration of questions of identity, *Dois Perdidos* features only two Brazilians (the two leads) and it therefore does not, in fact, examine the life experiences of the wider Brazilian community in New York or the United States more broadly. Henrique Goldman's UK–Brazil co-production *Jean Charles* is the only fictional feature film to document the lives of a group of Brazilian immigrants abroad. This snapshot of a community is constructed around the true story of Jean Charles de Menezes, the Brazilian who in 2005 was killed in London's Stockwell Tube station when he was mistaken by police for a terror suspect.

What *Jean Charles* shares with *Terra Estrangeira* and *Dois Perdidos Numa Noite Suja* is a refusal to shy away from the question of illegality: it is worth noting that even in the more substantial body of fiction in print form, there is little discussion of illegal Brazilian immigration.[8] This is mirrored in social science research, where it is acknowledged that firm data on undocumented migrant workers is hard to come by and much scholarship is therefore based on guesswork.[9] As we will see, *Jean Charles* acknowledges the blurred lines between legality and illegality and how these are negotiated by Brazilian migrant workers in London. This issue is made all the more significant by the importance given to real-life Jean Charles's visa status (was he or wasn't he in London illegally?) in press reports at the time of his death.

Making *Jean Charles*

Jean Charles began as a BBC-backed project involving London-based Brazilian director Henrique Goldman and his own production company, Mango Films. After reaching the script stage, however, BBC Films withdrew from the project. The parting of company with the BBC appears to have been brought about as a result of Goldman's determination to focus on the Brazilian community in London: 'It was a really difficult relationship because I was always looking at things from the Brazilian point of view and they wanted something with an English take on things'.[10] This 'English take on things' would have been a focus on the holding to account of the Metropolitan Police and their role in the death of Jean Charles. Changes in personnel at BBC Films and potential legal issues (the case against the Metropolitan Police was still ongoing at the time) were also blamed for the project stalling in 2006. The same year, the *Panorama* documentary 'Stockwell: Countdown to Killing' (dir. Peter Taylor) appeared to take care of the BBC's desire to tell the story of the killing of Jean Charles by concentrating exclusively on the actions of the police.[11] After parting company with the BBC, but keeping Stephen Frears as Executive Producer, Goldman rewrote the script, together with London-based Brazilian scriptwriter Marcelo Starobinas, to concentrate exclusively on Brazilian characters.[12] It is interesting to note that the working title of Goldman's film, until just months before its release, was *Brazucas*, a slang term used to refer to Brazilians abroad.[13]

In order to draw from their experiences of life in London, both Henrique Goldman and later actor Selton Melo, who plays Jean Charles, spent time with the London-based friends and members of Jean Charles's family. With the exception of Selton Melo, Vanessa Giacomo (cousin Vivian) and Luis Miranda (cousin Alex), the Brazilians who appear in the film were recruited from among London's Brazilian community, and their interactions with the main characters therefore bring a documentary feel to the film, which situates the film within a tradition of using social realism to depict the immigrant experience.[14] Jean Charles's cousin and flatmate Patricia Armani and one-time boss and friend Mauricio Varlotta both play themselves in the film, to good effect.

Brazilians in London

There are an estimated 200,000 Brazilians resident in the UK, with the vast majority residing and working in London. The small but nevertheless useful amount of research carried out on this burgeoning diaspora divides migration from Brazil into two waves.[15] The first, smaller wave was made up of mostly middle-class Brazilians who could afford the expense of the transatlantic flight to London and who came predominantly to study English, take postgraduate qualifications or as a kind of 'gap year', to work in restaurants, for example, and then travel through Europe. Henrique Goldman himself was part of the earlier 'professional' emigratory wave, arriving in London in 1992. Goldman has dual nationality through marriage and continues to work in both the UK and Brazil.

The second wave, taking place after both credit and specifically air travel had become more accessible to Brazil's lower-middle and skilled working classes, consisted mostly of young men and women seeking greater opportunities to make money. Many Brazilians in London experience 'occupational downgrade' and tend to work in the gig economy, for example as motorcycle couriers delivering food.[16] The Brazilian *motoboys*, as they are known, were the focus of an article in Brazilian daily *O Globo* after one was murdered in London in 2019.[17] These 'second-wave' Brazilians largely do not figure in the UK Census because they are either temporary residents, working illegally or both. The real-life Jean Charles came to the UK in 2002 as part of the second wave, after failing to secure a visa to enter the United States. This failure may well be linked to the fact that Jean Charles was from Gonzaga, a small town in the state of Minas Gerais which lies within the metropolitan area of Governador Valadares, a city notorious for the number of citizens who emigrated, most often illegally, to the United States.

Under a reciprocal agreement Brazilians can enter the UK as tourists for up to six months without a visa. As well as those who overstay and work on tourist visas, some Brazilians travel to London and work legally with European passports acquired by virtue of Portuguese, Italian, Spanish and German ancestry, for example, and thus are not registered as Brazilian upon entry.[18] Most are subsumed into the UK Census's unhelpful 'white other' racial and ethnic category. Despite the size of the community (one of London's largest minority groups) there has been relatively little research carried out on them, especially if we compare this to the growing body of work on Brazilians in the USA.[19] The film *Jean Charles* serves as a useful document for understanding the London-based Brazilian diaspora and, as we will see, many of the details of the protagonists' daily lives are corroborated by the (admittedly scant) scholarship on this community.

The Brazilian community in *Jean Charles*

Jean Charles opens with an extreme close-up of the face of a nervous-looking young woman. We hear two voices off-camera: first, the voice of what is quickly understood to be an immigration official speaking English and then a Brazilian interpreter speaking Portuguese. While the officer utters politely worded questions about intentions, finances and so on to the young woman he addresses as Vivian (played by Vanessa Giacomo), the interpreter goes off script, asking her if she thinks they are stupid and threatening her with three months in jail if she does not tell the truth. At this point the camera pulls back to reveal the arrival in the room of Vivian's cousin, Jean Charles (Selton Melo), who in fluent English explains how Vivian has come temporarily to help his wife, after their baby, of whom he has a photo on hand to show the immigration official, was born prematurely. As the officer stamps Vivian's passport, Jean Charles effusively thanks him. Cut to outside the airport: 'The English are really thick', laughs Jean Charles, as he proceeds to coach Vivian in telling well-told lies, in order to survive the 'brutal system' in London (Jean Charles is neither married nor has a child). It is only then that the spectators are 'situated' within London: we see conventional iconic overhead shots of the city, the touristic capital, as the film credits run, including the River Thames, Trafalgar Square, the Houses of Parliament, the London Eye and the West End. Thus, in the first four minutes of *Jean Charles*, Goldman establishes the key themes of his movie: the focus on survival strategies of Brazilians within a 'brutal' system; questions of language and identity, and in particular, the place of Portuguese as a marker of Brazilianness for Brazilians abroad; the role of lies and deception in the unfolding story; and iconic London as removed from the experiences of immigrant workers in the UK.

In the film, Vivian's professional status shifts from dental secretary back home in Gonzaga to informal work cleaning toilets and serving food in a café run by a racist Italian couple.[20] Jean Charles is a qualified electrician and that is the profession he pursues in London. He works mostly with other Brazilians, and occasionally with other members of London's immigrant communities (predominantly South Asians). When he is down on his luck, he is prepared to take on any paid work, such as cleaning taxis in the early hours and distributing leaflets advertising Brazilian businesses. When questioned about this, he repeats his earlier statement made to Vivian: 'o sistema é bruto' (the system here is brutal). The Brazilians we see are mostly male, none are marked as being in a relationship (other than with partners back home in Brazil) and frequent reference is made to sending money home to support their families.[21] Maintaining links with Brazil and in particular family back home is emphasised by regular telephone calls. The characters' working lives, then, share little in common with the lives of characters in the films cited by Thomas Elsaesser as depicting global cities, wherein migrants occupy interstitial spaces and are caught up in criminal subcultures involving drugs, sex, human trafficking and organ transplants.[22] Elsaesser was likely referring first and foremost to Steven Frears's *Dirty Pretty Things* (2002), one of the most cited films to depict immigration to London, and one which takes as its focus the work of migrants, specifically within the hospitality industry, as 3D (dangerous, dirty and demeaning).[23]

After Jean Charles gives Vivian her 'first lesson' on life in London at the airport on her arrival (how to lie effectively), she is offered practical advice on crossing the road (the importance of looking left) and finding her way round an English kitchen (this is a kettle; this is a George Forman; no one cooks here so use the microwave). After settling into the small but comfortable flat that Jean Charles shares with two cousins (Patricia and Alex), Vivian heads out into the London streets with Jean Charles. In a scene typical of Goldman's take on life for Brazilians in London, actor Selton Melo strikes up spontaneous conversations, always in Portuguese, with real-life Brazilians working in the centre of London as motorcycle couriers and selling Brazilian street food. Vivian comments that London is full of Brazilians. Jean Charles replies that Brazilians are like Gremlins: throw some water and 300 more appear.

The idea of home-away-from-home is further captured in *Jean Charles* when Vivian bumps into a neighbour from her village back home. While this is not articulated directly, one gets a clear sense that in London this neighbour has the freedom to explore his sexuality that he could not have enjoyed in the conservative state of Minas Gerais: in London he can wear tight, cropped t-shirts, is comfortable holding hands with his male partner in the street and works in a sex shop. The comparative sexual conservatism of life back home is highlighted more directly in the film by Jean Charles's reaction of displeasure when Vivian returns to the flat at daybreak after a night out with a male friend from work.

The tropes and clichés with which Brazilians are frequently associated and through which they frequently forge links with host communities (capoeira, Brazilian jujitsu, carnival and samba, and Brazilian evangelical churches with global reach such as the Universal Church of the Kingdom of God, for example) are missing from this account of Brazilians in London. In their place we have references to more kitsch cultural expressions associated in Brazil with the so-called emerging class (frequently dismissed as having money but no taste), such as popular foodstuffs (*pão de queijo, brigadeiro, goiabada*), the much-maligned but ever-popular *brega* music style, as witnessed in the performance of real-life star Sidney

Magal, oversized plasma television sets and even a *suruba*: an orgy/party thrown by Jean Charles's Brazilian boss for his Brazilian workers to celebrate securing a valuable contract.

The storyline in *Jean Charles* makes clear that, despite being one of the world's top tourist destinations, the Brazilian main characters struggle to relate to London as anything other than a place of work. Jean Charles and his cousins' one attempt in the film to socialise together and enjoy some sightseeing (on London's South Bank) proves to be disastrous: having convinced a depressed Vivian to come out on her day off, she and Jean Charles end up arguing, with Vivian declaring that, far from living the dream, London is a shit city ('merda de cidade') where she earns a pittance.

Despite the ease with which Brazilian characters interact in Portuguese with fellow Brazilians, the importance of learning English is underscored throughout the film. Vivian is at a marked disadvantage compared with Jean Charles when she arrives at the airport in the opening scene. Jean Charles himself is dismissive of Brazilians who work all day, never go out and thus do not learn English. Vivian is almost turned down for work that Jean Charles had secured for her in a café because, in the words of the unfriendly Italian café owner, 'she doesn't speak a word of English'. She does move on to a better position as a waitress on a boat-bar on the Thames and it is implied that this is due to her investing in English lessons. Vivian's ability to feel settled, gain less degrading employment and appreciate what London has to offer is ultimately determined by her acquisition of English (she is depicted as taking her English lessons seriously and she allows herself a moment of sightseeing pleasure when finishing her shift on the boat-bar on the Thames).

It is interesting to note that the Brazilian community depicted in London in *Jean Charles* is largely autonomous: we see no interaction, for example, with Spanish-speaking members of London's sizeable Latin American community, into which Brazilians are frequently lumped for auditing purposes.[24] Jean Charles and Vivian both communicate with the Italian café owner in English rather than Portuguese, despite the linguistic similarities between the two romance languages. In the film, Jean Charles speaks English only to work clients, none of whom is a native speaker. The only time Vivian is seen mixing with native English speakers is while serving them, being taught English by them or being informed by them of her cousin's death. Significantly, Jean Charles and his cousins are clearly marked in the film as not acculturated into the wider community of 'Londoners'.[25] This is made manifest through the manner in which they react and relate to the London 7/7 bombings in 2005, being initially dismissive of their effect on their daily lives and viewing the impact of the bombs via television news media reports. Even when they are directly caught up in the aftermath of the terror bombings, they are forever 'othered' in the city through the erroneous associations made between them and the terrorists.

Jean Charles goes some way towards demystifying the notion of legality/illegality within the Brazilian diaspora. The director, Goldman, has openly acknowledged that he spent three years living and working illegally in the United States in the 1980s, and marrying in order to secure a Green Card, before moving to Rome and then London.[26] Jean Charles's visa status is brought into question already in the opening scene of the film: he claims that the permanent leave-to-remain stamp in his passport was acquired through marriage to a British citizen. Jean Charles serves as a kind of informal trafficker in the film, having facilitated the migration of three cousins to London, which also demonstrates the extent to which familial and personal ties influence mobility and make London a de facto home, an adopted place where their Brazilian enclave thrives and coexists in this megacity. He is approached by two workmates who have heard that he could arrange permanent visas, thus giving the clear impression that he has carried out this illegal activity before. He uses a Brazilian contact, Cleusa, operating at the back of a Brazilian beauty salon, but, having taken the workmates' passports and their cash, she disappears, possibly as a result of being arrested.

Selton Melo had come to the role of Jean Charles fresh from his success playing a real-life middle-class cocaine dealer and lovable rogue in *Meu Nome Não É Johnny* (My name ain't Johnny; dir. Mauro Lima, 2008). Despite the fact that the real-life Jean Charles was said to have been shy, unassuming and quietly spoken, Melo's version of the character, like 'Johnny', oozes charm and is supremely confident and at ease in social situations. At one point, having negotiated a lucrative contract to refurbish a restaurant from under the nose of his employer, he dons a smart coat and Bluetooth and struts through the streets, catching the eye of female passers-by.

> In his wily way, he reps the best and brightest of the immigrant spirit: His endless resourcefulness, his genuine love for his adopted home of London, his embrace of the English language (he scoffs at those who don't even try to learn it) and his sky's-the-limit belief in individual potential are qualities to be admired.[27]

The way Jean Charles operates, erasing the lines between the institutional and/or professional and the personal, or to put it another way, between the public and the private, is reminiscent of the concept of *cordialidade* (cordiality), a mainstay in theories of Brazilian cultural identity. According to the theory of cordiality, elaborated by historian Sérgio Buarque de Holanda, Brazilians personalise relationships in the public sphere as they would in the private, and in so doing create a veneer of friendliness and intimacy.[28] Everyone that Jean Charles does business with is superficially treated as a close friend.

Jean Charles's problem solving also could be seen as reflecting typically Brazilian tropes, and in particular the interrelated concepts of the *jeitinho*, *permuta* and *malandragem*, all of which suggest varying degrees of rule bending to get a result.[29] Jean Charles applies the concept of *jeitinho* (quick fix) when he uses his electrical skills to save a show in which real-life singer Sidney Magal is due to perform.[30] He demonstrates *permuta* (exchanging services for payment) when he offers to fix things in the Bar Bruno café in exchange for employment for Vivian, and then when he offers to sort two workmates' visas if they come and work for him on the refurbishment of the Indian restaurant. His tricking of the Italian owners of the Bar Bruno into employing Vivian in the first place (when she couldn't speak English), as well as his deception of his boss in order to gain the Indian restaurant contract, are both examples of his *malandragem* (a kind of wide-boy trickery).

Friendly veneers can slip, of course, and as Buarque de Holanda warns, the origin of the term cordiality is *cordis*, from the heart, pointing to the potential exploding of emotions. In the course of the film Jean Charles's behaviour results in him going from 'o cara' (the main man) to 'moleque' (scoundrel) when the disgruntled workmates lose their passports and get their revenge by destroying the newly inaugurated Indian restaurant, and when Mauricio finds out he betrayed him.

Jean Charles and London's war on terror

In July 2005 London was on high alert, as a result of a series of bombs which exploded on Underground trains and a bus in Bloomsbury in a coordinated attack by Islamist suicide bombers, resulting in 52 deaths and over 700 injuries.

> The atmosphere of fear for those living and working in the capital cannot be over-estimated. The United Kingdom had never experienced suicide bombings, but within 24 hours of the widespread joy felt in the capital of London being selected as the city to host the 2012 Olympic Games there was a state of fear and panic.[31]

In *Jean Charles* shots of tourists in Trafalgar Square cut to a familiar scene of pigeons, which fly off in reaction to a barely perceptible bang. It then transpires that the bang was one of the 7th July bomb blasts (on a bus in nearby Tavistock Square). We are made aware of this because Vivian receives a call on her mobile phone while at work from family in Brazil asking if she is OK. The details of the bombings, and the failed follow-up bombings two weeks later, are relayed via real TV news footage. Rather than an atmosphere of fear, then, life carries on as normal for the cousins, other than having to rethink their journey home from work because of the disruption to the Underground. While watching the news at home, Vivian distractedly flirts with her boyfriend on the phone and the other cousins tuck into their TV dinners on trays on their laps. The only commentary, other than from police and politicians on the TV, comes from Alex, in a reference to Iraq: England should not have got involved in a war that wasn't theirs to fight, he says: 'They have their eye on their oil. They're hypocrites'.

It is only two-thirds of the way through the film that the focus shifts to the events leading to Jean Charles's death, with a recreation of his final movements: arriving at Brixton Tube station; discovering it is closed; hopping on a bus, and then descending the escalator at Stockwell. It is made manifest in the film that we are gearing up to Jean Charles's tragic end through the use of British Indian composer Nitin Sawhney's haunting extra-diegetic score. The handheld camera that has accompanied Jean Charles's passage through London throughout the film now swaps between shots of him from behind (we are made aware both that he is being followed and by whom) and those that show others' reactions to him, suggesting both an increased wariness on the part of the public and a hint at the suspicion with which he and other Brazilians are potentially observed by others in the city. Jean Charles is unaware that he is being both observed by fellow passengers and followed by members of the Met and actor Selton Melo does an effective job of demonstrating this. In what must be a conscious effort to dispel widely held beliefs propagated by the police and the media at the time of his death, Jean Charles on screen does *not* run, is *not* wearing a bulky jacket or backpack, does *not* jump the barrier and does *not* resist arrest. His last moments are captured in a point-of-view shot from his position on the floor of the carriage, having been repeatedly shot, before a brief fade to black, to be replaced by a CCTV image of an empty carriage apart from Jean Charles's dead body.

Audio reports in different languages confirming that a man has been killed are played over slow-motion images of Londoners (the majority non-white) moving through the city. The effect of the scene is twofold: the city of London is marginally slowed down (but not halted) by the shooting and, in the words of Cressida Dick, head of the operation that led to Jean Charles's shooting, there is no guarantee that another innocent person will not be killed in the future.[32]

Jean Charles's cousins hear first about the shooting of a suspected suicide bomber via the same television news reports. The film incorporates footage of the press statement of Police Commissioner Sir Ian Blair, at the time London Metropolitan Police's highest-ranking police officer. In it, he describes the connection of the shooting with ongoing investigations into terrorist attacks in London and how the suspect had refused to obey police instructions, using carefully worded expressions such as 'the information that I have available' and 'as I understand it'. Although it was never proven in court, investigations into the shooting highlighted the likelihood that Blair was already aware of the Met's error when addressing the press in this instance.[33]

Some of those same falsehoods are repeated by the two officers tasked to explain the circumstances of Jean Charles's death to Vivian and Alex: that their relative had been under surveillance as a suspected terrorist and that he had resisted arrest. The scene to an extent mirrors the film's opening sequence in which a nervous Vivian is interrogated by a border official. On this occasion, however, both officers are white English and there is no interpreter present, resulting in one of the officers attempting to explain the word 'morgue' to Vivian and Alex and resorting to broken Spanish in order to do so ('lugar de muertos' – literally the place of dead people), making the delivery of the news particularly callous. The sense of mirroring the opening sequence of the film is further suggested if we recall Jean Charles's remarks about the British authorities: that they would believe anything and that, for lies to work, they need to be well told.

Action shifts briefly to Brazil and Jean Charles's funeral.[34] The images are accompanied only by Sawhney's melancholic music. From the funeral we cut to a visit by the British Ambassador, a representative from the Metropolitan Police and an interpreter to Jean Charles's family home in Gonzaga. The formal, rather stuffy tone adopted by the British representatives is undercut by Alex, who thanks them for their visit and for the £15,000 contribution to the funeral costs but who then, talking over the top of a startled-looking interpreter ('there's no need to translate. We don't get a translator when we're over there!'), he declares that he will return to London and go after them until they are all in prison. As we leave Gonzaga the camera pans up to a sign being installed above the main road, remembering Jean Charles and stating 'Aqui priorizamos a vida' (Here, life means something).

An intertitle informs us that three years have now passed. The final bird's-eye view of London gives way to scenes outside Stockwell Tube station. Vivian, in large dark glasses, discreetly observes the real-life permanent memorial to Jean Charles outside the station. A protest, led by a Black British man, reveals that justice has still not been served and that the fact that Jean Charles was mistaken for a Muslim points to the racism inherent in the British security forces. This is the only reference, albeit tangential, made in the film to Jean Charles's ethnicity.[35] At the time of Jean Charles's death, imperial history scholar Richard Drayton reflected thus:

> Had Africa's signature not been visible on the body of the Brazilian Jean Charles de Menezes, would he have been gunned down on a tube at Stockwell? The slight kink of the hair, his pale beige skin, broadcast something misread by police as foreign danger.[36]

Despite the fact that a member of the police surveillance team had initially identified Jean Charles, as he left his flat on Scotia Road in Tulse Hill on the morning he was shot dead, as IC1 (white), at least one other member of the team stated that he was the suspect (Jean Charles's neighbour, Ethiopian Osman Hussain). The IC codes used by British police are necessarily based on visual assessment rather than self-definition, the latter being the method used in Brazil to establish racial identity. Jean Charles's (mixed-race) cousin Alex stated, in relation to the police error, that Jean Charles was 'white, not mixed-race'.[37] The implications of the British police's inability to distinguish between a white Brazilian and a Black Ethiopian have barely been discussed in the light of Jean Charles's death.

Less than twenty minutes of the film's running time (of a total of ninety minutes) are dedicated to the events surrounding Jean Charles's death in London. The last ten minutes return the focus to the broad subject of immigration, with a bored Vivian having given up her unexciting life in Gonzaga and subsequently returning to London, but this time on her own terms, with the intention of working to travel and using London as a gateway to visit mainland Europe. The final scenes show a more confident and determined Vivian retracing Jean Charles's steps but, unlike Jean Charles, she is able to enter Brixton Tube station unobserved and, importantly, she is carrying a very large rucksack on her back. While the film's images end on a positive note, returning the focus to how Brazilians negotiate their lives abroad and stand to gain from being in places like London, it does close with a series of intertitles that update the audience on the ongoing battle to get justice for Jean Charles

Concluding remarks

One-third of *Jean Charles*'s running time is filmed on the streets of London, and as the film progresses the bird's-eye view shots and streets scenes become increasingly nondescript. On the whole, then, it is a generic city space that is captured by Goldman's lens, in which 'an overhead shot of a cityscape looks no different from the circuit board of a computer'.[38] London is equally represented as a 'city state' as defined by Keith Wagner in the introduction to this volume: there is, for example, no mention in the film of the existence of a country beyond the capital; and when Brazilians in the film leave London, it is to return home or travel in continental Europe. There are no real attempts in the film to contrast the lifestyles of Brazilians with the host community, and there is little interaction between Brazilians and non-Brazilians.

In London, Brazilians more often than not work, rest and play with other Brazilians. In *Jean Charles*, when Brazilians are exploited, it is by other Brazilians (including Jean Charles himself). When things go wrong for Jean Charles, it is as a result of his own actions (his efforts to make a quick buck by undercutting his boss and offering to procure fake passports for his workmates), and it is to his fellow Brazilians that he has to answer – until, that is, post-national forces denominated radical Islamic terrorism spoil this slice of Brazilian life in London, and he is shot dead. Herewith London becomes, after New York and Madrid, the next target of large-scale suicide bombers, both homegrown and recruited from the Middle East and North Africa. It is at this point in the film that the language focus notably shifts to (white, native-born) English, and London is transformed. Jean Charles, by dint of living next door to Muslims and not being quite white enough, becomes collateral damage in a war being waged on an international stage. The fact that the British authorities denied any wrong-doing and that no police officer was ever brought to justice over Jean Charles's death ultimately serves to make manifest the asymmetric power relations associated with global cities.[39]

Notes

1 OECD, *Latin American Economic Outlook 2010* (Paris: OECD Publishing, 2009), https://doi.org/10.1787/leo-2010-en (accessed 2 July 2019).
2 Brazilian diaspora scholar Maxine Margolis estimated that already in 2001, two million Brazilians were resident abroad: 'Involving the Brazilian Diaspora in Brazilian Studies', *Lasa Forum*, 36.2 (2005), pp. 11–12.
3 Maria Fernanda Garcia, 'Brasileiros no Exterior Em 2018 Representam o Dobro dos Imigrantes do Pais', *Observatorio do Terceiro Setor* (27 December 2018), https://bit.ly/3V4OTHf (accessed 27 March 2020).
4 Stephanie Dennison, *Remapping Brazilian Film Culture in the 21st Century* (London: Routledge, 2020), p. 174.
5 Ibid., p. 151.
6 They range from box-office successes of the 1970s such as comedian Amácio Mazzaropi's *Meu Japão Brasileiro* (My Brazilian Japan; dir. Glauco Mirko Laurelli, 1965), a light-hearted and deeply caricatured portrait of one of Brazil's largest immigrant communities in the twentieth century, to the Oscar-nominated

O quatrilho (dir. Fábio Barreto, 1995), set in the early twentieth century among Italian settlers in southern Brazil.
7 Karla Adriana Martins Bessa, 'Perdidos, Marginais e Exóticos: Uma Reflexão sobre Como a Filmografia Enquadra Alteridades e Fronteiras', *Século XXI: Revista de Ciências Sociais*, 9.1 (2019), pp. 195–222 (202). Bessa draws attention in her article to fact that on-screen Brazilians who go abroad tend not to manage to return home.
8 Claire Williams, 'Something to Declare: Illegal Immigrants in Contemporary Brazilian Literature', in *Living (Il)legalities in Brazil: Practices, Narratives and Institutions in a Country on the Edge*, ed. Sara Brandellero, Derek Pardue and Georg Wink (London and New York: Routledge, 2019), pp. 144–59 (144). José Joffily's 2009 film *Olhos Azuis* (Blue eyes) deals with illegal immigration through the eyes of an airport border official.
9 International Organisation for Migration Data Portal, available at www.migrationdataportal.org/; see also Michael Samers, 'Immigration and the Global City Hypothesis: Towards and Alternative Research Agenda', in *Global Cities Reader*, ed. Neil Brenner and Roger Keil (London and New York: Routledge, 2006), pp. 385–91.
10 Marco Aurélio Canônico, 'BBC Cancela Filme Sobre Jean Charles', *Folha de S Paulo Ilustrada* (5 February 2021), www1.folha.uol.com.br/folha/ilustrada/ult90u68186.shtml (accessed 8 August 2019).
11 Sally Stott lists three plays staged in London about Jean Charles that were produced in quick succession not long after his death. It is interesting to note that all three focus on the actions of the police: 'Why Are There So Many Plays about Jean Charles de Menezes?', *Guardian* (10 November 2009), www.theguardian.com/stage/theatreblog/2009/nov/10/stockwell-shooting-theatre-de-menezes (accessed 29 March 2020).
12 Frears directed the London-based feature on migrant workers *Dirty Pretty Things*, a BBC Films co-production, in 2002.
13 *Brazucas* was also the title of the TV series that Goldman was in negotiations with Brazil's TV Globo to make in 2011 (the series was never made).
14 Will Higbee, 'Interstitial Cityspace and the Immigrant Experience in Contemporary French Cinema', in *Global Cinematic Cities: New Landscapes of Film and Media*, ed. Johan Andersson and Lawrence Webb (London and New York: Wallflower, 2016), pp. 201–17 (201).
15 See, for example, Gustavo Dias and Angelo Martins Jr, 'The Second Brazilian Migration Wave: The Impact of Brazil's Economic and Social Changes to Current Brazilian Migration to the UK', *Século XX1: Revista de Ciências Sociais*, 8.1 (2018), pp. 112–43.
16 Angelo Martins Jr, '"Differentiated Journeys": Brazilians in London beyond Homogenising Categories of "the Migrant"', *Plural*, 37.1 (2020), pp. 114–44 (120).
17 'Morte de brasileiro expõe rotina arriscada de motoboys em Londres', *Epoca Negócios* (25 June 2017), https://bit.ly/41DphUn (accessed 21 October 2019).

18 Agência Brasil, 'Em 15 anos, 170 mil brasileiros conseguem cidadania europeia', *UOL Noticias* (26 July 2019), https://bit.ly/40I2ndb (accessed 24 October 2019).
19 Significant scholarship on Brazilians in the UK includes the following: Yara Evans, Jane Wills, Kavita Datta, Joanna Herbert, Cathy McIlwaine, Jon May, Father José Osvaldo de Araújo, Ana Carla França and Ana Paula França, *Brazilians in London: A Report for the Strangers into Citizens Campaign* (London: Queen Mary, University of London, 2007); Dias and Martins Jr, 'The Second Brazilian Migration Wave'; Martins Jr, 'Differentiated Journeys'. For the USA see, for example, the far-reaching work of Maxine Margolis: *Little Brazil: Brazilian Immigrants in New York City* (Princeton, NJ: Princeton University Press, 1994); *An Invisible Minority: Brazilians in New York City* (Boston, MA: Allyn and Bacon, 2009); and *Goodbye Brazil: Emigrés from the Land of Soccer and Samba* (Madison, WI: University of Wisconsin Press, 2013).
20 The couple's racism is aimed specifically at Muslim customers: in one instance the male owner spits on a Muslim family's food, and Vivian is expected to serve it to them. This incident ostensibly drives her to seek alternative employment.
21 In the scholarship, while remittances are an acknowledged part of the Brazilian migrant worker experience in the UK, almost equal numbers of men and women have constituted the second wave of immigration: see Evans et al., *Brazilians in London*, p. 6.
22 Thomas Elsaesser, 'In the City but Not Bounded by It: Cinema in the Global, the Generic and the Cluster City', in *Global Cinematic Cities: New Landscapes of Film and Media*, ed. Johan Andersson and Lawrence Webb (London and New York: Wallflower, 2016), pp. 19–35 (21–2).
23 See Stephen Castles, *Ethnicity and Globalization: From Migrant Worker to Transnational Citizen* (London: Sage, 2000).
24 See, for example, the No Longer Visible project of 2011: Cathy McIlwaine and Bruno Bunge, *Towards Visibility: The Latin American Community in London* (London: Queen Mary/Trust for London, n.d.), www.trustforlondon.org.uk/documents/65/Towards-Visibility-full-report_QqkSbgl.pdf. This perhaps surprising autonomy is reinforced by the lack of any reference to the Latin American community in the *Brazilians in London* report referred to above.
25 In contrast with Rachid Bouchareb's 2009 film *London River*, also set against the backdrop of the London bombings. What the two films do share is an effective use of found news footage of the bombings and their aftermath.
26 Canal Londres, 'Henrique Goldman: Diretor de Cinema', *YouTube*, www.youtube.com/watch?v=t8kxjtgNNiw (accessed 30 March 2020).
27 Justin Chung, 'Jean Charles', *Variety* (18 September 2009), https://variety.com/2009/film/markets-festivals/jean-charles-1200476062/ (accessed 2 November 2019).
28 Sérgio Buarque de Holanda, *Raízes do Brasil* (São Paulo: Editora Schwarz, 2004 [1936]).
29 For a fascinating, detailed reading of these tropes, see Georg Wink, 'Jeitinho Revisited' in *Living (Il)legalities in Brazil: Practices, Narratives and Institutions*

in a Country on the Edge, ed. Sara Brandellero, Derek Pardue and Georg Wink (Abingdon: Routledge, 2020), pp. 52–71.
30 The real-life version of this tale is not quite so dramatic: Jean Charles was called upon by a friend to fix an electrical fault at a restaurant that was about to receive a celebrity visit by the singer Zeca Pagodinho.
31 Independent Police Complaints Commission, 'Stockwell One: Investigation into the Shooting of Jean Charles Menezes at Stockwell Underground Station on 22 July 2005' (London: IPCC, 2007), http://policeauthority.org/metropolitan/downloads/scrutinites/stockwell/ipcc-one.pdf (accessed 31 March 2020).
32 In 2007 Dick was cleared of any individual blame for the death of Jean Charles. Ten years later, she was appointed Commissioner for the Met, despite protests from Jean Charles's family.
33 Blair's initial refusal both to refer the case to the Independent Police Complaints Commission and to grant access to the crime scene raised many observers' suspicions. Despite an open verdict being returned at the inquest into Jean Charles's death, Blair was only forced out of the commissioner role in 2008 due to lack of support from then London Mayor Boris Johnson. Since 2010 he has held a crossbench life peerage.
34 The scenes of Jean Charles's funeral were recreated in Paulínia in upstate Sao Paulo, then being fiercely marketed as an audio-visual production centre.
35 It is worth observing that actor Selton Melo is physically quite different from Jean Charles: bigger framed, lighter skinned and Caucasian-looking. At the same time, the multi-racial make-up of Brazil is arguably represented through the casting of Black actor Luiz Miranda to play Jean Charles's cousin Alex.
36 Richard Drayton, 'The Wealth of the West was Built on Africa's Exploitation', *Guardian* (20 August 2005), quoted in Gláucia de Oliveira Assis, 'De Gonzaga para Londres: etnicidade e preconceito na história de Jean Charles de Menezes', *Confluenze: Rivista di Estudi Iberoamericani*, 3.1 (2011), pp. 174–87 (184).
37 Marcia Maria Cruz, 'Advogada e família de Jean Charles lamentam decisão de isentar policiais pela morte do mineiro', *Estado de Minas* (31 March 2016), https://bit.ly/3V9xI7n (accessed 19 October 2019).
38 Thomas Elsaesser, 'In the City', p. 26.
39 See Saskia Sassen, *The Global City: New York, London, Tokyo* (Princeton, NJ: University of Princeton Press, 1991).

8

A critical analysis of the Nollywood film *Osuofia in London*

Uchenna Onuzulike

Introduction

This chapter aims to understand how the Nigerian movie industry, popularly known as 'Nollywood', synthesises African (Nigeria, Igbo) and Western (United Kingdom, British) cultures in the film *Osuofia in London* (Ogoro, 2003/4), within the contexts of hybridity and postcolonial theory. This study takes a critical stance on the power dynamics characterising the Global North and the Global South in film and in the media. It explores the notion of globalisation between the West and emerging countries.

Sorrells articulates globalisation as the complex web of economic, political and technological forces that have brought people, cultures, cultural products and markets, as well as beliefs, practices and ideologies, into increasingly greater proximity to and con/disjunction with one another within inequitable relations of power.[1] She also contends that globalisation is 'deeply rooted in colonial histories and discourse'[2] and creates inequitable systems, as evidenced in *Osuofia in London*. Even though *Osuofia in London* is one of the most popular and best-selling Nollywood productions and has provided the industry with its greatest opportunity for international exposure,[3] the film has not received sufficient critical analysis.

In other ways, this chapter identifies only four studies that have critically and specifically examined this film, which are Okoye's study of European ethnographic discourse and negative representations of Africa; Okome's recent reading of the film via a postcolonial lens; Kilian's comparative study of *Xala* (1974), an auteur film, and *Osuofia in London*, a video film; and my study, 'Nollywood Video Film's Impact on Nigerian and Other African Cultures and Environments'.[4] Clearly, the Western or former colonisers' ideological domination over the former colonies has not been critically explored through the lens of African, Western and hybrid practices simultaneously.

This chapter explicates power relations by utilising hybridity and postcolonial prisms simultaneously to show how the film challenges and reproduces colonial stereotypes that continue to dominate Nollywood movies. Nollywood has been a cultural phenomenon since the production in 1992 of *Living in Bondage*.[5] This film, which has been credited by many with ushering in Nollywood, was produced by Okechukwu 'Paulo' Ogunjiofor, directed by Chris Obi Rapu (as 'VocMordi') and successfully marketed by Kenneth Nnebue's NEK Video Links.[6] The movie was produced on tape (VHS) due to the high cost of celluloid and depicted Nigerian cultural and social discourse. The traditional Yoruba Travelling Theatre of the 1980s, pioneered by directors such as Chief Hubert Ogunde and his contemporary Ola Balogun, has been acknowledged as setting the stage for Nollywood. Now, Nollywood produces virtually all its movies using video and digital technologies, although sometimes celluloid is used. But *Osuofia in London* was not made on celluloid.

Osuofia in London is a comedy shot in Nigeria and in the UK, featuring Nollywood star Nkem Owoh as Osuofia. It is the type of Nollywood film which, in spite of 'its populist, local and material concerns, not only "looks back" at mainstream colonialist discourse and negative representations of Africa in popular Western media, but also manages to reciprocate colonialist gesture by proffering a popular Nigerian representation of European Otherness'.[7] In alignment with the above assertion, this chapter utilises a critical approach to explore how the film challenges Western ideology and power in the context of African, Western and hybrid practices. More generally, some of the formulations here contribute to Nollywood studies by illuminating the power dynamics of globalisation in the film between former colonisers and the formerly colonised as it explores how Igboness is produced within the cultural constraints of globalisation.

Nollywood within the context of hybridity and postcolonial theory

At the theoretical level, hybridity, which mirrors postcolonial theory, is used to guide this study. Scholars have explored hybridity in the context of postcolonial discourse.[8] In this chapter, cultural hybridity is cast as a fusion of two cultures.[9] As Kraidy articulates: 'Since hybridity involves the fusion of two hitherto relatively distinct forms, styles, or identities, cross-cultural contact, which often occurs across national borders as well as across cultural boundaries, is a requisite for hybridity'.[10] It is also a part of postcolonial theory, where colonised cultures meld with the colonisers' culture. Haynes agrees with Barber, who states that, 'in the "postcolonial" theory developed principally in the West, cultural hybridity and transnational networks are celebrated as positive'.[11] Hybridity is a vital premise of postcolonial studies. As Kraidy observes:

> The postcolonial turn took up hybridity as a central dimension of the literary and cultural productions of Africa, Latin America, Asia, and diasporas in the West. Standing on the shoulders of the disciplines that debated syncretism, mestizaje, and creolisation, postcolonial theory re-popularised the term 'hybridity' to explicate cultural fusion.[12]

This statement suggests that the postcolonial existence of hybridity is essential to understanding how former colonised countries and their diasporas shape their cultures and identities. Nollywood serves as an example of hybridity. Even though the notion of hybridity 'come[s] together in the production of colonial legacies and practices', Nollywood as cultural hybridity has also created an avenue for colonised societies to tell their stories.[13]

Similarly, cultural hybridity can provide a pertinent tool for addressing transnational dialectics in intercultural communication.[14] The intercultural dialogue in *Osuofia in London* (between the Igbo/African and the British) is primarily fluid and uneven. Hence, the implication of power for relations of hybridity is acknowledged here. In terms of the politics of hybridity, Pieterse argues:

> Relations of power and hegemony are inscribed and reproduced within hybridity for wherever we look closely enough we find the traces of asymmetry in culture, place, [and] descent. Hence, hybridity raises the question of the terms of mixture, the conditions of mixing. At the same time, it's important to note the ways in which hegemony is not merely reproduced but refigured in the process of hybridization.[15]

This statement indicates that hybridity is uneven because it shows that when two cultures are combined, one tends to dominate the other, as evidenced in *Osuofia in London*. Okome argues that 'this film [*Osuofia in London*] fights the notion that is fashionable in some quarters that popular arts cannot be pressed to yield any sustained critique of the postcolonial condition because of the rowdiness of their uncritical push toward hybridity'.[16] He further articulates that '*Osuofia in London* offers a critical reading of the pro-filmic world from a postcolonial standpoint.'[17] In support of the above two assertions, I further argue that the film represents an ideal Africanist who wants their cultural heritage and identity to be acknowledged across the globe in the age of globalisation. It undermines the behaviour of Africans and their descendants who are in denial of their heritage and identity in relation to hybridity. Also, hybridity fits with the globalisation discourse of uncontrolled 'economic exchanges and the supposedly inevitable transformation of all cultures'.[18]

Some previous studies have connected Nollywood with hybridity.[19] Okome argues that while Nollywood exhibits hybrid characters that are evidenced in numerous 'forms of African popular arts, it is its acute notation of locality that gives unprecedented acceptability as the local cinematic expression in Nigeria and indeed in Africa'.[20] This statement shows that, just like other African arts, the mixture of Nollywood cinematic elements with non-African elements gives rise to irresistible hybridity, especially when it exhibits an African indigenous flavour. Möller claims that 'combining elements of traveling-theater film, telenovellas, Bollywood, Hong Kong, and Nigerian theater and TV (with their professionally trained actors), video films are strange and fascinating hybrids'.[21] He notes that Nollywood is adaptable and ready to incorporate a wide variety of cinematic practices, while using and transforming any new concepts that venture its way.

Elsewhere, I contend that the cultural hybridity of Nollywood is evident in the mixture of African and Western cultures found in Nollywood video films.[22] I also note that the hybridisation of traditional religions (cultures) and Christianity occurs in the films. In other words, a mixture of African traditional beliefs and Christian dogma are present in some Nigerian movies. Nollywood provides one avenue for Africans in the diaspora to keep in touch with their home cultures. Hybrid Nollywood movies function as a transnational practice for homeland and diasporic filmmakers. Nollywood serves as a hybridity both within Nigeria, and more broadly within Africa, and beyond African shores. Further, to some extent Nollywood can be viewed as a tool that brings different ethnic groups together, both on screen and in the film narratives. In Africa, it brings different African ethnicities and African countries together through co-productions. Outside of Africa, it bridges different cultures through more limited co-productions. In essence, this notion of hybridity is present in *Osuofia in London*.

The concept of power in relation to traditional culture

Martin and Nakayama postulate that 'power is pervasive in communication interactions, although it is not always evident or obvious how power influences communication or what kinds of meaning are concerned'.[23] They further note: 'dominant cultural groups attempt to perpetuate their positions of privilege in many ways. However, subordinate groups can resist this domination in many ways too'.[24] Hall posits that there are three common manifestations of culture, which are worldview, values and norms. They can be influenced by external power and 'are related to each other in many ways, but one important way in which they differ from each other is in terms of their level of abstraction'.²⁵ The differences and the level of construct are explored in the analysis section. In *Osuofia in London*, the protagonist, Osuofia, uses several methods of resistance, challenging and negotiation to question the dominant power of the West, hybridity and colonialism. In the same vein, in *Osuofia in London*, the concept of power is pervasive in relation to traditional culture and how it is communicated, lived and practised.

Arguably, there are two types of power that can be associated with *Osuofia in London*. The first one is power associated with traditional culture; the second one is power associated with colonialism, Westernisation and, to an extent, globalisation. The type of power I would like to give attention to in this analysis is the latter. This is because it has heavily eroded and impacted the former. Colonialism and neocolonialism continue to impact African traditional values, as demonstrated in the analysis in the chapter. Just like each society that experienced colonialism, Nigeria 'continues to suffer the throes of cultural upheaval stemming from and trailing after centuries of British rule'.²⁶ The British Empire, other European powers and the concept of colonial superiority have contributed to the dislocation of traditional cultures of the colonised and to the creation of cultural synthesis. The concept of power and its relations to the traditional culture are evidenced in the film and are articulated in this chapter.

Film synopsis

Osuofia in London is about Osuofia, a local, poor and arrogant hunter, who is married with five daughters. His life suddenly changes when he learns that he has been named as the beneficiary of the estate of his younger brother, Donatus, who recently died in London. Osuofia and the other members of his village are excited that an illustrious son will be travelling to London; this is very uncommon in their village. Friends and family members bid farewell to him by bringing food items for him to consume in London. Osuofia travels there to meet his brother's fiancée, Samantha, in order to sign a document releasing Donatus's money – the wealth that Osuofia has inherited. Osuofia experiences culture shock, including the unavailability of his native food at a McDonald's restaurant and a cashier's rejection of Nigerian currency as payment there. Further, his host does not have a toilet that Osuofia is familiar with. He also has a troubling encounter with a leggy teenager while she sits on the stairs outside a downtown building when he criticises her miniskirt and cigarette-smoking.

Meanwhile, Ben Okafor, a second-generation British Igbo who is Donatus's accountant, has agreed to split the money with Samantha at the ratio of 10 per cent to 90 per cent, respectively. After Samantha successfully convinces Osuofia to sign the document, Ben tells her that she will instead get 10 per cent while he gets 90 per cent. An argument ensues, and Samantha grabs the document from Ben's desk, rushes downstairs and boards a waiting limousine. When she arrives at home, she pleads with Osuofia to hurriedly pack his bag and accompany her to Africa. She explains that Ben is trying to dupe him. She promises to marry him, too. They rush to the airport as Ben arrives at Donatus's residence, only to discover that Samantha and Osuofia are on their way to the airport, en route to Africa.

Arriving back at his village, Osuofia and Samantha get married with jubilant villagers in attendance. Osuofia's African first wife, Uremma, and her daughters despise Samantha, who even learns how to prepare African dishes in order to convince Osuofia to give her some of the money. As Samantha is in the process of poisoning Osuofia's food in order to get hold of the cheques, one of his daughters sees this and runs to tell her mother, Uremma. They both tell Osuofia but he argues with them, pointing out that Samantha does not have the heart to poison him. Osuofia does, however, agree to exchange the possibly poisoned food with safe food. When he gets home and starts to eat the food with excitement, he praises Samantha for being such a great cook. He suddenly pretends to fall ill and pass out. Samantha tries unsuccessfully to snatch the chequebook from his right hand. The family rushes in and Uremma accuses Samantha of killing Osuofia. He is rushed to the hospital, where the doctor unsuccessfully tries to open Osuofia's hand. Then, the doctor says that the only way to get the chequebook he has been holding so tightly since passing out is to cut Osuofia's hand off, which Samantha agrees to. As he is about to surgically remove Osuofia's hand, Osuofia jumps up and expresses his disappointment in Samantha as well as in the doctor. Samantha apologises and Osuofia agrees to give her the money she requested and throw a send-off party for her. Samantha reaches over to Osuofia and kisses him while Uremma looks on with open-mouthed bewilderment and gives a sigh of discontent. Finally, Samantha expresses her regret for what she has done and praises the people of Nigeria.

As demonstrated in this chapter, *Osuofia in London* 'makes full use of the hybrid popular language and proves that it is possible to press it to deal with serious social, political, and cultural issues'.[27] Thus, this chapter seeks to address the following research question: how does *Osuofia in London* reveal, challenge or manage power in the context of African, Western and hybrid practices?

Study design, film selection and analytical procedures

A critical approach, some influences of postcolonial theories and those of transnational theories were used to analyse *Osuofia in London*. This approach and influences call on Gramsci's method of ideological critique or analysis, which focuses on cultural power, on hegemony and particularly on how meaning upholds the social order.[28] Gramsci's 'emphasis on the creation of a popular natural hegemony is a central feature of his attempt to build a theory of social change … [on] behalf of the people'.[29]

Just like any basic, qualitative, thematic or content analysis, the analysis of *Osuofia in London* is grounded on the three platforms of (i) themes, (ii) categories and (iii) codes.[30] I purposely used three predetermined categories or concepts, namely (i) African (ii) Western and (iii) hybrid. These tenets serve as a lens through which ideological tensions between the West and developing countries are questioned, challenged and managed.

Explaining the criteria that are used to establish the boundaries of traditional, Western and hybrid cultures is necessary to understand the analysis of the film. These concepts may be intertwined to a certain degree – they are not exclusive. I would like to point out that cultures evolve and are not static, specifically in terms of notions of traditional culture. Thus, native or traditional culture consists of the ways of life that are known to Igbo people living within the context of Nigeria and the rest of Africa. Traditional culture encompasses the pre-colonial, colonial and postcolonial periods – although the word 'traditional' marks it as distinct from Western or hybrid culture. This time frame is important to bear in mind because native or traditional ways of life may have evolved over time; cultures are not stagnant. Western or colonialist culture is the culture brought upon the colonised that may continue until today through forms of neocolonialism and globalisation. Hybrid culture or hybridity is a combination of traditional culture and Western culture or ideology. This is because they are intertwined at several levels.

To understand how cultural identity is represented in Nollywood, I selected the movie *Osuofia in London* for the analysis. It is specifically about the Igbo ethnic group culture, which generally shares cultural aspects with other ethnic groups in Nigeria and Africa. The language in the film is English, with some Igbo soundbites. The selection of *Osuofia in London* represents a convenience sample because it draws upon my knowledge of available movies and my discussions with Nollywood enthusiasts and critics. Basically, *Osuofia in London* was chosen because of its hybridity and transcultural setting. Furthermore, it is one of the most popular Nollywood comedy movies, and it needs more attention.

In terms of the analytical procedures, this study uses a critical approach, supplemented by qualitative content analysis. 'Content analyses are not necessarily stand-alone designs'.[31] Content analysis is defined as 'a systematic examination of the contents of a particular body of material for the purpose of identifying patterns, themes, or biases'.[32] To select the salient themes for the study, I employed the following amended analytical procedure.[33] In the first stage (open coding), even though I had watched *Osuofia in London* several times, I viewed it three additional times in order to determine its relevance and to identify twenty-one pertinent attributes (scenes). In the second stage (axial coding), I watched the film again to identify discrete connections between attributes and sub-attributes. In the third stage (selective coding), I watched the film again to identify core attributes and develop emerging themes.

Analysis and interpretations

The film was critically read to reflect 'African/Nigerian/Igbo', 'Western/British' and 'hybrid' cultures. The following five themes emerged during the coding: (i) African/folk belief systems and Christianity; (ii) traditional Igbo attire and English garb; (iii) African/folk and Western music; (iv) African and Western food and drinks; and (v) African/traditional and modern medicine. These themes were coded for African/Nigerian/Igbo, Western/colonialist and hybrid cultural practices. The movie juxtaposes Osuofia's village of Neke Ama Nasa with London in the opening shot, with parallels between these two spheres emphasised by a narrator, who tells us about life in an African village and that in a city like London. As suggested by the film narrative, the village signifies traditional culture; Lagos, Nigeria signifies hybrid culture; and London signifies Western culture. Although *Osuofia in London* is set in Nigeria and England and thus is inherently hybrid at some level, it utilises the colonialist's language (English) and only soundbites from the native language (Igbo). In other words, 'the confrontation with the European norms and conventions of former colonial power is paradigmatic in [*Osuofia in London*] for the complexity of relationships in the postcolonial context'.[34] The film, being in English, signifies ideological dominance. It has been documented that some Igbo children do not speak Igbo. Even though parents have been blamed for failing to pass down some elements of their cultural heritage to their children, one should not forget the impact of colonialism and neocolonialism that continues to affect the culture and the people of Africa.[35]

African/folk belief systems and Christianity

African indigenous practices in the movie signify traditional culture, although churches in Nigeria are hybrid. Missionaries introduced Christianity to Nigeria but since the church is Nigerian, the members are predominantly Nigerians, and it has been Africanised. An example of the Africanisation of churches in Nigeria is the utilisation of African musical instruments and languages for services.

Osuofia's oracle can be perceived as involving both traditional and hybrid cultures. Because it involves folk beliefs, it is considered African. On the other hand, because it has crossed overseas, it could be regarded as hybrid. Performing the acts of African traditions in a foreign land may not carry the same effect as if they were carried out in Africa. Even though the film may not have elements of vivid religious significance, they are embedded in the film, as portrayed in dressing in Igbo traditional attire and the Christian wedding ceremony at Osuofia's village. As Mbiti articulates, religion is embedded in the culture and in the people of African societies.[36] However, it varies based on demographic orientation. Regardless of the variation, in the eastern part of Nigeria where the Igbo (and Osuofia) live, Christianity is dominant and the majority of the people there are Christian.[37] Since the arrival of the missionaries, Christianity has impacted African traditional belief systems. Even though Christianity has been hybridised, the imbalance of power involved is clear: African elements are superimposed upon the Western-based religion.

Traditional Igbo attire and English garb

During Osuofia's wedding with Samantha, both are dressed in English garb. Samantha wears a wedding gown while Osuofia wears a wedding suit. However, there are several traditional and hybrid practices evident in the ceremony. First, the festivity starts with Osuofia and Samantha dancing in the street along with other villagers in celebration of the wedding. The crowd is dressed mainly in traditional Igbo attire. In addition, there are other aesthetic elements – such as music – that signify Igbo culture. The presentation of the wedding signals that cultures can be mixed in a haphazard fashion. Similarly, Okome notes in his analysis of the film:

> There is a lot to say about the paralinguistic coding of Osuofia's traditional Igbo attire, which he adorns proudly when he visits the lawyer, Ben Okafor, for the first time. Complete with the red cap that is the privilege of chiefs, his costume serves as the counterpoint to that of the lawyer, who is in a European suit.[38]

This statement supports the significance of Igbo cultural attire in the film as an assertion of identity. The notion of attire as a means for representing consciousness of one's self is articulated by Okome as follows:

> In London, the cultural politics, which his attire elicits, is radically different. He is no longer the bearer of the ways of the English. This conscious display of his 'Igboness' in London is, I would argue, a reiteration of his cultural well-being. In this cultural frame, he is no longer himself. He does not represent himself. He represents something more and other than himself. He is an assertion, a cultural assertion. In this sense, Osuofia's performance of culture, especially during this meeting with Ben Okafor, demonstrates the politics of cultural reproduction of homeland. A postcolonial subject, Osuofia recognizes the national culture as his social and cultural anchor.[39]

Osuofia, by asserting his Igboness through various means in this film, represents more than himself: he represents his ethnicity (Igbo), his nation (Nigeria) and his continent (Africa). Nonetheless, Western clothing increasingly continues to be the norm for the people of Africa. For example, at the annual Africa Movie Academy Awards (AMAA), the majority of the actors and other stakeholders dress in Western garb even though the event is held in Africa. This action signifies the dominant power exhibited by Western culture.

African/folk music and Western music

The opening score of the film represents traditional music (with the sound of drums). The Pidgin English songs represent hybrid culture, while English songs represent Western culture. However, the reggae music can be classified as hybrid because it uses African and Western instruments and the musicians are the descendants of enslaved Africans in Jamaica. Jamaican reggae is music based on African roots; it is noteworthy that these Jamaican singers are Black. Also exhibiting hybridity, traditional African folk rhythms are used to support Western forms/genres of music while, conversely, Igbo musicians have obviously borrowed some Western instruments. The power of the West again permeates and dominates on this level of hybridity because it is not uncommon for some contemporary African musicians to sing in the colonisers' languages.

However, Okoye views the traditional drum music from another perspective. He contends: 'The musical background for the opening credits of *Osuofia* is indeed evocative of "a wild barbaric nature." To a large extent the same order obtains in the very early part, as well as in the chorus, of the musical background of *Sanders of the River*.'[40] Further, he argues that one should wonder whether the chorus line 'Aiokooo egede-e', other than sounding 'wild barbaric', means anything in any Nigerian language.[41] Okoye bases his argument on the manner in which colonialists have characterised Africa. Is the characterisation of Africa by the West still practised? Is Ogoro (the film's director) trying to illuminate present-day Africa or is he basically repeating the same discourse of the colonialists?

If African music is tagged as a music that has 'a wild barbaric nature',[42] we should look to the concepts of hybridity and globalisation, and then articulate the style of music that is thriving the most or that the world is bound to imitate. It can be argued that not everyone accepts this characterisation of African music, which is nevertheless emulated and transmitted across the globe. The so-called 'jungle sound' might not sound strange to those Africans who lived or are still living in the traditional culture. The main thing is to create or recreate a discourse that will change the meaning of the dominant discourse created by the West in a way that promotes the maintenance of Igbo values and culture. It is difficult for individuals to fully separate themselves from colonial practices (power) while trying to preserve traditional culture.

African and Western foods and drinks

The traditional food that was prepared in the village represents African culture. The McDonald's food chain is Western because it does not have Osuofia's traditional food. It also represents globalisation – the new global culture. The manner in which Samantha prepares the native food could be regarded as African, Western or hybrid. Based on the conceptualisation and definitions of the above words, it shows that the food and recipes are native while the scene is hybrid since Samantha speaks English and some Igbo words.

Concerning drinks, palm wine in the village represents traditional culture. The liquor (e.g. Schnapps) represents Western culture and power. For example, Osuofia tells a local palm wine seller that when he returns from London, she will cease to sell palm wine in favour of liquor. Although this fits within the three aspects of cultural film analysis, Osuofia is implying that local wines are less precious than foreign ones. In other words, he perceives Western wines as superior to African wines. This indicates the ideological domination of the West over former colonialists or over the former colonies. However, as Kilian observes, the film 'focus[es] on the individual's responsibility in postcolonial power structures'.[43] But even though Osuofia challenges the power structures, he sometimes becomes part of the power structures that disparage African cultures, here represented by palm wine.

African/traditional medicine and modern medicine

A local herbalist represents traditional culture, while a local hospital in the city in Nigeria represents hybrid culture and a London hospital represents Western culture. This distinction is made clear when Samantha tells Osuofia that she needs £25,000 to travel to London to see her doctor, because she is afraid that she has caught some disease. Osuofia tells her that a native doctor who is known as 'Ọ̀ tụ̀lụ̀ọ̀gbajíẹ́' could cure her illness. There is also hybridity when considering the Western hospital in Nigeria where Osuofia is taken after supposedly suffering from food poisoning. Samantha demonstrates that she does not trust or recognise African traditional medicine or healing practices. Osuofia tries to convince her but she personifies the domination of Western medicine over African medicine. Okoye parallels *Osuofia in London* to *Sanders of the River* and *Nionga*, films that degrade Africa.[44] He notes that:

> [the] first part set in Osuofia's Nigerian village clearly repeats as well as subverts those dominant tropes in colonialist discourse in evidence in such films as *Sanders of the River* and *Nionga*. First, *Osuofia* creates the impression of a remote primitive village unpolluted by processes of cultural advancement and impervious to the vagaries of the outside world.[45]

The present study adds to Okoye's analysis by viewing this film through the lens of hybridity and globalisation, and posing a challenge to the colonialist discourse of painting Africa as primitive. Each African society has a unique way of life and the Western characterisation of these cultures as backward is a form of hegemony. Further, when a Nigerian Nollywood filmmaker portrays Africa in a positive or negative way, this choice should not primarily be blamed on the West. Rather, Nollywood stakeholders should be held responsible for appropriating stereotypes of Africa. Ideological positions of Nollywood stakeholders tinted by colonial and Western discourse should not be treated as innocent or erroneous. This shows the power modern medicine commands over traditional medicine.

Discussion

This study via hybridity invokes colonial, postcolonial, neocolonial and globalisation debates by suggesting that the colonialist's discourse on Africa can be deconstructed to facilitate positive cultural transformation. Since cultures are not stagnant, a positive and progressive hybridity is necessary to keep African cultures relevant in the face of globalisation.

Nollywood hybrid practices provide an avenue for producing just such an evolving African society. Okome contends that 'Osuofia represents the rural archetype of the postcolonial, and as a character, he functions as one who is designed to reverse the stereotype of the rustic who is seen as the epitome of the unintelligent being'.[46] This statement indicates that Nollywood has mediated Osuofia as worthy of emulation in the fight against imperialism. As Okome further argues: 'Unlike empire films, *Osuofia in London* provides a multilayered discursive platform to do this type of deconstruction. It gives the viewer the critical view of Osuofia's gaze as it is positioned as a critique of what is alluded to.'[47] In other words, the film models Osuofia as a desirable example of deconstruction or constructive hybridity.

The concept of power in relation to traditional culture in *Osuofia in London* is manifested in the analysis. The manifestation of power is consistent in the film. Western aspects of culture – rather, power – are ever-present both in Nigeria and in the United Kingdom. Even when showing a traditional African way of life, the film presents a Western orientation and power over traditional African culture. Even though dominant Western culture is pervasive, Osuofia attempts to challenge Western cultural power through hybridity. Hence, it can be argued that hegemony cannot exist in isolation where hybridity occurs. Just as in Nollywood films and most African cultures, a Western orientation usually provides the standard when it comes to hybridity. Literally, the concept of power to the traditional culture results in inequality, likewise hybridity.

Some have argued that hybridity blurs authenticity. In *Osuofia in London*, hybridity involves challenges to imperialism but it is also seemingly complacent in the face of Western ideology. Even though Osuofia challenges Western ideology in London, he tells the woman who sells liquor in his village that when he comes back from London, she will cease selling local palm wine and switch to Western liquor. In this case, hybridity serves to both push and pull.

According to Pieterse: 'Hybridities with or without a center are polarities of a continuum. Again, it is difficult to think of an example of completely free-floating mixture, for even at a carnival the components are charged with different values, polarities'.[48] Using this stance to evaluate *Osuofia in London* indicates that hybridity is not a balanced exchange or mixture of two cultures. This fact highlights the inequality of globalisation because mainstream culture usually dictates what is accepted as popular culture while non-mainstream culture usually accepts the dominant one. The ideology of the mainstream is usually the dominant force. He further argues that 'the significance of hybridity extends only so far as the reach of the boundaries that it transgresses'.[49]

Cultural gatekeepers can and should be mindful of the paradigms they subscribe to. African, Western and hybrid cultures are critically essential in the face of globalisation because of an underlying concern, which is explained by the Igbo proverb, 'Áká ńrī kwọ́ọ́ áká ekpe`, áká e` kpe`` akẁ ọ́ọ́ áká ńrī'. This proverb literally means that when the right hand washes the left hand, the left hand washes the right hand. Figuratively, each culture should be complementing the other via hybridity. Yet, colonial and neo-colonial power relations are reinforced and reflected in Nollywood films. Despite the colonial power relations and Western cultural dominance, *Osuofia in London* shows that Nollywood's expression of Igboness 'is contingent on the valorization of Igbo identity'.[50]

This chapter contributes to the debate on the mediated representation of Africa, and particularly on the othering of the African continent, and highlights its impact on the process of identity formation. It promotes the visibility of African culture in the communication field, and specifically in critical intercultural communication. This chapter can encourage and guide others who evaluate mediated texts from a critical or intercultural perspective. It allows colonised people and others to (re)construct colonised and/or suppressed cultures – in other words, it gives a voice to 'other' cultures and can be used to understand how cultural layers have evolved in the face of globalisation. This also contributes to critical film studies by challenging the hegemonic tendencies of mainstream culture, power and ideology.

There is value in the promotion of diversity within film as well as communication studies. 'Increased disparities serve to structure and bind intercultural relationships in terms of power, privilege, and positionality'.[51] This film gives voice to two distinct cultures to interact despite their different positions. The contribution of this analysis of *Osuofia in London* to our overall understanding of Nollywood films demonstrates that these films are reshaping and adding to a global film discussion. Even though Nollywood aspires to attain Hollywood levels of production, it inevitably retains some of its unique cultural identity and production style, which brings diversity to communication studies, as well as the hope that hybridity rather than pure Western culture and ideology will continue through Nollywood.

Concluding remarks

A critical analysis of *Osuofia in London* via the prisms of 'African/Nigerian/Igbo', 'Western/British' and 'hybrid' cultures evidences power dynamics in challenging, questioning, managing, participating in and reproducing Western stereotypes and orientation. One weakness of the film is that it at times belittles Igbo culture and its people, while succumbing to Western ideological domination. Even though the hybrid practice of Nollywood is about how Nigerian and other African cultures are experienced, (re)created, verbalised and encountered inside and outside Nigeria through a mediated format, '[a] dialectical contradiction always exists between local [native] and global [Western] and the two are constantly interpreting [hybrid] each other'.[52] This contradiction is present in several scenes of *Osuofia in London* – for example, in the depiction of the syncretism of African traditional beliefs and Christian dogma. Due to colonialism, neocolonialism and globalisation, inequitable relations of power exist and appear in every layer of interaction.

Regarding the hybridity in Osuofia challenging Western culture and values, there are not enough instances in the movie. One possible exception is Osuofia being polygamous – in his case, it is a part of African traditional culture, which directly challenges a fundamental Western value and interpretation of marriage. Similarly, there are other minor elements, such as when Osuofia challenges the restaurant cashier about why African food is not sold, and when Osuofia questions the cashier's refusal to accept Nigerian currency. He also challenges Ben Okafor, a second-generation British Igbo, for refusing to acknowledge Nigerian currency during a meeting in the latter's office regarding the will. On the other hand, the fact that Osuofia is intelligent challenges stereotypes but is very much in tune with the Western value of individualism. What is lost most importantly with hybridity as exemplified in *Osuofia in London* is the Igbo language. Hybridity could have been used to challenge Western ideology as well as neocolonialism, but the movie falls short of critically challenging it.

In a wider framework, *Osuofia in London* is a tool for exposing the Western power and ideological dominance that Osuofia encounters, challenges or negotiates. It demonstrates that globalisation, as a powerful force, is an inequitable expansion of communication links among different regions, which can occur via various forms, including cultural text and cultural product as well as in physical and virtual spaces. Kilian deems the film 'a masterpiece'. To me, even though Nollywood genres are fairly fragmented and still evolving, *Osuofia in London* is a focal point of identity negotiation for many Igbo, many Nigerians and possibly even many other Africans.

Notes

1 K. Sorrells, 'Re-imagining Intercultural Communication in the Context of Globalization', in *The Handbook of Critical Intercultural Communication*, ed. T. K. Nakayama & R. T. Halualani (Malden, MA: Wiley-Blackwell, 2010), p. 171.

2 Ibid., p. 176.
3 W. Connors, 'Nollywood Babylon: Nigeria's Movie Industry Is Winning Global Attention, but DVD Piracy May Bring It Down', *The Wall Street Journal* (22 May 2009).
4 C. Okoye, 'Looking Back: Nigerian Video Film Anthropologises the West', *The Leeds African Studies Bulletin*, 72 (2010), pp. 76–92. O. Okome, 'Reversing the Filmic Gaze: Comedy and the Critique of the Postcolony in *Osuofia in London*', in *Global Nollywood: The Transnational Dimensions of an African Video Film Industry*, ed. M. Krings and O. Okome (Bloomington, IN: Indiana University Press, 2013), pp. 139–57. C. Kilian, 'Worth a Closer Look: A Comparative Study of *Xala* and *Osuofia in London*', *Journal of African Cinemas*, 5.1 (2013), pp. 55–71. U. Onuzulike, 'Nollywood Video Film's Impact on Nigerian and Other African Environments and Cultures', *Explorations in Media Ecology*, 13.3&4 (2014), pp. 279–92.
5 U. Onuzulike, 'What's Wrong with Igbo-language Nollywood Film?', in *Perspectives on the Igbo: Multidisciplinary Approaches*, ed. A. P. Nwauwa and C. J. Korieh (Glassboro, NJ: Goldline and Jacobs Publishing, 2015), pp. 237–48.
6 See for example: A. L. Abah, 'One Step Forward, Two Steps Backward: African Women in Nigerian Video-Film', *Communication, Culture & Critique*, 1.4 (2008), pp. 335–57; P. J. Ebewo, 'The Emerging Video Film Industry in Nigeria: Challenges and Prospects', *Journal of Film and Video*, 59.3 (2007), pp. 46–57; J. Haynes, 'Introduction', in *Nigerian Video Films*, ed. J. Haynes (Athens, OH: Ohio University Center for International Studies, 2000), pp. 1–36; J. Haynes, *Nollywood: The Creation of Nigerian Film Genres* (Chicago, IL: University of Chicago Press, 2016); Onuzulike, 'What's Wrong with Igbo-language Nollywood Film?'.
7 Okoye, 'Looking Back', p. 81.
8 See H. Bhabha, *The Location of Culture* (London: Routledge, 1994); M. M. Kraidy, 'Hybridity in Cultural Globalization', *Communication Theory*, 12.3 (2002), pp. 316–39; M. M. Kraidy, *Hybridity, or The Cultural Logic of Globalization* (Philadelphia, PA: Temple University Press, 2005); J. N. Pieterse, 'Globalization As Hybridization', *International Sociology*, 9.2 (1994), pp. 161–84; J. N. Pieterse, *Globalization and Culture: Global Mélange* (Lanham, MD: Rowman & Littlefield Publishers, 2004).
9 Kraidy, *Hybridity, or The Cultural Logic of Globalization*.
10 Ibid., p. 5.
11 Haynes, *Nigerian Video Films*, p. 77.
12 Kraidy, *Hybridity, or The Cultural Logic of Globalization*, p. 57.
13 R. Shome, 'Internationalizing Critical Race Communication Studies: Transnationality, Space, and Affect', in *The Handbook of Critical Intercultural Communication*, ed. T. K. Nakayama and R. T. Halualani (Malden, MA: Wiley-Blackwell, 2010), p. 150.
14 Kraidy, 'Hybridity in Cultural Globalization'.
15 Pieterse, *Globalization and Culture*, p. 74.
16 Okome, 'Reversing the Filmic Gaze', p. 155.

17 Ibid., p. 155.
18 Kraidy, *Hybridity, or The Cultural Logic of Globalization*, p. 1.
19 See O. Möller, 'A Homegrown Hybrid Cinema of Outrageous Schlock from Africa's Most Populous Nation', *Film Comment* (2004); O. Okome, 'The Popular Art of African Video-Film', *NYFA Quarterly* (2001).
20 Okome, 'The Popular Art of African Video-Film', p. 1.
21 Möller, 'A Homegrown Hybrid Cinema', p. 12.
22 U. Onuzulike, 'Nollywood: Nigerian Videofilms As a Cultural and Technological Hybridity', *International Journal of Intercultural Communication Studies*, 18.1 (2009), pp. 176–87.
23 J. N. Martin and T. K. Nakayama, *Intercultural Communication in Contexts*, 5th ed. (New York: McGraw-Hill, 2010), p. 110.
24 Ibid., p. 112.
25 B. J. Hall, *Among Cultures: The Challenge of Communication*, 2nd ed. (Belmont, CA: Thomson-Wadsworth, 2005), p. 30.
26 S. N. Mohammed, *Communication and the Globalization of Culture: Beyond Tradition and Borders* (Lanham, MD: Lexington Books, 2013), p. 15.
27 Okome, 'Reversing the Filmic Gaze', p. 155.
28 A. Gramsci, *Selections from the Prison Notebooks*, trans. H. Quintin and G. Nowell-Smith (New York: International Publishers, 1971).
29 M. Landy, *Film, Politics, and Gramsci* (Minneapolis, MN: University of Minnesota Press, 1994).
30 J. Corbin and A. Strauss, *Basics of Qualitative Research: Techniques and Procedures for Developing Grounded Theory* (Thousand Oaks, CA: Sage Publications, 2007); N. K. Denzin and Y. S. Lincoln, *Strategies of Qualitative Inquiry*, 3rd ed. (Thousand Oaks, CA: Sage Publications, 2007).
31 P. D. Leedy and J. E. Ormrod, *Practical Research: Planning and Design*, 8th ed. (Upper Saddle River, NJ: Pearson-Prentice Hall, 2005), p. 142.
32 Ibid., p. 142.
33 Ibid., p. 141.
34 Kilian, 'Worth a Closer Look', p. 61.
35 Onuzulike, 'Nollywood: Nigerian Videofilms As a Cultural and Technological Hybridity'.
36 J. S. Mbiti, *Introduction to African Religion*, 2nd ed. (Oxford: Heinemann Educational Publishers, 1991 [1975]).
37 U. C. Siugo-Abanihea, J. A. Ebigbolaa and A. A. Adewuyia, 'Urban Nuptiality Patterns and Marital Fertility in Nigeria', *Journal of Biosocial Science*, 25.4 (1993), pp. 483–98.
38 Okome, 'Reversing the Filmic Gaze', p. 151.
39 Ibid., p. 151.
40 Okoye, 'Looking Back', p. 82.
41 Ibid., p. 82.
42 E. Sandon, 'Projecting Africa: Two British Travel Films of the 1920s', in *Cultural Encounters: Representing 'Otherness'*, ed. E. Hallam and B. V. Street (London: Routledge, 2000), pp. 108–47.

43 Kilian, 'Worth a Closer Look', p. 66.
44 Okoye, 'Looking Back'.
45 Ibid., p. 84.
46 Okome, 'Reversing the Filmic Gaze', p. 146.
47 Ibid., p. 146.
48 Pieterse, *Globalization and Culture*, p. 108.
49 Ibid., p. 86.
50 Ravi, p. 50.
51 Sorrells, 'Re-imagining Intercultural Communication', p. 177.
52 R. Chuang, 'Dialectics of Globalization and Localization', in *Communication and Global Society*, ed. G. Chen and W. J. Starosta (New York: Peter Lang Publishing, 2000), p. 28.

9

Poetics of double erasure: British East/South-East Asian cinema and *Lilting*

Victor Fan

The lived experiences of British East/South-East Asians in London are best summarised by Vietnamese American filmmaker and scholar Trinh Minh-ha: 'You try and keep on trying to unsay it, for if you don't, they will not fail to fill in the blanks on your behalf, and you will be said.'[1] As Glen G. Mimura argues, Trinh's 'poetic mixture of intimate anger and critical insight concisely captures the predicament, that of ceaselessly speaking against your own erasure, that unavoidably haunts marginalized media'.[2]

What Mimura calls 'erasure' is an ongoing process by the hegemonic social discourses to render Asian American (in her case) and British East Asian/South-East Asian (BEASEA) lives, images and other cultural productions sociopolitically and economically precarious. As Felicia Chan and Andy Willis point out, such a process of erasure has been etched onto the bodies and psyches of BEASEA lives through physical violence, day-to-day micro-aggressions, systemic exclusion from the discourses of both the unmarked dominant and marginalised communities and deprivation of institutional funding. For the same reasons, the critical discourse of BEASEA cinema and media, either by academic scholars or practitioners, is still inchoate. For Chan and Willis, such discourses often struggle to maintain a position 'even on the margins' of the larger debate on British cinema and media.[3]

In this chapter, I turn to another meaning of 'erasure', provided by Jacques Derrida, who argues that an act of erasure does not simply efface the presence of a text and create a clean slate for its replacement. Rather, as in a palimpsest, an act of erasure always leaves a trace of the effaced text as a ghostly image that continues to haunt what comes to *overlap* with it. The result is the presence of an absence that renders visible and sensible the contestation between the two textual layers.[4]

The reason for my paying attention to Derrida's understanding of erasure is pragmatic. BEASEA cinema and media, unlike their US counterparts, have not had the same degree of historical infrastructure of activism, identity politics, independent film movements and public institutional support.[5]

Furthermore, the precarity of the community has been consolidated by decades of postcolonial *white*-centric British identity promoted by the Conservatives, followed by a neoliberal understanding of multiculturalism practised since the New Labour administrations.[6] As Daniel York argues, BEASEA cultural practitioners are surrounded by a brick wall that has been increasingly consolidated by what Laurent Berlant calls 'cruel optimism'. For Berlant, neoliberalism is an economic and sociopolitical ecology that systematically deprives *free* members of a neoliberal society of living opportunities and resources. Yet, under such precarious conditions, these 'free' members continue to maintain a cruel optimism that there is no systemic failure. There are only free individuals who fail to work hard enough to attain what they could have achieved.[7] Against this brick wall, my question is not *how* we (BEASEAs) can or should be represented and made representable in a media ecology that has systematically and systemically rendered us invisible but rather, how a perpetual process of erasure can be re-examined as a productive force: a potential field of immanence that can foster new creativities.[8]

The case study I analyse in this chapter is Hong Khaou's *Lilting* (2014). This film was a festival, box office and critical success on its release in London. As I will point out, *Lilting* does not consistently pass the test of representational politics. Among many points of contention (which I shall discuss), the dead second-generation British Cambodian Chinese protagonist Kai (Andrew Leung) is featured as a memory of either his *white* partner Richard (Ben Whishaw) or his first-generation British Cambodian Chinese mother Junn (Cheng Pei-pei).[9] In other words, Kai has no corporeality but only a ghostly presence in the processes of memory revision and rehearsal conjured up and by two embodied consciousnesses that constantly erase and rewrite him in their own terms. However, instead of condemning the film's effacement of Kai's corporeality and the lived experience he is supposed to embody, I argue that *Lilting* offers us a user manual in terms of how a BEASEA film (and filmmaker) negotiates the *affect* of someone who is constantly being doubly erased by multiple contesting forces.

BEASEAs: a history of double erasure

The sociopolitical, cultural and economic position of BEASEAs – as biopolitical lives – is best understood as that of double erasure. As Chan and Willis argue, in the larger sociopolitical sphere and the critical discourse of the cinema, BEASEAs are not only rendered invisible by the unmarked dominant but also 'overlooked' by other minoritised communities.[10]

To begin with, there has never been an internally coherent and unified BEASEA community in London and the rest of the UK. As Ashley Thorpe and Diana Yeh, and Gregor Benton and Edmund Terence Gomez point out in their respective works, until the 1990s, the colonial classification of *Chinese* as a racialised group that encompassed individuals of East/South-East Asian descent had remained unquestioned. Those who have been racialised as Chinese include UK-born Britons of East/South-East Asian descent; early Cantonese-speaking settlers from Hong Kong's New Territories in the 1950s and 1960s; Singaporeans of Chinese descent who came to the UK after Operation Coldstore in 1963; Vietnamese and Cambodian Chinese who left their countries due to Sinophobic persecutions; Mandarin-speaking Mainland Chinese and Taiwanese; and, today, Hong Kongers who seek refuge from the tightening security of the People's Republic of China (PRC).[11]

In this sense, the label 'Chinese' has been historically imposed in Britain – or sometimes internalised voluntarily or under sociopolitical pressure – by individuals who have different family or personal histories, regional and linguistic backgrounds, levels of education, political values and in-group loyalties. The term 'British Chinese', which began to gain circulation among intellectuals and activists in the 1990s, did not fundamentally challenge such a colonial racial category.[12] Instead of serving as an identity that offers individuals with diverse experiences a sense of in-group cohesion, the term 'British Chinese' sometimes puts individual and communal differences under erasure: a label that signifies one's sense of *un*belonging. Not only does the term designate a zone of exception, every biopolitical life within this community is an exception of an exception. Yet, as I will discuss later, in London, the socioeconomic, political and cultural diversity within the 'British Chinese' community, together with the city's celebration of multiculturalism, cosmopolitanism and global position, has indeed nurtured an environment in which artists and activists could foster a stronger sense of communal cohesion.[13]

The general sense of belonging neither to the social hegemony nor to a shared marginalised position is comparable to that of the Asian American experience. As Peter X Feng argues, 'Asian American' is not meant to be an umbrella term that puts differences and contradictions aside. Rather, it embraces and expresses all the contestations between individuals while acknowledging a shared history of marginalisation. Hence, for Feng, instead of being a point of convergence to which one belongs, the term is better regarded as a process of becoming constituted by differences.[14] Regarding the UK, Lau Cheuk Wai also argues that in spite of its neoliberal ideological basis, multiculturalism – especially the idea of 'superdiversity' in London – has encouraged BEASEA activists and cultural producers to rethink multiculturalism not as a measurement against monoculturalism but as an opportunity to foster a sense of communal cohesion and national belonging through inter- and intra-cultural exchanges.[15] Based on the same reasoning, the term 'British East Asian/South-East Asian' has gained popularity since the rise of COVID-19-related racialist violence in 2020, as the wider community now needs a more cohesive term that can address the heterogeneity and diversity of its members.

As Thorpe and Yeh point out, British Chinese identity has been historically grounded in the imperial history of British identity itself. Thorpe and Yeh trace this back to Winston Churchill's definition of the British aerial victory against Nazi Germany as the 'survival of Christian civilization ... British life, and the long continuity of *our* institutions and *our* Empire'.[16] Such an understanding of Britishness once underlined the Conservatives' version of nationalism during the Thatcher era. Historically, the UK policy of Chinese exclusion and the official colonial policies in Hong Kong, Singapore and Malaya that Chinese people were biologically and naturally unassimilable as British citizens are still actively shaping both governmental policies and popular imagination today.[17] Within such a framework, multiculturalism in the 1980s was defined by Margaret Thatcher's administration as a set of relationships that has been historically tied to white Britain through colonialism.

Chan and Willis argue that during the 1970s and 1980s, the critical discourse of Chinese identities, art and culture was supposed to be part of what Stuart Hall calls the 'black experience', which denotes 'a way of referencing the common experience of racism and marginalization in Britain and came to provide the organizing category of a new politics of resistance, amongst groups and communities with, in fact, very different histories, traditions and ethnic identities'.[18] Nevertheless, as Eddie Chambers argues, Chinese in Britain often 'disappeared' from the practical and critical discourses of Black art and cinema.[19] As Chan and Willis observe, both journalistic and scholarly studies of Black art and cinema during this period omitted representations of BEASEAs with no scholarly justification.[20]

With the publication of the *Future of Multi-Ethnic Britain* (also known as the Parekh Report) in 2000 under New Labour, multiculturalism was acknowledged, though depoliticised, under neoliberalism.[21] Multiculturalism under New Labour introduced discourses of postcolonialism, concepts of institutional racism and individual unconscious bias and concrete policies to improve racial equity and the socioeconomic life quality of many people of colour. Many of these ideas and policies have been carried forward by the Conservative governments that succeeded New Labour. However, Arun Kundnani argues that the colonial ideological infrastructure of this new mode of multiculturalism has remained intact.

Kundnani argues that, by giving Britain's postcolonial ethnic and cultural diversity a name, multiculturalism was configured as a social symptom that could be 'institutionalized, managed and reified'.[22] As Shih Shu-mei argues, multiculturalism reduces the complex political asymmetries and colonial histories to a matter of cultural differences. These differences are further reduced to commodities for white Euro-American consumption.[23] Under neoliberalism, ethnic minorities are told that they can overcome the existing sociopolitical and economic asymmetries by working hard in a liberal society with equal opportunities. Meanwhile, individuals of colour are systematically deprived of actual opportunities to participate in the economy, society and politics. Historically, as British television and independent films have been increasingly critical of racism and as more public funding opportunities have been dedicated to ethnic minority artists and filmmakers, the erasure of BEASEA works and representation became even more conspicuous. In 2011, the Yellow Earth Theatre co-founded by David Tse and Kumiko Mendi lost all its Arts Council funding. As Tse argues, although British Chinese constitutes the third largest ethnic group in the UK, its complete disappearance from both hegemonic and marginal discourses has remained unchallenged.[24]

Between the Beijing Olympic in 2008 and the tightening of the PRC's global cultural policy in 2021, public institutions like the British Film Institute (BFI) and private cinemas had become more supportive of cinema from Mainland China. The London-based Chinese Visual Festival, for example, promoted Chinese independent films to the London audience during this period. Meanwhile, the London East Asian Film Festival also featured commercial films from China and other Sinophone regions. With the increasing number of students and immigrants from the PRC, sales agents also became increasingly willing to distribute Mainland and Hong Kong commercial films theatrically. Yet, the growing visibility of cinema from China and other Sinophone regions, which is often promoted as the *real* Chinese experiences, has ironically rendered BEASEA works even more indiscernible. Moreover, some of these works have reinforced the sociopolitically and historically constructed East–West dichotomy, which many BEASEAs have worked hard to deconstruct in their artwork and daily experiences.[25]

BEASEA cinema

There is an absence of historiographical work on BEASEA filmmaking before the 1980s. Even today, the BFI's account of British Chinese cinema still uses Leong Po Chih's 1986 feature *Ping Pong* and Mike Newell's 1988 film

Soursweet as their starting point.²⁶ Jun Okada aptly points out that Asian American film- and video-making was able to grow into a movement in the 1960s and 1970s because of a synergy between individual talents and institutional support, known as Triangle Cinema, in the Bay Area of California. This cinema was made by Asian Americans and targeted Asian Americans across the United States. Such institutional support was mainly instigated by the publication of the Carnegie Commission on Educational Television in 1967 and the subsequent establishment of the Public Broadcasting Service (PBS) in 1969.²⁷ Meanwhile, UK institutions that were supposed to support minority representation have often disqualified BEASEAs from the margin. This situation was eventually improved with the establishment of Film London in 2003 and with the British Broadcasting Corporation (BBC) issuing its first diversity policy in 2009.

The two BEASEA feature films that I mentioned earlier are in fact significant milestones, which bring to the fore the politics of representation in their respective ways. Leong was born in London, and during his production process he made a point of hiring British Chinese actors and crew members.²⁸ In the film, Elaine Choi (Lucy Sheen), an East London–born lawyer with a cockney accent, is asked to execute the will of a British Chinese businessman. As Choi visits different members of the deceased's family, she needs to negotiate the linguistic, cultural and socioeconomic differences between first and second generations of British Chinese. The film's mixture of humour, mystery and 'kitchen-sink' reality enables spectators to delve into the uneasy tensions between British Chinese of different class backgrounds, with various senses of belonging and purposes of life in Britain. Like Wayne Wang's *Chan is Missing* (1982), *Ping Pong* uses self-satire to confront the heterogeneity of British Chinese lives and put into question each viewer's notion of 'British Chineseness'.

Soursweet is based on Timothy Mo's award-winning novel of the same title. The novel is about a family who have settled in Soho, London from the New Territories of Hong Kong. The family owns a Chinese takeaway, and the text employs a modernist strategy of narrating alternately between different family members' perspectives and sometimes from the restaurant's perspective. The novel has often been considered an authentic representation of British Chinese immigrant life in the 1960s and 1970s, including its portrayal of Chinatown gang wars. Nonetheless, by simply regarding the novel's representation as realistic, these critics overlook the novel's frequent shifts between reality and fantasy, and the unreliability of the narrators.²⁹

Adapted by Ian McEwan and directed by Mike Newell, *Soursweet* was both praised for its realism and criticised for the loss of Mo's authentic voice.³⁰ The film also features Taiwan actor Sylvia Chang (who later became a permanent resident in Britain). Unlike *Ping Pong*, *Soursweet* is not a self-representation by BEASEA filmmakers and actors. By turning the novel into a *realistic* representation of hard-working first-generation Hong Kong immigrants, the film loses the novel's self-irony and the ambiguous boundary between fantasy and reality when it comes to the multiplicity and contestability of what it means by BEASEA's lived experiences.

Today, *Soursweet* is still fondly remembered as one of the few films that represent some form of British Chinese experience on screen. Chan and Willis argue that self-representation of BEASEAs did not re-emerge in British cinema until the release of Ray Yueng's *Cut Sleeve Boys* (2006) – often hailed as the 'first gay British Chinese film' – and the films of Guo Xiaolu.[31] Guo, who grew up in Wenling, Zhejiang and moved to London in 2002, has tried to reconcile and formulate her dual-cultural identities. Her work stands out from other BEASEA feature films not only through her tendency to represent migrant workers (especially sex workers) from China and other Sinophone regions but also because of her tendency to use on-location shooting, handheld camera and long takes, which are idiomatic of the generation of Chinese independent filmmakers from the 1990s and the early 2000s. Her films, in general, attract a larger audience in international film festivals (especially Rotterdam), art museums and academic circles and many of these films resonate as London migrant films.[32]

Ping Pong and *Soursweet* illustrate the politics of representation outlined by Gayatri Chakravorty Spivak in her article 'Can the Subaltern Speak?' (1988). In the narrative of *Ping Pong*, Choi is supposed to speak from the BEASEA community and advocates for a deceased man from within it. Yet, she finds herself not being equipped with the diverse linguistic and cultural skills due to her position as a subaltern (someone who has been educated within the epistemic space of the coloniser) and to her difference *from* those individuals for whom she is supposed to speak. Eventually, all members of the deceased's family and Choi herself find their own voices, identities and personal freedom in their own processes of executing or struggling against the will. Meanwhile, *Soursweet*, a literary text written by a British Chinese writer is ventriloquised by filmmakers and actors from outside the community. But if BEASEAs are constantly erased both by the hegemony and by other marginalised communities, elements from Timothy Mo's text speak through these ventriloquised bodies, and it is up to its BEASEA spectators to reclaim Mo's text via their diverse lived experiences.

Double erasure as a poetics

The struggle for representation and visibility in the cinema is undoubtedly the primary target for which artists, activists and audiences must fight.

But my discussion above also demonstrates a systemic problem: that within the epistemic space of British race relations, BEASEAs are posited in a position that is *unrepresentable*, not because their bodies and voices cannot be put onto the screen but because, as Spivak argues, the subaltern can only speak in those terms that have been filtered through colonialism and postcolonialism.[33] However, as Homi Bhabha argues, such unrepresentability is precisely a process of *splitting* that makes visible and sensible the failure of the two dimensions of the imaginary nation state: (1) the pedagogical power of the nation state to interpellate individual biological lives as subjects and (2) the performative power of the nation state to inscribe a sense of collective historicity that each individual life would misrecognise as their internal subjectivity.[34]

Why is it important to make this process of splitting visible and sensible? As Thomas Elsaesser argues, every biopolitical life is doubly occupied by contesting or even irreconcilable forces and beliefs. Elsaesser calls this 'double occupancy', which he initially applied to filmmakers and spectators of European films, who posit the cinema as a site where they can rehearse, revisit and rewrite their relationships with conflicting notions such as the national and the regional, the European and the local, the unmarked dominant and the precarious working-class and migrant experiences.[35] In *Extraterritoriality* (2019), I argue that under postcolonialism a precarious biopolitical life is not only doubly occupied by conflicting juridico-political forces but also doubly ostracised by them. For example, a Hong Konger is always doubly occupied by their British colonial past and the PRC's authorial claim over their biopolitical existence. While the British authority has historically posited Hong Kong as a colony that is both part of the empire and *outside* its nation state proper, the Chinese authority does the same by designating Hong Kong as a special administrative region. These juridico-political forces therefore occupy these lives in an extraterritorial position that neither belongs to nor is completely severed from the larger national imagination, and such occupation is precisely made possible by ostracising them to this liminal, undefinable and unrepresentable space. I further argue that while a member of the unmarked dominant community may treat subjectivity, individuality and (political) autonomy as their *point de départ*, a colonised life is always desubjectivised, deindividuated and deautonomised. In fact, every public discourse and institution is configured for the purpose of depriving these lives of any opportunity to subjectivise, individuate and autonomise.[36]

One must therefore pay attention not only to representation on screen but also to how the process of double erasure, which renders BEASEA lives unrepresentable in the larger imagination of British cinema, is made visible and sensible. And this is the reason I want to turn to *Lilting* as an example.

166 Global London on screen

At the centre of *Lilting*'s narrative is the death of Kai, who was run over by a bus on his way to fetch his mother, Junn, from the nursing home to his home in East London for dinner. His plan was to introduce his lover, Richard, and come out to his mother. The spectator never gets to see and experience this traumatic incident. Rather, the film as an image – or, as Gilles Deleuze argues, a *consciousness* (an embodied experience that includes the body, the embodied thinking process and the associated milieu which is often taken by the body as its object) – is gradually in-formed (put into forms) as Richard visits Junn and tries to establish a connection with her based on their shared pain.[37]

The film image unfolds according to Henri Bergson's first schema of time in *Matière et mémoire* (Matter and memory, 1939) (see Figure 9.1). In this schema, O is the very *object* that the body intuits (a direct contact between those particles and energies that constitute the body and those that constitute the associated milieu), which rewrites the relationality between the body and the milieu, the constitution of the body itself and its memories. Yet, such an intuition (in the case of the film, the visually and sensually effaced traumatic incident) is never processed as the way it is. Rather, a perception A is in-formed based on those memories from the past that help constitute it and an anticipation of a future that has yet to come. Such a

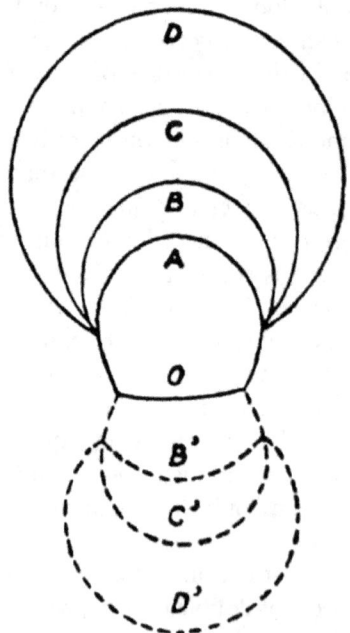

Figure 9.1 Henri Bergson's first schema of time

perception *protentionally* produces perceptions B, C, D and so forth, which the body takes as actual, and each actual perception rewrites – and is rewritten by – a virtual circuit of memory-anticipation (B', C', D' and so forth).[38]

In *Lilting*, when Richard pays his first visit to Junn, he realises that she cannot speak to him in English and seeks help from an interpreter, Vann (Naomi Christie). Yet, being able to communicate to each other verbally deepens Junn's mistrust of Richard, whom Junn believes to be a 'bad influence' who contributed to Kai's drifting away from her. Junn eventually refuses to see Richard again. These actualised experiences are intertwined with Richard's and Junn's respective memories (sometimes fantasies) of Kai. In Richard's memory, Kai stubbornly refuses to come out to Junn. In Junn's memories, Kai's love for Richard is responsible for her alienation, even though Kai and Richard invited her to move in with them.

The film's textual surface can be seen as ethnically and culturally problematic. As I mentioned in the introduction to this chapter, Kai is never corporealised in the image as an actual life; rather, he is momentarily corporealised – and, therefore, ventriloquised and fantasised – in Richard's and Junn's memories. Contextually, while Junn is played by Hong Kong veteran martial art film actor Cheng Pei-pei, who has no personal connection to BEASEA life, Richard is played by Ben Whishaw, who made the production bankable and marketable. In other words, Kai, the key BEASEA character in the film, is reduced to a ghost who never speaks as or for himself and is only perceived through the two national perspectives that contribute to his double erasure.

However, Kai's double erasure (by his boyfriend and by his mother) is the very position occupied by BEASEAs. Here, a Deleuzian understanding of the cinematographic image is helpful in the way that the film is not to be understood as a text or an image *out there* that represents an object. Rather, as the body perceives, recognises and conceptualises the image as a consciousness, it is engaged in a process of becoming with its associated milieu (an overall *dispositif* or network of social practices and discourses and personalised experiences). On the one hand, the film draws the perceiving body into the melancholy and nostalgia of the loss of a young gay man's life; on the other hand, it enables the body to acknowledge the constructedness of Richard's and Junn's memories. As a result, the doubly erased BEASEA body is made visible as an inscription of a network of memories and fantasies that are constantly revised by Richard's and Junn's senses of loss and regret.

The constructedness of Richard's and Junn's memories is foregrounded by their *mise-en-scène*. Richard's memories of Kai take place in bed covered with immaculately white sheets. Their naked bodies are intertwined between the sheets, with a strong backlight from the windows behind them. The interior of the room is brightly lit, giving the two bodies almost identically white skin tone and suggesting that 'Kai' is a mirror image of Richard. Both Kai and Richard have similar facial hair and physique, and the extensive use of medium close-ups of their faces, torsos, legs and feet draw the perceiving body not to them as individuated beings but as an affective intensity: the sensation of two pieces of human skin brushing against each other, a lover's desirable body odour, the coldness or warmth of each other's feet, the subtle and erotic smell of a lover's breath. These memory sequences therefore encapsulate the perceiving body neither in what happened and what was being said in the past, nor in what will happen and what can be said if there were a future. Rather, they indulge the perceiving body in a memorised/fantasised sensation here and now, from which the body of Kai is individuated from Richard's own image (or self-image).

Likewise, Junn's room in the nursing home is decorated in the style of a 1950s middle-class living space, with yellow, beige and brown flower-patterned wallpaper and furniture from that period. In one sequence, Junn plays Li Xianglan's (Yamaguchi Yoshiko) rendition 'Yelaixiang' (Chinese violet; released in 1944) on a vinyl record. Junn's room can therefore be regarded not as a realistic representation of a nursing home room but as a materialisation of her childhood memory (Cheng herself was born in 1946). Hong Khaou confesses that, for him, Junn does not live in what we would call reality; rather, she lives in a *sensation* of the past.[39] It is out of this pure sensation that bodies and relations between bodies are transindividuated (inter- and intra-individuated). Towards the end of the film, over a piece of music, a 360-degree rotating camera first shows Richard and Kai dancing intimately. As the camera rotates beyond them, it shows the bodies of Richard and Vann, and eventually Kai and Junn. The interchangeability of bodies in a singular relationality (a pair of intimately dancing bodies) signals that what we call reality – that is, an image-consciousness – is in-formed out of a perpetually changing process of affective intensity. And an affective intensity is an actualisation of a memory of a past sensation or, sometimes, an attachment to a sensation that is constructed *afterwards* when one is incapable of remembering or grasping the very object of memory as the way it is.

In *Cinema Illuminating Reality* (2021), I argue that the formational process of the cinematographic image, in terms of Buddhist philosophy, is karma. Karma is best understood, in Yogācāra terms, as an assemblage of impulses (past memories that serve as productive potentialities) that in-form – and are in turn in-formed by – the consciousness's process of becoming. In Buddhist philosophy, one's inability to become mindful of how consciousness constantly drives – and is driven by – karma, initiates an attachment to the process of becoming itself as though it existed with permanence and substantiality. In short, it is an attachment to the self and an inability to let go and let be one's constructed and revised past that affects how one perceives, recognises and builds one's knowledge of the self and other.[40]

In *Lilting*, it is during Junn's visit to Richard and Kai's shared house that their living space is given a *body*. I use the word *body* in the Deleuzian sense: the corporeality, materiality and sensorial intensity of an assemblage of molecular changes – or a milieu – which constitute the *subjectivity* of the space itself and the lives that occupy it.[41] Junn requests some time alone to be in 'Kai's room' so that she can smell the lingering trace of Kai's corporeal presence. However, the spectator, by this point in the film, has long identified this room *as* the smell emanated from the two young lovers' intimate bodies. Therefore, what Junn reminisces is a smell that is a sensation of her past, to which she is attached, and this past sensation gives forms to every being, object and moment of existence in relation to the constructed memory of her own son. Before this sequence, Junn asks Richard for Kai's ashes. While Richard initially refuses, after this sequence he eventually lets go and lets be those karmic impulses that compel him to cling on to the ashes of his lover's body.

In this sense, the presence of the absence of the BEASEA body can be understood as an instantiation of Richard's and Junn's karmic impulses. They both attach themselves not to the *here and now* (i.e. every lived present) of Kai when he was alive but to the sensations of intimacy, tactility and smell that linger and are revised in their memories. It is tempting to read this film allegorically: that the BEASEA body is, politically and socially, *nobody*. Instead, it is a projection of all those people who claim that they have the right to speak *for* and construct this body. Such an allegorical reading, however, is secondary to the structure of feeling encapsulated by Kai's presence of absence: the sense of desubjectivisation, deindividuation and deautonomisation when there is no body for a BEASEA that can emit a voice. Kai's absented body is ironically ostracised by its lover's and mother's claims for their right to *care for* this non-existent imagined body.

It is important to remember that Vann is also a BEASEA character, and she serves as an interlocutor between Junn and Richard. Vann initially seems to be more sympathetic to Richard, as they are both around the same age with the same London upbringing. In fact, East London as a community that has been historically more open to the BEASEA community is foregrounded by her cosmopolitanism. After Richard's first visit, the film shows Vann and Richard walking along a canal, with a mixture of the more recently developed apartment buildings and Victorian-Edwardian row houses, which characterise the East London landscape. East London therefore serves as a space where racial equity and mutual understanding can be achieved precisely through the neoliberal understanding of multiculturalism.

Yet, when Richard presses Junn to recognise his relationship with Kai, Junn swears at Richard. Vann translates Junn's swear words faithfully, as though she is transmitting Junn's anger through her own body. Richard's shock is empathetically conveyed by a cut to a medium close-up of his face with a look of incredulity. *Lilting* is often interpreted by white British critics as a film about 'lost in translation'.[42] In the film, there is no suggestion of translational problems. Richard walks into Junn's room knowing exactly how she feels about his relationship with Kai and the loss of her son, and Junn is not oblivious to her son's relationship with Richard and how he must have felt. The problem in this scene is not about mistranslation but about translating everything too literally. Junn's anger is triggered by Richard's insistence on over-translating everything (from every word Junn speaks to his proposal to take care of Junn as though he were her son) in terms that would make sense only to him, terms which he authorises. His plight before Kai's death was Kai's refusal to come out to his mother in what Richard thought was the only right thing to do. In this sense, Vann, a BEASEA who is 'hired' by Richard to be an interlocutor between him and Junn, performs and translates the very frustration and anger Kai must have felt: that not every act, thought and speech must be translated into terms that feel *right* by someone who claims their authority over the terms of translation.

It is important to note that, although the film is set in East London, the film only shows East London overtly *once* in the aforementioned scene between Vann and Richard. London, however, resurfaces as a trace in Vann's fashionable outfit, in the café where she meets Richard, in the tastefulness of Kai's interior design and, precisely, in the interracial relationship between Kai and Richard. In this sense, the film leaves the spectator a taste of hope that East London can serve as a cradle where racial equity and the recognition of a BEASEA consciousness can be *approached*, not as a fixed identity or essence to be achieved but as a process that works hand-in-hand with the city – and the nation state at large – as a constantly growing and changing imagined community.

Conclusion

The poetics of double erasure is not an end but only a means to a further stage of struggle for visibility. As BEASEA artists Lucy Sheen, Daniel York and David Tse would argue, Hong Khaou's successes are few and far between. Also, let us not forget that *Lilting* received its primary attention in the United States, not the UK. The status of BEASEAs being doubly occupied and ostracised by both the unmarked dominant groups and the marginalised communities is still part of *our* lived experiences. Nonetheless, the poetics of double erasure at least enables the spectator to become mindful of the process of double erasure itself. It also makes visible and sensible that the subalterns are always being spoken for, spoken about, with all the blanks and omissions filled in by those who claim to care for them. These speakers often attach themselves to a projection of their own image, speaking for the *other* in a language authorised by the speakers' own terms.

Notes

1 Trin T. Minh-ha, *Woman, Native, Other: Writing Postcoloniality and Feminism* (Bloomington, IN: Indiana University Press, 1989), p. 80; qtd in Glen M. Mimura, *Ghostlife of Third Cinema: Asian American Film and Video* (Minneapolis, MN: University of Minnesota Press, 2009), p. xv.
2 Mimura, *Ghostlife of Third Cinema*.
3 Felicia Chan and Andy Willis, 'British Chinese Cinema and the Struggle for Recognition, Even on the Margins', in *Contesting British Chinese Culture*, ed. Ashley Thorpe and Diana Yeh (Cham, Switzerland: Palgrave Macmillan, 2018), pp. 152–60.
4 Jacques Derrida, *De la grammatologie* (Paris: Les Éditions de Minuit, 1997 [1967]).
5 See Jun Okada, *Making Asian American Film and Video: Histories, Institutions, Movements* (New Brunswick, NJ: Rutgers University Press, 2015), p. 3.
6 Ashley Thorpe and Diana Yeh, 'Introduction: Contesting British Chinese Culture', in *Contesting British Chinese Culture*, ed. Thorpe and Yeh, pp. 8–17.
7 York frequently posts on his Facebook forum British East/Southeast Asian (BEASEA) Actors and Artists Discussion Forum, www.facebook.com/groups/940972859300342 (accessed 17 August 2021). For a discussion of York's position, see Chan and Willis, 'British Chinese Cinema', p. 156. For 'cruel optimism', see Lauren Berlant, *Cruel Optimism* (Durham, NC: Duke University Press, 2011).
8 For the idea of the cinematic consciousness as a field of immanence, see Gilles Deleuze, *Cinéma 2. L'image-temps* (Paris: Les Éditions de Minuit, 2017 [1985]).
9 The word 'white' is highlighted here in order to foreground its constructedness and contestability.
10 Chan and Willis, 'British Chinese Cinema', pp. 152–60.
11 Thorpe and Yeh, 'Introduction', pp. 7–8; Gregor Benton and Edmond Terence Gomez, *The Chinese in Britain, 1800–Present: Economy, Transnationalism, Identity* (Basingstoke: Palgrave Macmillan, 2008).
12 Yeh, 'The Cultural Politics of In/Visibility: Contesting "British Chineseness" in the Arts', in *Contesting British Chinese Culture*, ed. Thorpe and Yeh, pp. 31–56. For the idea of identity as imposition, see David L. Eng and Shinhee Han, *Racial Melancholia, Racial Dissociation: On the Social and Psychic Lives of Asian Americans* (Durham, NC: Duke University Press, 2019), p. 38.

13 Tariq Modood and Nasar Meer, 'Framing Contemporary Citizenship and Diversity in Europe', in *European Multiculturalism(s): Cultural, Religious and Ethnic Challenges*, ed. Anna Triandafyllidou, Tariq Modood, and Nasar Meer (Edinburgh: Edinburgh University Press, 2011), pp. 33–60.
14 Peter X Feng, *Identities in Motion: Asian American Film and Video* (Durham, NC: Duke University Press, 2002), pp. 4–5. Here, Feng refers to José Esteban Muñoz, *Disidentifications: Queers of Color and the Performance of Politics* (Minneapolis, MN: University of Minnesota Press, 1999), p. 6.
15 Eric Chek Wai Lau, 'The Ownership of Cultural Hybrids: Creativity, Culture, and Performance', in *Interculturalism: Exploring Critical Issues*, ed. Diane Powell and Fiona Sze (Oxford: Inter-Disciplinary Press, 2004), pp. 121–5.
16 Winston Churchill, 'Their Finest Hour' [18 June 1940], www.winstonchurchill.org/resources/speeches/233-1940-the-finest-hour/122-their-finest-hour (accessed 23 November 2015); qtd in Thorpe and Yeh, 'Introduction', p. 1. My emphases.
17 See Benton and Gomez, *The Chinese in Britain*, pp. 54, 56, 69, 79, 86, 95, 107, 114, 127, 136 and 147. Evidence of the linguistic policies in Hong Kong and Singapore can be found in their respective government documents housed in the National Archives, Kew.
18 Stuart Hall, 'New Ethnicities', in *Black Film British Cinema*, ed. Kobena Mercer (London: ICA, 1988), p. 27; qtd in Chan and Willis, 'British Chinese Cinema', p. 153.
19 Eddie Chambers, *Black Artists in British Art: A History Since the 1950s* (London: I.B. Tauris, 2014), p. 61; qtd in Chan and Willis, 'British Chinese Cinema', p. 154.
20 Chan and Willis, 'British Chinese Cinema'.
21 Runnymede Trust, *The Future of Multi-Ethnic Britain: The Parekh Report* (London: Profile Books, 2000); discussed in Thorpe and Yeh, 'Introduction', p. 12.
22 Arun Kundnani, 'The Rise and Fall of British Multiculturalism', in *Resituating Culture*, ed. G. Titley (Strasbourg: Council of Europe, 2004), p. 106; qtd in Thorpe and Yeh, 'Introduction', p. 11.
23 Shih Shu-mei, 'Global Literature and the Technologies of Recognition', *PMLA*, 119.1 (January 2004), pp. 22–9.
24 David Tse Ka-Shing, 'It's Time to Put British East Asian Theatre in the Spotlight', *Guardian Theatre Blog* (6 November 2008), www.guardian.co.uk/stage/theatreblog/2008/nov/06/british-east-asian-theatre (accessed 22 August 2011); qtd in Chan and Willis, 'British Chinese Cinema', p. 158.
25 I speak with my experience as Film Consultant of Chinese Visual Festival from 2013 to 2021.
26 Dylan Cave, '10 Great Films about Chinese People in the UK', *BFI* (19 February 2015), www.bfi.org.uk/lists/10-great-films-about-chinese-people-uk (accessed 22 August 2021).
27 Okada, *Making Asian American Film and Video*, p. 3.
28 My conversation with Lucy Sheen in 2013.

29 See, for example, Shirley Geok-lin Lim, 'A Conversation with Timothy Mo', *World Englishes*, 29.4 (21 November 2010), pp. 557–70.
30 See Cave, '10 Great Films'.
31 Chan and Willis, 'British Chinese Cinema', p. 160.
32 My conversation with Guo in 2014.
33 Gayatri Chakravorty Spivak, 'Can the Subaltern Speak?', in *Marxism and the Interpretation of Culture,* ed. Cary Nelson and Lawrence Grossberg (Urbana, IL: University of Illinois Press, 1988), pp. 276–86.
34 Homi Bhabha, 'DissemiNation: Time, Narrative, and the Margins of the Modern Nation', in *Nation and Narration*, ed. Bhabha (London: Routledge, 1990), p. 297.
35 Thomas Elsaesser, 'Real Location, Fantasy Space, Performative Place: Double Occupancy and Mutual Interference in European Cinema', in *European Film Theory,* ed. Temenuga Trifonova (New York: Routledge, 2012), pp. 47–62.
36 Victor Fan, *Extraterritoriality: Locating Hong Kong Cinema and Media* (Edinburgh: Edinburgh University Press, 2019), p. 13.
37 Gilles Deleuze, *Cinéma 1. L'image-mouvement* (Paris: Les Éditions de Minuit, 2015 [1983]), pp. 84–5.
38 Henri Bergson, *Matière et mémoire: Essai sur la relation du corps à l'esprit* (Paris: Presses Universitaires de France, 2019 [1939]), p. 115; Deleuze, *Cinéma 2*, p. 65.
39 My conversation with Hong Khaou, January 2021. Rey Chow might see it as a form of 'sentimental fabulation'. See Rey Chow, *Sentimental Fabulations, Contemporary Chinese Films: Attachment in the Age of Global Visibility* (New York: Columbia University Press, 2007).
40 Victor Fan, *Cinema Illuminating Reality: Media Philosophy through Buddhism* (Minneapolis, MN: University of Minnesota Press, 2022).
41 Deleuze, *Cinéma 2*, pp. 246–91.
42 See, for example, Jonathan Romney, '*Lilting* Review: When Love is Lost in Translation', *Guardian* (10 August 2014), www.theguardian.com/film/2014/aug/10/lilting-review-when-love-lost-in-translation-ben-whishaw (accessed 22 August 2021); Laurence Barber, 'Loss in Translation: Hong Khaou's *Lilting*', *Metro Magazine,* 186 (2015), pp. 14–19.

10

Global Hollywood and the London set piece

Lawrence Webb

At the climax of a high-octane rooftop chase sequence in *Mission: Impossible – Fallout* (Christopher McQuarrie, Paramount, 2018), a dizzying aerial shot captures Ethan Hunt (Tom Cruise) surveying the London skyline from the chimney of Tate Modern as his antagonist, John Lark (Henry Cavill), escapes in a helicopter. Over the previous seven minutes, we have watched Cruise/Hunt run at full pace through St Paul's Cathedral, climb onto its roof, pull off a series of hair-raising leaps between buildings, almost but not quite miss a key jump, make a brief detour into an office interior, drop from a third-floor window, sprint across the Thames over the top of Blackfriars railway bridge and ascend the Tate building using the emergency ladder of a service elevator. Moving from one historic landmark (St Paul's) across another (the River Thames itself), the film takes us to a more recent addition to the capital's globally familiar iconography, the contemporary art museum Tate Modern (formerly Bankside Power Station). The action is framed by a sustained panorama of London's transformed skyline and a roll-call of its most famous and controversial high-rise buildings, from 30 St Mary Axe ('the Gherkin', completed 2004) through to 122 Leadenhall Street ('the Cheesegrater', completed 2014), 20 Fenchurch Street ('the Walkie Talkie', completed 2014) and, on the south side of the Thames, the Shard (completed 2013). During this intense sequence, the architecture and infrastructure of modern, global London are briefly but memorably on display.

In this chapter, I will use this rooftop chase as the starting point for a consideration of London's role in the global film industry and its current status as a thriving production centre for Hollywood tentpole blockbusters. The chapter addresses a series of questions. Beyond its obvious merits as an impressive piece of genre spectacle, what does this scene have to tell us about the intersecting industrial, political-economic and cultural factors that shape the production of high-budget franchise films in the United Kingdom? What are the specific qualities and affordances of such spatially dynamic set pieces, and how do they relate to questions of industry, genre, aesthetics and politics? And how might we place this brief but impactful action sequence into the histories of London on screen that have been mapped out by scholars such as Charlotte Brunsdon?[1] Rather than focusing on an individual visiting filmmaker, this chapter examines the systemic relationship between Hollywood and the UK and considers the cinematic experience of London that arises from the industrial and cultural dynamics of that relationship.

To do so, I will zoom in on the phenomenon of what I call 'the London set piece' – intense, relatively self-contained chase and action scenes staged on the streets and in the public spaces of the capital – as a means of understanding the intersections between global Hollywood and contemporary London. For blockbusters such as *The Bourne Ultimatum* (Paul Greengrass, Universal, 2007), *Mission: Impossible – Rogue Nation* (Christopher McQuarrie, Paramount, 2011), *Fast and Furious 6* (Justin Lin, Universal, 2013), *Thor: The Dark World* (Alan Taylor, Walt Disney Studios, 2013), *Edge of Tomorrow* (Doug Liman, Warner Bros, 2014), *Jason Bourne* (Paul Greengrass, Universal, 2016), *Doctor Strange* (Scott Derrickson, Walt Disney Studios, 2016), *Mission: Impossible – Fallout* and *Spider-Man: Far From Home* (Jon Watts, Sony, 2019), London is not only a hub for studio production and visual effects work but also a stage for location-based action. Although the city only appears for a relatively short duration on screen, these are nevertheless among the most prominent images of London in contemporary cinema for international audiences. In addition to the rooftop chase in *Mission: Impossible – Fallout*, this chapter will analyse another action-thriller set piece in detail: the Waterloo station scene in *The Bourne Ultimatum*. Placed roughly a decade apart, these two films span from the introduction of the UK film tax credit (in 2007) to near the present time of writing (before the COVID-19 pandemic shut down production). Whereas *M:I – Fallout* plays with the iconic qualities of tourist landmarks, *The Bourne Ultimatum*'s railway station chase displays a self-consciously restrained approach to London's urban landscape. Yet, as I'll show, both chase sequences use their set piece status to mobilise ideas about spectacle, authenticity and realism. In what follows, I'll consider how these attention-grabbing scenes employ the city as a production space, a stage for genre action and a multivalent cultural signifier.

London as Hollywood's offshore service centre

But what brings Tom Cruise to Tate Modern – or, in other words, how do we explain the apparent success of the UK as a service centre for Hollywood? Cruise's personal love affair with London is a well-worn topic for the press but the star's predilection for the city might be read as a synecdoche for the ongoing industrial romance between Hollywood and the English capital.[2] Paramount's *Mission: Impossible – Fallout* is one of many Hollywood blockbusters produced (in whole or in part) in London in recent years. According to data published by FilmLA in 2019, the UK was the most popular single destination for US overseas production in 2018, accounting for nearly a quarter of all international shoots that year (a total of thirty-seven theatrical feature films) and 12.7 per cent of all narrative features (overseas and domestic combined).[3] When the focus is narrowed to top-grossing films, the numbers increase: at 43.2 per cent, the UK outperformed California and New York as the production location for box office hits.[4] Measured in terms of budget, at least, the UK has become the number one centre for Hollywood production in the 2010s and early 2020s. The British Film Institute estimates the combined inward investment for 2019 at £1.74 billion, a staggering 89.3 per cent of annual production spend for the British film industry.[5] As these statistics suggest, the UK is among the most successful production hubs for high-budget Hollywood filmmaking.

Untangling the British film industry from US influence is not easy but there are nevertheless some specific factors that have pushed London to the top of Hollywood's offshore production pipeline in the twenty-first century.[6] Foremost among these is the substantial tax relief offered by the British government, which subsidises qualifying productions at up to 25 per cent. Established in 2007, the UK tax credit is the most expensive film incentive programme in the world, costing the UK treasury more than £500 million annually.[7] The availability of high-specification studio infrastructure is equally important. Blockbuster movies require capacious sound stages for green-screen work as well as access to high-tech post-production services. The UK offers approximately 3.5 million square feet of stage space – though that figure is growing rapidly – much of it concentrated in Greater London and the home counties, including world-class facilities such as Pinewood Studios, Shepperton Studios, Longcross Studios and Warner Bros Studios Leavesden. Though there is more stage space in Southern California overall, the UK boasts the highest number of large-capacity stages (defined as over 30,000 square feet).[8] Those soundstages are increasingly filled with Hollywood projects and US–UK co-productions, as long-term leases signed by Disney at Pinewood and Netflix at Shepperton demonstrate.[9] Alongside the twin attractions of tax credits and infrastructure, London offers above-the-line talent, skilled below-the-line labour and industry-leading visual effects houses such as Soho's Framestore, and its relative affordability for overseas investment has only been improved by the declining pound in the wake of the Brexit referendum. Less tangible but likely important are the 'soft' qualities that sweeten the deal for producers, directors and stars:

London is a globally networked transport hub and an attractive tourist destination with all the allures of a tier-one global city (five-star hotels, Michelin-starred restaurants, high-end shopping).[10] Whether one considers finance, infrastructure, labour or cultural amenities, the Greater London region is geared to service the production of big-budget Hollywood franchise films (such as *Mission: Impossible*, *Star Wars* and Marvel movies) and glossy serial television dramas (such as *The Crown* (Netflix, 2016–23)).

London's appeal to Hollywood has been almost uniformly framed in a positive light by industry representatives and politicians such as Mayor Sadiq Khan, who has spoken widely about his vision for London as 'the world's most film-friendly city', but it's worth sounding a critical note here.[11] In brief, we might equally view London's Hollywood success story in relation to globalisation, offshoring, financialisation and neoliberal rentier capitalism. When it subsidises film production, the British state funnels public money into tax relief for the multinational corporations that own the Hollywood studios. In line with the broader financialisation of the media industries, those corporations primarily operate in the UK at a series of exclusive studio complexes that are now owned by equity funds such as Aermont Capital. From an investor's vantage point, studios have become financialised real estate assets in London's hyperinflated property market.[12] At the same time, the UK's generous tax credit scheme has played a key role in the global competition for US film production that has been accompanied by a 'race to the bottom' in terms of working conditions and regulations.[13] For many workers, the film industry remains badly paid and plagued by a culture of overwork and widespread safety problems.[14] And for some commentators on the British film industry, Hollywood's capture of major studio spaces has had negative effects on local production cultures.[15] In short, the transatlantic industrial romance could be construed in many ways as a toxic relationship.

London's success as a Hollywood production centre appears on the surface to have relatively little to do with its social and physical qualities as a city, but there are ways we might complicate that picture. In terms of its construction of a visible screen London, Hollywood's London output can be split into two main categories. First, there are films which are primarily produced in the Greater London studios but are not set in the city. For productions such as *Star Wars: The Force Awakens* (J. J. Abrams, Walt Disney Studios, 2015), filming in the UK is entirely disconnected from motivations of story and aesthetics. These films are primarily produced in front of green screens on sealed-off soundstages that are sequestered in suburban and semi-rural locations far from the urban centre, with excursions to more 'exotic' overseas locations taken as required. In some cases, such productions do venture onto London locations to construct fantasy or science-fiction environments in other times and places – we might think of the brief appearance of Canary Wharf Tube station in *Star Wars: Rogue One*, the Millennium Footbridge in *Guardians of the Galaxy* (James Gunn, Disney, 2014) or the Brent Civic Centre in *Avengers: Age of Ultron* (Joss Whedon, Disney, 2015) – but, for the average viewer, these are not legible as London.[16] Secondly, there are what Paul McDonald defines as 'British Hollywood' films, which are typically financed and distributed by the Hollywood majors but rely on British creative input and capitalise on British culture and identity as an overt part of their appeal to viewers. Displaying markedly British themes and settings, these films have no problems meeting the BFI's criteria to be categorised as 'culturally British' and are often identified as such for the purposes of the BAFTA awards.[17] McDonald's key example is *Notting Hill* (Roger Michell, Universal/Polygram, 1999), a film that was shot in UK facilities and uses 'identifiably London locations' to 'create a little fantasy world that was both London and not London'.[18] More recent examples include Universal/Working Title's period drama *Darkest Hour* (Joe Wright, 2017), set in London during World War II, and Disney's *Mary Poppins Returns* (Rob Marshall, 2018), which uses a combination of locations, studio sets built at Shepperton, visual effects and digital animation to update the fantasy London of the classic musical. Whereas many franchise blockbusters conceal their production location, British Hollywood films trade on their images of London as marketable elements of cultural specificity.

Films such as *The Bourne Ultimatum*, *M:I – Fallout* and the other titles listed in the introduction are closer to the first category but there are some areas of crossover with the British Hollywood film that arise from their location-filmed action sequences. In these high-budget spy thrillers, superhero films and science-fiction adventure pictures, London is both a production location and a narrative setting, though it typically appears during brief bursts of action rather than in dialogue-driven dramatic scenes. Although the city is usually just one among a series of interconnected settings for blockbuster franchise movies, whose high-stakes narratives tend to be framed at a transnational or even planetary scale, London is nevertheless highly significant to them both industrially and culturally. At an industrial level, filming in the city – especially using local labour – helps productions to score points on the all-important BFI test for tax relief. Points are allotted for a range of criteria, including employing UK cast and crew, the percentage of principal photography that takes place in the UK and the proportion of the film that is set in the UK (25 per cent is the key threshold).[19] There are therefore strong economic and institutional motivations for including different kinds of British content in blockbuster films and for increasing the percentage of material filmed in the UK. And these films strategically deploy their London set pieces, which often self-consciously engage with iconic urban landmarks, as a means to accrue some of the markers of cultural specificity that British Hollywood films mobilise. Taken together, these high-budget productions have channelled billions of dollars through the British film industry; perhaps unsurprisingly, given the generic patterns of franchise filmmaking, more money was spent in the UK between 2017 and 2019 on making action films than on any other category (40.3 per cent of the aggregate budget of UK-produced features).[20] London produces action films, then, but we might also ask what kind of London action films produce for the screen.

The set piece: industry, genre and marketing

The image of the city created by these films is shaped by the generic and industrial parameters of the set piece, which can be broadly defined as a spectacular, audio-visually expressive sequence that prioritises action, movement and display rather than dialogue.[21] Set pieces foreground visual and aural design and are intended to create visceral, affective responses in the audience. In this respect they are one of the traditional viewing pleasures offered by certain kinds of genre cinema. Set pieces create a dynamic relation to space that emphasises cinema's spatio-temporal capacities (we might think of Erwin Panofsky's famous elaboration of cinema's 'dynamization of space' and 'spatialization of time').[22] Crucially, a set piece is designed to stand out from the rest of the film; by definition, it highlights its semi-autonomous status. In that sense, set pieces are inherently self-reflexive: they ask the viewer to notice them and, by doing so, they draw attention to the process of production. By their nature, they flaunt their logistical and technical complexity. When viewing a set piece, we are likely to be reminded of the intensive labour and technological feats behind their staging, especially in challenging real-world locations such as the streets of a major city. Because they are intended to be broken out from the main body of the film and discussed separately, set pieces are often a site of reflection for film critics and a subject for behind-the-scenes promotional materials. In short, set pieces are visually and sonically expressive, spatially dynamic and industrially reflexive.

Recent scholarship on the action film has emphasised its spatial qualities. Nick Jones has made an extended case for action cinema as 'a cinema of space, a cinema that puts environmental knowledge and negotiation at the heart of its agenda'.[23] For Jones, one of the core appeals of action cinema is watching the protagonist master and appropriate space in a way that recalls Michel De Certeau's notion of tactics.[24] In some cases, Jones suggests, the on-screen negotiation of space can present critical or even subversive qualities, revealing 'the anxieties that surround contemporary space, its multiple pressures and threats, its alienating monumentality and its suffusion with surveillance devices and state-controlled systems of domination'.[25] Similarly, Lisa Purse has argued that 'the speed sequence' in action cinema 'offers the fantasy of mapping [...] urban space through assertive, self-directed movement, of pushing through the city's barriers, of rising out of its strictures'.[26] We should be careful to note, however, the difference between the pleasures of tactics offered by the protagonists' skilful navigation of narrative space and the underlying strategies of the Hollywood studios and other agents. As Jones argues, action films speak to viewers' utopian desires to overcome the abstract space of capitalism but they are inescapably located within its strategic frameworks.[27] And as Yvonne Tasker's work has explored, action is a highly gendered format; despite the rise of the female action hero in recent years, the London set pieces under examination in this chapter are almost exclusively masculine affairs.[28]

In the first instance, set pieces are designed to meet genre requirements for exciting and innovative action, often explicitly through their relationship to specific spaces and places – whether taking the audience to somewhere new or revelling in the reappropriation and revision of familiar sites. For the action thriller more specifically, there are deep genre roots to this kind of architectural drama, especially Alfred Hitchcock's memorable reconstruction of buildings and monuments such as the Statue of Liberty in *Saboteur* (Universal, 1942), Mount Rushmore in *North by Northwest* (MGM, 1959) and, in the specific context of London, the domed roof of the British Museum in *Blackmail* (British International Pictures, 1929).[29] Alongside such dynamic and spectacular engagement with the built environment, espionage thrillers naturally structure their narratives around international travel, a genre norm that dates back at least as far as the success of the James Bond films in the 1960s. Today, genre conventions work in dialogue (and sometimes in tension) with the industrial requirements of franchise filmmaking, which repurposes the familiar dynamics of repetition and difference in relation to intellectual property and proprietary branding. Nevertheless, there are strong patterns of influence and exchange as well as commercial differentiation between the Bond, Bourne and Mission: Impossible series, each of which has made international travel and breakneck chase sequences into a signature feature. As numerous reviewers observed in chorus, films like *M:I – Fallout* have evolved into streamlined 'delivery systems' for action: in the *Los Angeles Times*, Kenneth Turan noted that 'the storyline's essential function is to serve as an action sequence delivery system'; the *Washington Post* critic Ann Hornaday described the film as 'an efficient, attractive delivery system for the kind of spectacle we've come to expect from midcareer Cruise'; while

Slate's Sam Adams acknowledged that 'even the best *M:I* movies largely function as delivery systems for action sequences'.[30] However we interpret the metaphor of the delivery system – drugs and military hardware seem equally apt – critics agree that the set piece is, for better or for worse, more important to these films than traditional qualities of character and story. The primacy of the action set piece is reflected in the production process too: according to the cinematographer, Robert Elswit, shooting for the action scenes in *Mission: Impossible – Rogue Nation* kicked off some time before the final script had been completed.[31]

As Elswit's comments suggest, set pieces have a number of industrial functions that extend beyond genre. At the level of production, the inherently modular, 'plug in' quality of the set piece is perfectly suited to the fragmented, spatially dispersed nature of contemporary Hollywood's globalised supply-chain model. In this sense, the action set piece and the globetrotting of Hollywood production are symbiotically related. The need to film set pieces in global locations is one factor behind the dispersed geography of the action thriller but there are strong economic imperatives behind the globalisation of production too, from transnational financing deals, tax incentives and access to local markets to cheap labour and reduced regulations. Constructing a film as a series of semi-autonomous action set pieces therefore works smoothly with the requirements of genre and the geographical pressures of contemporary production. At the same time, the reflexive and modular quality of the set piece also lends itself to promotion (or, perhaps, to frame it the other way around, it is partly through promotional forms that set piece status is conferred and maintained). Set pieces and the architectural spectacle they often generate are tailor-made to be viewed, discussed, shared and listed separately from the rest of the film, and extra-textual materials about set pieces frequently promote a heightened awareness of space and place. *Architectural Digest*, for example, has published extended discussions of the architecture used in the *Mission: Impossible* series ('The Major Buildings Tom Cruise's Character Has Scaled, Landed on, or Fallen from in Every *Mission: Impossible* Movie') and in *M:I – Fallout* specifically ('The Actual Architectural Wonders Used in *Mission: Impossible – Fallout*').[32] Likewise, the special features on *The Bourne Ultimatum* DVD show how constructing the film as a series of modular set pieces makes it easy to break the text into promotional segments. A series of short behind-the-scenes films takes us on a parallel journey to the key locations for *Bourne Ultimatum*'s action sequences – Berlin, Paris, London, Madrid and Tangiers – providing both information about the locale (we learn about the complexities of filming in Tangier during Ramadan, for example) and technical detail about the staging of action and stunts.

The inside is on the outside: landmark London and operational aesthetics

The Lonely Planet–guide quality of the *Bourne Ultimatum* extras highlights the essentially touristic sensibility of the set piece. As the *M:I – Fallout* chase and its image of the skyline suggest, the London set piece typically invokes what Charlotte Brunsdon calls 'landmark London' – that instantly recognisable array of 'tourist hardware' that mostly dates to the nineteenth century (Tower Bridge, the Palace of Westminster, Nelson's Column) or earlier (St Paul's Cathedral, the Tower of London) but can now also include examples of 'millennial modernity' (such as the London Eye, Tate Modern, the Gherkin and the Millennium Footbridge).[33] It would therefore be easy to critique the fleeting engagements with London in these action films as touristic: they frequently display iconic, picture-postcard landmarks such as St Paul's Cathedral as geographical markers and are clearly not designed to engage with the everyday lives of citizens. Yet tourism is a somewhat shop-worn metaphor, as well as being imprecise – as anyone whose path has ever been obstructed by smartphone-toting visitors knows, tourism is an activity that tends to happen at a much more leisurely pace than these frenetic action sequences. And more importantly, there is a playful and self-conscious quality to the London set piece and its engagement with landmark London. To be immediately identifiable as London on screen, Brunsdon incisively observes, these sites must already be understood as clichés; as a result, there is a built-in sense of redundancy that means 'location-shot films may go to great pains to offer fresh views of familiar landmarks'.[34] The set piece amplifies this tension between conventionality and innovation. To some extent, these action sequences acknowledge and even encourage self-conscious reflection on the status of landmarks as cliché. In other words, such sequences are spectacular *because* they take place at such well-known places.

Set pieces therefore generate what the television scholar Jason Mittell defines as an 'operational aesthetic'. As Mittell argues, the principal pleasures of television viewing now include thinking about, discussing and hypothesising about the operations behind the text – considering 'How did they do that?' as much as 'What will happen next?'[35] But in contrast to Mittell's area of focus, 'complex television', the operational qualities of the franchise film's set piece are less about self-consciously baroque storytelling devices than the logistical challenges of the scene. The action set piece, which by definition draws attention to its staging, brings this 'operational aesthetic' to the surface. Set piece status is predicated partly on the performance of logistical difficulty that their staging requires: these sequences ostentatiously display the filmmaking coup of shooting in crowded public spaces (like Waterloo station) or inside world-famous historic buildings (like St Paul's Cathedral), working against the conventional status of the landmark as a means of orientation or a backdrop. Frequently, this involves going 'behind the scenes' at well-known sites via staff entrances, emergency stairs and service elevators – an engagement with the inner structures of the building that pushes against the typical use of landmarks as backdrop. Brunsdon notes that St Paul's Cathedral is used repeatedly across genres as an establishing signifier of London but 'not much actually happens there'; as she puts it, 'it is relatively rare for it to be used as a location within the imagined world of a film'.[36] Staging a chase scene in St Paul's, as *M:I – Fallout* does, both capitalises on the ready familiarity of the building to most audiences worldwide and plays with that familiarity. The well-known nature of these places is precisely the point: 'How did they film this action scene *there?*', we are invited to wonder. As Richard Brody writes in his *New Yorker* review of *M:I – Fallout*, 'Its feat of cinematic engineering invites admiration for its engineering: the infrastructure is on the outside, the seemingly tenuous threads that dangle its dramatic pendants are on view, and the delights that it offers are those of a production video, showcased not in a behind-the-scenes reel, but throughout the movie itself.' Or, as the subeditor succinctly frames it, 'Mission Impossible Fallout Is Basically a Two-and-a-Half Hour Making-of Sequence'.[37]

Whereas Tom Cruise's sprint takes us on an outdoor journey between two well-known public buildings, the London set piece in *Bourne Ultimatum* is a cat-and-mouse chase mostly staged inside Waterloo station. In the scene, Jason Bourne (Matt Damon) helps the *Guardian* reporter Simon Ross (Paddy Considine) navigate the teeming concourse while pursued by one of the CIA's Blackbriar agents, Paz (Édgar Ramírez). At the same time, CIA deputy director Noah Vosen (David Strathairn) tracks the operation from New York by tapping into the station's extensive CCTV network. Stations appear frequently in the film – Waterloo is the third, after Atocha in Madrid and Gare du Nord in Paris – and in the franchise more generally. A crowded mainline station has much to offer a chase sequence at a narrative level: it is recognisable and plausible as an everyday urban space, it is full of obstacles and challenges, and it offers possibilities for evasive manoeuvres and displays of tradecraft for the special agent. But it has set piece appeal for the audience too, as the UK location manager, Sam Breckman, observes: 'The best part of it is the smug satisfaction of being able to accomplish something like this, where people say, "How the hell did you get Waterloo station?" Waterloo station is a brilliant place to film in and it's a challenge.' Filming in a working railway station among real crowds was demanding but, as Greengrass explains, the location was chosen precisely for that reason. In the DVD commentary, Greengrass recalls that the logistical difficulty of the scene suited the spatial sensibility of the franchise. 'I didn't want to [...] move into town and create sanitised spaces, put a picket fence around the unit and make our film cut off from everyday life', he recalls, 'because that's not where the Bourne franchise lives. The Bourne franchise lives on the streets'. It also pushed them to work in a more stripped down style – pushing against the 'mainstream Hollywood mentality', as Greengrass saw it – with a small team of only fifteen to twenty people: 'it forced us to be true to our roots, to operate like a guerrilla unit, seizing shots on the run, in amongst everyday life – the teeming reality of big cities'. 'I think that gives this sequence its vitality', he adds, 'because very often we were literally making it up as we go along and grabbing shots as best we could in amongst the workings of the station'. Operating among the 'workings of the station' entailed not only moving from public space into the 'back stage' areas of the station, which Bourne memorably uses to evade and then neutralise his pursuers, but also patching into security cameras to access a live feed of surveillance footage ('It will be unmistakably real', Matt Damon observes, 'and I think that's what people like about these things'). As these quotations from the film's promotional apparatus show, shooting on location in the station provided an opportunity for overt reflection on the set piece in relation to the marketable qualities of authenticity and realism that they mobilise.

For Greengrass, who is British, the Waterloo set piece was explicitly intended to depart from landmark London. As he explains, 'I've always felt that London in big movies is too often presented to us as a land of Big Ben and the Houses of Parliament, and St Pauls, and London buses – a tourist London. And that's not the world of Jason Bourne.' Bourne, adds Greengrass, 'lives in the cities we all live in ... it's just an ordinary city'. As Greengrass suggests, the London scenes in *Bourne Ultimatum* are in many respects more 'ordinary' than the explicitly touristic display of *M:I – Fallout* and certainly more contained in their engagement with city space. London is established by a shot of the *Guardian* offices at their former location in Farringdon, for example, rather than through a more conventional panorama of the Thames. Sue Harris has developed this idea, arguing that the Bourne films develop an explicitly 'anti-touristic idiom' by removing the conventional functions of establishing shots and other markers of orientation and by fragmenting screen space.[38] For Harris, public space in the Bourne movies becomes 'flattened, in the face of unique cultural markers and national visual cues, into undifferentiated and indistinguishable canvases for the display of material and symbolic violence'.[39] Despite the fragmented visual style, however, there are still strong continuities with *M:I – Fallout* and other examples of the London set piece. Waterloo station was at that time the Eurostar terminal: hardly a postcard image but not entirely removed from tourist London either, and though the station makes up part of the daily commute for thousands of Londoners, its status as an international point of arrival and departure is central to its function within the thriller narrative.

Global networks: technology and authenticity

Thus, another way to reframe the inherently 'touristic' qualities of the London set piece emerges: by focusing on elements of the city that tourists often see, beyond landmarks – especially major railway stations, bridges and other kinds of transport infrastructure – these films grasp something of the technologically mediated nature of the city that is not always visible in prominent British Hollywood genres such as heritage films, romantic comedies or children's adventure films. As a by-product, they often capture more banal spaces of the British high street too, such as the glimpses of Superdrug on a side street in *M:I – Fallout*. In distinction to most British Hollywood dramas, the action set piece constructs London primarily as a global city rather than as a distinctively national space, engaging with infrastructural networks of transport, technology, communication and surveillance. As Christian Long notes, the chase sequence is typically preoccupied with transport, especially the 'multi-level, multi-modal transportation infrastructure' of major urban centres.[40] Adam O'Brien has also convincingly argued that set pieces often incorporate infrastructure – or, more precisely, that infrastructure on screen has a propensity to create a 'set piece effect'. Set pieces and infrastructure, O'Brien argues, have a special affinity.[41]

Both the *Bourne Ultimatum* and *M:I – Fallout* set pieces explore the infrastructural networks of the city. In each case, the chase takes place in public space that is continuously monitored by digital surveillance, establishing an immediate divide between action that is performed in one place and simultaneously tracked in another. In *Bourne Ultimatum*, Bourne's every movement is traced by the CIA's 'Deep Cover Anti-Terrorism Bureau' in New York, where Noah Vosen's team are able to tap remotely into Waterloo station's countless CCTV cameras ('Give me eyes on Waterloo Station!'). In *M:I – Fallout*, Hunt is supported by the faithful but not always competent IMF tech team led by Benji Dunn (Simon Pegg), who map his progress on an iPad and frantically attempt to direct him through his earpiece ('turn right!') The back-and-forth dynamics of this thriller trope, whereby the agent in the field and the audience are connected back to 'mission control', establish tension (in *Bourne Ultimatum*) and humour (in *M:I – Fallout*) but they also create a sense of coherence and legibility for the viewer. In *M:I – Fallout*, repeated close-ups of Benji's iPad show us Hunt's position and the route that the chase will take, though these digital maps are unreliable and their failures playfully acknowledge the disparity between 2D and 3D projections of space. Maps also appear in the Blackbriar control centre in *Bourne Ultimatum* – showing, for example, the route that Simon Ross will take to Waterloo in a taxi. In *Bourne Ultimatum*, there are two sets of communication occurring simultaneously: Vosen's team track Bourne via the US control room and their asset on the ground, while Bourne directs the movements of the journalist Simon Ross on his mobile phone. Bourne's constant instructions to Ross, which create a sense of him 'directing' the scene while participating in it, are especially important for maintaining legibility in light of the highly fragmented and almost chaotic visual style which shatters conventional screen space with its rapid cuts, frantic snap zooms and whip pans. As Greengrass observes, 'tempo without clarity is very, very unsatisfying'. The Bourne and Mission: Impossible series have distinct approaches to staging action, but there are a number of intriguing similarities between these sequences in the way that they mobilise technological systems as aesthetic and narrational strategies.

Although they are openly inauthentic in relation to the everyday life of the city, action sequences nevertheless trade on authenticity at a different level: the sense of locative presence and familiarity invoked by the set piece is part of a wider discourse of realism that attends the production of place (as well as performance and stunts) in the era of CGI. In the case of *M:I – Fallout* such an emphasis on the difficult and even hazardous nature of production intersects with a wider set of discourses circling around the film in relation to practical stunts and, in particular, Tom Cruise's own participation as a stunt performer. Reviews of the film typically place this knowledge about what the *New York Times* called 'persuasive markers of authenticity' centre stage (emphasising, for example, that 'his ability to continue to do all his own stunts becomes remarkable' and that 'he famously insists on doing his own stunts').[42] As Sam Adams's review for *Slate* suggests, this 'preference for practically based stunts over computer-generated spectacle' connects the 'authentic' feats of the star's ageing body to pervasive discourses of realism in the digital age.[43] Nowhere was this clearer than when news emerged of Cruise injuring himself while on location. The star had broken his ankle when landing awkwardly for one of the London rooftop jumps but in a characteristic public display of professionalism he completed the take, still mobile but visibly limping. Not only did the shot end up in the final version of the film but footage of the incident was also released by the studio and purposefully imbricated into the film's promotion: it circulated widely in the press and on social media and was discussed by Cruise himself on television chat shows such as the BBC's *Graham Norton Show*. The relatively unusual level of publicity attending an aspect of failure in the production – especially given that accidents and deaths of stunt performers are routinely played down – speaks not only to audience fascination with Cruise's insistence on doing his own stunts but also to the discursive value of the location set piece. Location shooting, in this case on London rooftops, is just one of many ostensibly 'analogue' elements that structure the film's promotional presence: stunt work, practical effects and the use of 35mm film. All of these components have gained value in counterpoint to critical discourses about the over-use and perceived inauthenticity of digital visual effects.[44] The value of these ideas can also be gauged by watching the various short behind-the-scenes films made to promote *Mission: Impossible – Fallout*, which return repeatedly to rhetoric about realism, location and authentic performance (McQuarrie: 'The language of *Mission: Impossible* is all about going to real locations'; Cruise: 'It's all about practical action').

The fall from the London rooftop pinpoints not only the persistence of long-standing values of believability and seamlessness that have always been central to Hollywood's version of realism but also the promotional value of the material versus the digital. Creating a sense of materiality and plausibility – 'they really did this' – is central to the audience's affective relationship with the set piece and its operational aesthetics. Set pieces can, of course, be driven by digital visual effects too, and we should remember that the rhetoric of authenticity and practical stunts elides the extent to which CGI is used for location work. *M:I – Fallout* contains around 2,000 VFX shots and lists 300 digital artists on the credits; even at the most basic level, the rooftop jump needed digital tools to remove the safety ropes from view and to match the colour of the sky across different footage (Cruise's accident meant that they filmed at different times of year). In London, where Hollywood film production primarily takes place using green screens on large-capacity sound stages, the set piece shows how locations have an important role to play in the way that place and space are created, promoted, viewed and discussed.

Conclusion

In this chapter, I've argued that the London set piece is both a product and a projection of Hollywood's strategic investment in London. In the first instance, these intensive location-based sequences are a by-product of the success of the UK film tax credit and the London studios. Because set pieces draw attention to the production process – a quality that is amplified by their heightened presence in promotional materials – they operate as branding not for London in toto but more specifically for the city as a media production centre. The effect is not necessarily intentional, of course, because there are multiple factors that play into the construction of the set piece. Nevertheless, staging logistically complex and challenging shoots on the city's streets gives the city a type of visibility and global presence that readily meshes with the mayor's vision for 'the world's most film-friendly city' and Film London's strategic goal of 'promoting London on an international stage as an attractive base for film and media production'.[45] Thus they are productive both for the city and for Hollywood. For the studios, filming a short but impactful sequence on location has a number of potential industrial functions: in some cases, using local crew and shooting on the city streets helps productions to accrue points on the BFI's cultural test for tax relief; it provides narrative justification for the choice to work in London, which is primarily motivated by other, less artistic concerns; and it plays into realist discourse and other promotional agendas about the authenticity of locations, stunts and practical effects in the CGI era. The set piece mobilises reflexive engagement with urban space, folding the narrative of production back into the experience of the film itself. Though there is some complexity to the way that the films engage with landmark London, the set piece is designed to draw attention to landmarks and play with their iconicity. And through their engagement with infrastructure and technology, set pieces symptomatically reveal a distinctive image of the city as a globally networked space that is not always so present in other types of British Hollywood filmmaking. Whether we celebrate the ingenuity of their staging or critique them as branding exercises that elide the more negative aspects of the film industry, action set pieces are crucial components of London's screen presence in the early twenty-first century.

Notes

1. See Charlotte Brunsdon, *London in Cinema: The Cinematic City since 1945* (London: BFI, 2007); Pam Hirsch and Chris O'Rourke, eds, *London on Film* (London: Palgrave Macmillan, 2017).
2. See, for example, 'Tom Cruise on London Life: "I Love it Here … It's a Wonderful Place to Live"', *Evening Standard* (18 December 2012); Kevin Maher, 'Why is Tom Cruise Everywhere?', *The Times* (13 July 2021), www.thetimes.co.uk/article/why-is-tom-cruise-everywhere-fr38c9sjk (accessed 2 May 2020).
3. Anne Wurts and Philip Sokoloski, 'FilmLA. Feature Films: A Profile of Production' (2018), p. 6.
4. Ibid., p. 14.
5. 'Screen Sector Production', British Film Institute, p. 5.
6. On the economic relationship between Hollywood and the UK, see John Hill, '"This is for the *Batmans* as well as the *Vera Drakes*": Economics, Culture

and UK Government Film Production Policy in the 2000s', *Journal of British Cinema and Television*, 9.3 (2012), pp. 333–56.
7 For example, film tax relief expenditure amounted to £595 million in 2018–19. See www.gov.uk/government/statistics/creative-industries-statistics-august-2019 (accessed 4 June 2021).
8 Wurts and Sokoloski, 'Film LA. Sound Stage Production Report', pp. 10–12.
9 See, for example, Louise Tutt, 'The Walt Disney Co Signs Long-Term Lease for Entire Pinewood Studios Site in the UK', *Screen Daily* (9 September 2019), www.screendaily.com/news/the-walt-disney-co-signs-long-term-lease-for-entire-pinewood-studios-site-in-the-uk/5142713.article; Mark Sweney, 'Netflix Strikes Production Deal with Shepperton Studios', *Guardian* (3 July 2019), www.theguardian.com/media/2019/jul/03/netflix-strikes-production-deal-with-shepperton-studios (accessed 23 October 2019).
10 On London as a global city, see Saskia Sassen, *The Global City: New York, London, Tokyo* (Princeton, NJ: Princeton University Press, 2001).
11 'Mayor Sets Out Vision for London to Be World's Most Film-Friendly City', *Mayor of London / London Assembly* (31 January 2017), www.london.gov.uk/press-releases/mayoral/new-raft-of-measures-to-invest-in-talent (accessed 16 November 2019).
12 On the London studios and the property market, see the report produced by the consultancy firm Lambert Smith Hampton: 'Sites, Camera, Action! The UK Film & TV Studio Property Market 2018' (2018). On studios and equity finance, see Konrad Putzier, 'Blackstone Sees Film-Production Facilities as a Hot New Real-Estate Play; The Company Wants to Own the Places where Amazon, Apple and Others Are Making Content', *Wall Street Journal* (29 June 2020), www.wsj.com/articles/blackstone-sees-film-production-facilities-as-a-hot-new-real-estate-play-11593433803 (accessed 2 June 2021). I develop this analysis further in 'Studio Urbanism', in *The Routledge Companion to Media and the City*, ed. Erica Stein, Germaine R. Halegoua and Brendan Kredell (London: Routledge, 2022), pp. 299–308. Though he does not discuss film studios, Andrew DeWaard analyses the broader process of financialisation in the media industries; DeWaard, 'Financialized Hollywood: Institutional Investment, Venture Capital, and Private Equity in the Film and Television Industry', *Journal of Cinema and Media Studies*, 59.4 (2020), pp. 54–84. On the rentier economy, see Brett Christophers, 'The Rentierization of the United Kingdom Economy', *Environment and Planning A: Economy and Space* (2019), DOI: 10.1177/0308518X19873007.
13 See Michael Curtin and Kevin Sanson, eds, *Precarious Creativity: Global Media, Local Labor* (Oakland, CA: University of California Press, 2016), pp. 1–18.
14 Paul Evans and Jonathan Green, 'Eyes Half Shut: A Report on Long Hours and Productivity in the UK Film and TV Industry', *BECTU*, https://members.bectu.org.uk/advice-resources/library/2363 (accessed 2 June 2021).
15 Mark Sweney, 'Hollywood and TV Put the Squeeze on UK's Low-budget Film-makers', *Guardian* (31 May 2017), www.theguardian.com/film/2017/may/31/hollywood-and-tv-put-the-squeeze-on-uks-low-budget-film-makers (accessed 23 June 2023)

16 For a discussion of Marvel scenes filmed in the city, see 'London Scenes in the Marvel Cinematic Universe Films', *Londonist*, https://londonist.com/london/film/mcu (accessed 24 June 2021).
17 Paul McDonald, 'Britain: Hollywood, UK', in *The Contemporary Hollywood Film Industry*, ed. Paul McDonald and Janet Wasko (Malden, MA: Blackwell, 2008), pp. 220–31. See also James Russell, 'Hollywood Blockbusters and UK Production Today', in *The Routledge Companion to British Cinema History*, ed. I. Q. Hunter, Laraine Porter and Justin Smith (Abingdon: Routledge, 2016), pp. 377–86.
18 McDonald, 'Britain', p. 224.
19 See the BFI's website: www.bfi.org.uk/apply-british-certification-tax-relief/cultural-test-film (accessed 2 June 2021).
20 'Screen Sector Production', British Film Institute, p. 9.
21 Adam O'Brien provides an in-depth exploration of the set piece in 'Energy and Eventhood: The Infrastructural Set Piece', *Journal of Aesthetics & Culture*, 11.1 (2019), pp. 1–8.
22 Erwin Panofsky, *Three Essays on Style* (Cambridge, MA: The MIT Press, 1995), p. 96.
23 Nick Jones, *Hollywood Action Films and Spatial Theory* (London and New York: Routledge, 2015), p. 3.
24 Ibid., pp. 34–9.
25 Ibid., p. 3.
26 Lisa Purse, *Contemporary Action Cinema* (Edinburgh: Edinburgh University Press, 2011), p. 65.
27 Jones, *Hollywood Action Films*, pp. 36–9.
28 Yvonne Tasker, *Spectacular Bodies: Gender, Genre and the Action Cinema* (London: Routledge, 1993).
29 See Steven Jacobs, *The Wrong House: The Architecture of Alfred Hitchcock* (Rotterdam: 010 Publishers, 2007).
30 Kenneth Turan, 'Review: Tom Cruise Returns, Crazy Stunts and All, in "Mission: Impossible – Fallout"', *Los Angeles Times* (13 July 2018), www.latimes.com/entertainment/movies/la-et-mn-mission-impossible-fallout-review-20180712-story.html; Ann Hornaday, '"Mission Impossible – Fallout" Is Big, Convoluted and Exhausting. It's Also Good', *Washington Post* (24 July 2018), www.washingtonpost.com/goingoutguide/movies/mission-impossible--fallout-is-big-convoluted-and-exhausting-its-also-good/2018/07/24/2920a0b2-8b84-11e8-85ae-511bc1146b0b_story.html; Sam Adams, 'The New *Mission: Impossible* Understands the Secret of the Franchise's Action Sequences', *Slate* (12 July 2018), https://slate.com/culture/2018/07/mission-impossible-fallout-starring-tom-cruise-reviewed.html (accessed 2 June 2021).
31 Michael Goldman, 'Going Rogue', *American Cinematographer* (August 2015), p. 33.
32 Marc Malkin, 'The Actual Architectural Wonders Used in *Mission: Impossible – Fallout*', *Architectural Digest* (6 August 2018), www.architecturaldigest.com/story/the-actual-architectural-wonders-used-in-mission-impossible

fallout; Marc Malkin, 'The Major Buildings Tom Cruise's Character Has Scaled, Landed on, or Fallen from in Every *Mission: Impossible* Movie', *Architectural Digest* (9 August 2018), www.architecturaldigest.com/story/the-major-buildings-tom-cruises-character-has-scaled-landed-on-or-fallen-from-in-every-mission-impossible-movie (accessed 2 May 2021).
33 Brunsdon, *London in Cinema*, pp. 21–3.
34 Ibid., p. 21.
35 Jason Mittell, *Complex TV: The Poetics of Contemporary Television Storytelling* (New York: NYU Press, 2015), pp. 41–4.
36 Brunsdon, *London in Cinema*, p. 52.
37 Richard Brody, '"Mission: Impossible – Fallout" Is Basically a Two-and-a-Half-Hour Making-Of Sequence', *New Yorker* (28 July 2018), https://bit.ly/3LvB4hK (accessed 2 December 2021).
38 Sue Harris, 'Conspiracy, Surveillance, and the Spatial Turn in the *Bourne* Trilogy', in *Globalization, Violence and the Visual Culture of Cities*, ed. Christoph Lindner (Abingdon: Routledge, 2010), p. 167.
39 Ibid., p. 171.
40 Christian Long, 'Chase Sequences and Transport Infrastructure in Global Hollywood Spy Films', in *Global Cinematic Cities: New Landscapes of Film and Media*, ed. Johan Andersson and Lawrence Webb (New York: Wallflower, 2016), pp. 235–51.
41 O'Brien, 'Energy and Eventhood'.
42 Manohla Dargis, '"Mission: Impossible – Fallout" and the Bliss of the Hyper-Human Tom Cruise', *New York Times* (25 July 2018), www.nytimes.com/2018/07/25/movies/mission-impossible-fallout-review-tom-cruise.html (accessed 4 May 2020); Turan, 'Review: Tom Cruise Returns'.
43 Adams, 'The New *Mission: Impossible*'.
44 See Lisa Bode, *Making Believe: Screen Performance and Special Effects in Popular Cinema* (New Brunswick, NJ: Rutgers University Press, 2017).
45 'Mayor Sets Out Vision for London to Be World's Most Film-Friendly City', *Mayor of London / London Assembly* (31 January 2017); Film London (2021), https://filmlondon.org.uk/what-we-do (accessed 23 June 2023).

11

Performative liveness in *Lost in London*: cinematic streaming and the digital happening in globalising London

Michael A. Unger and Keith B. Wagner

As a cinematic-cum-multimodal audio-visual-orbital feat, livestreaming is nothing less than presentational wizardry and a narrative storytelling that works against the clock. This type of filmmaking is admirably embodied as premise and constraint in Woody Harrelson's directorial debut, *Lost in London* (2017). Advertised as a site for live experience in the black box by utilising the aesthetics of the long take,[1] this feature film creates what we refer to as a digital 'happening': it situates the profilmic event of shooting a long-take film with the technological caveat that one camera records the entire film as it develops in real time. This single long-take premise also required that *Lost in London* was shot entirely on location and set in the theatre district of London in the early morning of 20 January 2017, while streamed simultaneously into 550 theatres in the United States and one in London. In this regard, the perceived temporal authenticity and site-specific aspect of a long-take film shot on location in London is billed as an *international livestreaming film event*.

With that in mind, Harrelson's rendition of London is no longer a 'landmark city' in Charlotte Brunsdon's famous coinage because this film lacks the iconic red buses and letterboxes and aerial establishing shots of regal architecture associated with the Houses of Parliament and London Bridge. Countering this further, we argue that *Lost in London*'s livestreamed praxis is intent on traipsing viewers through the memories of one wild night by a Hollywood A-list actor whose on-screen talent often exceeds his everyday recognisability; the *Schadenfreude*, or the farcical moments derived from the calamity of Harrelson's alleged real-life high jinks – a drunken escapade at the Chinawhite club in Soho scooped by the raunchy British tabloids in 2002; this night becomes *his* event that is demarcated through the very re-enactment of that evening and visualised at street level. Thus, the camera eye takes audiences 'live' through Covent Garden, Holborn and Soho, areas known for their nocturnal entertainment of both legal and sordid varieties, places which can easily absorb and befuddle most tourists or cloak many international and sometimes British celebrities in anonymity compared with other megacities like New York or Tokyo (as was the case for Harrelson in this film).[2] Like a remora fish that rides in the slipstream of the apex predator shark, paparazzi trail celebrities relentlessly, but the intensity and anonymity of central London provide greater concealment for those well-known people walking among us. While tabloid coverage of celebrities' personal lives is often seen as sensationalist journalism, invasively exposed with the *News of the World*'s phone-hacking scandal, Britain's capital offers a smaller number of celebrity chasers than other global cities, despite the complaints made by those in the limelight.

In other ways, *Lost in London* also pays homage to creative industry talent as well as articulating the well-to-do modern *flâneur* and thespian enthusiast that call WC1 their cultural or even real home; a film that goes from the high culture of theatre at its start to Harrelson being caught up with other men out on the prowl, 'A Rake's Progress' in a contemporary Hogarthian sense. While accompanying these randy men, Harrelson is seen trying to reconcile his own polyamorist behaviour days earlier, which his wife discovers through a conversation overheard in the toilet of an upscale restaurant, making his infidelity harder to forgive. This triggers the wild set of events in the film (presumably different to how his real-life wife might have been told about or discovered Harrelson's affair). This changes the tone from the original event and sets Harrelson's character as another version of himself, thus sending him down a new path: uninhibited by too many libations after the fictional (but fact-based) affair is plastered across UK newspapers, which ultimately triggers the row and his retreat in shame; and perhaps his transgression becomes a 'live' apology to his wife and children for his past indecent conduct as he is lost emotionally in London.

The focus of this chapter is how *Lost in London* constructs its immediacy of liveness by utilising the two elements of continuous cinematic time and space: a live 100-minute long-take film stunt shot within a radius of two square miles in the theatre district of London as a live stage or theatre for its inception.[3] Cinematic time and space are thus presented in *Lost in London* as unaltered by the livestreaming of the long take, contributing a dual sense of immediate connectivity to the viewing of the film rather than a remediation of their materiality and cinematic representation within the film. These two facets together showcase *Lost in London*'s performative allure of liveness through a mediatised experience on different screens: in the multiplex and later on YouTube and Netflix. But it also recasts London, inadvertently and read by us, as the media capital for all forms of audio-visual experimentation in the twentieth and twenty-first centuries: from the BBC Television Service, which on 2 November 1936 became the first television broadcast in Europe from its studios at Alexandra Palace in North London; to the first live television signal beamed around the world using the Telstar 1 satellite, for which most technological support and assistance was provided by engineers and personnel in the BBC headquarters in Portland Place and Langham Place, in central London; to *Lost in London* as yet another cultural and mediatic milestone as the city continues to dominate as a place of extraordinary creative and technological ingenuity.

Defamiliarising views or rather showing audiences a street-level unfolding of action in *Lost in London* lends to the very title of the film a certain bafflement of London's Zone 1 topography. Others who know the topography derive pleasure from traversing the same streets themselves as Harrelson did, a sign of being a cosmopolitan compared with the average confused tourist. Lesser-known landmarks dominate the *mise-en-scène* as well as heritage landmarks at the conclusion of the film, where more traditional English architecture gives way to the sculptural qualities of the South Bank and its angular geometries. Sites are occupied by a motley crew of multicultural characters, establishing London's superdiverse demographic and its fusion of ethnic cultures. Taken together, London's globalness remains unmatched through these and other countless mediatic and cultural milestones.

A brief account of liveness in screen media

At the structural level, this chapter explicates the notoriously slippery term 'live', in order to illuminate the power of real-time broadcasting and streaming that often promotes itself as a live event through shared simultaneity and co-presence made possible through broadcast content. Therefore, the live sports event garners its moniker because it comes to remediate that event – a professional game watched by thousands on a given television network – by inhabiting a reality which is inscribed by a mass media infrastructure from the camera to satellite and then beamed to a public. This technological hardware and apparatus thus present a reality as it happens in fractionally delayed seconds in real time. Analysing the epistemological and techno-mediated contours of liveness, Nick Couldry reminds us that liveness is not a 'natural category but a constructed term, its significance rests on a whole chain of ideas'. He goes on to argue that we gain liveness to 'access the now, not later; live access is not random; that the media is the privileged means for obtaining that access'.[4] Like Couldry, Auslander offers the use of instant replay in sports events or live musical performances in stadiums replete with large video screens projecting music video imagery of the performers on stage as two contemporary examples where the viewer's experience of the live event is transformed by creating a mediated performance; that is, when the instantaneous nature of the live event is fused with media technologies of recording and reproduction.[5]

These monumental occasions, which have become ubiquitous across network television networks starting in the 1950s with live broadcast events, constitute more broadly media globalisation. Now with livestreaming services like Periscope part of our 'app culture', these simultaneously recorded and broadcast events offer, in real time, new production and reception responses by industry and audiences, which since the 2010s have been a mark of platformisation and media that elicit further our global interconnectedness. Thus the revival of live broadcasts is apparent not only on 'planetary TV'[6] as event televisual culture – for example, NBC's string of live musicals in the United States in 2013,[7] the recent three-minute live segment in an episode of the animated series *The Simpsons* in 2016,[8] or the fifty-second live commercial ad by Snickers during the 2017 *Super Bowl* featuring Adam Driver – but liveness is also being flaunted within other forms of media: from the livestreaming of operas and performances held at the Royal Opera House in Covent Garden in London, beamed to cinemas across the globe since 2014, to digital platforms that also offer livestreaming content such as Facebook (with Facebook Live), Snapchat (Live Stories) and video games (Twitch). In the context of documentary filmmaking, Sam Green and Joe Bini's 'live documentary' entitled *A Thousand Thoughts* (2018) traces the work of the Kronos Quartet with the band playing the score live in a theatrical venue and Green himself providing narration on stage while archival footage, interviews and photos about the group are projected on screen. While not a livestreamed event per se, it does combine live performance with cinematic non-fiction forms that changes with each presentation. Such hybrid filmic work also expands the possibilities of liveness with the documentary medium beyond that of the live transmission of observational events, performances and interviews in broadcast journalism and internet platforms.

Comparatively, *Lost in London*'s livestreamed capabilities to other long-take films such as *Victoria* (Sebastian Schipper, 2015) show similar ambition but on a smaller scale. This German crime thriller reveals that it was an antecedent moment at liveness for movies due to its prolongation of its live action. But unlike *Victoria*, *Lost in London* was the first feature-length film to succeed in combining its large-scale production through multiple locations shoots (including a variety of vehicles to shuttle Harrelson around central London) and the employment of an army of industry and creative labour: for example, 30 professional actors, 300 crew members and 500 extras to create its simulacrum-like London.[9] Both films thus belong to a category of long-take feature filmmaking, namely 'bravura' filmmaking that showcases the director's skills by relying on dramatic and cinematic showmanship involving elaborate staging and camera movement. *Timecode 2000* (Mike Figgis, 2000), for example, is comprised of four separate 97-minute-long takes of different characters shot simultaneously on location in the city of Los Angeles. The four shots are presented together in a multiscreen format with the sound design mixed to highlight certain dramatic moments from each of the four stories. *Russian Ark* (Alexander Sokurov, 2002) consists of a 96-minute Steadicam long-take shot in the Winter Palace in St Petersburg where the camera moves through a series of stately rooms, populated with fictional and real characters from the city's history and choreographed through the complex technique of the unseen fourth wall device that is repeatedly broken and restaged off screen.

Other films, such as *Birdman* (Alejandro Iñárritu, 2014) and *1917* (Sam Mendes, 2019), present the illusion of a long-take feature film by disguising their edits through action wipes and other techniques and employ a fade-out to denote the passage of time from night to day to extend story time in relation to its actual screen time. Such long-take films are renowned for their cinematic virtuosity rather than their observational endurance that they demand from the viewer.[10] Koepnick comments that such long-take films 'may not be perceived as long at all as a result of the frantic action of a hypermobile camera'.[11] Nonetheless, they promote themselves as an unusual cinematic spectacle by calling attention to their specific profilmic challenges of shooting a feature film in an actual or supposed long take as a distinguishing caveat of their narrative content. They are akin to what we would describe as a film stunt where the act of filmmaking as a difficult physical feat or achievement distinguishes it from other types of narrative filmmaking – a particular cinematic excess which, in the words of Bruce Isaacs, 'displays the virtuosity of the filmmaker over and above the requirement of narrative unfolding'.[12]

In line with these other live-like filmic experiences, *Lost in London* advances the long-take feature one step further into the realm of a film event, or what we refer to as a 'digital happening'. According to C. W. E. Bigsby, Alan Kaprow coined the term 'happening' in 1959 'to describe a presentation which had its roots in art but which has taken the artist in the direction of theatre'.[13] We find this definition noteworthy because it indicates a performative factor involving integrated space and the unfolding of real time. 'Happening' refers to the traditional sense of performance art or an art event that encourages spontaneity and/or audience participation in the same physical space as an essential factor of its creation and reception. We include the word 'digital' in our terminology to indicate that the viewer witnesses the art event at the same time as its creation but in a different space through livestreaming. The term also connotes an exciting or unusual art event that occurs only once but can possibly go haywire, and in this particular context the film event of shooting *Lost in London* as a long-take streamed event means that chance plays a role, as something could go wrong and usually does.

This notion of chance was a primary marketing factor in its promotion and reception. *Lost in London*, while shot and performed in London, was simultaneously transmitted initially to several different viewing audiences in different time zones and via an array of movie theatres in the United States. This transforms the viewer's experience of the black box as a site in which they watch a pre-recorded film that does not change in terms of content, to that of a live event mediatised through the contemporaneous shooting and streaming of a long-take film both for the filmmakers and the viewers. Harrelson reveals that *Lost in London* is indeed indebted conceptually in part to the long-take German feature film *Victoria*, which also features a nocturnal narrative adventure that takes place in another city. Shot in a single continuous take of 138 minutes on location in Berlin, *Victoria* provided a cinematic and technological model for Harrelson to shoot a long-take feature film on location at night in a city.[14] Nevertheless, Harrelson in an interview states that he did not want to simply create a London version of *Victoria* but to accomplish the long take in a way that would distinguish it from its predecessor: 'Harrelson then came up with the idea of combining elements of theatre and live streaming [with] *Lost in London* to cinemas as it is being shot.'[15]

Zone 1 as playground/exquisite enclave for the cosmopolitan/Hollywood A-lister

Zone 1 locales are the heart and soul of *Lost in London*'s urban topography. Capturing key central London neighbourhoods, Covent Garden, Holborn and Soho, these iconic places are portrayed as likenesses without totality in this film and are thus recast as a playground for Harrelson's debauchery. Known as 'Hollywood's wildest wild child, a raw-foodist and eco-crusader and Iraq-war protester and marijuana-legalization champion', according to *Esquire* magazine, having also had several brushes with the law in the United States, Harrelson's reputation precedes him. But all his rowdy partying and high jinks fail to conceal Harrelson's thoughtful, intelligent choices in roles for film and stage and his commitment to politics and environmentalism that often bubble up in his screen personas.

Yet the event taken from the tabloid front pages in Britain, another one of his missteps off screen, is re-presented fascinatingly in *Lost in London*. Harrelson's London becomes a personalised geography, one with subtler landmarks identifiable to a more refined audience in Britain or the United States, which works to conceal his identity while also showing his cultural engagement with London's urban core. For example, the old site of Central St Martin's School of Art and Design on Southampton Row is transformed in the film into the trendy nightclub Chinawhite, with the building and Harrelson's identity as another version of himself. This then invites reflexivity to not only the site of the now relocated art school to King's Cross but also, in this scene, Harrelson's 'TVQ', or television quotient – what he describes in a line of dialogue as 'a read of how popular you are in a given culture' – perhaps signalling he is no global celebrity. Yet the way this phrase invites reflexivity is cleverly deployed: the bouncer regards this fictional Harrelson as an under-the-radar talent, unaware of the Hollywood A-lister's fictive/real accolades. He was nominated for three Academy Award for his performances in *The People vs Larry Flynt* (Miloš Forman, 1996), *A Scanner Darkly* (Richard Linklater, 2006) and, most recently, *Three Billboards Outside Ebbing, Missouri* (Martin McDonagh, 2017). Here, Harrelson's decade-defining work in television also comes to resonate with the sophisticated tastes of its cinephile audiences: his earlier career in the 1980s American television show *Cheers*, a smash hit and Emmy-winning sitcom set in a Boston bar (via a Hollywood lot).

Watching this live film and being 'in the know' at this moment about Harrelson's achievements contrasts with the well-knownness, to invoke Dyer, of global stars Tom Cruise and Brad Pitt who use London as a set piece for action and a city they openly adore.[16] These other white mega-celebrities and genre-bending performers whose cinematic work is globally consumed – and who often use London as a backdrop (see Chapter 10) – would more likely, unlike Harrelson, cause throngs of fans to follow this type of production and make filming in central London impossible. In other ways, audiences presumably chuckled away, as many of our more mature students did in our classroom screenings, at this ageing Hollywood actor not being recognised. In the downplaying of location and himself, Harrelson's protagonist pokes fun at his 'extraordinary ordinariness', to borrow from Raymond Williams, and his own view of television's cultural appeal.[17]

Aware of television history, Harrelson's film makes an appeal to an early model of live television in the United States, which sought to distinguish itself from the dominance of the black box as a site of filmic consumption by offering the spectacle of transmitting events as they occur contemporaneously to the viewer. This applies not only to news programmes that broadcast actual events as they unfold in real time but also to live, televised fictional drama. Lenox R. Lohr highlights this distinction between cinema and television in that 'the instantaneous nature of the broadcast gives television drama a certain superiority over filmed drama. The spectator knows that he is seeing something actually taking place at the same moment'.[18] This perceived immediacy encourages in the viewer feelings of connection to or presence at the mediatised event, even though that event spatially occurs elsewhere from the viewer. Sarah Atkinson, in her research on audience reception of *Lost in London*, contends that the primary motivation viewers cited for attending the screening of the film was due to its 'liveness' as a viewing experience. She points out that 'the respondents indicated a great deal of perceived or "virtual" presence through a sense of "proximity"'.[19] *Lost in London*, we wish to stress here, is not an unplanned event but one that is explicitly staged for its mediatisation through live broadcast and also as a document or recording of the digital happening for later consumption through other pre-recorded cinematic platforms such as DVDs and digital streaming on Amazon. The film also encapsulates a re-enactment of a filmmaking stunt which effaces its own production – one that has been meticulously planned, coordinated and rehearsed by its filmmakers prior to viewing for the sake of its live broadcast.[20] This gives *Lost in London* its performative intention as a mediatised management of a live recording of what could be described as 'street' theatre contained within a specific geographical space that is also managed. In other words, liveness is constructed. Perhaps a more apt title for the film would be *Live in London* since its intentionality belies the fictional conceit of Harrelson's character being physically lost or psychologically disoriented within its diegesis of London which is site-specific; and yet also a cinematic representation of a particular aspect of that city.

London as a performative space

It is no coincidence that Harrelson decided to shoot his live film in Soho and the West End theatre district of London, and here we will outline the cinematic cartography of his film to discern the difference between the cinematic space of the film and the actual physical space of location where it was shot, which the long take seeks to efface. The film begins with Harrelson taking a bow with a cast of actors after taking a curtain call for his play in Soho.[21] We see a half-empty theatre containing some slumbering spectators. He walks into his dressing room where he changes from his costume to his normal attire off screen while his assistant Jake discusses the performance with him and debates the merits of comedic vs dramatic acting. The two exit the theatre with the camera first following and then leading them onto the adjoining street as Harrelson signs autographs to theatregoers who have just watched the play. In the background of the camera frame, the viewer can see the facade of Aveda Lifestyle located on 174 High Holborn in the West End, which places the location of the street with an exact geographical reference point. One can then assume that the theatre they left is the Shaftesbury Theatre, reputed to be the biggest independent theatre in the West End, with its red velvet seats and ornate box seats that briefly appear during the opening curtain call, although this is not specifically mentioned or revealed in the film.[22] The two set off on foot together down a narrow street away from Aveda to a restaurant opposite a high-end lingerie store, where Harrelson meets his family for a late dinner. One can discern in the background the number 77 outside the restaurant which most likely places it at 77 Grape Street.

After the incident that occurs with his wife inside the restaurant boils over into a public row, Harrelson leaves and sees a Banksy graffiti that the camera captures through his point of view by panning from Harrelson to the graffiti and then briefly lingering on it for a second before panning back to Harrelson's reaction. Banksy's graffiti states: 'If graffiti changed anything it would be illegal' with a stencil of his iconic city rat below. This graffiti was actually created in 2011 and located at the BT Tower on the end of Clipstone Street in Fitzrovia, central London, rather than where it appears in the film, visually placing the film temporally during millennial London.[23] Woody takes an eight-minute car ride with an Iranian prince and his sons to a club standing in for the exclusive Chinawhite club, which was originally located between Piccadilly Circus and Soho until 2008 when it moved to 4 Winsley Street in Fitzrovia under the new title Libertine at Chinawhite. After an extended sequence inside the club, he exits the building onto a square where we can see briefly in the background the neon blue sign of the Holborn Hotel which is located at 16 Princes Street before he enters a black taxi. He tells the taxi driver to take him to the Sloane Hotel, located in Sloane Square in the well-heeled West End, but ends up in a nondescript corner park with a children's playground somewhere in its vicinity where Woody hides on the slide but is quickly discovered and apprehended by the Metropolitan Police. From there he is escorted by the police in a van and driven to an unidentified police station where he spends the night in a lock-up. The next morning, with London still enrobed in darkness, he is released from his holding cell and takes another van ride (presumably the same vehicle that he previously arrived in) to Waterloo Bridge where the climax of the film occurs and where he reconciles and is reunited with his family.

Although presented in the long take as a disoriented but linear journey from one actual location to another, an unused building in the centre of London in fact was used by the filmmakers to house two assorted locations markers in the form of constructed sets: a replica of the Chinawhite club and the police station with cells and an interview room. Both are populated by film extras who never look at the camera as it moves through those spaces as an invisible but omniscient observer to maintain the illusion of the fourth wall in narrative cinema and theatre.[24] By connecting the actual exterior locations with the fabricated interior ones, the long take serves as a counterweight to give credibility and authenticity to the latter. There is also actually little foot traffic that occurs in the film; most of the travelling Harrelson does from one location to another takes place in an assortment of vehicles to give the illusion of the extended city space of the West End that he traverses in the film. Furthermore, when he arrives at the club in a van, two police officers on motorcycles have followed the picture car and placed 'road closed' signs to prevent other unplanned vehicles from driving into the shot.[25] The glimpses of the actual exterior locations by the moving camera are themselves brief and do not reveal beyond their frame how these exterior locations were controlled or managed by the filmmakers or crew for the shoot – giving them an aura of a live, uncontrolled urban space.

It is noteworthy that *Lost in London* is shot at night in order to minimise the possibility of unpredictable interference by actual onlookers, pedestrians and traffic within the demarcated shooting locations and routes of central London. The only features of the locations beyond the control of the filmmakers were the weather conditions (fortunately it did not rain), the potential for losing the location of the Waterloo Bridge a few days before the shoot, due to the discovery of an unexploded munitions device from World War II, and the timing of the traffic lights which the filmmakers misjudged in one ride early on in the film, preventing the vehicle from proceeding for five minutes and forcing the actors to improvise their lines to fill in the dead screen time.[26]

From national landmarks to global spaces in *Lost in London*

Beyond the parameters of a film production on location transforming or altering the physical spaces, however briefly, with its rehearsals and shooting, the creation of cinematic space in the words of Mark Shiel and Tony Fitzmaurice as a 'spatial system' of culture gives that urban space a more lasting impact through its cinematic depiction as a cultural site-specific by-product.[27] The intersection between 'space in film' and 'film in space' is intertwined in both its cinematic production and representation.[28] Building on Shiel and Fitzmaurice's scholarship, Johan Andersson and Lawrence Webb in *Global Cinematic Cities* (2016) maintain that this intersection builds upon 'locating film texts, industries and cultures in specific local geographies, while simultaneously reframing and decentering the traditional category of national cinema within global networks of transnational flows'.²⁹ Due to the current widespread distribution and availability of media through streaming services, a majority of the global population can first encounter any given city through its various media representations. Today, viewers never have to physically step foot in a city because cinema, TikTok, Instagram, even AR can depict urban space in their own fascinating ways, but those who do visit may recall their prior actual experiences in a reflexive manner by viewing *Lost in London*.

To return to Andersson and Webb, they make the provocative statement that within the intersection of urban and cinematic discourses cities such as London must be 'viewed as "cinematic"' and thus 'be understood as a necessary precondition for global city status'.³⁰ For example, the climax of the film takes place at Waterloo Bridge where the viewer encounters a series of iconic London buildings and global landmarks from its moving camera that combines different entities of historical London and of London's evolving cityscape. With government and corporate architecture surrounding Harrelson and providing an imagined, and thus imaginative, set of events for liveness to take place, all of this is dependent on global communication and the city itself as one central facilitator to media's transcontinental reach. Each day, the BBC World Service uses London's iconic and globalising cityscape as its on-air backdrop. Such an imagery of global London reinforces not only the gold standard for communication since the first media wave in the inter-war years but also that London and its media image continue to be a source of legitimacy and place of newsworthiness.

To relate this to the literature devoted to cinematic London, Brunsdon describes such landmarks as 'Landmark London' which 'like that of capital cities, is an historically formed, multi-media iconography which is always about location but never just about location'.³¹ Waterloo Bridge itself connotes a past imperial London that commemorates the British, Dutch and Prussian victory over Napoleon at the battle of Waterloo in 1815. It has also served as the closing shot for such films as *Alfie* (Lewis Gilbert, 1966) and the closing scene of *Trainspotting* (Danny Boyle, 1996) and is the primary location for the film *Waterloo Bridge* (James Whale, 1931; Mervin LeRoy, 1940; and the renamed *Gaby*, Curtis Bernhardt, 1956), which demonstrates how 'films set in London are in a constant dialogue with existing and often stereotyped images of the city whether these are constructed by earlier filmmakers or in other cultural forms'.³² Waterloo Bridge thus is reputed to have the best tourist views of London, which is inscribed by the camera movement from Harrelson's film: the police van finally pulls away from the camera and passes by, situated in the background, the brightly lit London Eye Ferris wheel on the South Bank of the Thames river. This architectural icon is a direct manifestation of millennial London that opened to the public in 2000 and was reputedly the most popular tourist destination in the United Kingdom in 2014.[33] As the camera continues to pan, it ends in its last seconds of the entire long take of the film on an establishing shot of the eastern view of the Thames with the City of London and Canary Wharf in the background. Facing south, the National Theatre is directly behind Harrelson in this final scene. It is no coincidence that the National Theatre bookends this film. It is a reminder to Londonphiles like us and others that brutalist spaces for theatre are preserved even in a site where high finance continues to transform the cityscape and its topography via its newly erected skyscrapers and expanding real estate. Our historical understanding is that the National Theatre was part of a much more social democratic municipal plan for a pre-neoliberal London. According to Clement, brutalist architecture maintained a 'ruthless adherence to one of the basic moral imperatives in design: honesty in form'.[34] Liveness, like brutalism, we would argue, values form and a tightness of vision as it glorifies its own visuality. Today, luckily, heritage sites like these in London are safe, unlike in other global cities, particularly New York, where nothing is off-limits to real estate developers.

In other ways, these global landmarks, we believe, situate the film not only within the parameters of the cinematic history of London but also as part of the history of the city itself housing a British and global film history. Some landmarks are located directly off screen too. In perhaps another unintended commentary on cinema history, below the Waterloo Bridge on the South Bank of the Thames where Harrelson stands in this final scene is the British Film Institute (BFI). Formed in 1933 as a film and television charitable organisation, its primary institutional function is to archive and promote British and world cinema to its public in London and beyond. Housed adjacently to the National Theatre, in arguably a less regal facility (though it recently had a facelift to its front entrance and remains a popular summer haunt for tourists and cinephiles having outside drinks, providing luxurious views of the north side of the Thames river and the Strand), the BFI is a reminder of the British film industry's global reach and its place in a city that has a glittering international reputation for fostering cutting-edge culture: from film festivals to academic conferences to on-location shooting for overseas filmmakers. The BFI is truly a global hub for all things cinematic.

Referencing that global popularity of British fantasy-inspired blockbusters as the camera lingers for about five seconds on this view of the National Theatre (and sits on top of the BFI), it finally fades out while the van, supposedly off screen, continues towards the Harry Potter set – a fictive and off-screen set of spaces that evokes the worldwide success, as well as a specific franchise, of London's film industry recognised by not only cinephiles but also the public at large as a celebrated cultural reference. In the film's coda, an interview from the actor Daniel Radcliffe then appears on screen, separate from the long take and shot in a different digital format, in which he recounts Harrelson's actual visit to the set in 2002 as a possible ruse or escape from his circumstances depicted in the film.

Lost in London also depicts a specific locale, namely the West End, as a prominent location both in its cinematic depiction and within the popular mediatised consciousness of London as a metonym for the British theatre world: its rich history and its adoration by citizens across the globe establish it as a global cultural institution. But the film's finale is on the South Bank, designed by architect Sir Denys Lasdun; the buildings which occupy this place remain egalitarian and erected for the purpose of serving the cultural needs of the British and global public. The theatre district in London often 'performs itself'[35] or presents itself as a cinematic location for the mecca of British theatrical industry ranging from high-brow serious dramas and mainstream kitschy Broadway entertainments to vaudeville and striptease. Brunsdon, in examining films that feature the West End, argues that it 'is a cinematic location [that] recurs throughout the twentieth century, signified through and signifying neon, music, clubs, dancing, shopping, gambling, strolling crowds and sex' – in one word, as she puts it, entertainment.[36] Harrelson's character within that neighbourhood in *Lost in London* performs in a theatre, dines in a restaurant, dances in a nightclub, kisses a self-proclaimed gypsy woman that he meets at the club, is chased by the paparazzi hot on the scent of the latest Hollywood sex scandal involving Harrelson, is thrown into jail and released the next morning. In his journey Harrelson encounters a population (through a supporting cast) that consists of a literal cross-section of locals, immigrants and foreigners, connoting a cosmopolitan district inhabited by different nationalities and ethnicities. Brunsdon argues that 'Soho is the most signifying of this West End and is figured as a site of cosmopolitanism' and this complicates notions of the city's landmark qualities on screen.[37]

Conscious to London's unrivalled multiculturalism and his own predilection for sharing in this worldly diversity, Harrelson's wife Laura is played by Eleanor Matsurra, a Japanese-born British actress; his real-life second wife, Laura Louie, is of East Asian descent. Their children together are of multicultural heritage. Harrelson's deep understanding and view of difference is representative in who was cast in *Lost in London*: the Roma woman Zrinka is played by Zrinka Cfitesic, a Croatian film, television and theatre actor. The Iranian prince is played by Al Nedjari. Paddy the Irish policeman is played by Martin McCann, an actor from Northern Ireland, and the two bouncers that make fun of Harrelson's film career are played by Tobi Bamtefa and Youssef Kerkouri who were born and raised in Morocco, just to name several of its performers from a highly international troupe of actors, though most are situated in the British film and theatre industry, which also adds to the aura of its cinematic depiction as a foreigner's enclave and tourist destination. Altogether, *Lost in London* constitutes not only an example of an auteur's gaze on the neighbourhood within its diegesis but also a cultural artefact that reflects the global reach of the West End in its cultural economy.

Conclusion

Woody Harrelson is one of many visiting or foreign filmmakers who have contributed to the ongoing international cinematic representations of global London and its globalising iconography on the small and large screen. Interpersonally, and it terms of global star studies, Harrelson's celebrity is expressed in his own mobility in the film, which the long take encapsulates: his self-regarded and so-called dwindling recognisability allows him to enter a famous club in Soho (relocated to Holborn) only through the uber-moneyed elite in London who recognise him and his Hollywood credentials. Though Harrelson's credentials on their own fail to get him through the door, he does encounter older admirers and fans for whom he promises autographs, replete with personal anecdotes, to the delight of the authorities who arrested him. Thus, Harrelson is able to move freely once again in global London. Harrelson himself says to the Iranian prince character that 'Hollywood is like royalty without borders', which enables the character (and, sometimes, Harrelson in real life) to move through different spaces and meet a variety of different types of characters (real people) within the film's diegesis (and in real life outside the diegesis). Harrelson also uses his own persona as the dramatic conceit for the financing and creation of *Lost in London* as both its first-time director and lead actor, which constitutes an essential factor for enticing people into multiplexes and art houses to experience this first large-scale feature film to be streamed live to a global audience.

As a technological marvel of live digitalisation, *Lost in London* transforms the virtuosic creation of a long-take feature film into the realm of a live film event through livestreaming as an international digital happening occurring in real time in London. By transmitting its own formulation as a cinematic event being filmed in the moment, *Lost in London* expands the notion of digital liveness within the black box as a spectacle; it provides an innovative model for future long-take feature films as a medium for live broadcast framed as a theatrical, virtual experience for the viewer. Add to this the spectacle itself of transmitting this 'film' to audiences in the United States and such technologisation of vision by Harrelson is remarkable and a stunning achievement in cinema history. As Paddy Scannell reminds us: 'it is the distinctive aspect of our common humanity that we can and do arrange to *give* ourselves experiences in order to have them'.[38] Understood in this context, the intentionality of liveness in *Lost in London* is not reliant on a performer–viewer interaction directly, but it is mediated through a virtual co-presence of integrated cinematic time and space that the filmmaker and the viewer share through livestreaming.

Lost in London's globality is also unmistakable: It is not just a feat of ingenuity due its liveness but the city's global status and superdiversity are put on display. Its placeness (architecture and locations in central London) and demographic richness (BAME characters and extras) become key tropes to ponder, and they complement and reinforce London's multicultural supremacy. Whether we can consider Harrelson a 'woke' white Hollywood celebrity is not for us to decide, but we can stress that it is remarkable to view his four decades–long filmic output through a multicultural lens: *White Men Can't Jump, Money Train, The High-Lo Country, No Country for Old Men, Nanking, Seven Pounds, Bunranku, The Hunger Games, Lost in London* and *Three Billboards Outside Ebbing, Missouri*. These films, set in the United States or other parts of the world, put viewers into a cross-cultural and intercultural orbit, their narratives dealing with a variety of themes such as racism, xenophobia, biracial love, extra-nationalism, altruism, mixed-race identity, whiteness, Asianness, Latinxness and Blackness. Thought of in this regard, these Harrelson films seem to convey a hope for greater tolerance and racial acceptance. Harrelson's honest approach to London's superdiversity in this film is not just an American filmmaker's appropriation of this global city's geography but one that expands London's global status as a tourist and also a multicultural hotspot, unparalleled in our world system of cities. Thus, globalisation in practice is detectable and mediated in *Lost in London*'s dense material and urban fabric: both in architectural form and in the cast and ethos of its characters found on screen, each a beacon to a city like London's enduring globality. As a theatrical film stunt physically staged and simultaneously filmed within the spatial parameters of a specific London neighbourhood through orbital live transmission, *Lost in London*'s construction does visualise the notion of liveness as a glocalised, cinematic space in the making. Most importantly, it showcases liveness as a performative interaction between filmmaker and viewer to create a cinematic artefact – a one-off moment – that captures both event and experience but also culture and geography with aplomb.

Notes

1 For example, see Chris Gardner's review 'Inside Woody Harrelson's Ambitious, Groundbreaking Live Film Screening "Lost in London"', *The Hollywood Reporter* (20 January 2017), https://bit.ly/3oSwtO4 (accessed 24 May 2019).

2 For an account how this district first evolved as a pleasure district, see Rohan McWilliam, *London's West End: Creating the Pleasure District, 1809–1914* (Oxford: Oxford University Press, 2020).
3 Betsy Sherman, 'Film Review: Woody Harrelson's Movie – A So-So Nocturnal Odyssey' *Artsfuse* (27 January 2017), https://artsfuse.org/154623/film-review-woody-harrelsons-movie-a-so-so-nocturnal-odyssey/ (accessed 2 June 2019). The very word 'theatre' refers to not only the performative act but also its specific site or place, from the ancient Greek 'theatron' meaning 'a place of viewing'. In this sense one could infer that all long takes are theatrical when viewing a performance recorded by the camera with the continuity of the actors' performances left intact in real time, rather than a performance compiled through classical Hollywood continuity film editing from different shots, takes and disparate performances filmed at different times and later cut together to create the illusion of continuous space, time and performative action.
4 Nick Couldry, 'Liveness, "Reality," and the Mediated Habitus from Television to the Mobile Phone', *The Communication Review*, 7.4 (2004), pp. 353–61.
5 Philip Auslander, *Liveness: Performance in a Mediated Culture* (New York: Routledge, 2022).
6 See Lisa Parks and Shanti Kumar, eds, *Planet TV: A Global Television Reader* (New York: New York University Press, 2003).
7 The NBC network started this genre of live broadcast musical performances in 2013 with *The Sound of Music*, which was watched by nearly twenty million viewers. See Lesley Goldberg, 'Network TV's Live Musical Boom Hits a Sour Note', *The Hollywood Reporter* (13 February 2019), www.hollywoodreporter.com/live-feed/network-tvs-live-musical-boom-hits-sour-note-1186035 (accessed 7 June 2020).
8 On 15 May 2016, *The Simpsons* aired at the end of an episode a three-minute live segment featuring the animated character Homer Simpson answering questions from fans through motion capture animation that featured the character with the voice actor Dan Castellaneta in real time with its broadcast.
9 Steve Weintraub, 'Woody Harrelson on Filming "Lost in London" in Real Time and in a Single Take', *Collider* (25 May 2018), https://collider.com/woody-harrelson-interview-lost-in-london/ (accessed 1 June 2020).
10 *Birdman* received at the 87th Academy Awards the Oscar for Best Picture, Director and Cinematography while *1917* won the Academy Award for Best Cinematography at the 92nd Academy Awards.
11 Koepnick, *The Long Take*, p. 40.
12 Bruce Isaacs, 'Reality Effects: The Ideology of the Long Take in the Cinema of Alfonso Cuarón', in *Post-Cinema: Theorizing 21st Century Film*, ed. Shane Denson and Julia Leyda (Falmer: Reframe Books, 2016), https://reframe.sussex.ac.uk/post-cinema/4-3-isaacs/ (accessed 21 May 2020).
13 C. W. E. Bigsby, *A Critical Introduction to Twentieth-Century American Drama* (Cambridge: Cambridge University Press, 1985), p. 45.
14 Cat Dragoi, '"Lost in London": Woody Harrelson Discusses His Directorial Debut with Street', *34th Street* (24 January 2018), https://bit.ly/40MfjPk (accessed 10 July 2021).

15 Ryan Gilbey, 'Live-shooting with Woody Harrelson at 2am: "There's something about the terror of it I love"', *Guardian* (17 January 2017), www.theguardian.com/film/2017/jan/17/woody-harrelson-lost-in-london-live-film-interview (accessed 5 March 2020).
16 Richard Dyer, *Stars* (London: BFI Publishing, 1979).
17 Raymond Williams, *Television: Technology and Cultural Form* (London: Routledge, 1974).
18 Lenox R. Lohr, *Television Broadcasting: Production Economics, Technique* (New York: McGraw Hill, 1940), p. 72.
19 Sarah Atkinson, '"You sure that's a film, man?": Audience Anticipation, Expectation and Engagement in Lost in London LIVE', *Participation: Journal of Audience and Reception Studies*, 14.2 (2017), p. 703.
20 It should be noted that *Victoria* was first shot in a more conventional approach due to the demand of its investors and then afterwards as a long take three times over the course of three different nights before the director chose the third take as the finished product. Harrelson rehearsed shooting *Lost in London* twice the night before shooting the actual long take for live broadcast. See Weintraub, 'Woody Harrelson on Filming "Lost in London"'.
21 Harrelson was in London rehearsing the debut of the play *On an Average Day* with Kyle MacLachlan on 6 June 2002 during the night re-enacted in the film, as reported in Kaleem Atfab, 'Lost in London: How Woody Harrelson's Crazy Night Out Inspired His Directorial Debut', *Independent* (8 May 2017), https://bit.ly/420Zqp0 (accessed 30 March 2019).
22 Shaftesbury Theatre website: www.shaftsburytheatre.com/about-us/about-the-theatre/.
23 Matt Randal, '10 Banksy Street Art Pieces in London', *Widewalls* (4 September 2014), www.widewalls.ch/magazine/10-banksy-street-artworks-in-london (accessed 19 May 2021).
24 Gilbey, 'Live-shooting with Woody Harrelson at 2am'.
25 Ibid.
26 Gardner, 'Inside Woody Harrelson's Ambitious, Groundbreaking Live Film Screening'.
27 Mark Shiel, 'Cinema and the City in History and Theory', in *Cinema and the City*, ed. Mark Shiel and Tony Fitzmaurice (Oxford: Blackwell Publishers, 2001), pp. 5–6.
28 Ibid., p. 5.
29 Andersson and Lawrence Webb, 'Introduction: Decentering the Cinematic City – Film and Media in the Digital Age', in *Global Cinematic Cities*, ed. Johan Andersson and Lawrence Webb (New York: Columbia University Press, 2016), p. 1.
30 Andersson and Webb, 'Introduction: Decentering the Cinematic City', p. 8.
31 Charlotte Brunsdon, *London in Cinema: The Cinematic City since 1945* (London: British Film Institute, 2007), p. 22.
32 Pam Hirsch and Chris O'Rourke. 'Introduction: Film Londons', in *London on Film*, ed. Pam Hirsch and Chris O'Rourke (London: Palgrave MacMillan, 2017), p. 10.

33 John O'Ceallaigh, 'London Eye: Complete Visitor Guide', *Telegraph* (1 May 2014), https://bit.ly/3n0hEbE (accessed 2 June 2021).
34 Alexander Clement, *Brutalism: Post-war British Architecture* (Marlborough: The Crowood Press, 2018).
35 This is in direct reference to Thom Anderson's video essay *Los Angeles Plays Itself* (2003) in which the director explores the various ways the city is represented in films and how it serves at times as a character itself.
36 Brunsdon, *London in Cinema*, p. 90.
37 Ibid., p. 94.
38 Paddy Scannell, *Television and the Meaning of Live* (Cambridge: Polity Press, 2014), p. 187.

12

Borders and cosmopolitanism in the global city: *London River*

Ana Virginia López Fuentes

Introduction

The increasing mobility of people, goods and information around the globe has resulted in an increasingly interconnected world with a high potential for cosmopolitan encounters. This is particularly true in the so-called global cities where people from all over the world meet and interact on a daily basis. No longer restricted to the geographical lines dividing two countries, borders play a key role in the contemporary scenario. Both dividing lines and borderlands, they have the potential to either curtail or promote cosmopolitan moments of self-transformation. The so-called 'border films' structure their narratives around different types of borders, usually highlighting their paradoxical nature.[1]

This chapter looks at *London River* (Rachid Bouchareb, 2009) as an example of a border film that can be inscribed within the category of 'cultural exchange' narrative as theorised by Deborah Shaw, Tom O'Regan and others.[2] The film tells the story of two parents: Ousmane (Sotigui Kouyaté), a Black Muslim from Mali, and Elisabeth (Brenda Blethyn), a white Protestant from the Channel Islands, looking for their children in the city of London after the 7th July terrorist attacks. Borders feature prominently in the film. The narrative crosses various geographical borders and was filmed in different locations: France, London and one of the Channel Islands (Guernsey). It was a French–British co-production and it features a multinational cast and crew, including a French director of Algerian origin working in London. This chapter looks at the film's representation of today's extremely complex borders, in society in general and particularly in global cities. As will be argued, the movie constructs different spaces of the city of London as both dividing lines and as borderlands, emphasising the dual nature of borders theorised by border scholars such as Gloria Anzaldúa, Mike Davis and Anthony Cooper and Christopher Rumford.[3] Elijah Anderson's concept of 'cosmopolitan canopy' and Gerard Delanty's 'moments of openness' will be used to analyse the articulation of cosmopolitanism in the different constructed spaces displayed in the film.[4]

Cosmopolitanism and borders

Critical theorisation on the border has noticed its intrinsically paradoxical nature since the line that separates two countries or territories is also what they have in common. Anzaldúa's foundational text *Borderlands/La frontera* distinguishes between border and borderlands. While the term 'border' emphasises the division between two contiguous territories, 'borderlands' refers to the hybridity and fruitful encounters that are also consubstantial to any border. As she puts it, the borderlands 'are physically present whenever two or more cultures edge on each other, where people of different races occupy the same territory, where under, lower, middle and upper classes touch, where the space between two individuals shrinks with intimacy, created by the emotional residue of an unnatural boundary'.[5] Borders can be seen as both sites of separation and exclusion and of confluence and openness to the Other. They can act as sites of oppression and violence but also as 'connective tissue'; they can be both enriching and destructive.[6] Anthony Cooper and Chris Rumford argue that 'the border is a prime site for connecting individuals to the world, bringing them into contact with Others and causing them to reassess their relations with the multiple communities to which they may or may not belong'.[7] In this sense, borders are one of the privileged sites where cosmopolitan encounters take place.[8]

Cosmopolitan theorists have developed a growing interest in borders over the last two decades. Cosmopolitanism is based, on the one hand, on the notion that all human beings are equally valuable, positing borders as a site of connection between individuals.[9] However, when diverse cultures get together, differences may be exacerbated and reinforced. The contact with the non-nationals in cities can result in an open disposition and a fruitful interaction, a type of self-transformation that Delanty refers to as 'the cosmopolitan moment'.[10] However, this encounter may also trigger an anti-cosmopolitan reaction of rejection and fear. Cosmopolitanism is a contested term that also includes several critiques and theoretical approaches by scholars Craig Calhoun, David Miller and Eddy Kent and Terri Tomsky.[11] For instance, David Miller considers cosmopolitanism as an imperialist project in which existing cultural differences are nullified or privatised.[12] For his part, Calhoun talks about this project as unrealistic and utopian, and he claims that real people are necessarily situated in particular webs of belonging, with access to particular others but not to humanity in general.[13] Celestino Deleyto argues that contemporary movies attempt to make sense of the world in a context of globalisation and its economic, social and cultural consequences, and as such they can be interpreted under a 'cosmopolitan lens'.[14] Borders are an intrinsic element of cosmopolitanism and, therefore, need to be looked at in order to analyse films from a cosmopolitan point of view.

Global cities have become one of the recurrent sites to explore cosmopolitan and border dynamics. As a consequence of the increasing flow of border-crossers towards them, global cities are traversed by borders. According to Saskia Sassen, global cities like London are a consequence of the weakening of the concept of the nation as a spatial unit due to the privatisation and deregulation of territories as well as the strengthening of globalisation.[15] Global cities emerged as a strategic site for the transnationalisation of labour and the formation of translocal communities and identities.[16] In the field of cinema, Mendes and Sundholm mention how transnational films embody 'dimensions of border crossing, including its locales, its constraints and its affective aspects'.[17] For his part, Deleyto imagines London as a border city, 'a city crossed by borders and constantly reshaped by borderwork'.[18] Borderwork is the process whereby borders are constantly transformed by the daily activity of ordinary people.[19] Charlotte Brunsdon argues that the city of London has suffered (and benefitted from) a transformation from imperial capital to global city and this is portrayed in twenty-first-century films.[20] Global cities become not only microcosms of a global world but actual borderlands, constantly crossed by fluctuating borders, exclusions and exchanges.

London can be considered such a borderland, one which includes the city's cultural diversity while at the same time witnessing the proliferation of various types of borders between its citizens, among them economic barriers. Doreen Massey, in her book *World City*, explores these two parameters of the city of London.[21] Massey describes the global city as a place that is part of a larger system, with advanced producer services in a context which involves banking, accountancy, law and advertising.[22] London is undoubtedly a significant centre of coordination of the global economy, trade and financial flows, based on its neoliberal economy. Historically, the city reinvented itself as a world financial centre after a mid-twentieth-century decline.[23] First industrialisation and then financial power meant an increase in the possibilities of work. Therefore, its resurgence is a product of deregulation and privatisation/commercialisation, along with internationalisation. This has attracted migrants from all over the world, particularly but not only the old colonies of the British Empire, which in turn has produced a cultural diversity that contemporary discourses on the city exploit to provide a positive spin on its ruthless deregulatory financial activity.[24] British governments implemented restrictive immigration policies throughout the 1970s and 1980s, so in the 1990s employers began to call for easing of restrictions on the use of foreign labour to meet demand.[25] At the same time, migration increased, partly as a result of the expansion of the EU but also because of the growth in refugees and asylum seekers.[26] Thus, the proportion of foreign-born residents in London rose dramatically during the 1990s, to account for approximately 29 per cent of the city's total population by 2001.[27]

In the city of London more than 270 nationalities coexist and over 250 languages are spoken. The interface between the Anglo majority and other ethnicities in London is regulated by what Davis has called the 'third border'.[28] The third border is the invisible line that deprived foreigners come across every day in their interactions with other communities, a reminder that their lives are under constant scrutiny.[29] This third border restricts the use of public space by poorer citizens, building boundaries inside the inner city between neighbourhoods with a different economic development and based on racial segregation. Simultaneously, the process of gentrification has built an exclusionary wall around the entire city of London. Neil Smith describes gentrification as a 'global urban strategy' socially organised in the twenty-first century, which portends a displacement of working-class residents from urban centres.[30] It is a practice through which whole urban neighbourhoods are appropriated by real estate and business concerns, property values skyrocket and, as a consequence, the low-income families that lived in those neighbourhoods are displaced.

London was at the height of its self-refashioning as a global city when the 7 July 2005 bombings took place. Global terrorism is one of the three axes of conflict that, for Ulrich Beck, are central to the 'world risk society', a term he uses to describe a contemporary social order affect by manufactured and unexpected risks that are global in nature.[31] The risk society, Beck argues, creates a generalised feeling of threat and, in the case of global terrorism, fear of the Other. The perception of terrorist threats replaces active trust with active mistrust, which undermines trust in fellow citizens, foreigners and governments all over the world.[32] Consequently, racial issues and cultural disagreement between different cultures are increased.

However, the perceived risk of global terrorism has also had the opposite effect, Beck claims, since it has marked the beginning of a new phase of globalisation: the globalisation of politics, the moulding of states into transnational cooperative networks.[33] Even in the state of mistrust produced by terrorist attacks, terrorism can be considered a form of cosmopolitanism because it not only separates societies: it also reunites them. 'What can unite the world?' asks Beck. The answer suggests that unity to confront the threat is possible between different social groups: 'alliances are forged across the opposing camps, regional conflicts are checked and so the cards of world politics are reshuffled'.³⁴ Although, it is necessary to distinguish between the risks and the opportunities presented by these dangers, alliances between different cultures have been created to combat the threat and differences have been laid aside, at least in some respects. As others like Carrie Tarr have suggested, *London River* uses the bombings as a 'catalyst for the exploration of cultural difference in London'.³⁵

A film like *London River* portrays London as both a city crossed by internal borders and, at the same time, a fruitful borderland where cosmopolitan encounters take place. It shows how global terrorism and fear of the Other can both separate and unite people. *London River* is not the only contemporary film to deal with these issues. Recent border films such as *Amreeka* (Cherien Dabis, 2009), *The Reluctant Fundamentalist* (Mira Nair, 2012), *Crossing Over* (Wayne Kramer 2009) and *Ae Fond Kiss ...* (Ken Loach, 2004) present multiple social borders inside different global cities, like culture, religion and race. Most of these borders are based on prejudices towards the Other, on account of the fact that, while borders permit a new human sensibility, at the same time they restrict certain forms of expression. Movies set in the British capital – *Breaking and Entering* (Anthony Minghella, 2006), *It's a Free World ...* (Ken Loach, 2007) and *Eastern Promises* (David Cronenberg, 2007) – portray a city of London characterised by extreme wealth, unrestrained capitalist practices and borderwork. Although away from geopolitical borders, this is, in Anzaldúa's terms, a borderland where people of different ethnic origins come together, interconnectedness being balanced by violence and intolerance.³⁶ As a whole, these films contradict the view of the city as a harmonious multicultural place where various cultures coexist without any problem. They offer a sense of the global city as a borderland of encounters and exclusions, spaces of globalisation and mobile borders, where cosmopolitanism exhibits its complexity and contradictions. It is within this context of contemporary cinematic representations of the British capital as a bordering and cosmopolitan place that I would like to place my study of *London River*.

Cosmopolitan and border moments through urban constructed spaces

In *London River*, the city is presented as a border place where the action happens in several important spaces. It is a geography of power that produces an unequal geographic democracy.³⁷ This geography of inequality is produced by the gentrification of the city in different neighbourhoods that are classified by the nationalities and cultural origins of their citizens. In Bouchareb's film, most spaces depict Muslim communities, separated by the existence of the third border. In this part of the analysis, the chapter explores the main multicultural urban spaces of London used in the movie in which the encounters and disagreements of different cultures occur. It is necessary to remark how the *mise-en-scène* helps to display the global city of London as a place characterised by inner borders between different groups of society but also by blossoming intercultural encounters. In a different register, the film articulates complex cross-border interactions, reflecting the evolution of the characters whereby they become more cosmopolitan and open-minded due to the coexistence of different cultures and participation in moments of openness.

A central trope in *London River* is its topographic adherence to place which provides a realistic effect with the use of real London locations. Like an A–Z London map, we land on Blackstock Road in Finsbury Park. This space is introduced with a handheld camera and a bumpy framing from inside the car in which Elisabeth is travelling from the ferry port to Jane's flat. The shot offers a glimpse of the film's documentary style, which is sustained throughout the whole narrative. Once the taxi stops at Jane's address, we see a point-of-view shot of the neighbourhood from Elisabeth's eyes that suggests disapproval of her new environment. Then the camera follows the direction of her eyes and shows the sign of the halal shop, Butcher El Baraka, above which Jane's flat is located. Elisabeth observes this Middle Eastern enclave in North London with scepticism. At this point, the window of the halal shop functions as a border. Elisabeth looks through the shop window and metaphorically a border is crystallised, in Elisabeth's eyes, between her Anglophone roots and the Islamic world. The framing makes her look provincial, submissive and frightened. Moments later, the camera follows Elisabeth with a close-up, detailing her alienated state. This first representation of the street offers the viewer a clue about the possible position of Elisabeth – namely, her rejection of her multicultural surroundings.

In a later scene, Blackstock Road is presented very differently. When Ousmane and Elisabeth come out of the travel agency, thinking that their children are safe on a trip to France, the street is particularly highlighted, with natural light illuminating the road, which is further enhanced by the characters who are brimming, temporarily, with happiness. They sit on a doorstep, sharing an apple that Ousmane slices with his penknife. She cleans the first piece that Ousmane shares with her but not the second one. It is the first moment in the film in which there is no physical border between the characters: they commiserate with each other, relieving their pent-up dread. It is also the first time in which they do not need to hold onto the belongings that define who they are: a briefcase and a walking stick in the case of Ousmane and a handbag in the case of Elisabeth. The apparently good news provides temporary solace and liberates previous anxieties in each other's presence; each has learnt to coexist with the culture and customs of the other. In this climax, Elisabeth even ventures to introduce some chirpy comments about Ousmane's appearance, specifically his long hair. The London street becomes a space with the potential for multicultural encounters like this one.

A thorough analysis of the street enables us to see more examples of extensive intercultural exchange. For example, the representation of women from different cultures in a city like London is remarkable. In the following scene, Elisabeth observes the street at length, and she sees a group of women with different ethnic origins and colorisms. The film gives an image of a relatively privileged position for women in a global city like London. One of these strolling women, for example, is using her mobile phone while wearing a burka, which, to some, may represent something repressive and traditional. However, in contrast with this positive view of a multicultural space, the third border is again presented in this neighbourhood as a tool to control the mobility of foreigners. In this image of multiple women from different origins, the film captures not just the diversity of the area but also the reality of this borderland led by a discriminatory border system that has the aim of maintaining and reinforcing the status quo of certain empowered citizens and the patriarchal system. The border is established here; the foreign population could be perceived as being socially and culturally subordinate to white British and larger Anglophone customs and hegemonic societal norms.

This third border, exclusionary and tinged with racist attitudes, is seen as gradually counterpoised with the presence of what Anderson has described as 'cosmopolitan canopies': urban sites that offer a special environment conducive to interethnic dialogue and communication.[38] An example of a cosmopolitan canopy is seen in the memorable and heartening scene – contained in one of London's many green spaces – where the two protagonists are sitting on a bench in Finsbury Park. This becomes one of the most important settings of the film because parks historically in London can de-emphasise the border that has separated ethnic/diasporic classes and groups and eventually unites Ousmane and Elisabeth. The narrative conscientiously tries to create this type of accepting, cosmopolitan space, not only as environments where people from different cultures meet and pass by one another but also as kinds of spaces where the protagonists search for each other's presence. In the film director's words, 'in France, Finsbury Park in North London is well-known as a place where a lot of Muslims live, and a lot of people from Algeria and Morocco, too'.[39] Finsbury Park has, therefore, the right cross-cultural characteristic for *London River*'s setting. The scene begins with a close-up of Elisabeth's face used to emphasise a moment of tension that develops into a moment of freedom in this gratifying green space. Then, we are presented with a long shot which frames the characters sitting on a park bench (Figure 12.1). This technique is used to emphasise the arduous situation in which the characters are living in the aftermath of the London bombings, both of them navigating the city without any clue of where their children could be. Widely attributable to a search for a post-7/7 London, the film connotes what Jan Nederveen Pieterse calls '"intermestic" (international-domestic) affairs [which] is a general trend. Global multiculture means engagement with conflicts worldwide'.[40] Through close-ups of both characters, Bouchareb emphasises the fruitful moment they manage to create and the 'cosmopolitan canopy' into which the scene turns. It is a natural space where they feel comfortable as it is more similar to their usual environments. The movie constructs this park as a 'heterotopic place',[41] considered as a space for otherness that only lasts a few moments, in which the protagonists open up to each other, share their concerns about their children and start to know each other deeply. In this moment, they realise that they are not very different from one another and, despite their obvious differences, their ways of life share numerous similarities.

If we turn our attention once again to the first time that Elisabeth arrives at Blackstock Road, there is another important space involved, which is conceptually and geographically counterpointed with urban and domestic spaces: the entrance to the flat and the gate. The entrance functions as a cosmopolitan space where sexual and ethnic differences are challenged at some point. In the first scene, Elisabeth is framed standing in the entrance;

Figure 12.1 Finsbury Park and the cosmopolitan canopy

it is as if she were trapped or entering a cage. The fences on the right and at the back of the frame, together with the high walls, form an oppressive framing. It portrays her feelings of panic and unease. Suddenly, she moves backwards as the Muslim shopkeeper approaches her, until she is unable to move any further because of the wall – she is totally trapped. Then, the owner says that he is the landlord of Jane's house and, with amiability, offers to give Elisabeth a key to the flat. At this point, Elisabeth becomes more comfortable with his presence, yet she is wracked by doubt.

Later, the same setting seems to be transformed, transmitting very different feelings – security, freedom and borderlessness. The final scene of Ousmane and Elisabeth together aims at moving the audience. The figure of Ousmane hugging Elisabeth, protecting her and consoling her, helps us to see how devastated both of them are but also how they have finally transgressed the borders between them. Importantly, at this point, no fences are shown in the frame, just the two protagonists. In this shot, it is possible to appreciate how Ousmane is enveloping Elisabeth, meaning that he has already transmitted his sense of otherness to her. Ousmane's height exceeds the level of the walls that previously separated them and made Elisabeth feel trapped. His otherness and tolerance have been transmitted to Elisabeth through a feeling of protection and respect.

Central to the transnational sensibility of this globally attuned film, there are other familiar locations which foreground the presence of Muslim diasporas in London, for instance the mosques. Mosques in real life are often identified from a Christian perspective as places of inscrutable 'otherness'. Nowadays, there is a well-known conflict over the Islamisation of the public space in Britain, which often reveals major fears about the erosion of the 'British way of life' in an age of global migration and ethnic pluralism.[42] There is a certain rejection by the Western world of Muslim religious symbols and places of gathering, which represent one of the main borders between different cultures in today's society. *London River*, however, portrays mosques as places where fruitful encounters and flourishing forms of cosmopolitanism take place. There are two mosques shown in the film: the Central Mosque of London and Finsbury Park Mosque, where Jane and Ali take Arabic classes. The first place where Ousmane receives help is the London Central Mosque, at the hands of the Imam (Sami Bouajila). Later, he receives help from the teacher of the Arabic class in the Finsbury Park Mosque and also meets with Elisabeth there. Furthermore, it is here that the Imam tries to bring the two parents together, explaining to Elisabeth that their children know each other and making gestures to encourage her to reconsider her position towards Ousmane. Barta and Powrie comment on how Ousmane finds a 'network of solidarity' in this space.[43] To this, I would add the idea of a network of cultural and religious solidarity where, despite not knowing each other, the Muslim community tries to help their brother Ousmane.

The last remarkable space that reappears several times throughout the narrative and is consciously constructed as a border place is the bridge that crosses Haringey train station. This railway station is located off Wightman Road in the borough of Haringey, in North London. It is presented as one of the most important physical borders during the entire film. The train station separates both protagonists according to the part of the city with which they are initially associated: where Ousmane is staying (Shelton Hotel) and where Elisabeth is staying in her daughter's flat. The bridge is a figurative border with a double functionality; it is the means whereby Ousmane and Elisabeth are reunited and separated depending on the moment that they cross it.

In the opening scenes, the bridge is presented as a threatening place, starting with a long shot and ending with a close-up of Elisabeth. In this frame her tension is exacerbated when she sees the photocopied 'missing' signs attached to the walls of the bridge. The thunderous sound of the railway makes it an acoustically terrifying moment. In this moment she realises the magnitude of the terrorist attack and also how common it is for someone to go missing in this global city. The presence of people of all sexes, colours and origins suggests that the bridge is a sort of no-man's land and that all people, regardless of their social status, are equal in a situation of terror. It is a space in between two different worlds, which are, in this case, the world of Ousmane and her world. After moments of openness like the ones we have previously analysed, this border is forgotten as an exclusionary weapon and is transformed into a space of unity. The initial separation of spaces reinforces their differences. Once the two parents realise that they are not so different, they are reunited through the bridge. The borders that separate them are transcended when they start living together, just as their children did. After they decide to live together, we see Ousmane crossing the bridge. The demographical border between them disappears, showing the character of Ousmane walking over the bridge with his suitcase in his hand, past the xeroxed 'missing' posters (Figure 12.2). This important framing highlights Ousmane's figure as he crosses the bridge and portrays the disappearance of his and Elisabeth's differences.

Domestic spaces as a microcosm of the global city

After analysing the different urban spaces discovered and relocalised in London by the protagonists, this section explores domestic spaces – namely, the flat where Jane and Ali live together. The flat, the setting

Figure 12.2 Ousmane crossing the bridge to live with Elisabeth in Jane's flat

for numerous scenes in *London River*, is representative of the concept of 'borderlands', in which one can observe the cooperation, collaboration and adaptation between two different cultures. The different cultures are represented by the white British Protestant Elisabeth and the Black African Muslim Ousmane and, before them, their children who coexisted in this same space: a double articulation of coupling and interculturalism. The presence of this cinematic space leads us to realise that Ousmane and Elisabeth are a reflection of a multitude of global forces of which they are unaware, foregrounded by the wall map of the world found in the flat. Their situation reflects the current state of the world: a fragile multiculturalism in a post-9/11 world, where interculturalism still seemed possible. However, unlike her daughter's perceived openness, at first, Elisabeth rejects Ousmane. She often manifests racist superiority and suspicion of non-Anglophone cultures. However, this situation progressively changes. The film demonstrates that globalisation is far from resolving the differences between cultures. In fact, it suggests that cultural borders can be transgressed easily although the *mise-en-scène* shows contradictions. The closing minutes of the film try to suggest that we have already achieved a tenuous situation of worldwide 'convivial multiculturalism', to borrow from Paul Gilroy, with the blossoming moment that Elisabeth and Ousmane *could* live together.[44] The truth is that real citizens, including the protagonists, are not that close. Consequently, *London River* uses the flat to express an opinion: this is a state in which inequality persists and is even reinforced by white majority countries towards other ethnicities, despite the discourses of multiculturalism accredited to London.

The flat acts as a place of gathering for different religions and cultures and as a microcosm of the global world where polycentrism over ethnocentrism can be read as imagined or, sadly, short-lived – a kind of accommodation between Islam and Christianity, majoritarian and ethnic minorities communities. The physical changes in it provide an accurate view of the evolution of the characters in the film. Lighting is used in *London River* to shape the way in which Jane's flat changes its appearance, reflecting the moods of the protagonists. At first Jane's absence makes Elisabeth feel anxious and she is also disturbed by her daughter's Muslim neighbours. The initial shadows signal all the things that Jane is hiding from her mum, such as her relationship with a BAME, Muslim man. Elisabeth realises that she no longer knows her daughter. At first, blue and purple colours are highlighted. In the final moment in this flat, there are lighter tones that combine with intensified lighting, showcasing that both characters are in a cosmopolitan space where they have learnt to coexist. Elisabeth has been transformed by the moments of openness, which in many cases were produced by the terrorist bombings.

Props situate the protagonists within their new environment and introduce the unseen characters, Ali and Jane. An African musical instrument that Elisabeth finds inside the flat will become a remarkable element of union between the four. In the opening minutes Elisabeth holds the instrument in her hands with a surprised expression on her face. When the police come to the flat, Ousmane comments on the fact that the instrument used to belong to him, and later he says it was a present for Ali. This musical instrument is called a *kora*: a traditional West African stringed instrument that is played in Mali, where Ousmane was born. The *kora* is an important prop because it is a very specific item from Ousmane and Ali's culture. It makes the parents realise that their children are living together. A copy of a book in Arabic additionally denotes Jane's interest in and openness towards African and Arabic culture.

Other important objects are found inside the flat as well as photographs of the young couple in the city – more specifically, in a bar, sitting on the grass and walking along a street. These images provide a way for their parents to start to know their unknown children. The pictures denote their children's appreciable adaptation to the metropolis. The flat seems to be their own cosmopolitan space, where they interact and coexist in a seemingly egalitarian manner. When Elisabeth enters the bathroom, she sees men's bathroom accessories. The framing displays Elisabeth's discomfort. She is not likely to see the truth: her daughter has had a relationship with a man and is living in a multicultural neighbourhood with him, without giving her any information. Elisabeth's face can only be seen reflected in the mirror. The curtain obstructs our view of her face, functioning as a border and suggesting her mistrust of her daughter.

The film builds a representation of the global world around this space. It projects its ideology onto a small location where both cultures coexist and intersect, with the hope of a happy ending. Elizabeth and Ousmane through their interactions in the flat come to 'experience the materially local urban reality which at the same time is inevitably conditioned by the global forces that transcend the local'.[45] The limitations encountered at the beginning are blurred and the protagonists manage to adapt to each other. To contradict this view, it is possible to observe exclusionary borders inside the same living space. The main borders are seen when Ousmane and Elisabeth are together in the flat and they are related to their different cultural backgrounds, which will be explained in the following paragraphs through the analysis of different scenes. The flat is a 'borderscape', a concept which Deleyto characterises as 'social space defined by its borderliness and by a border ideology'.[46]

A noteworthy scene inside this space is when the police arrive to take DNA samples (Figure 12.3). They illuminate the truth: namely, that it is definitely possible that their children were living together in the flat and were in a relationship. Ousmane and Elisabeth open their eyes. The police give light to the flat, in a metaphorical and literal way. As we can observe in the framing, the intensified lighting contrasts with the dark presentation of the space offered previously. The wooden table separates both protagonists and the wardrobe divides the framing in two parts,

Figure 12.3 The flat as a 'borderscape' when the police arrive to take DNA samples

with the Muslim inspector on the side of Ousmane and the English on the side of Elisabeth. This framing divides both groups of society into two clearly differentiated groups by culture, race and, possibly, religion. This is a moment of tension reinforced by the African items found by the police inside the flat. The African instrument described above turns out to be a present from Ousmane to his son and, importantly, is the proof that Elisabeth needed. There is also the book written in Arabic which Elisabeth discovers at that same moment. The Union Jack beside the world map also offers a vision of openness through the character of Jane. However, in this case, instead it is representative of what the world is like for Elisabeth, comparing the large size of the flag with that of the world map. At this point in time, the police are used to open her mind and make her comprehend that the global city of London is a place of interaction between cultures but also, through the *mise-en-scène*, the film portrays how borders have been established towards the Muslim community, thereby segregating them.

A crucial moment in the flat, which contrasts with the scene with the police, occurs when the protagonists come to live together and have dinner in the apartment. Elisabeth, apparently free of her prejudices, opens up to Ousmane and explains her anguish about how her husband died in the war and how she has brought up Jane by herself. Her fear about her daughter's disappearance can be seen in her face. The movie gives the impression that the borders between the characters have now disappeared. Their relationship is presented as a fruitful encounter. The *mise-en-scène* presents a good example of this on the right-hand-side wall, which shows the world map without any British flag. This portrays their intention to become citizens of the world beyond narrow nationalisms. The wooden table once positioned the protagonists opposite each other. Now they sit at the table side by side during dinner. The parents simulate their children's way of life. This is the turning point: from this moment onwards, the two remain together until they eventually receive the fatal news. On the other hand, after eating, Elisabeth lights a cigarette and again a physical border is placed between them: the hob. Once again, borders are being reinforced by their cultural differences. A woman smoking in front of a man is an uncommon sight for Ousmane. These apparently unimportant differences will continue to divide them until the end of the movie; it is hard for them to understand each other. Cosmopolitanism also transmits this view and includes borders in its discourse – borders that are impossible to eradicate. People cannot be equal in all aspects of their lives because every human being is different and unique. Not all individuals think in the same way or have the same qualities. There will always be components of a culture that the other one will not understand.

London River produces meaning through this differentiation of people during specific moments inside Jane's flat. Elisabeth is described by Barta and Powrie as an active representative of the 'host society'.[47] Elisabeth is the one who seems to be the owner of the flat, and charity may be seen as the reason why she accepts Ousmane as a guest, because he cannot afford to stay at the Shelton Hotel. Their shared occupancy signals an advance in Elisabeth's prejudices after the cosmopolitan moment in Finsbury Park where she opens her mind to the other. She is likely to tolerate the presence of Ousmane, but at night he sleeps in a separate bed and space, in the living room on the sofa. Elisabeth sleeps in the bed. Again, the *mise-en-scène* separates the two protagonists. Only through this element can we see that the position of Elisabeth is privileged with respect to Ousmane's position. Besides, Ousmane's affirmation that he will take Ali back to Africa as soon as he finds him makes Elisabeth smile. Both parents, in spite of trying to plan what might be seen as a life together, continue trying to keep their children apart. They cannot come to terms with their transnational relationship.

The final moments of the film seem to eradicate any chance of future coexistence for the two protagonists. The link between them is broken along with the knowledge of the deaths of their children. Ultimately, although it seems that their lives have undergone a real change, they still return to their separate homes. These scenes contrast with the final scene of the pair inside the flat, when a farewell song is sung in Malian by Ousmane. It creates an emotional moment that seems to bring a close to their relationship with their feelings of devastation. However, their relationship is also offered an opportunity, with the meaning of the song pointing out the uncertainty of the future: 'Will I die in a city or a forest?' The truth about the protagonists is known: they have many similarities but they are also truly different. It is a moment of entire openness in which they feel the same desperation and uncertainty about what will happen to them in the future.

Conclusion

New borders have been constructed through transnational encounters between the local and the global today in certain spaces, 'borderlands'. These new borders are often related to race, religion and language. These characteristics of a culture are the ones that mark the difference between what a group of human beings consider 'Us' and what they consider the 'Other' or 'Them'. The drama of difference is challenged in *London River* with the portrayal of two very different characters learning to coexist in the same spaces and enjoy each other's presence. The devastating attacks have been the link between them but also the means of their separation due to their children's deaths.

Muslim communities all over the world are enduring the devastating consequences of terrorism as well as racist attitudes in cities like London and others. Borders are established with the Other, which in this case is identified with the Muslim culture and the character of Ousmane. These borders are present in global cities through the 'third border' and 'gentrification', excluding foreigners from certain areas. This is shown in the movie in the use of spaces with a Muslim majority, like Blackstock Road, Haringey borough and Finsbury Park. Framing indoors and outdoors work together with lighting and props to underline barriers and designate borders.

The complexity of the borders portrayed in the movie is also a problem seen in today's society. *London River* is an accurate representation of the complex social networks occurring in large cities all over the world. In the film, this is especially reflected in the most intricately developed space, which is Jane and Ali's flat, where the fruitful and, in some cases, fraught relationship between their parents is played out. Multiple processes of globalisation are presented inside the flat, the crossing of cultures and moments of openness. Ultimately, this is the essence of global human interaction: sets of complex relationships separated and reunited by different situations and conditions.

Notes

I would like to thank Marimar Azcona and Celestino Deleyto for their help with earlier versions of this chapter. I am also very grateful to the *Journal of English Studies* for publishing this text previously as an article.

1 A. C. Mendes and J. Sundholm, 'Walls and Fortresses: Borderscapes and the Cinematic Imaginary', *Transnational Cinemas*, 6.2 (2015), pp. 117–22; C. Deleyto, 'Women on the Border: A Cosmopolitan Approach to Representations of Femininity in It's a Free World …', 21st SERCIA Conference, Masculine/Feminine: Gender in English-Language Cinema and Television, Artois University, Arras, France, 3–5 September 2015; C. Deleyto, 'Looking from the Border: A Cosmopolitan Approach to Contemporary Cinema', *Transnational Cinemas*, 8.2 (2017), DOI: 10.1080/20403526.2016.1168117.

2 Deborah Shaw, 'Deconstructing and Reconstructing "Transnational Cinema"', in *Contemporary Hispanic Cinema: Interrogating the Transnational in Spanish and Latin American Film*, ed. Stephanie Dennison (Woodbridge: Tamesis, 2013), pp. 47–65; Tom O'Regan, 'Cultural Exchange', in *A Companion to Film Theory*, ed. T. Miller and R. Stam (Oxford: Blackwell, 1999), pp. 262–94.

3 Gloria Anzaldúa, *Borderlands/La Frontera: The New Mestiza* (San Francisco, CA: Aunt Lute Books, 1999 [1987]); Mike Davis, *Magical Urbanism: Latinos Reinvent the U.S. City* (London and New York: Verso, 2000); Anthony Cooper and Christopher Rumford, 'Cosmopolitan Borders: Bordering as Connectivity', in *The Ashgate Research Companion to Cosmopolitanism*, ed. Maria Rovisco and Magdalena Nowicka (London: Ashgate, 2011), pp. 261–76.
4 Elijah Anderson, *The Cosmopolitan Canopy: Race and Civility in Everyday Life* (New York: W. W. Norton, 2011), pp. 14–31; Gerard Delanty, 'The Cosmopolitan Imagination: Critical Cosmopolitanism and Social Theory', *The British Journal of Sociology*, 57.1 (2006), pp. 25–47.
5 Anzaldúa, *Borderlands/La Frontera*, p. 25.
6 Christopher Rumford, 'Introduction: Citizens and Borderwork in Europe', *Space and Polity*, 12.1 (2008), pp. 1–12.
7 Cooper and Rumford, 'Cosmopolitan Borders', p. 262.
8 Rumford, 'Introduction'.
9 Ulrich Beck, 'The Cosmopolitan Perspective: Sociology of the Second Age of Modernity', in *Conceiving Cosmopolitanism: Theory, Context, Practice*, ed. S. Vertovec and R. Cohen (Oxford: Oxford University Press, 2002), pp. 61–85; Z. Skrbis, G. Kendall and I. Woodward, 'Locating Cosmopolitanism, Between Humanist Ideal and Grounded Social Category', *Theory, Culture & Society*, 21.6 (2004), pp. 115–46; Rumford, 'Introduction'.
10 Delanty, 'The Cosmopolitan Imagination', p. 29.
11 Craig Calhoun, '"Belonging" in the Cosmopolitan Imaginary', *Ethnicities*, 3.4 (2003), pp. 531–53; Craig Calhoun, 'Cosmopolitanism and Nationalism', *Nations and Nationalism*, 14.3 (2008), p. 427; David Miller, 'Cosmopolitanism: A Critique', *Critical Review of International Social and Political Philosophy*, 5.3 (2002), pp. 80–5; David Miller, *National Responsibility and Global Justice* (New York: Oxford University Press, 2007); Eddy Kent and Terri Tomsky, *Negative Cosmopolitanism: Cultures and Politics of World Citizenship after Globalization* (Montreal and Kingston, London and Chicago: McGill-Queen's University Press, 2017).
12 Miller, 'Cosmopolitanism'.
13 Calhoun, '"Belonging" in the Cosmopolitan Imaginary'.
14 Deleyto, 'Women on the Border', p. 2.
15 Saskia Sassen, 'The Global City: Introducing a Concept', *Brown Journal of World Affairs*, 11.2 (2005), pp. 27–43 (27).
16 Ibid., p. 38.
17 Mendes and Sundholm, 'Walls and Fortresses', p. 120.
18 Deleyto, 'Women on the Border', p. 6.
19 Cooper and Rumford, 'Cosmopolitan Borders', pp. 262–4.
20 Charlotte Brunsdon, *London in Cinema: The Cinematic City since 1945* (London: British Film Institute, 2007).
21 Doreen Massey, *World City* (London: Polity, 2007).
22 Ibid., pp. 33–5.

23 Ibid., p. 32.
24 Ibid., p. 44.
25 Don Flynn quoted in Cathy McIlwaine, *The Postcolonial Practices of International Migration: Latin American Migration to London* (London: Department of Geography, Queen Mary, University of London, 2008), p. 8.
26 P. Rees and P. Boden quoted in McIlwaine, *Postcolonial Practices of International Migration*.
27 L. Spence quoted in McIlwaine, *Postcolonial Practices of International Migration*, p. 35.
28 Davis, *Magical Urbanism*, p. 59.
29 Ibid., p. 71.
30 Neil Smith, 'New Globalism, New Urbanism: Gentrification as Global Urban Strategy', *Antipode*, 34.3 (2002), pp. 427–50 (440).
31 Ulrich Beck, 'The Terrorist Threat: World Risk Society Revisited', *Theory, Culture & Society*, 19.4 (2002), pp. 39–55 (41).
32 Ibid., p. 44.
33 Ibid., p. 46.
34 Ulrich Beck, 'The Cosmopolitan State', *Der Spiegel*, 15 (2001), pp. 1–4.
35 Carrie Tarr, 'The Mediation of Difference in *London River* (Rachid Bouchareb, 2009)', in *Bicultural Literature and Film in French and English*, ed. Peter I. Barta and Phil Powrie (London: Routledge, 2015), p. 60.
36 Anzaldúa, *Borderlands/La Frontera*, p. 25.
37 Massey, *World City*, p. 119.
38 Anderson, *The Cosmopolitan Canopy*, p. xiv.
39 Rachid Bouchareb quoted in D. Gritten, 'London River: Why We Filmed in Finsbury Park', *Telegraph* (12 July 2010), https://bit.ly/41FJrNs (accessed 13 July 2016).
40 Jan Nederveen Pieterse, *Globalization and Culture: Global Mélange* (Lanham, MD: Rowman & Littlefield, 2009).
41 Michel Foucault, *The Order of Things* (New York: Vintage Books, 1971).
42 S. McLoughlin, 'Mosques and the Public Space: Conflict and Cooperation in Bradford', *Journal of Ethnic and Migration Studies*, 31.6 (2005), pp. 1045–66 (1046).
43 P. Barta and P. Powrie, 'Introduction: Being In-Between', in *Bicultural Literature and Film in French and English*, ed. Peter Barta and Phil Powrie (New York: Routledge, 2015).
44 Paul Gilroy, *After Empire: Melancholia or Convivial Culture?* (Abingdon: Routledge, 2004).
45 Carolina Sánchez Palencia, 'Cosmopolitan (Dis)encounters: The Local and the Global in Anthony Minghella's *Breaking and Entering* and Rachid Bouchareb's *London River*', *Vo. Cultura, Lenguaje y Representación*, 11 (2013), p. 121.
46 Deleyto, 'Women on the Border', p. 10.
47 Barta and Powrie, 'Introduction'.

13

Utopia as a cosmopolitan method in Alfonso Cuarón's *Children of Men*

Mónica Martín

Utopian cosmopolitan discourses are gaining momentum in twenty-first-century cinema at the same time as global social movements like Occupy Wall Street, Fridays for Future and International Women's Strikes reflect the consolidation of intersectional alter-globalisation imaginaries.[1] Whereas open-ended post-apocalyptic films of the 2000s like the Matrix series, *Children of Men* and *Blindness* fit the 'critical dystopia' theorised by Raffaella Baccolini and Tom Moylan, in post-recession (2010–) movies like the *Hunger Games* series and *Mad Max: Fury Road* utopia is more explicitly articulated as an achievable political task that concerns us all and the ecological space we inhabit as a species.[2] The protagonists in these contemporary films forge cooperative networks of resistance – across gender, racial and class categories – that illustrate what Baccolini and Moylan define as 'a new form of political opposition': 'an alliance politics that speaks back in a larger though diverse collective voice'.[3] As a response to widening social inequalities, oligarchic political bodies and environmental crises, these twenty-first-century movies are restaging utopia as a cosmopolitan method to transform non-sustainable paradigms of progress and individualist worldviews according to inclusive and ecological principles.

This chapter analyses Alfonso Cuarón's *Children of Men* as an illustrative example of cinematic cosmopolitan utopianism in the light of Tom Moylan's and Ruth Levitas's dialogical and holistic conception of utopia, and Ulrich Beck's and Gerard Delanty's critical articulations of cosmopolitanism. Moylan's outspoken defence of 'the social value of utopia' assumes that 'our dreams and hopes impact on our present reality and on the actual future into which we, now as a global population, are moving'. According to Moylan, utopia 'empties the present of its absolute authority' with a critical 'totalizing lens' that is better thought of 'in terms of the epistemology of ecology, rather than the rule of totalitarianism' and envisioned as a process rather than a place.[4] Similarly, Levitas endorses utopia as a dialogical sociological method 'concerned with the potential institutions of a just, equitable and sustainable society'.[5] Defending a no-alternative-to-utopia argument that finds echo in Zygmunt Bauman's later *Retrotopia*, Levitas sustains that utopia as method can help us to reflect on 'the connections between economic, social, existential and ecological processes in an integrated way'.[6] Social theorists Delanty and Beck, for their part, argue that critical cosmopolitanism is the methodological perspective necessary to address global challenges such as climate change and to forge dialogical social cultures 'based on the principle of world openness'.[7]

In contrast to post-9/11 films like *I Am Legend*, *War of the Worlds* and *Cloverfield*, in which apocalyptic circumstances are imputable to zombie or monstrous Others (even an American-centric monopolisation of trauma, its McDonaldisation of terrorism à la Ritzer),[8] *Children of Men* engages in a speculative critique of non-sustainable global neoliberalism that rejects alien scapegoats, as happens in other contemporary titles such as *The Happening*, *The Road*, *Never Let Me Go*, *Snowpiercer* and *Elysium*.[9] Cuarón's film portrays an undeniably dystopian future set in the year 2027 in London, a megacity afflicted by armed violence, pollution, anti-immigration policies and governmental surveillance. One of the most recognisable global cities in the world, the British capital in the film stands for an ecocidal neoliberal society that has turned infertile and is now unable to give birth to future generations. Following this thread, this chapter complements as well as departs from earlier investigations into more prismatic examinations of the film: from 'postcoloniality and detention' to 'bio-reproductive futurism' and 'states of exception', among other in-depth studies.[10] It therefore concentrates on how *Children of Men* forms a distance from the anti-utopian bias of late twentieth-century cultural texts and social theories – a demise of utopian thinking fostered by, among other causes, the postmodern questioning of grand narratives of progress, utopia's equation with totalitarian projects, its co-optation by individualist market logics and celebratory end-of-history capitalist discourses which sustain this critique, acknowledging the 'disengaged imagination' of global neoliberal elites.[11] The film's catastrophic backdrop seems incompatible with any utopian aspirations but, against all odds, a pregnant illegal immigrant named Kee (Clare-Hope Ashitey) brings the possibility of hope to a dying human species and also to Theo (Clive Owen), a pessimistic middle-aged Londoner who will try to help Kee and her baby reach human rights activists. In addition to Kee's centrality as character and the possibility of what Barbara Korte calls 'envisioning a black tomorrow', there are many other utopian disruptions to the prevailing dystopian order in the film.[12] The following pages examine, first, a stressed sense of directionality forward and elsewhere in the evolution of the narrative and the protagonists. Then, the analysis focuses on how the film's aesthetics and use of spaces argue against exclusion and locate utopian aspirations outside the borders of the national.

Finally, *mise-en-scène* and sound will be explored, tracing specific moments when the film places the marginal in the spotlight to celebrate the utopian potential of dialogical and inclusive cultures.

Articulating the rebirth of utopia: narrative and protagonists move forward and elsewhere

Theo, the main character in the film, undertakes a journey of political awakening into utopian possibility – a quest for hope rooted in historical consciousness, social awareness and acceptance of responsibility, drawing on Baccolini's description of the protagonist in the critical dystopia.[13] Closely monitored by a handheld camera from the beginning of the film, Theo evolves from an alienated spectator of disaster – disaffected and bitter about his past political involvement and the loss of his own child – to later be mobilised into a utopian actor. In the film's opening scene, a news reporter's voice is heard over a black screen informing about the siege of Seattle, the deportation of immigrants and closure of borders, followed by the more personal details of the murder of an eighteen-year-old Argentinian man, dubbed 'Baby Diego' by the media and the youngest person on earth. The camera remains practically still in front of a group of petrified spectators fixing their gaze on the TV screen of a coffee shop while Theo orders a drink, apparently less affected than the others. At this early point in the film, Theo is a sceptical spectator of global dystopia – a global citizen consuming, though reluctantly, the everyday reality of the 'world risk society' theorised by Beck.[14]

As Theo moves to the door, the handheld camera follows him out of a scruffy café, leaving him off screen to show, without cuts, a main street of 'London, 16th November 2027' (according to a caption; filmed on Oxford Street, Central London, for greater locational awareness among audiences). Panning left back to Theo, the camera moves behind the protagonist as he walks by bobbies, heavy traffic, rubbish bags and other pedestrians, then waits by his side when he stops to pour some whisky into his coffee. After an explosion in a building nearby the protagonist retreats to the wall, seeking protection and spilling his drink on the road, and the handheld camera moves away from him in order to get closer to the source of the detonation. Among debris and injured bodies, a woman walks towards the camera holding her amputated arm, while the post-blast whirring sound in Theo's ears becomes louder. The whirring bridges a cut to the title of the film on a black screen and then to a different scene in which Theo submits to rigorous identity checks at the entrance of his workplace in the Ministry of Energy. More distant from its subject now, the handheld camera shows

Theo passing by governmental posters that sponsor 'Jobs for Brits' and, as the whirring decreases, calling on the boss's office to ask for a day off, pretending to be affected by the tragic news of Baby Diego's untimely death. This way, spectators make the transition from the opening scene to the one after the title through Theo's aural focalisation (the post-blast ringing that he hears) but, rather than figuring as a victim of circumstances whose perspective of the world is privileged – white, male, middle class, British – he is critically introduced as an emotionally detached bureaucrat, contributing indirectly to sustaining the dystopian status quo and the state's orchestration of it; he is a civil servant who tries to make it through his hopeless everyday reality, disregarding the injustice of mass deportation and displacement, refugee camps and opposition to the anomie.

The apocalyptic surrounding context, though, does begin to affect him little by little. After the scene at his workplace, we see Theo on a train trying to ignore governmental TV ads asking people to 'report all illegal immigrants'. Suddenly, an object thrown by protesters at his barred window wakes him up from his self-imposed lethargy and lingering hangover. The blow hits the protected glass at the same moment as the train passes by a graffiti tag that states 'The last one to die, please switch off the light' – an apocalyptic joke that illustrates his cynical hopeless attitude so far. Then, after he disembarks the train and walks along a platform crowded with jailed illegal migrants and military police, he hugs his friend Jasper (Michael Caine) outside the station. The first ray of sunlight in the film shines upon the two friends' faces as they embrace, welcoming the protagonist's first true display of affection and a break in the overcast bleakness of London and the wider United Kingdom in autumnal and wintry seasons. The warmer *mise-en-scène* outside the militarised station evokes the ontological turn that awaits the protagonist once he resolves to help Kee, an illegal migrant: Theo is about to move beyond his nihilist 'comfort zone' as a *flâneur* of dystopia to embark on an eye-opening voyage to underprivileged realities lived by marginalised Others.

In the context of the Christian references that permeate the film ('Theo' means 'gift of God', 'the Fishes' recalls the secret symbol adopted by early Christians and the baby's birth alludes to the nativity of Jesus, to name but a few), the protagonist's cosmopolitan awakening can be read in the light of Alain Badiou's theorisation of St Paul's conversion and his universalist conception of the Christian subject beyond legal and cultural individual considerations. According to Badiou, St Paul offers a model of militancy based on 'universal singularity' that is alternative to the 'party militant' of 'bloodstained' communist experiences – a universalist militant figure that can be recuperated to oppose the social 'fragmentation' that capitalism and identitarian politics foster today.[15] Theo's cosmopolitan 'militancy' can be said to represent a model of inclusive universalism that, instead of invoking afterlife salvation, relies on the disruptive political potential of the utopian to negate the absence of global systemic alternatives and vindicate 'a break', as Fredric Jameson puts it.[16] As embodied by Theo's non-violent commitment and Kee's maternal care, a cosmopolitan utopian break demands cooperative, nurturing and dialogical relations, rather than belligerent revolutionary dialectics and individualist strategies. Within the post-secular society that the film depicts, Theo's utopian turn is not prompted by faith in a specific religious doctrine or political ideology but is motivated by a moral allegiance to the right to life of others and the hopeful vision of a cosmopolitan down-to-earth hereafter for the human species beyond his own lifetime.

As Theo's outlooks and attitudes become less self-centred, the camera will get closer to him, often documenting empathically, at an eye-level angle, his efforts to get his feet in the mud and walk in others' shoes (explicitly so since he will find his toes deep in mud at one point and will need to borrow shoes from an illegal migrant). At first carried by others (in cars, trains, vans, a double-decker bus and governmental vehicles), Theo will then accept the responsibility to help Kee reach the ship *Tomorrow* to bring her baby safely into the world. Later, the ocean at the conclusion becomes a desirable borderless world, where totalitarian states like England have no jurisdictional control to stifle the humanitarian charting of a new course away from land. After Jasper and Julian (Julianne Moore), Theo's ex-wife and leader of the pro-refugee resistance group 'the Fishes', are killed by members of her own underground organisation, he will have to drive the car himself and lead the mission to guide Kee through a refugee camp and to the sea. In the camp, at last, Theo eventually becomes the Other in the eyes of the military officers and spills his blood (rather than just his coffee, as he did at the beginning) for a cause worth his sacrifice – the welfare of Kee and her newborn, who embody the possibility of hope for a dying humanity.

In the foggy waters of the closing scene, the narrative journey, which so far has followed a distressed and what Mbembe calls 'death worlds' directionality forward, now reaches its final stage by heading elsewhere, toward new world-building.[17] Fatally wounded at this point, Theo rows a small wooden boat through a dark tunnel and into the open waters while Kee holds her baby in her arms. In the grey foggy *mise-en-scène*, we see Theo holding Kee's hand and asking her to keep her baby close 'whatever they say'. It is their survival, not his, that matters to him. Bleeding and in pain, he smiles when Kee tells him she is going to name her girl Dylan after Julian and Theo's son, who died during a flu pandemic. With that last smile on his face, Theo loses consciousness while the boat starts to take distance from the camera. However, Theo's death does not signal the end of the story but the beginning of another: a possible cosmopolitan future now seen from the perspective of Kee. A point-of-view shot that displays the ship on the horizon from her perspective and another shot where she tells her baby 'you are safe now' point at a utopian directionality elsewhere, embodied by the Black female illegal migrant and her baby girl. The last shot in the film – a low-angle shot of the crew on a ship clearly named *Tomorrow* – is followed by the title of the film on a black screen, accompanied by a score of children laughing instead of the post-blast whirring of the beginning. This time, the ending seems to suggest, the future should not lie in the hands of white men conquering and spoiling wild 'promised land' but in the arms of a Black woman who stands for the dispossessed and the marginalised. If Theo has died a radically different man from the hopeless and passive Londoner we saw at the beginning of the film, utopia, likewise, re-emerges amidst the ashes of ecocide and bigotry reformulated as a cosmopolitan method.

Expanding utopia: filming cosmopolitan openness – spaces, framing and editing

The way Theo's journey ends and baby Dylan's starts – in borderless waters – illustrates the opening process that accompanies the rebirth of utopia in the movie. Hope resides, like baby Dylan's survival in the film, in the crossing of borders: geographical (Kee is an illegal migrant who needs to escape the confinement of the refugee camp) and interpersonal (Theo and Kee have cooperated as equals beyond gender, national, class and racial differences). As the ship's name in the closing shot suggests as it heads towards Kee's boat, a just and sustainable global tomorrow requires international institutions, like the Human Project in the film, that are able to place social welfare, egalitarianism and ecology before particular economic interests and nationalist outlooks.

The apartheid-like spaces of London in the film – refugee camps, detention areas and elitist inner-city neighbourhoods, among others – operate under the logics of what Beck defines as a 'risk regime', one that 'is not national, but global' and conforms to the 'world risk society'.[18] Risk contention legitimises the restriction of liberties, the militarisation of the government and the closure of borders in the movie. London 2027 hosts a 'fear society', which, as defined by Steve Macek, exploits 'deviant, threatening, or troubling objects … produced by particular social agents in particular contexts for specific purposes'.[19] The main deviant objects in this case are illegal migrants, portrayed by neoliberal nationalist power elites and the media as criminal parasites on a nation with limited resources. The privileged, meanwhile, enjoy pleasant everyday lives in restricted spaces such as St James's Park and the exclusive building where Theo's high-rank cousin lives. When Theo pays him a visit to ask for transit papers for Kee, the spotlessly white interiors of the cousin's living quarters and the magnificent works of art inside – Picasso's *Guernica* and Michelangelo's *David* – stand for an extractive Western global neoliberalism that has appropriated common resources. This economic elite controls public institutions like the military, uses violence to protect its interests (as conveyed by the cousin's growling dogs) and ignores eco-social welfare. Unaffected by the crowded slums and polluted Thames waters on the other side of his walls, Theo's cousin overlooks others' suffering from his ivory tower like the piggy-bank balloon work of art that contentedly floats in the air outside his residence – an image that evokes the cover of Pink Floyd's 1977 album *Animals*, its critique of Margaret Thatcher's neoliberal conservatism and its allusion to George Orwell's satirical appraisal of class-based societies and totalitarian revolutionary leaders in *Animal Farm*.

Together with Jasper's John Lennon hippie looks and Lenin's ornamental profile (placed by Christian iconography in a Russian lady's home in the refugee camp), *Guernica*, *David* and the inflatable pig form a decontextualised pastiche of past cultural symbols of resistance. Leftist for the most part, these neutralised mementos of gone utopian aspirations comment on the decay of utopia and the need to renew utopianism beyond the nostalgic remembering that Jasper's 1960s countercultural outfit represents. Riddled with memories of the good old utopian days, Jasper's isolated rural cottage offers Theo and Kee a momentary escape from the chaotic reality of London – a 'retrotopian' evasion, drawing on Bauman's term, of the complexities of multicultural social conflict and neoliberal urbanisation, a flight from reality that does not bring utopian transformation.

The counterviolence strategy that the Fishes employ to fight for the rights of refugees proves, in turn, as sterile for eco-social progress as the neoliberal paradigm represented by Theo's cousin. When Theo is kidnapped by some members of this activist group (which is directed by his ex-wife Julian) and taken to their hideout in an old church attic, the roofless dome structure above their heads can be read as a spatial metaphor for the moral holes and ineffectiveness of their violent methods. Despite being grounded on solid ideological foundations and aspiring to good causes, the radical activists use aggressive and utilitarian tactics similar to those of the government. Their paramilitary actions and internal struggles for power within the group (Julian is later killed by members of her organisation) eventually turn out to be as useless to society as the naked dome is to protect those inside from the cold and the rain.

Against the enclosed spaces of power elites, retrotopian evasion and radical activists described above, the editing and framing call for dialogical openness in social relations and sociopolitical outlooks. As Theo learns to connect and cooperate with others, the framing changes. If, at the beginning of the film, medium and long shots of the protagonist highlight his social alienation when walking in the city, entering his office and waking up at home, two shots of Theo and Jasper laughing in the car and the long take inside Julian's vehicle after he meets Kee convey the affective bonds he is forging with others. At the end of the movie, another long take in a battle scene at the refugee camp, in which different armed factions fight, endorses holistic approaches to convoluted conflict issues. While the military attack a rebel refugee group and the Fishes shoot Theo to capture Kee, the cut-less editing and criss-crossing bullets articulate the interconnection of the different agents and issues involved in the struggle. As happens with the film's opening scene, the long take ties individuals and actions to the space around them but now Theo takes responsibility for the apocalyptic situation rather than trying to evade it, as he did at the beginning. The fragility of the newborn in such a hostile environment points at the pressing necessity to abandon dialectical aggressive relations with the Other and to develop, instead, dialogical and cooperative cosmopolitan cultures. The future of humanity depends on it, according to the film, as much as on our capacity to reverse the ecocidal 'progress' that images of filthy streets, car-congested urban spaces, dead cattle and polluted rivers and skies denounce throughout the movie.

Commenting on how the film's blend of ethics and aesthetics results in a piece of political protest similar to Picasso's *Guernica*, Samuel Amago holds that 'Cuarón turns *Children of Men* into a call for individual action, a hopeful prayer for peace, and an encouraging example of what cinema might do to change the world.'[20] Yet, although the narrative focuses on Theo's personal transformation and growing engagement, the long takes described above and the borderless waters in which the film ends can be said to call for collective cosmopolitan action rather than individual action. Shifting the protagonist's perspective to Kee's and naming the Human Project's ship *Tomorrow* in the last scene, the film claims the allegorical nature of the narrative and its main character. Individuals' ethical actions and everyday politics are consistently vindicated throughout the movie, but *Children of Men* ultimately calls for political and ethical paradigms that transcend the individual realm, the tribe and the nation. Theo's sacrifice and Kee's baby alone cannot guarantee humanity's fertility in the same way that Britain cannot effectively manage pandemics and environmental crises. If individuals' actions can reform the world it will happen thanks to intercultural cooperative strategies like Theo and Kee's and cosmopolitan institutions like the Human Project in the film.

Utopian aspirations are to be framed from cosmopolitan prisms, as the ending hints. The fact that *Children of Men* refers critically to early twenty-first-century neoliberal globalisation, its ecocidal economics and post-9/11 fear discourses does not imply the film supports anti-globalisation stances. Rather, the film calls for the rebirth and expansion of utopia in a global society that already shares an environmental framework in crisis and can no longer effectively prevent the mobility of underprivileged people. If at the beginning of the film utopia seems to have 'no topos', as Bauman lamented, and hope is a luxury only a few can afford, the end of the movie redraws utopia from a cosmopolitan point of view.[21] Against fear-ridden apartheid solutions and anti-utopian perspectives of the global that foreclose propositional speculation, *Children of Men* argues that the hope for a better life should be retrieved as a political task tied to inclusive and ecological progress. This implies that imaginaries need to shift from neoliberalism, nationalism and economic materialism to ecology and cosmopolitanism.

As Manfred B. Steger and Paul James assert in *Ideologies of Globalism*, in the early twenty-first century 'competing ideologies of globalization articulate a tangled, but generalizing, global imaginary that, more readily than ever before, cuts across class, gender, race, and state-based, geopolitical and cultural differences, postcolonial divides and other social boundaries'. This global imaginary, they argue, 'has become relatively encompassing, translated into differing political programs by competing *globalisms*' – market globalism, justice globalism, religious globalism, imperial globalism – and including many of the previously called 'anti-globalization' movements, which now 'describe themselves as part of the "alter-globalization" movement'.[22] In line with earlier theories on the global flow of ideas such as Arjun Appadurai's 'ideoscapes', the 'globalisms' Steger and James propose would be 'woven' into a 'global social imaginary' that constitutes 'the dominant social imaginary of our time (albeit still contending with the weakening national imaginary) from within all contemporary political belief systems must be understood and analyzed'.[23] Contemporary social imaginaries, they explain, are 'patterned *convocations* of the lived *social whole*' that used to be tied to national communities alone but now call together 'meanings, ideas, sensibilities' around 'an almost pre-reflexive sense that at one level "we" as individuals, peoples, and nations have a common global fate'. Thus, 'normative contestations continue, but they tend to have a common implicit point of reference – the global'.[24]

Drawing on Steger and James, *Children of Men* partakes of the global social imaginary that permeates contemporary life, articulating what could be labelled as 'cosmopolitan globalism' or, using these authors' terminology, 'justice globalism' – 'an alternative vision of globalisation based on egalitarian ideals of local-global solidarities, distributive justice, and ecological sustainability'.[25] The film's closing scene advocates for the consolidation of a cosmopolitan alternative to a 'market globalism' with imperial undertones, as Steger and James call it, which is unequivocally portrayed as dystopian and contextualised in early-century global politics (images of tortured prisoners in the refugee camp echo the pictures taken by US soldiers in the Iraqi Abu Ghraib prison during the Bush administration). The cosmopolitan outlooks in the film also confront a nationalist globalism that relies on risk-based global imaginaries to justify its anti-immigration politics, as more recently seen in Trump's presidential campaign and the Brexit process.

This way, although *Children of Men* illustrates the anxieties and eco-social crises of early-century neoliberal globalisation – as explored by Julia Echeverría's analysis of the long takes in connection with Bauman's 'liquid fear' and Michael Hardt and Antonio Negri's 'global state of war' – the ending's location (fluid waters) and the formal highlighting of relational bonds among characters and their environment (especially through the use of long takes) endorse the utopian opening process that characters undergo.[26] The film's use of spaces and formal choices prompts viewers to expand their utopian horizons and desire cosmopolitan futures, regardless of how bleak the international panorama might look, as suggested by the foggy open waters of the closing scene.

Reformulating utopia as cosmopolitan method: *mise-en-scène* and sound embrace the stranger

The cosmopolitan aspirations articulated in *Children of Men* involve the reformulation of utopia as a holistic and dialogical method. As happens in Ruth Levitas's social theory, *Children of Men* conceives utopia as an open-ended speculative sociology concerned with the world, nature, others and the future.[27] The cosmopolitan attitudes Theo and Kee perform in their apocalyptic everyday feature as a utopian yet effective method to transform the world. In line with the 'cosmopolitan imagination' theorised by Gerard Delanty, the protagonists' utopian cosmopolitanism replaces the us/them dialectics of apartheid conceptions of utopia (be they nationalist, oligarchic, patriarchal or xenophobic) with dialogical relations with the Other that bring about self-transformation.[28] The film's narrative and formal devices locate the 'strangers at our door', as Bauman referred to the rising numbers of 'migration crises', in a central cinematic place.[29] Kee, as hinted at by her name's phonetics, is a 'key' to Theo's conversion – a marginal object of fear that turns into an essential subject for narrative continuity. Her pregnancy, the first in the last two decades, states that humanity's survival depends on lifting up the borders that separate us as a species, as Bauman did in *Retrotopia*.[30]

The film's lighting insists on this matter binding hope and inclusion together. When Kee shares the news of her pregnancy with Theo for the first time, we see a medium shot of her naked body surrounded by wired milk cows in a barn, with her belly contour illuminated by the warm light of fluorescent lamps. As she comments on how cows' teats are cut to fit the milking machine, the *mise-en-scène* interconnects cosmopolitan, feminist and ecological aspirations as part of a single utopian agenda. Later, there is a long shot of her sitting on a playground swing under the sunshine, seen through a broken window from Theo's perspective. Framed by the sharp angles of the broken glass, in what used to be a school, the shot composition conveys the hostile context illegal migrants face and the carelessness of a social order that has not been able to protect children. The lighting, though, suggests that hope can resist the harshest circumstances and pictures, once again, the possibility of post-apocalyptic futures from a cosmopolitan point of view. Likewise, when Kee gives birth to baby Dylan in the refugee camp, a lamp next to her draws a circle of illuminated exception within the total darkness around. In the middle of the frame and under the spotlight, Kee's pregnant Black body, assisted by Theo's white hands, heralds the cosmopolitan promise of a human future able to overcome the dialectics of the Other through egalitarian cooperative paradigms that discard white saviourism and patronising patriarchal stances.

As far as utopian uses of sound go, pleasant sounds break up and disrupt, in some scenes, the otherwise intrusive, unidirectional and violent daily score of governmental propaganda messages, police officers' cursing and explosions. One of the most remarkable examples is the harmonic entanglement of three different languages in a scene when Kee, her baby and Theo stay at a Russian woman's home in the refugee camp. Although the characters do not share a common language, they participate in a shared emotional conversation that associates cosmopolitan dialogics with the ethics of care. Another key moment takes place in the battle scene at the refugee camp, when bombs and shootings are suddenly interrupted by the newborn's cry. As the people inside the building and the soldiers outside stop their fighting to hear the baby's unmistakable wailing, they open up a spontaneous silent humanitarian corridor for Kee, Dylan and Theo to get out of the battle. Though warfare is swiftly resumed, the brief relieving parenthesis of silence signals that cosmopolitan understanding can only happen when one is willing to listen to the Other.

Once the protagonists effectively reach 'the light at the end of the tunnel' and access the open sea in the closing scene, there is a noticeable absence of background noise and a bare *mise-en-scène* where the boat floats in a thick fog and diffuse light. The end features as a blank canvas that, at first, seems to herald unpromising prospects for the characters: there are no safe points for the fragile wooden boat to cling on to amidst the inhospitable humid atmosphere and Theo dies, leaving Kee and Dylan floating adrift. Yet, as the big sturdy ship *Tomorrow* moves steadily ahead to rescue Kee and her daughter, the blank *mise-en-scène* can also be read as the empty space of a future that is yet to be drawn. It is a space of utopian possibility occupied by characters that embody intersecting underprivileged positions – a poor Black female illegal migrant and her baby girl; a kind of 'migrant image' discussed in other contexts by T. J. Demos.[31]

As argued by Celestino Deleyto and María del Mar Azcona, many contemporary films build their narratives around the 'pervasiveness of border experience in contemporary societies', documenting its injustices and how borders play a central role in developing a 'transnational consciousness'.[32] In *Children of Men*, the relay of perspectives in the final scene (from Theo's to Kee's) and the sound and lighting formal choices described above articulate what Sandro Mezzadra and Brett Neilson call 'seeing like a migrant': displays of 'the subjective viewpoint of border crossings and struggles' that can serve to develop 'border as method' in order to rethink 'questions of organization, political action, and contestation' in an emergent 'political world beyond the nation-state'.[33] According to James M. Hodapp, the migrant's baby in the film represents 'a postcolonial, fragmented, and contested subject' that is proclaimed 'the true globalized citizen'.[34] If, as Debbie Olson states, the child in post-apocalyptic cinema 'is the intersection of our past, present, and future, the manifestation of who we were, who we are, and who, or what, humanity can become', baby Dylan would be imbued with cosmopolitan aspirations critical of colonial and patriarchal histories of oppression, and ecocidal, economised global presents.[35]

Still, drawing on Nicole L. Sparling's and Sarah Trimble's biopolitical readings of the film, the fact that Kee remains a rhetorical vehicle for imagining our collective future as a species – the holder of a reproductive power whose specific history of racial and gender oppression is subdued by the cosmopolitan survival narrative – should prompt guarded reflection on the need to overcome whitened and patriarchal forms of cosmopolitanism.[36] As opposed to the confident sailing of the white male activists onboard the potent ship *Tomorrow*, which brings to mind histories of the transatlantic slave trade and colonialism, Kee's physical exposure while caring for her baby in a fragile wooden boat might evoke a safer utopian route into a cosmopolitan future: an ecofeminist shift that Cuarón's later films *Gravity* and *Roma* vindicate more clearly via female protagonists whose cooperative ethics and utopian resistance feature allegorically as essential values for the sustainability of the species.[37]

After witnessing the Great Recession, the Brexit process, Donald Trump's anti-immigration policies and climate-change negationism, the rising popularity of nationalist parties in countries like France, Italy and Poland, the resilience of systemic racism and gender abuse in developed countries (as illustrated by George Floyd's killing and the Harvey Weinstein case) and the COVID-19 pandemic, the cosmopolitan horizon that *Children of Men* dared to envision in the mid-2000s remains an urgent utopian task. *Children of Men* hopes and asks for a cosmopolitan remapping of the global city beyond the frameworks provided by anti-utopic, nationalistic, risk-prone societies under neoliberalism. This way, Cuarón's film ends posing a global political challenge: the construction of a cosmopolitan social space. As Henri Lefebvre argued, 'what is an ideology without a space to which it refers, a space which it describes, whose vocabulary and links it makes use of, and whose code it embodies? ... Ideology *per se* might well be said to consist primarily in a discourse upon social space'. *Children of Men* ultimately invokes 'the space of the human species', as Lefebvre put it: 'a planet-wide space as the social foundation of a transformed everyday life open to myriad possibilities'– that is, an inclusive and sustainable world order for the 'children of men' *and women*, of all races and origins, for other species and habitats across the world and into the future.[38]

Notes

1 See Manuel Castells, *Networks of Outrage and Hope: Social Movements in the Internet Age* (Cambridge: Polity Press, 2012); Camil Alexandru Parvu, 'Contestatory Cosmopolitanism, Neoliberal Rationality and Global Protests', *Globalizations*, 14.5 (2017), pp. 776–91; and Cinzia Arruzza, Tithi Bhattacharya and Nancy Fraser, *Feminism for the 99 Percent: A Manifesto* (London: Verso, 2019).

2 The Matrix series, directed by the Wachowskis (Warner Brothers, 1999–2003); *Children of Men*, directed by Alfonso Cuarón (Universal Studios, 2006); and *Blindness*, directed by Fernando Meirelles (Twentieth Century Fox, 2008); Raffaella Baccolini and Tom Moylan, 'Introduction: Dystopia and Histories', in *Dark Horizons: Science Fiction and the Dystopian Imagination*, ed. Baccolini and Moylan (New York: Routledge, 2003), pp. 1–12; *The Hunger Games*, directed by Gary Ross (Lionsgate, 2012); *The Hunger Games: Catching Fire, The Hunger Games: Mockingjay – Part 1* and *The Hunger Games: Mockingjay – Part 2*, directed by Francis Lawrence (Lionsgate, 2013–15); and *Mad Max: Fury Road*, directed by George Miller (Warner Brothers, 2015).

3 Baccolini and Moylan, 'Introduction', p. 8.

4 Tom Moylan, 'To Stand with Dreamers: On the Use Value of Utopia', *Irish Review*, 34 (2006), pp. 3–10, 17.

5 Ruth Levitas, *Utopia As Method: The Imaginary Reconstitution of Society* (New York: Palgrave Macmillan, 2013), p. xviii.

6 Zygmunt Bauman, *Retrotopia* (Cambridge: Polity Press, 2017), pp. 153–67; Levitas, *Utopia As Method*, pp. xii, 19.

7 Ulrich Beck, *World at Risk* (Cambridge: Polity Press, 2009), pp. 61, 188; Gerard Delanty, 'The Cosmopolitan Imagination: Critical Cosmopolitanism and Social Theory', *British Journal of Sociology*, 57.1 (2006), pp. 27, 39, 44.
8 George Ritzer, *The McDonaldization of Society* (Thousand Oaks, CA: Pine Forge Press, 2011).
9 *I Am Legend*, directed by Francis Lawrence (Warner Bros Pictures, 2007); *War of the Worlds*, directed by Steven Spielberg (Paramount Pictures, 2005); and *Cloverfield*, directed by Matt Reeves (Paramount Pictures, 2008). *The Happening*, directed by M. Night Shyamalan (20th Century Fox, 2008); *The Road*, directed by John Hillcoat (Dimension Films, 2009); *Never Let Me Go*, directed by Mark Romanek (Fox Searchlight Pictures, 2010); *Snowpiercer*, directed by Bong Joon-ho (The Weinstein Company, 2013); and *Elysium*, directed by Neill Blomkamp (Sony Pictures, 2013).
10 Shohini Chaudhuri, 'Unpeople: Postcolonial Reflections on Terror, Torture and Detention in Children of Men', in *Postcolonial Cinema Studies*, ed. Sandra Ponzanesi and Marguerite Waller (London: Routledge, 2011), pp. 191–204; Heather Latimer, 'Bio-reproductive Futurism: Bare Life and the Pregnant Refugee in Alfonso Cuarón's *Children of Men*', *Social Text*, 29.3 (2011), pp. 51–72; Dale Chapman, 'Music and the State of Exception in Alfonso Cuarón's *Children of Men*', in *The Oxford Handbook of Sound and Image in Digital Media*, ed. Carol Vernallis, Amy Herzog and John Richardson (Oxford: Oxford University Press, 2013), pp. 288–309.
11 On postmodern questioning see Krishan Kumar, 'The Ends of Utopia', *New Literary History*, 41.3 (2010), p. 559. On utopia's equation with totalitarian projects see Gregory Claeys, *Searching for Utopia: The History of an Idea* (New York: Thames and Hudson, 2011), pp. 200–7. On utopia's co-optation see Moylan, 'To Stand with Dreamers', p. 2. And on 'disengaged imagination' see Zygmunt Bauman, 'Utopia with No Topos', *History of the Human Sciences*, 16.1 (2003), pp. 11–25.
12 Barbara Korte, 'Envisioning a Black Tomorrow? Black Mother Figures and the Issue of Representation in *28 Days Later* (2003) and *Children of Men* (2006)', in *Multi-Ethnic Britain 2000+*, ed. Lars Eckstein, Barbara Korte, Eva Ulrike Pirker and Christoph Reinfandt (Leiden: Brill, 2008).
13 Raffaella Baccolini, '"A useful knowledge of the present is rooted in the past": Memory and Historical Reconciliation in Ursula K. Le Guin's *The Telling*', in *Dark Horizons*, ed. Baccolini and Moylan, pp. 114–19.
14 Ulrich Beck, *World Risk Society* (Cambridge: Polity Press, 1999).
15 Alain Badiou, *Saint Paul: The Foundations of Universalism*, trans. Ray Brassier (Stanford, CA: Stanford University Press, 2003), pp. 1–15.
16 Fredric Jameson, *Archaeologies of the Future: The Desire Called Utopia and Other Science Fictions* (New York: Verso, 2007), pp. 231–2.
17 Achille Mbembe, 'Necropolitics', *Public Culture*, 15.1 (2005), pp. 11–40.
18 Beck, *World Risk Society*, p. 3.
19 Steve Macek, *Urban Nightmares: The Media, the Right, and the Moral Panic over the City* (Minneapolis, MN: University of Minnesota Press, 2006), p. xiv.

20 Samuel Amago, 'Ethics, Aesthetics, and the Future in Alfonso Cuarón's *Children of Men*', *Discourse*, 32.2 (2010), p. 231.
21 Bauman, 'Utopia with No Topos', pp. 19–23.
22 Manfred B. Steger and Paul James, 'Introduction: Ideologies of Globalism', in *Globalization and Culture*, vol. 4: *Ideologies of Globalism*, ed. Steger and James (Los Angeles: Sage, 2010), p. ix.
23 Arjun Appadurai, 'Disjuncture and Difference in the Global Cultural Economy', *Theory, Culture and Society*, 7.2–3 (1990), pp. 295–310.
24 Steger and James, 'Introduction', pp. xvi–xvii, xxvii.
25 Ibid., p. ix.
26 Julia Echeverría, 'Liquid Cinematography and the Representation of Viral Threats in Alfonso Cuarón's *Children of Men*', *Atlantis*, 37.2 (2015), pp. 137–53; Zygmunt Bauman, *Liquid Fear* (Cambridge: Polity Press, 2006); and Michael Hardt and Antonio Negri, *Multitude: War and Democracy in the Age of Empire* (New York: Penguin Press, 2004).
27 Levitas, *Utopia As Method*, pp. 217–20.
28 Gerard Delanty, *The Cosmopolitan Imagination: The Renewal of Critical Social Theory* (Cambridge: Cambridge University Press, 2009), p. 12.
29 Zygmunt Bauman, *Strangers at Our Door* (Cambridge: Polity Press, 2016).
30 Bauman, *Retrotopia*, p. 167.
31 T. J. Demos, *The Migrant Image: The Art and Politics of Documentary during Global Crisis* (Durham, NC: Duke University Press, 2013).
32 Celestino Deleyto and María del Mar Azcona, *Alejandro González Iñárritu* (Urbana, IL: University of Illinois Press, 2010), p. 118.
33 Sandro Mezzadra and Brett Neilson, *Border As Method, or, The Multiplication of Labor* (Durham, NC: Duke University Press, 2013), p. 166.
34 James M. Hodapp, 'The Specter of the Postcolonial Child and Faux Long Takes in Cuarón's *Children of Men*', in *The Child in Post-Apocalyptic Cinema*, ed. Debbie Olson (Lanham, MD: Lexington Books, 2015), pp. 172, 177.
35 Debbie Olson, 'Introduction', in ibid., p. xiv.
36 Nicole L. Sparling, 'Without a Conceivable Future: Figuring the Mother in Alfonso Cuarón's *Children of Men*', *Frontiers: A Journal of Women Studies*, 35.1 (2014), pp. 160–80; and Sarah Trimble, 'Maternal Back/grounds in *Children of Men*: Notes Toward an Arendtian Biopolitics', *Science Fiction Film and Television*, 4.2 (2011), pp. 249–70.
37 *Gravity*, directed by Alfonso Cuarón (Warner Bros Pictures, 2013); and *Roma*, directed by Alfonso Cuarón (Netflix, 2018).
38 Henri Lefebvre, *The Production of Space*, trans. Donald Nicholson-Smith (Malden, MA: Blackwell, 1991), pp. 44, 422–3.

Epilogue:
The rise of sourdough bread: *The Street,* gentrification and Brexit

Charlotte Brunsdon

Zed Nelson's 2019 film *The Street*, filmed in the East London borough of Hackney, has a deceptively simple project: to track the transformations in inner-city Hoxton Street over the four years of filming. Through this undertaking, Nelson tells a rather more complicated story than the familiar narrative of the changing built environment of the cinematic city. His achievement is to record a micro-history of the changing street as long-established businesses like Anderson's the Bakers and Lawrence's the carpet shop close, to be replaced with bars and galleries, in a broader context of the continuing spread of the City of London into adjacent previously working-class areas. Framing the changes in the street within the 2010 coalition government's austerity project and the 2016 Brexit referendum, Nelson explores, using only the careful editing of his informants' words, the way in which voting to leave Europe could be understood as a response to the loss of a familiar way of life, a familiar street, to the hipsters and incomers of gentrification. Although austerity, the referendum and the following years of political fractiousness form the film's political anchor, for a film much concerned with where people live and the loss of social housing, the tragedy of the 2018 Grenfell Tower fire erupts as a temporal marker of a different kind, and Nelson shows some of his participants reacting to the events in West London as news of the lives lost filters through news media on an August morning. The film finishes, as it began, with Serge, the philosophical, erudite inhabitant of the defensible space under the foot of a bridge over the nearby River Lea. Serge's home, with its carefully accumulated possessions, which we have come to understand, through the process of the film, to be a more autonomous and satisfactory space than some other people's living spaces, has been vandalised and burnt out.

While contemporary politics contextualise the film, it is always the inhabitants of the street, Nelson's informants, who are its concern, particularly the elderly Colleen, who reappears throughout the ninety minutes, becoming progressively more housebound as the film proceeds. Nelson makes an embodied history of the street, attentive to the ceaseless refurbishment of an accelerated period of aggressive gentrification, but attentive to these changes through the experience and reflection of the people living there as they see their world transformed. This project of an embodied history is established in the opening minutes of the film with the juxtaposition of some introductory titles and the first appearances of the people in the street who will be Nelson's informants. The titles appear in three tranches, like a slide show. First, the identification of the street:

> Hoxton Street is a traditionally working-class street in Hackney, one of London's poorest boroughs.

Then, the juxtaposition of the post-crash austerity programme with London property price inflation:

> As property prices reached unprecedented levels in the capital, the government's austerity programme cut £30 billion from social services across the UK in the nine years starting in 2010.

And finally, the introduction of the EU referendum:

> At a time of growing social polarisation and widespread mistrust of the political establishment, David Cameron announced the EU referendum.

The final slide in this sequence is a long steady shot of Hoxton Street in the early morning, showing the skyscrapers of the City of London to the south with the rising sun reflecting off the glass towers like a flame (Figure 14.1).

Figure 14.1 The repeated shot of Hoxton Street looking south towards the City of London (Courtesy of Zed Nelson)

Hoxton Street was the main shopping street in an area of historic 'significant social deprivation' close to both the City of London (the financial district) and Islington, the area discussed by Ruth Glass in her classic 1964 study of gentrification.¹ Hoxton, despite its proximity to both Islington and East London's 'Silicon' (Old Street) roundabout, remained a working-class place for longer than adjacent areas, despite significant artist gentrification in the south round Hoxton Square (one end of Hoxton Street). In an analysis of creative industries and urban regeneration, Andy Pratt points out that the Hoxton of hipsterdom, 'one of the coolest places on the planet' (according to *Time Magazine* in 1996), 'is technically Shoreditch', located mainly south of Old Street, bounded by Great Eastern Street and Shoreditch High Street.² It is this area, the Shoreditch triangle, which was home to the YBAs as well as many new media start-ups, while Hoxton Square itself housed the LUX cinematheque (1997–2001) and the White Cube Gallery (2000–12). In his case study of the brief flame of Hoxton's 1990s Cool Britannia celebrity, Pratt dates the beginning of the end to 2000–1 and, writing in 2008, observes, 'North of the square, Hoxton proper is as poor as it ever was.'³ Badly bombed in World War II, with a mixture of council estates and older terraced housing, the key artery of 'Hoxton proper' is the street of the film's title.⁴ It is the colonisation of this space that the film documents, while the filmmaker's choice to omit the word 'Hoxton' in his title avoids the connotations of *fin-de-siècle* trendiness that the name of the district now suggests. Pratt notes that an essential element in the 1990s gentrification he analyses was that Hoxton offered 'space and grime, and little regulation'.⁵ The new context of the post-2007–8 economic crash, in combination with this historic erosion of regulation which might protect established, but poor, residents and businesses, provides the background to the stories of *The Street*. As the film proceeds, even some of the beneficiaries of the flexibility of live/work planning protocols are recorded expressing concern about Hackney's failure to control redevelopment.⁶

A photographer's film: 'It's not my world, it's your world'

The film's maker, Zed Nelson, has won international recognition for his work as a photographer with projects such as *Gun Nation* (2000) and *Love Me* (2009). *The Street* develops concerns already manifest in the series *Disappearing Britain* (which includes portraits of shipbuilders, Cornish fishermen, boxers and foxhunters) and *Hackney – A Tale of Two Cities*. The Hackney series, which was published as a successful book, *Portrait of Hackney* (2014), and is described as ongoing, 'reflects on the extraordinary contemporary social situation in the borough, where fashionable young hipsters, yuppie developments and organic cafés co-exist awkwardly with Hackney's most underprivileged'.[7] The biography to the Hackney book identifies Nelson as having 'lived in Hackney all his life', and his work demonstrates a mundane familiarity with the streets he photographs, attentive to minor shifts and changes in the everyday landscape. The time-based medium of film enables Nelson's continuing meditation on the 'beauty and ugliness that co-exist in the borough today' to be framed historically – a record of a particular, violent, period of transition.

Nelson's photographic experience has two discernible effects on the film. First, as an accomplished portrait photographer, he is practised in enabling his subjects to feel at ease. For this film, Nelson was not just making a portrait but also eliciting the views of Hoxton Street residents about their neighbourhood. His evident achievement is to create an atmosphere in which his informants feel relaxed enough to comment frankly, even though, as made wryly explicit by Bill Lawrence, proprietor of the carpet shop, Nelson himself is recognised as being of a different social class.[8] Nelson paid attention to the people with whom he was working, and the quality of the attention is recognised in their responses, which sound like their thoughts and voices rather than just answers to his questions. Secondly, and perhaps more obviously, Nelson has an eye for a telling detail and is not frightened of a still image. He understands how the texture of place, and the homeliness of that place, is made through little choices and repetitions. In his attention to Serge's dark, cluttered under-bridge home, he reveals how Serge can move confidently to reach his books. In footage of Anderson's the Bakers, the camera dwells in close-up on individual handwritten labels which give the prices of the 'proper bread and cakes at proper prices': 'pineapple tarts', 'jam tarts', 'Bakewell Tart' (Figure 14.2).

Near the beginning of the film, the camera rests on the wooden memorial to the war dead in St Anne's Church as Father Christopher explains its origins. The memorial, difficult to read – a faded, painted black, with layers of flaking gold inscription – is offered as emblematic of the poverty of the parish. 'It's always been a poor parish', the priest explains, decoding the hieroglyphics to reveal that it is the underlying pub sign, repurposed to serve as the memorial, which is becoming more visible than the names of the war dead: 'The original materials for the pub sign were much better quality'. The camera pauses on the image, enabling the viewer, with this new contextual information, to understand the initially mysterious writing of different eras and to see indeed that this sign now speaks more of the poverty of the parish than the memory of the dead.

Nelson's use of composed, carefully framed images enables him to build up, throughout the film, some rhythms of repeated, but transformed, views of this urban landscape as redevelopment gathers pace and the

The Street, *gentrification* and Brexit

Figure 14.2 Cakes and cake prices in Anderson's the Bakers

shopfronts change. Some of the change is so radical that it becomes impossible to remember what went before, although the repeated view from the pie and mash shop provides one vantage point, as do the churches and Colleen's home. He captures residents staring at a notice in the window when the bakery disappears, but Paula's café, the one place where original residents sit outside to smoke, is replaced by so many eateries with outdoor tables serving a quite different clientele that its location blurs. The views of low-rise council housing are obscured by the rising towers of luxury condominiums, and the camera dwells on the images of the limber, laughing white people with gleaming teeth and shiny hair which populate the hoardings that surround the building sites. In the context of the street which Nelson has provided, these representations of the proposed new inhabitants appear like a grotesque eugenic population transfer.

Cinemas of gentrification and redevelopment: 'us old ones, we don't want to move'

Within the London canon, *The Street* most obviously recalls Robert Vas's 1961 short film, *The Vanishing Street*. *The Vanishing Street* too is set in one street, Hessel Street, just east of the City boundaries near Aldgate in what was then, still, the Jewish East End.[9] Each film gestures to the 'day in the life of a city' format used in city symphonies the world over – the awakening of the street, the empty streets which will become busy, shutters rolling up, premises being unlocked, street traders preparing their wares. The opening of the film matches the beginning of the day for those on the street, and, in each case, by the end of the film, there is a sense of a different kind of day-end closing. In *The Vanishing Street*, the cross-hatch lens of the surveyor's glass appears in the second minute, foreshadowing the future, while in *The Street* passers-by are shown standing in respect as a traditional glass-sided funeral coach is drawn by white-plumed horses past Hays and English, Funeral Directors. In *The Street*, these early sequences, particularly of the white goods shop, JimGo, show the labour involved in the display of goods. The small shop, overnight crammed with cookers, fridges and washing machines, must, each day, be emptied out onto the pavement, the heavy units wheeled out and positioned individually so that customers can walk between items, assessing sizes and comparing prices. This is filmed from the proprietor's arrival, when he prays before he opens the shop door, through the process of setting out the machines, which he explains – while working – takes about forty-five minutes each day.

While there are similarities of structure and focus in these two films, particularly the overwhelming sense of the loss of an East London community which haunts each, their context and temporality is different. *The Vanishing Street* is a film of redevelopment, while *The Street* is a film of gentrification. The ladies who shop in Hessel Street, speculating about the 'slum clearance' which is taking place around them, express no fear about population replacement: they understand that their own fate may be the newly built towers which loom over their market street but do not anticipate no future provision for themselves. The context of the destruction of their environment is the post-war project for the amelioration of housing stock. Problematic as many of the strategies within this project may have turned out to be, it was still envisaged within a broader understanding of the responsibilities of the state (both national and local) for the provision of housing for the less well-off.[10] *The Street*, in contrast, tracks the progressive elimination of residents and businesses who understand themselves, accurately, as in the way of the 'fast people' to whom the city now belongs.

The violent gentrification depicted in *The Street* is not the same process that Ruth Glass described in her study of nearby Islington. In the 1960s, Glass observed the way in which middle-class people purchased and refurbished nineteenth-century terraced houses in what were, in the mid-twentieth century, working-class areas. The houses, cheap, in poor condition and usually multi-tenanted, were restored, often by their new owners themselves, to single-family residences.[11] The middle-class incomers were, in Glass's study, the initiating agents of a change which, 'once it starts in a district, goes on rapidly until all or most of the original working-class occupiers are displaced, and the whole social character of the district is changed'.[12] In the extensive debates about whether gentrification as a process and term still has validity, questions of agency and causality have dominated.[13] Tom Slater usefully sidesteps these arguments to propose that 'what is still relevant from her [Ruth Glass's] classic statement' is 'the political importance of capturing a process of class transformation', 'the fine empirical details of her historically and geographically contingent definition'.[14] Several of Nelson's gentrifying interviewees, particularly in the early part of the film, explain that they have been priced out of nearby Shoreditch and Clerkenwell but that this part of Hoxton has been 'left behind' or is still 'untouched'. This sense of an opportunity for the incomer proprietor of a small business has affinities with classic gentrification, although not phrased in quite the language of restoring a Georgian terraced house: 'it was a shit-hole, but a shit-hole we could afford', as a coffee bar proprietor observes. However, the large capital-intensive residential towers which are dominating the landscape by the end of the film are a quite different proposition, signifying the shaping involvement of City money in the redevelopment of the area, which is also demonstrated in the interviews with investors looking for lucrative buy-to-let residential property investment. As most gentrification scholars agree, even if they dispute causes and terms, the processes are now being driven by international capital, often in collaboration with state actors.[15] These state actors, committed to projects named anything but gentrification ('regeneration') are both national and local.[16] In a historically poor area such as the London Borough of Hackney, there is immense pressure on the local state to sell assets such as playing fields, housing estates and cultural buildings as a way of (short term) balancing the books in a period of intense, nationally legislated austerity with the key characteristic of deep cuts to local government.[17]

By the end of *The Street*, Aviva, the financial services giant, has arrived in Hoxton. Nelson's cumulative method, in which the duration of his engagement with the street testifies to the quality and extent of its transformation, is exemplified in the way in which he is able to piece together a narrative, through images and interviews, in which the new Aviva premises are the end of a story which begins with one of his most engaging informants, Errol, the proprietor of the Cremer garage. Like the pie and mash shop with its addition of 'Vegan pie and mash' to the menu, or the bakery with its 'no trans fats', Errol registers the demands of the new residents with a notice explaining that he does not undertake bicycle repairs or jobs such as pumping up tyres, but clearly feels under pressure (Figure 14.3). Gesturing to the demolition and construction in process on either side of his building, he refers to himself as 'the last man

Figure 14.3 Errol and his garage: last man standing

standing' and recounts the multiple weekly offers he receives to buy his property. As with all the long-established interviewees – Errol has had the business for twenty-seven years – passers-by greet him as he talks and he explains about watching whole families growing up in the locality. Errol is introduced in the establishing first third of the film, when the street is shown to contain all that would be needed to sustain a local life – the bakery, the laundrette, JimGo the white goods shop, the pubs, the carpet shop. When he reappears in the second part of the film, after the announcement of the referendum, the bakery has already gone (after 130 years), more pubs are closed and the old inhabitants feel their days are numbered. 'We're the last of a dying breed, we're the dinosaurs', says the milkman, asking who will do the road-sweeping for the new inhabitants if no low-paid workers can live there. Errol declares that 'London now is for the fast moving people' and soon the garage is locked up, with a farewell notice from Errol posted outside, explaining that it would have been too painful to say goodbye in person.

Errol doesn't appear again, but his garage does. First, we see its demolition, and all the accumulated interior décor – the calendars, the scraps of paper, a framed print, job-sheets – piled into rubble as the walls come down. And then finally, in the last part of the film, when the early days of craft beer and coffee shops have been superseded by the enormous million-pound apartment towers and even City property speculators are explaining how Hackney council has no protection in place for low-income residents or the abuse of live/work planning permission, the garage makes one last appearance. Nelson films a long interview with a senior manager in Aviva, the insurance company which has by this time acquired most of Hoxton Square. She is proud of the company's expansion of its Hoxton premises, feeling that the location will encourage 'smart thinking and working', and is relaxed about explaining, with expansive gestures round the square, how very much of the area they now own. The redevelopment has been sympathetic, she feels, with, for example, the retention in the floor of the part of the Aviva estate called 'The Garage' of the hexagonal, textured metal covering of what was once Errol's mechanic's pit. Nelson's archive has enabled him to tell a continuous story about one patch of land which knits together characters who don't know each other but who between them document the shift from mechanical labour to financial services.

The music which is played over the opening of the film, and which recurs at the end, is Rachel Portman's 'Life Is Sweet' theme, written for Mike Leigh's 1990 film of the same name. Leigh made *Life Is Sweet* two years after his Kings Cross–set gentrification film, *High Hopes*. *High Hopes* too features an old lady out of step with the transformation around her, and the characterisation of the ghastly gentrifiers who have moved in next door has some similarities with the portrayal of an aspirant hipster artist and gallerists in *The Street*. The connection between the two films is no more than a musical allusion, but it situates *The Street* within a tracery of gentrification films.[18] *The Street*, though, documents not just the disorientation of an old lady who has locked herself out of her house and gets little succour from her new neighbours but the destruction of an environment so that the very landmarks that would allow orientation for long-term residents have been erased.

Brexit and the hubris of London

In the years documented in *The Street*, which Fintan O'Toole, in his collection *The Brexit Chronicles*, calls 'Three years in hell', there was considerable public discussion of the cultural and political geography of the UK.[19] London voted overwhelmingly to remain within the European Union, and there were London Remainers who voiced the view that the city should secede from the UK to stay part of the larger union of Europe. Modern, liberal, cosmopolitan London was set against backward, xenophobic, left-behind places like the north of England which had voted to leave. It was almost as if it was the right of Remainer Londoners to get the result they had voted for, and the rest of the country could deal with the consequences of their own vote. In the Remainer morality play, there was a felt injustice in the failure of the city's economic and cultural dominance to be translated into a continuation of the status quo in relation to membership of the European Union. London's status as a world city is dependent on the centrality of the City of London to the financial markets. Once the City could no longer house the headquarters of global financial institutions because it no longer had privileged access to the EU markets, this status was threatened.

'Get Brexit Done' could be a plausible, and successful, slogan for Boris Johnson in his 2019 election landslide because the period since the Brexit referendum (June 2016) – the three years in hell – had been distinguished by failure, at a number of levels, to agree on the terms for leaving the EU. Before I discuss the way in which the Brexit vote looms over *The Street*, I want to spend a little time on the place of London within the UK and how this is conceptualised.

Firstly, I want to reiterate the centrality of London to all UK geographies. The often unconsciously entitled way in which Londoners assume the normality of the pre-eminence of, and provision for, their city has every justification except for their tone.[20] As the researchers of the 'great British Class Survey' put it in 2015:

> What comes out of our analysis therefore is a complex geography which operates across several dimensions; urban-rural; north-south; and the metropolitan capital of London versus the rest. All these divisions ultimately articulate the central power of London itself. We might, crudely, characterize earlier periods as having contrasted different spatial imaginaries in which London might have been dominant, but in ways which were contested. The power of provincial, county and regional identities was strong. However, London now operates as the unquestioned centre of elite geography.[21]

London, however, despite this dominance, is not unitary, and Doreen Massey makes some crucial connections between the characterising of London and the rest of the country. In her celebrated 2005 essay on the throwntogetherness of place, Massey offers a penetrating analysis of the function of the word 'but' in discussions which compare London with the rest of Britain while also seeking to recognise the unevenness of London. She identifies a clear rhetorical strategy in which the contrast is acknowledged: '"London is a successful city", they aver, "but there are still areas of poverty and exclusion".'[22] While Massey is sympathetic to the impulse to recognise the existing deprivation in the city, she argues that the 'but' in this formulation misrecognises causality. It is 'and' not 'but' which comes closer to revealing that the poverty and exclusion in London is produced in part by the dominance, in London, of global financial industries and its drive to world city status since the mid-1980s. Just as the wrecking of the regions is partly the consequence of policies which make manufacturing too expensive – in comparison to financial services – to pursue, so the inflation of property and land prices in London produces homelessness and destitution in London. *The Street* is a film situated in the terrain of the relationship between the 'but' and the 'and' of Massey's argument. It documents the everyday lives of people who live in a poor district of London, showing their progressive exclusion from what was once their street – as the proprietor of the pie and mash shop describes the market, 'that's where they lived, that's where they shopped, that's where they drank' – as it is transformed around them to serve the interests of incomers who want coffee, craft beer and sourdough bread more than they need a laundrette. The film documents the causality of which Massey speaks: it tracks the simultaneous erection of new condominiums and the consequent diminution of resources and spaces for residents of more modest homes. The imaginative failure of some of the new entrepreneurs – even those of the best liberal, Remainer opinions – to understand their role is captured in a vignette on the night of a gallery opening. The newly stripped interior, all white walls and relevant artwork, is illuminated against the dark street, providing a focus for a group of soup-kitchen regulars who huddle outside. A man from this group raises his hand, making the shape of a gun, and 'shoots' the gallery guests. The gallery director, with her glass of wine, waves back, evidently misunderstanding the gesture.[23]

The vividness of the antagonism to the new commodities – '"craft beer": what's that when it's at home?', the assertion of 'proper bread' – correctly identifies that the new businesses cater to a different type of consumer and threaten the existing residents. However, as Sharon Zukin argued about New York loft-living pioneers in the 1970s, these new types of artisan food are the tangible signs of a much more substantial struggle 'for the reconquest of the downtown' in which the craft-brewers and bakers are merely a supporting – if pioneering – cast.[24] Middle-class agency in the new scenarios of gentrification is often as consumers – the heavy-lifting of transformation is driven by financial capital in various modes. The novelist Hari Kunzru observed of Broadway Market, another Hackney market street, '[P]eople like me – writers and artists – have softened Hackney up. Now comes the real money'.[25] The rhetoric within the Brexit campaign of regaining control, getting something back, restoring a golden age, has an emotional resonance for people who see their paltry share diminishing daily and, indeed, find the necessities of life increasingly beyond reach. Stefan, the German proprietor of the craft beer shop – a very early new business, and gone by the film's end – recalls weeping on the morning of the result of the Brexit referendum, and there is an awkward scene when the filmmaker has brought Stefan together with Joe Cooke in his pie and mash shop (which is opposite Stefan's business) to discuss Brexit. This, very unusually for the film, feels like a set-up; people who wouldn't be having this conversation naturally, because of an understanding that they are on different sides of an argument, brought together for the film.

The awkwardness of this conversation nevertheless reveals something of the way in which the legitimation of xenophobia by the Brexit campaign and the preceding government policy of a 'hostile environment' for immigrants have contributed to a kind of ecumenical causality, in which the blaming of the others – foreigners, yuppies, immigrants – can coexist with older nationalist and racist formations. Nelson unearths the long history of white politics in the area in the testimony of the Reverend Gloria about vigilante harassment of the worshippers at the (mainly West Indian) Bethel Tabernacle in the 1970s. Hoxton had a substantial National Front (fascist) presence at this time, when the Front was active in many parts of Britain. The Reverend Gloria, at that time one of the worshippers at the Bethel Tabernacle, describes the attacks on their church, recalling, with the memory of terror both present and controlled in her voice and demeanour, how the congregation had to keep a vigil in the chapel and eventually erect steel gates to safeguard the building and themselves.

These are uncomfortable histories which coexist with difficult and contested views of history and community, through which Nelson treads a careful path. He manages to neither deny their existence nor suppress them, instead showing something of the contexts and everyday multiculturalism of these opinions. Nelson has, I guess, made some clear decisions to exclude explicit racist comments from his informants, but also, as is shown in a conversation discontinued as he walks into Colleen's flat, maybe his informants have chosen to withhold some of their views from someone who they would anticipate does not share them. Living with difference may involve a little more mutual withholding of divergent views in banal coexistence than is always recognised. One reviewer called the Hoxton Street shown in this film 'Brexit Britain in microcosm'.[26] It is certainly more helpful to have the contradictions of the 'three years in hell' revealed in all their local complexity, rather than caricatured as 'Progressive internationalist London' versus the 'Reactionary Rest' of the country.

'Not love but anger'

At the end of the film, the vicar of St Leonard's, the Reverend Paul Turp – who has spoken with passion and foreboding of the way in which the London housing crisis is destroying neighbourliness and feeding anti-immigrant feeling – is finally leaving his church at the mandated retirement age of seventy and will be unable to afford to stay in the area. The churches have been shown to be among the few institutions in the area still providing succour to local residents as austerity cuts reduce support by both local council and state. Cuts, in combination with the move to internet provision, exclude many needy and elderly parishioners from any access to remaining services. Websites and phone-lines are little use to those without computers or mobile phones. At St Anne's, Father Christopher, with his volunteers, organises food and somewhere inside to eat, and it is evidently through these meals that Nelson meets some of the people whose lives he explores in the film. At nearby St Leonard's, the Shoreditch Church, in his final appearance in the film, the Reverend Paul explains his vocation: 'My motivation as a priest is not based on love, it's based on anger'.[27] The manifest injustice of so much that has featured in the film – so that Nelson has captured even some of the beneficiaries of this property and population transfer expressing anxiety – has not been presented with outrage. Instead, Nelson has worked through the careful editing of his archive of film footage and interviews gathered over the four years of the film's making. Individual interviews are cut up and spaced throughout the film, juxtaposed with other interviews and images. The tranquillity of the opening of the film is assaulted by the noise of demolition and construction. 'Acquired for Development' signs are juxtaposed with the reduction of familiar spaces and a changed geography emerges. Nelson's accomplishment is that this slow accumulation of detail seems to speak for itself. Instead of cookers and washing machines laid out on the pavement, there are, by the end of the film, tables laid for dining. As Joe Cooke, the proprietor of the pie and mash shop, points out, there are now thirty food outlets on this street, 'and not one butcher'. No proper bread, no white goods, no carpets, no car repairs. No Poundland. No Cashbrokers. Of the filmmaker's original informants, only Reverend Paul,

Joe Cooke, Colleen and Serge last through the film. At the end, Colleen's door is boarded up, Serge has been burnt out and the priest is leaving.

This is a quietly devastating film about lives wrecked by government policies and responses to wider economic and political shifts. It records, in Tom Slater's terms, 'the fine empirical detail' of a process of class transformation in an inner London district at a particular historical moment. It shows why, when given an opportunity to express a political will in the Brexit referendum, this will was 'no'. The film could be seen to indict the eaters of sourdough bread (and I am one) for not understanding the cost of their bakeries. It accumulates details which might disturb the complacency of some London Remainers' contempt for their opponents, suggesting that Remain views, in Hoxton, in 2016, might be lifestyle choices not unlike sourdough bread. In Doreen Massey's terms, the recent Brexit vote in London was majority Remain and – not 'but' – there was a substantial Leave vote in the city. However, it would be a mistake to understand this film as, in any simple sense, a Brexit film. Brexit provides, almost coincidentally, a referential structure, but it is a longer government-supported financialisation of housing, as documented by Rowan Moore, Loretta Lees et al., Anna Minton and Rowland Atkinson, which underlies the film's concerns.[28] It is the rapid acceleration of this process in the twenty-first century – the 2010 government's austerity project, the plundering of the public realm, the selling of the social city to capital – which is the film's main concern. The devastating consequences of these policies, and the erasure from public debate of alternatives other than the continuous placation of the super-rich, resonate for all who do not wish to live in such an increasingly segregated world. This is a film about Hoxton Street between 2014 and 2019 which is granular in its attention to particular premises, characters, locations and events. The detail of this documentation, with the careful contextualisation of so many of its characters, is what makes the film vivid and compelling. Individual voices linger on, with their rich registers of emotion and attitude, long after the images – and their homes and businesses – have faded. It would be a foolish mistake, however, to understand it as a film which is just about Hoxton Street.

Notes

1. Ruth Glass, 'London: Aspects of Change', in *Clichés of Urban Doom* (Oxford: Basil Blackwell, 1989 [1964]), pp. 133–58. First published as the introduction to the edited book *London: Aspects of Change* (London: Centre for Urban Studies, 1964).
2. Andy C. Pratt, 'Urban Regeneration: From the Arts "Feel Good" Factor to the Cultural Economy: A Case Study of Hoxton', *Urban Studies,* 46.5/6 (May 2009), pp. 1041–61.

3 Ibid., p. 1048.
4 For bomb damage, which mainly accurately predicts subsequent council housing, see 'Map 51, Shoreditch, Hoxton and Haggerston', in *London County Council Bomb Damage Maps 1939–45*, ed. Lawrence Ward (London: Thames and Hudson, 2015), pp. 82–3.
5 Pratt, 'Urban Regeneration', p. 1053.
6 Live/work planning permission can mean that the designated properties evade regulation for each of residential, business and industrial premises, while also, for instance, in England, sidestepping the requirement to provide a proportion of affordable housing. While planning and legal systems are different, Rebecca Solnit's account of the role of live/work in San Francisco is illuminating. See *The Siege of San Francisco and the Crisis of Urbanism* (London: Verso, 2000).
7 Zed Nelson, 'Introduction to *Hackney: A Tale of Two Cities*', https://zednelson.com/?Hackney:text (accessed 2 July 2021).
8 Several of Nelson's interviewees make social difference explicit in their comments, as does Colleen in the observation used as an epigraph to this section: 'It's on the up now, it's near the city, that's why all these yuppies are coming down, it's not my world, it's your world.'
9 On *The Vanishing Street,* see Charlotte Brunsdon, 'Sites of Melancholy: London in Transition', in *London on Film*, ed. Pam Hirsch and Chris O'Rourke (Cham, Switzerland: Palgrave Macmillan, 2017), pp. 223–8.
10 British cinema and television of the 1960s and early 1970s, looked at from a certain angle, is suffused with images of 'slum clearance' and redevelopment, from London-set films like *Up the Junction* (BBC, 1965) and *The Optimists of Nine Elms* (1973) to Alan Plater's melancholy Hull drama, *The Land of Green Ginger* (BBC, 1973).
11 For a discussion of a 1970s televised encounter between a gentrifier and an Islington skilled worker, see Charlotte Brunsdon, 'Taste and Time on Television', *Screen*, 45.2 (2004), pp. 124–8.
12 Glass, 'London', p. 138.
13 The contours of these debates are outlined in Loretta Lees, Tom Slater and Elvin Wyly, eds, *The Gentrification Reader* (London: Routledge, 2010). Neil Smith's influential writings on gentrification are resonant here: 'New Globalism, New Urbanism: Gentrification As Global Urban Strategy', *Antipode*, 34.3 (1987), pp. 427–50; 'Of Yuppies and Housing: Gentrification, Social Restructuring, and the Urban Dream', *Environment and Planning D: Society and Space*, 5 (2002), pp. 151–72.
14 Tom Slater, 'The Eviction of Critical Perspectives from Gentrification Research', in *The Gentrification Reader*, ed. Lees, Slater and Wyly, p. 579.
15 Loretta Lees et al. argue that in the international context, the state is now more important than individual gentrifiers, often undertaking the preparatory work for corporate gentrifiers to follow. See Loretta Lees, Hyun Bang Shin and Ernesto López-Morales, *Planetary Gentrification* (Oxford: Polity, 2017), p. 87.
16 In Britain, this generally means the redevelopment of council (social) housing by private contractors with only a paltry amount of social and 'affordable'

housing retained in what becomes a private development. See John Broughton, *Municipal Dreams: The Rise and Fall of Council Housing* (London: Verso, 2018). Hoxton Street is north of the River Thames; the process has been at its most radical in London on the South Bank where the class composition of the area is being completely transformed. On the conceptualisation of VNEB (Vauxhall Nine Elms Battersea), see Rowan Moore, *Slow Burn City* (London: Picador, 2016), pp. 452–73. And on the extensive documentation of the fate of the Aylesbury and Heygate Estates, for example the residents' stories at heygatewashome.org, see Moore, *Slow Burn City*, pp. 195–222; and Ben Campkin, *Remaking London: Decline and Regeneration in Urban Culture* (London: I.B. Tauris, 2013), pp. 77–104.

17 The separate issue of the pre-Austerity financial record of Hackney Council, the 2001 audit (which revealed a debt of £72 million) and the financial measures then put in place has also been significant in this area, as suggested by the testimony, allegations and inquiry into the 2005/6 Broadway Market property transactions. As Hari Kunzru argued at the time, 'what is best value?' See Hari Kunzru, 'The Battle for Tony's Café: An Everyday Story of Gentrification', *Guardian*, G2 (7 December 2005), pp. 8–11 (online version titled 'Market Forces').

18 There is also an old lady – the key victim character in gentrification cinema – central to the New York–set gentrification film **batteries not included* (1987/8), in which assistance in resisting eviction is provide by extra-terrestrials. Johan Andersson and Lawrence Webb suggest that the history of gentrification 'runs like a thread' through their book on film and post-industrial culture, *The City in American Cinema*. See Johan Andersson and Lawrence Webb, *The City in American Cinema* (London: Bloomsbury, 2019), p. 7. For further discussion of *High Hopes,* Kings Cross and gentrification, see Charlotte Brunsdon, *London in Cinema* (London: British Film Institute, 2007), pp. 210–19.

19 Fintan O'Toole, *The Brexit Chronicles: Three Years in Hell* (London: Apollo, 2020).

20 For example, London Transport is the only metropolitan public transport in Britain that has not been privatised and, in comparison to anywhere else in the country – particularly the actual country – works wonderfully.

21 Mike Savage, Niall Cunningham, Fiona Devine, Sam Friedman and Daniel Laurison, *Social Class in the Twenty-First Century* (London: Penguin Random House, 2015), p. 295.

22 Doreen Massey, 'Throwntogetherness: The Politics of the Event of Place', in *For Space* (London: Sage, 2015), p. 156.

23 One of the employees in this gallery, interviewed early in the film, is the young artist from West London, Khadiye Saye, who died in the Grenfell Tower. The gallery is later shown to make a memorial garden for her.

24 Sharon Zukin, *Loft Living: Culture and Capital in Urban Change* (London: Radius, 1988 [1982]), p. 175. Joy White gives an equally vivid account of the role of farmer's markets and organic foodshops in the creation of white enclaves in Forest Gate in the London Borough of Newham. Here it is the planned arrival

of Crossrail, rather than proximity to the City of London, which makes the area desirable to new residents. See Joy White, *Terraformed: Young Black Lives in the Inner City* (London: Repeater, 2020).
25 Kunzru, 'The Battle for Tony's Café'.
26 Steve Rose, 'A 50p Cuppa and a £2m Flat', *Guardian*, G2 (22 November 2019), p. 7.
27 The website of St Leonard's Shoreditch (the 'Shoreditch Church') hosts a short interview with Zed Nelson over extracts from the film: https://shoreditch.saint.church/heritage (accessed 28 June 2019).
28 Moore, *Slow Burn City*; Loretta Lees, Tom Slater and Elvin Wyly, *Gentrification* (London: Routledge, 2008) and *The Gentrification Reader*; Anna Minton, *Big Capital* (London: Penguin, 2017); Rowland Atkinson, *Alpha City* (London: Verso, 2020).

Index

A–Z map of London xvi, 12
A Child from the South 62
A Rake's Progress 193
Ackroyd, Peter 3
Africa 4, 140–57, 224
African traditional beliefs 142
Akomfrah, John 73, 74
Algeria 21, 201, 216
Anglocentrism 14
anti-discrimination 15
anti-immigration policy 229, 237, 239
American *see* United States 14, 31, 44, 61, 71, 127, 131, 163, 170, 192, 195, 197, 198, 206
Appadurai, Arjun 82, 83, 91, 236
Apter, Emily 13
aura of indispensability 4

Ballard, J. G. 44, 47, 58
BAME (Black, Asian and Minority Ethnic) 16, 206
Banaji, Shakuntala 20, 107
Basic Instinct 2, 5
Bauman, Zygmunt 236
BBC 7, 33, 41, 89, 117, 126, 137, 193, 194, 202
Beck, Ulrich 213, 233
Bethnal Green 99, 102
Black Audio Film Collective 19, 72, 90, 91
Black and Asian diaspora in Britain 73

Bollywood 107–12, 122, 123, 143
Bouchareb, Rachid xvi, 20, 138, 201, 214, 217, 227
Brazil 13, 124–9, 132, 134, 135, 139
Brexit vii, 2, 3, 24, 72, 88, 89, 90, 92, 176, 237, 239, 245, 247, 249, 251, 252, 254, 255, 256, 258
BRIC countries 20
Britain 1, 26, 28, 29, 31, 32, 33, 40, 41, 80, 85, 88, 160, 161, 198, 235, 253, 255, 258
Britishness 108, 161
British Chinese 28, 161–73
British colonialism 108, 109, 165
British East Asian/South–East Asian (BEASEA) 158–71
Brunsdon, Charlotte 10, 11, 22, 23, 36, 47, 93, 182, 183, 192, 202, 204, 212
brutalism 6, 7, 48, 83, 101, 203, 209

Canada 1, 10, 31, 37, 101
Chan, Felicia 158–61, 171–3
Chek Wai Lau 14, 15, 23
China 1, 160, 162, 164
Chinatown 28, 82, 163
Children of Men 21, 228–42
Christie, Ian 12, 23, 40
cities xvi, 1, 2, 6, 7, 8, 10, 11, 17, 21, 22, 31, 33

city film 46, 47, 52, 75, 83, 89, 125, 129, 136, 137, 138, 184, 191, 193, 201, 202, 203, 211, 212, 225, 245
City of London 29, 80, 95, 101, 118, 133, 203, 210, 212–15, 223, 243, 244, 245, 252, 259
cityscape 3, 9, 10, 17, 19, 43, 46, 87, 90, 113, 135, 202, 203
class exploitation 50
claustrophobia 4, 52
colonialist culture 146
convivial multiculturalism 220
co-productions with Europe 2, 124, 125, 143, 176
cosmopolitanism 12, 26, 109, 122, 160, 169, 204, 210–14, 218, 223, 226, 228, 229, 236, 237, 239, 240
Couldry, Nick 194
council housing 247, 258
Covent Garden 195
COVID-19 3, 15, 18, 24, 72, 161, 175, 240
creative industries 6, 8, 245
cross-cultural 4, 5, 14, 20, 141, 216
Cuaron, Alfonso 228–42
Cut Sleeve Boys 164

decadence 4, 44
deglobalisation 3
delocalisation 1
demography xvii, 2, 5
Dennison, Stephanie 124
deportation 16, 85, 230, 231
Desi British 107
destination-scape 17
desubjectivisation 165, 169
digital happening 20, 192, 196, 199, 205
Dirty Pretty Things 17, 51, 120, 137
diversification of diversity 4
Doctor Strange 175
dynamization of space 179
dystopia 21, 228, 229, 230, 231, 236, 240

Englishness 45
entrepreneurial city 7, 23
erasure 159, 162, 164, 167, 170
essayistic film 73, 74, 75, 77, 84, 85
essentialism and exclusivity 2
exclusion 4, 9, 17, 47, 159, 161, 211, 212, 213, 214, 216, 222, 229, 253
extraterritoriality 13

Fan, Victor 19, 158
Fast and the Furious 6, 175
Finland 1, 99
Finsbury Park ix, xvii, 21, 215, 216, 217, 218, 224, 225, 227
Flanagan, Kevin M. 44
flâneur 193, 231
foreigner 16, 36, 204, 205, 213, 216, 225, 254
France 1, 8, 30, 63, 93, 173, 210, 215, 216, 226, 239, 254, 257, 258, 259
Fuentes, Ana Virginia Lopez 210

gangsters 5, 19, 35, 48, 51, 93, 102
gentrification 5, 9, 12, 19, 74, 77, 81, 88, 89, 94, 100, 105, 213, 215, 225, 227, 243, 244, 245, 247, 248, 249, 251, 254, 257, 258, 259
geographical markers 182
Germany 9, 45, 161
Gilroy, Paul 85
global
  global art cinema 2, 21, 23
  global celebrity 198
  global cinema 2, 22
  global city 4, 8, 9, 15, 23, 24, 39, 72, 83, 88, 111, 122, 177, 185, 202, 212, 213, 214, 216, 223
  Global Hollywood viii, 6, 20, 22, 174–91
  Global London 1–13, 19–20, 22, 72–92, 107–24, 140, 175, 192–209, 211–27, 229–42
  Global North 13, 140
  Global South 2, 140

globalisation 2, 3, 5, 8, 13, 15, 16, 18, 22, 72, 73, 82, 83, 84, 89, 140, 141, 142, 144, 146, 150, 151, 152, 153, 154, 177, 181, 195, 206, 212, 213, 220, 225, 228, 235, 236, 237
glocal/glocalisation xviii
Goldfinger, Erno 6
Goldman, Henrique 124
Grenfell Tower 243
Guha, Malini 19, 22, 72

Hackney 94, 99, 243–58
Hall, Stuart 14, 19, 78, 112, 161, 172
Harrelson, Woody 192–209
heterogeneity 14, 15, 31, 161, 163, 217
High-Rise 48
hipsters 19, 243, 246
Hirst, Pam 11, 23, 58, 188, 208, 257
Hogarth, William 193
Holborn 192, 197, 200, 205
Hollywood 5, 7, 9, 10, 46, 58, 61, 98, 108, 118, 153, 174–91, 197, 198
homogeneity 3, 13, 121, 137
Hong, Khaou 159
host society 224
Houses of Parliament 10
Housefull 3, 107
Huyssen, Andreas 5
hybridity 75, 141–54

I Hired a Contract Killer vii, xvii, 5, 19, 93–106
Igbo culture 145
illimitable space 2, 3
immigration 11, 14, 17, 25–43, 110, 112, 124–39, 158–73, 231, 237, 239, 254, 255
Imperial past 10, 24, 28, 73–89, 107–23
India 89
infrastructure 5, 6, 7, 72, 83, 158, 161, 174, 176, 177, 185, 188, 190, 194
Instagram 3, 202

interculturalism 4, 7, 23, 24, 29, 142, 153, 154, 155, 156, 172, 206, 215, 216, 220, 235
intersocietal interaction 3
Islam 111, 132, 136, 215, 218, 221

Jab Tak Hain Jaan 108
Jean Charles 124
Johnson, Boris 88, 90, 252

Kaurismaki, Aki xv, 19, 93–106
King's Cross 100
Knightsbridge 3
Koolhaus, Rem 7
Kraidy, Marwan 141, 155

Lack, Roland-François xvi–xviii, 12, 45
'landmark London' 11, 100, 103, 179, 182, 184, 202
Lefebvre, Henri xvii, 240, 242
Lilting 158–73
live-streaming 192–209
London 9, 11, 18, 63, 110, 117, 194, 195, 197, 198, 200, 201, 206, 230
  central London 9, 11, 18, 63, 110, 117, 193, 195, 196, 197, 198, 200, 201, 206, 230
  global London 1–13, 19–20, 22, 72–92, 107–24, 140, 175, 192–209, 211–27, 229–42
  'landmark London' 10, 11, 36, 47, 52, 94, 99, 100, 101, 103, 114, 174, 175, 179, 182, 183, 184, 185, 188, 192, 194, 198, 201, 202, 203, 204, 251
  local London 1–2, 38, 93, 243–59
  London-centrism 48
  millennial London 17, 200, 202
  multisited London 1, 2
  'off-centre London' 12, 19, 93–106
  preservationist view of London 2
  'the London set piece' 174–91
  unfamiliar London 97, 105

London as wonderland 15
London as 'the world's most film-friendly city' 177
London Docklands 94, 101
London Eye 3, 114, 115, 117, 128, 182, 202, 209
London River xvi, 20, 210–27
London Underground 50, 59, 104, 107, 132, 139
Losey, Gavrik 61–71
Lost in London 20, 192–209
Love, Actually 18

Martin, Mónica 21, 228
Marylebone 9
Masrani, Rahoul 107
Massey, Doreen 83, 212, 253
May, Theresa 72, 89, 90
Mayfair 9, 11, 17
McDonaldisation 13, 229
media capital 6, 174–91, 193
megacity xvii, 5, 8, 12, 13, 15, 20, 21, 131, 193, 229
Mexico 1
Mezzadra, Sandro 239
migration 4, 13, 212, 219, 221, 255
Miracle in Soho 25–43
Mission: Impossible – Fallout 183
mixture of two cultures 152
mobility 15, 131, 205, 210, 216, 236
Modi, Narendndra 119
Monk, Claire 93
multiculturalism 1–24, 34, 109, 110, 113, 118, 121, 159, 160–69, 172, 194, 204, 206, 214, 215, 216, 234, 254
multilingualism 4, 15, 22
Muslim *see* Islam

nationalism 107, 116, 119, 121, 123, 161, 206, 223, 226, 236
Neilson, Brett 239
Nelson, Zed 243
neoliberalism 5, 12, 108, 110, 159, 162, 229

Netflix 176, 177, 189, 194
networks 3, 7, 73, 142, 185, 195, 201, 213, 225, 226, 240
Newland, Paul 61
New York 5–10, 22–3, 30, 39, 52, 61, 66, 125, 136, 176, 183, 185, 193, 203, 253
Nigeria 1, 17, 20, 87, 140–57
Nollywood 20, 140–57

offshore service centre 176–79
Onuzulike, Uchenna 20, 140
O'Rourke, Chris 11, 23, 45, 58, 141, 188, 208, 257
Osuofia in London 140
outsiders' views 44, 46, 47, 48, 51, 73, 76, 78, 82, 85, 86, 88, 94, 103, 105
Oxford Street 3

Pacemaker 11
Panofsky, Erwin 179
Papastergiadis, Nikos 17
Paris xvi, 7, 22, 30, 35, 42, 91, 104, 183
Penz, Francois 22
photogenic supremacy 3
Piccadilly Circus 3, 28, 32, 68, 108, 118, 200
Pinewood Studios 7, 34, 35, 41, 42, 176, 189
Ping Pong 11
Poland 1, 44
polyculturalism 15
polyvalent 2, 4
postcolonial 13, 91, 108, 110, 112, 141, 152, 159–65, 227, 229, 236, 239, 241
Pressburger, Emeric 25
privatisation 212
property market 66, 81, 177, 189, 213, 244, 250, 251, 253
psychogeography 6, 93, 94, 100, 104, 106
Purab aur Paschim 107

redevelopment 5, 12, 81, 100, 101, 105, 244–51
Regent's Park 6
relocalisation 1, 19, 219
River Thames 6, 76, 100, 128, 174, 258

Sarkar, Bhaskar 1
Sassen, Saskia 2, 8, 82
Schadenfreude 192
Scheiler, Merrill 9
segregation 2, 74, 86, 213
Shepperton Studios 7, 176, 189
She, A Chinese 17
Shiel, Mark xvii, 22, 201
Shohat, Ella 13
Shoreditch 99, 245, 249, 255, 257, 259
Skolimowski, Jerzy 50
skyscrapers 5, 6, 9, 10, 81, 108, 203, 244
sojourner 3, 8
South Asian masculinity 114
South Korea 1, 11
Spider-Man: Far from Home 175
Stam, Robert 13, 225
superdiversity 3, 15, 21, 85, 160, 206
Sweden 1
Swinging London 4, 19, 44, 85, 160, 206

Tate Modern 174, 175, 182
tentpole blockbuster 174
terrorism 9, 72, 136, 185, 213, 214, 225, 229
Thatcher, Margaret 5
theatre 31, 41, 137, 141, 162, 172, 192–204
The Bourne Ultimatum 175
The Long Good Friday 5
The Street 20, 243
the Shard 10, 108, 109, 115, 117, 174
TikTok 3

Tokyo 7, 8, 9
Tokyo! 8, 9
topography xvi, 2, 3, 15, 23, 81, 194, 197, 203
transmogrification 2
transnational 6, 9, 20, 21, 23, 91, 93, 95, 96, 101, 103, 105, 121, 138, 142, 143, 155, 178, 181, 201, 212, 213, 218, 224, 225, 239
Twilight City 72

Unger, Michael A. 192
United States 14, 44, 61, 131, 192, 195, 206
urban development 10, 12, 106
urban imaginaries 2, 4, 22, 37, 197
urbanism 3, 5, 6, 8, 9, 10, 15, 22, 26, 38, 40, 45, 50, 58, 59, 81, 83, 93, 110, 125, 175, 177, 180, 183, 185, 188, 198, 201, 202, 213, 216, 217, 222, 226, 234, 235, 245, 246, 257

Vertovec, Steve 4, 14, 22, 23, 91, 226
VFX shots 187

WC1 193
Wagner, Keith B. 21, 135, 192
Webb, Lawrence 22, 174
Westminster 11, 182
Whitechapel 99, 100, 102, 104
Willis, Andy 158, 159, 161, 164
Windrush generation 16, 17, 85
Wonderwall 44, 49, 53
world city 8, 95, 212, 227, 252, 253

xenophobia 4, 12, 89, 118, 206, 237, 252, 254

young British artists (YBAs) 5, 120, 121
Young, Jingan MacPherson 25

zones (zonal) 18, 194, 197

EU authorised representative for GPSR:
Easy Access System Europe, Mustamäe tee 50,
10621 Tallinn, Estonia
gpsr.requests@easproject.com

www.ingramcontent.com/pod-product-compliance
Lightning Source LLC
Chambersburg PA
CBHW051605230426
43668CB00013B/1993